CAPTAIN KIDD
✳ AND *the* WAR ✳
AGAINST *the* PIRATES

CAPTAIN KIDD

✳ AND *the* WAR ✳
AGAINST *the* PIRATES

ROBERT C. RITCHIE

BARNES & NOBLE

NEW YORK

© 1986 by the President and Fellows of Harvard College

This 2006 edition published by Barnes & Noble, Inc.,
by arrangement with Harvard University Press

ISBN-13: 978-0-7607-0840-8
ISBN-10: 0-7607-0840-1

Printed and bound in the United States of America

3 5 7 9 10 8 6 4 2

Preface

During the seventeenth century many a judge glowered at his jurors and admonished them to remember that "piracy is *merely* robbery committed at sea." As the law was defined, the judges were right; yet piracy was never *merely* robbery. Petty theft would not have swept the world and produced a host of scoundrels like William Kidd, Blackbeard, and Sir Henry Morgan. It would not have found a lasting place in our culture or our history. But the colorful and romantic aspects of pirate life have obscured the historical and political reasons for the rise of buccaneering.

By the mid-sixteenth century England, the Netherlands, and France were struggling desperately to overtake Spain and Portugal in the race for trade and empire. Through state sponsorship, by licensing of entrepreneurs, or simply by turning a blind eye to pillage, the challenger nations let their ships sail free. More and more mariners discovered the joys of plunder in locations far from their own shores. In time, some even preferred to live near the Caribbean or the Indian Ocean, beyond the control of their own governments. These men, as they expanded the scale and geographic range of their operations, became threats to all merchant ships.

William Kidd, famous in his own day, became still more notorious after his execution. His best-known voyage, to Madagascar in 1696, was sponsored by some of the most powerful politicians in England, and while their patronage granted him extraordinary privileges it also tied him to the fortunes of his benefactors. When the political tide turned against the Whig leaders, their government came under increasing pressure to regulate piracy. And Kidd epitomized the practices that would have to change.

Kidd's career swept from the Caribbean to New York, to London, to the Indian Ocean. Historians examining his life can observe the evolution of piracy as it changed from a state-sponsored to an increasingly autonomous activity. Through Kidd's exploits we can also learn about the men who became pirates and some of their reasons for doing so, the conditions under which they lived, the dangers they confronted, and the rewards they reaped.

By the early modern epoch piracy had spread worldwide; but it had become too dangerous to be supported by any nation as a policy against its rivals. The pirates grew more and more violent, thereby alienating previously sympathetic merchants and shipowners, who now joined the Royal Navy in hunting down pirate ships. In the end, the buccaneers would lose—but not before they became legendary figures who even today are important in popular culture. This book is about their fate as much as it is about William Kidd's.

Many years ago, while doing research in London, I first discovered material on piracy. In the course of other projects I continued to collect notes, even as colleagues wearied of hearing my pirate stories. Then a friend, Eugene S. Larson, asked me to give a lecture, thereby prodding me to think in systematic fashion about early modern piracy. William S. Goodman subsequently encouraged me to undertake a major study, and this book is the result.

Over the years I have become indebted to a large number of librarians who helped me utilize a variety of sources unknown to me when I began the project. At my own campus library Gena Peyton introduced me to the Kenneth E. Hill collection of Pacific voyages, and she and Lynda Claassen continued to make me welcome in the Special Collections department. I am deeply indebted to librarians and archivists at the Henry E. Huntington Library, where I spent a highly productive sabbatical year. Also helpful were the staffs of the Franklin D. Roosevelt Library at Hyde Park, New York City Hall of Records, New-York Historical Society, New York State Library, and Queens College Library, all in New York; the Beineke Library at Yale University; the Wichita (Kansas) Public Library; the James Ford Bell Library at the University of Minnesota; the Berkshire Record Office, Bodleian Library at Oxford University, British Library, City of London Record Office, Guildhall Library, India Office, Institute of Historical Research, National Maritime Museum, Nottingham University Library, Public Record Office, and Riegate Corporation Library, all in England; and the Algemeen Rijksarchief in The Hague.

Along the way I received advice and encouragement from many friends and colleagues: Dunbar M. Hinrichs shared his knowledge of Kidd with me; Julius Chodorow was my guide to the New York City Hall of Records; D. W. Jones and Jacob Price gave me invaluable aid in the Public Record Office; and Jo Elsinger helped me in Wichita. My late friend Andrew B. Appleby listened to many pirate tales and forced me to put them in a larger historical framework.

My studies have been generously supported by the Research Committee of the University of California, San Diego, and the Henry E. Huntington/National Endowment for the Humanities Program.

Aspects of this work have been presented at a number of seminars; I remember particularly a lively session led by Michael Zuckerman at the University of Pennsylvania, as well as others at the University of Cincinnati and the Huntington Library, and a conference of the Southern California Early Americanists. I am indebted to Robert Middlekauf and Gary B. Nash, who read and commented on the manuscript.

Others who shared their expertise with me were Donna Andrews, Larry Cruse, Mary Hoogterp, Eunice Konold, Patti Rosas, and Kristin Webb. Stanley Chodorow, Douglas Greenberg, Steven Hahn, Henry Horwitz, Karen Kupperman, and Scott Waugh have given me their counsel at various times. And Aida Donald, Elizabeth Suttell, and Vivian Wheeler of Harvard University Press have been especially thoughtful and informed in their comments on the manuscript.

The book is dedicated to the person who helped me the most:

Louise Nocas Ritchie

Contents

1. The Sea Peoples   1

2. From Pirate to Friend of the Junto   27

3. Voyage to Madagascar   56

4. The Pirates' Last Frontier   80

5. Life in a Pirate Settlement   112

6. Revenge of the Company   127

7. Cat and Mouse   160

8. Winners and Losers   183

9. The Trial   206

10. Of Death, Destruction, and Myths   228

Abbreviations   241
Notes   243
Index   299

Illustrations

page 28   The Atlantic Ocean

following page 94
A ship being careened
Sir James Vernon
Richard Coote, Earl of Bellomont
Citizens aiding the pirates
A mock Admiralty Court
The island of Ascension, drawn in
  1704
Captain John Kempthorne bat-
  tling seven Barbary pirates
The west coast of India, about
  1680
Jonathan Kempthorne's painting
  of the harbor at Johanna
The island of Johanna in 1689

page 81   The Indian Ocean

following page 170
Henry Avery and his famous prize
Edward Barlow's depiction of the
  Sceptre
Captain Mathew Lowth captures
  Samuel Burgess
Approaches to Saint Marie
An early map of the strait of
  Babs-al-Mandab
The bay of Saint Augustine,
  Madagascar, drawn in 1642
Watercolor of the *Charles Galley*
Dutch view of a tropical harbor
A pirate hanging at Execution
  Dock

page xi   Pirates carrying off stolen treasure. (Courtesy of the Henry E. Huntington Library and Art Gallery)

The sea serpent ornament appearing throughout the book is from Conrad Gesner's *Fischbuch*, first published in 1670. (Courtesy of the Museum of Comparative Zoology, Harvard University)

CAPTAIN KIDD
✳ AND *the* WAR ✳
AGAINST *the* PIRATES

ONE

The Sea Peoples

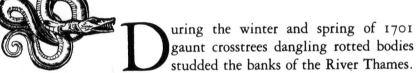

During the winter and spring of 1701 gaunt crosstrees dangling rotted bodies studded the banks of the River Thames. Each blackened corpse attested to one more pirate who had fallen into the clutches of the High Court of Admiralty. Past this grisly scene teemed the traffic of the great river: colliers from Newcastle, red-sailed Thames luggers, broad-beamed Indiamen struggling to complete their long and arduous voyages, hosts of weather-beaten snows, pinks, brigantines, and other craft that carried the trade of England's growing empire. Their crews could hardly fail to see the gruesome exhibits at the margins of the river, and the sailors no doubt made uneasy jokes about the local "bird food," or tried to ward off the evil eye, or muttered "There but for the grace of God . . ."

The Lords of the Admiralty had mounted the horrible display to remind sailors of the consequences of signing on as a pirate, and to comfort and reassure the merchant community of London, which was alarmed at the frightening surge of piracy in the Americas, Africa, and Asia. After such a sight no one could doubt the determination of the government to remove robbers from the sea-lanes and allow commerce to flow unimpeded, bringing wealth to merchants and revenue to the state. Most of the dead were Frenchmen from the crew of Captain Louis Guittar, whose ironically named ship, La Paix, had been taken off the coast of Virginia after a long fight with the Shoreham, a navy patrol ship.[1] The captain and twenty-three of his men had been "pushed off" (hanged) in one day, a spectacle that drew a particularly large crowd. Afterward four corpses, including that of Guittar, were strung along the Thames bank.

Toward the end of May another group of bodies washed back and forth in the tides, and while most of the corpses were those of simple seamen whose lives went unnoticed outside the records of the High Court of Admiralty, the exception was Captain William Kidd, whose body decorated Tilbury Point. Kidd's reputation was enhanced at the time of his hanging by two pamphlets known as broadsheets, which gave an account of his dying moments, and a ballad celebrating his career.[2] This publicity fed a public that doted on scandalous lives, particularly those that ended in some gruesome way. Kidd was already renowned in London (somewhat unjustifiably) as a ferocious pirate, and his name even today is a byword for piracy. He represents the heroic age of buccaneering so beloved in popular culture.

William Kidd is also a transitional figure. The very success and geographic expansion of piracy in the seventeenth century could not continue in an era of thriving imperial trade. The roistering buccaneer did not suit the hard-headed merchants and imperial bureaucrats, whose musty world of balance sheets and reports came into violent conflict with that of the pirates. Eventually the imperial powers would reform their methods of handling piracy and create new means of suppression. Not that piracy was wiped out, but the large groups of European deep-sea marauders ceased to exist. The means created to achieve this task would be useful later as the European powers, particularly the English, expanded their empires. Kidd's misdeeds helped to bring about the new policy; thus his life represents a turning point in the history of empire as well as in the history of piracy.

Ever since the waterways and seas of the world have been used for transport, there have been sea robbers ready to emulate their land-bound colleagues. There have always been those who relied on the seas to provide for their needs and who took the ocean's bounty to include those goods brought to their doorstep;

whether these came by shipwreck or by seizure mattered very little. Until recent times shipping was expensive and used only when necessary, so almost anything shipped by sea was either a luxury item or a desperately needed staple. Ships hugged the shoreline and rarely ventured into deep waters; if they did, it was for the shortest distances possible. They moved slowly from promontory to promontory, keeping a constant lookout. Every twist and turn of the coast could hide a marauding vessel waiting for the unwary or the ill prepared. A sudden flash of oars, blood-curdling shouts, a shower of projectiles, the crash of hulls were a prelude to surrender or bloody fighting. Prisoners were kept only if needed as slaves or for ransom; if they were unfortunate enough to fit neither category, they were killed. Life in general was nasty, short, and brutish; it was more so on the seas. The merchant ships were not always paragons of virtue either. They too were prepared to plunder any vessel that appeared to be weak, in distress, or in any way an easy target. A profit was a profit, no matter how it was earned.

Now and then a community decided that piracy provided a more profitable living than anything else available. It then made certain that its ships were faster and its men better armed than those of the potential opposition. Such communities created zones of great danger, best avoided by all but the most powerful. If they happened to be located near an important strait, such as Hormuz, Malacca, or Gibraltar, safe passage was achieved only via a strong ship or payment of a "fee." Sometimes the sea peoples were unsatisfied with control of local waters. Fast ships and fighting men could be used against stationary targets; any port, town, or village might become a tempting prize. Even though wealth was transported by sea, it was accumulated in the homes and warehouses of merchants and officials, and in these communities each and every person was a potential slave. The sea peoples terrorized all those on or close to the sea.

From time immemorial the Mediterranean Sea has suffered every kind of pirate community. Its narrow waters have carried goods of all kinds between Asia and Europe, and the large populations living on its shores have generated a substantial amount of trade. Nothing traveled with much certainty—particularly after 1200 B.C., when there was a general breakdown of order. Then, as Tritsch writes, "harsh-voiced and sullen-faced [men who] loved the groans and violence of war" rose to scour the sea and act as "sackers of cities." These men were immortalized by the Greek epic poets, who recorded their pirate deeds against a backdrop of contending gods and goddesses who furthered the goals of their special heroes while expressing malevolent displeasure with those favored by their enemies. So common was piracy to the Greeks that Aristotle and Thucydides spoke of it as a reasonable career, and Herodotus began his history of the Persian wars with an act of piracy.[3] Many peoples around the Mediterranean basin practiced piracy, but the Greeks made it the stuff of legend.

As trade and commerce flourished, so did the corsairs; the checks on them were few, and some were emboldened to terrorize large areas. The Samians had a large fleet and ferocious mariners, with which they controlled the balance of power among the Greek trading leagues. Their chief goal was to ensure that no league could grow strong enough to threaten their activities.[4]

The most famous pirate league of ancient history was that of Cilicia. Its members inhabited the coastline of southern Anatolia, where the rugged interior sheltered them from land attacks. By the middle of the last century B.C. the Cilicians had a fleet of some thousand ships that roamed the Mediterranean. They defeated a Roman fleet and plundered Syracuse; Ostia, Rome's own port, fell to them; two purple-robed praetors and their retinue were kidnapped while traveling on a coastal road; even the Roman legions risked dangerous winter voyages rather than face them. Mithradites and other enemies of Rome sought them out as allies. Scarcely a fishing boat, village, merchantman, or seashore path was free from their attacks. Even the young Julius Caesar fell victim to them, but he paid his ransom and later returned to take their goods and crucify them.

By 69 B.C. Ostia and Delos were looted; the grain ships from Africa were diverted, threatening Rome with starvation; other trade was at a standstill; and Roman politicians were on their feet demanding action. The result was the much feared revival of the powerful office of tribune and the appointment of the ambitious Pompey to fill the post of proconsul. Two years later Pompey had marshaled 270 ships, which roamed the Mediterranean seeking out the Cilicians. After securing the western end, with sixty selected ships he turned to Cilicia itself and crushed the home bases there. Subsequently the Romans built small outposts to protect shipping: each contained docks to shelter one or two galleys, and housing for the sailors and soldiers who manned them while patrolling local waters. The Pax Romana reigned at sea.[5] As long as Roman power was in the ascendant, piracy was kept under control; but as Rome declined, a wise captain regarded every other ship with deep suspicion as, once more, fast ships went to sea filled with hard-eyed men.

After the passing of the Roman hegemony in the fifth century the corsairs again flourished in the Mediterranean, and the unbridled, widespread piracy that was the norm elsewhere prevailed. Some of the pirate groups of the time have an established place in sea lore. The Vikings, for instance, plundered trading vessels, towns, and religious houses with equal fervor. Anyone within reach of their ships feared the end of winter because it brought a surge of men in long ships seeking land and plunder. While the Vikings were the most famous pirates of the Middle Ages, they were not the only ones. The English, the French, the Dutch, the Irish, the Muslims, and the Basques were notable hunters upon the seas. They did not range as far afield as the Vikings, but they threatened any traveler from Cape Finisterre in Spain to the North Sea approaches of the English Channel.[6]

A similar threat hung over any passage in the world where shipping congregated. The sea routes between East and West were always dangerous. Between India and the Middle East were two bottlenecks: the strait of Babs-al-Mandab between the Red Sea and the Arabian Sea, and the strait of Hormuz between the Persian Gulf and the Gulf of Oman. In these straits, or the approaches to them, lurked constant danger. Through the Babs-al-Mandab went ships bound for Egypt and, after the expansion of Mohammedanism, pilgrim fleets sailed cautiously from as far away as Southeast Asia to the port of Jidda, the last stop before Mecca. These fleets, along with a great variety of trade goods, carried thousands of the faithful, loaded with money to pay for their travel. They made a tempting target.[7] And the strait of Hormuz was an enormous funnel for the rich East-West trade from India to Persia.

Farther east lay similar stretches of treacherous waters. The

Malabar coast of India was frequented by pirates ready to intercept trade as it followed the coast northward. Still farther east, in the strait of Malacca, only the brave and the foolish failed to keep watch. The Malays and the Sumatrans controlled the Indian Ocean side of the strait, and the Dyaks and Arrakans harassed those who ventured on the eastern approaches. In fact, if a vessel started a voyage in Japan bound for Persia, it could only feel safe in mid-ocean; but because the trade routes hugged the coast, there were few locations where a captain could feel secure.

The traditional sea peoples threatened every trade artery from ancient times on. The names might change, the ships might change—but there were always those who waited for the unwary. As trade prospered, the numbers of these peoples grew; as it declined, so did they. Only occasionally, when they became too troublesome or overbearing, were they threatened by the land-based states. Pompey and the Roman assault on the Cilicians is one of several examples. During the Ming dynasty (1368–1644) the central government of China became alarmed by the increasing toll taken over a larger and larger area of the coast and inland waterways by the Wo-k'ou (Chinese and Japanese pirates operating off China's coasts). It mustered its resources to crush the marauders and alleviate the conditions that caused their increase. As a result, piracy reverted to a more localized if still persistent condition.[8] Venice at its height as a trading power suffered many raids by the Uzkoks. Eventually the government organized sufficient military and diplomatic support to isolate the Uzkoks, invade their base at Segna, and prevent them from terrorizing the Adriatic.[9]

Premodern states had to be deeply aroused before initiating such actions. Except for Venice, the major states were oriented to domination of land areas. For land and people created the wealth transported by sea, and societies were organized around the control of these resources. Military castes, whether knights or samurai, won glory and acquired social position in land battles. Deeds at sea counted for little.[10] Fighting ships also cost a great deal to build and maintain; creation of a navy resulted in exorbitant financial burdens. Rulers who did not prize control of the seas felt little need to indemnify themselves in this way. In fact, they frequently used pirate ships if they needed fighting vessels or transport for their armies. Even England used "unofficial" fleets before the creation of its modern navy.[11] Thus the sea people flourished and declined, cooperated with or attacked, the landed empires and states in a never-ending cycle. Then in the fifteenth century the situation changed dramatically. New states, bent on control of the seas, emerged in Europe and their rise also brought a new group of pirates to the coastlines of the world.

By the fifteenth century a variety of new shipping and navigation technologies allowed the mariners of Europe to sail farther and farther away from the coast with a high degree of certainty in retracing their route. The world opened to them, and the lengthy process of European expansion began. It was accompanied by new forms of piracy. To the rest of the world the nuances of this evolution mattered little, for *all* Europeans came to their shores as pirates. Witness the early career of the Portuguese, who were attracted to Asia by the spices, drugs, jewels, and exotic cloth of the East. When Vasco da Gama sailed into the Indian Ocean in 1498, he confronted an ancient trade network controlled by established merchant communities. Undaunted, da Gama attacked merchantmen, pilgrim ships, and rice carriers with equal ferocity. Sailors were mutilated and men, women, and children were burned to death with their ships.[12] This savagery was initiated by the Portuguese, and the Europeans who followed them simply adopted their techniques. Such outrageous behavior was not unknown in Europe; however, a growing web of international agreements tried to restrict atrocities to wartime.[13] These understandings were limited to European waters, and the Christians of western Europe never applied them to the Muslims who controlled much of the trade of the Indian subcontinent and the Spice Islands.

The Portuguese had their reasons. The wealthy societies of Asia had very little need for European goods such as heavy wool, olive oil, and minerals. If they wanted Asian commodities, the Portuguese had to either steal them, which in the long run was self-defeating, or pay for them with gold and silver—unthinkable as a permanent policy. The solution, developed by the Portuguese and emulated by those who followed them, was to dominate the local or native trade routes. To that end they seized ports such as Goa, Cochin, Hormuz, and Malacca. The trade between these ports, notably in Indian cloth that was exchanged in Malacca for spices, came under their control or was carried on only after duties were paid to them. The wealth generated by such trade and fees could be used to offset the chronic imbalance of payments in the East. All of the other European powers adopted similar schemes in Asia, the most odious of which was the opium trade utilized by the English to acquire an income in China.[14]

The great Asian empires were unable to forestall the Portuguese onslaught. By 1543 Portuguese ships had swept around Southeast Asia to make contact with China and finally Japan. Wherever they went, they attacked local shipping while negotiating concessions. Pugnacity, greed, a crusading spirit, and, above all, a superior marine technology guaranteed their success. The Portuguese had led western Europe in developing sturdy, maneuverable, well-armed ships that, properly handled, had no equal. The landed states could keep the Europeans from penetrating the interior, but they could not control their own coastlines.

The Mughal Empire in India, for example, exercised little or no control over the seas. Starting from a base in northern India, the Mughals slowly expanded southward until by the end of the seventeenth century their empire encompassed nearly all of the subcontinent. The emperors were absorbed with these conquests, and the few coastal states had to deal alone with the Europeans. The Kunjalis, the hereditary admirals of Calicut on the east coast, or the Gujaratis, on the west coast, were left to meet the Portuguese; although they registered a few early victories, they quickly succumbed to the superior ships of the enemy. The Gujaratis then requested aid from the Muslim world, and the declining Mameluk state of Egypt in 1509 sent a fleet that was quickly crushed. The Turks moved to help, but the Ottoman Empire was using its resources to expand to the west and northwest. The resources it was able to spare were enough to keep the Portuguese from penetrating very far into the Persian Gulf and the Red Sea, and the two sides learned to live with an uneasy truce.[15]

There had existed for a time one fleet capable of intimidating the Portuguese. Under the Yung-Lo emperor of the Ming dynasty the Chinese fleet numbered approximately thirty-eight hundred ships; the most powerful, the treasure ships, reached a length of 442 feet and a width of 180 feet and carried four hundred fifty to five hundred men. The Yung-Lo emperor sent his powerful war fleets on seven different expeditions—to remind the world of China's power, to trade, and to acquire knowledge. The leader of six of these voyages was the famous admiral Cheng-Ho. During the first of his voyages (1406–1407) he commanded 317 ships (including 62 treasure ships) and 28,870 men. This fleet ventured into the Indian Ocean and returned through the strait of Malacca, where the local pirates made the costly mistake of challenging Cheng-Ho's authority and power. In revenge he killed five thousand of them and took their leader to China where, after being taught the error of his ways, he was beheaded. The other expeditions visited Japan, Southeast Asia, many of the island kingdoms, India, Ceylon, Persia, and the Red Sea, and sailed down the African coast as far as present-day Tanzania. The size of these fleets and the complexity of the organization for such long voyages indicate that in the early fifteenth century China was the greatest naval power in the world. We can only speculate on what would have happened if the Portuguese had met one of these armadas, for by 1435 the Chinese fleet was rotting at the docks, abandoned by a new emperor who felt no need of contact with the rest of the world. In an era of European expansion Chinese naval power would never recover. The retreat of the Ming Empire to contemplation of the singular splendor of Chinese civilization was symptomatic of a general malaise in all the major landed states at this time, a situation that opened the way for further European expansion.[16]

If the vast land-based empires could not control the seas, neither could Portugal and Spain, the new imperial powers. Hardly had the carapaces of their empires been formed than others pried them open to share the wealth. The newcomers were England, France, and the Netherlands, all rising states of northwestern Europe with ancient maritime traditions. By the end of the sixteenth century these nations challenged Spain and Portugal in every corner of their hard-won empires, copying their techniques against local trade and using them also against the Iberians. Try as they might to keep the poachers out, the new empires failed. Portugal fell by the wayside, leaving Spain to fight the newcomers alone. While there were Spanish victories, there was no ultimate crushing defeat of its enemies.

The English, the French, and the Dutch also fought one another in declared and undeclared war, as each sought to protect its gains and fulfill its national aspirations. Small wonder that each could hurt the other, but none could deliver a death blow.[17]

One of the most important arenas in this conflict was the Mediterranean, and it illustrates all of the problems confronting Spain. For centuries Christians and Muslims had unleashed crusade after crusade to contest every inch of ground around the Mediterranean. Muslim advances had steadily pushed the Christian nations farther and farther west until, in the sixteenth century, Spain (now under Hapsburg leadership) organized the defenses of the West, and in 1571 Don Juan of Austria led the Christian navies to a victory at Lepanto. It proved to be one of those battles from which both sides recoiled, unable and unwilling to repeat the effort needed to continue the struggle. Spain became absorbed in the fight against the heretics in the Low Countries and in England, while the Ottoman Empire fell victim to internal reforms that weakened its government and its military organization. Although both were still formidable military powers, they ceased using the tactic of sending great battle fleets to smash the opposition. Instead, they allowed a situation to develop that has been called "war by other means"—war fought by irregular forces that preyed upon the enemy and kept them off balance at very little cost, and that created maximum peril to ordinary trade. This brutal conflict had few rules, as governments sanctioned many activities in the name of the true faith. In time, as the struggle for empire expanded, this situation spread beyond the Pillars of Hercules to engulf most of the world. The governments, not very powerful to begin with, found it ever more difficult to control their subjects. "Harsh-voiced and sullen-faced men" dominated the desperate struggle that followed.[18]

By the end of the seventeenth century several types of piracy were discernible: officially sanctioned piracy, commercial piracy, and marauding. They were not mutually exclusive, and the career of any given pirate might encompass all three. There was always the possibility too that what was sanctioned one day might be damned the next, so these three types should not be considered rigid categories, but only a mechanism for understanding the vast number of actions known as piracy.

Officially sanctioned piracy comprises acts that are clearly piratical under any system of law but that go unpunished because a particular government finds it convenient to ignore such activities or even secretly to sponsor them. The avarice of England, France, and the Netherlands was whetted by the rumors that leaked out of Iberia of enormous wealth in the New World. Then in 1523 Jean Fleury, commanding a French squadron, chased a heavily laden Spanish fleet struggling home from the Caribbean. He captured a few of the ships, and when the French broke into the sealed chests on board, their wildest fantasies were realized. Before their eyes were the treasures Cortez had plundered from the Aztec capital of Tenochtitlán.[19] As fast as wind and tide allowed, the story of Fleury's prize spread over Europe. Outsiders pondered the injustice of so much wealth in the hands of so few and decided it must be shared. The manner of redistribution was rarely discussed in the same breath as law and morality.

Prevailing opinion in England, France, and the Netherlands usually supported anyone who was successful. The legal mechanisms for control of wrongdoers outside the boundaries of the state were in their infancy. Still, there were a few rules. In wartime the privateering commission or letter of marque permitted privately financed warships to attack enemy shipping; in peacetime the letter of reprisal allowed merchants to recover their losses due to piracy. Reprisal recognized that princes did not maintain permanent embassies with one another so that it was impossible to pursue private grievances on a regular basis. Thus a letter of reprisal from a ruler allowed the aggrieved subject to steal from the subjects of the prince whose subjects stole his property in the first place. It was a rather crude way of compensating for losses at sea and illustrates the weak institutional structure of international relations at the time.

Both commissions created many opportunities for abuse. Privateers rarely recognized neutrals and seized the property of anyone trading with the enemy, no matter what their relationship with their own prince. In fact, it was common to regard anyone not in actual alliance with one's own country as an enemy. Professional privateers also sought commissions in the service of another prince if their own sovereign decided to opt for peace, so that it was difficult to tell who was a legitimate privateer and who was a pirate. The reprisal commission offered similar opportunities for cheating. Who would know if the same letter of reprisal appeared in a number of out-of-the-way ports to justify multiple seizures? Revenge was sweet, but also incredibly profitable.[20] Even if such a ruse was detected, enforcement was ineffectual. Corruption flourished everywhere, and there were problems in the nature of government. Piracy in southwestern England and southern Ireland, for example, lasted a long while after the creation of the Tudor state. The central government lacked authority because local magnates, who also controlled local offices, lived partly on the profits of brigandage. Their unwillingness to act severely restrained the power of the central government. When the Lord High Admiral colluded with local officials or pirates, and he did, the government was paralyzed.[21] Occasionally the navy received orders to patrol, but because of the expense involved in sending large ships, only small ones went out and frequently they were careful to avoid battle with the better-armed pirates.[22] Thus greed, corruption, and chronically weak treasuries hampered the institutions of central government, at the same time that the legal situation lacked clarity. All of these factors compounded the problems of control.

A host of other activities did not have the slightest patina of legality yet still received official sanction, or at least were greeted with temporary blindness. Among the most famous examples of this phenomenon is the circumnavigation of the world in 1577–1579 by the most renowned Sea Hawk, Sir Francis Drake. This voyage was a masterful piece of navigation, a great adventure—and a pirate voyage. Once Drake had entered the Pacific, where the Spanish dozed in the security of the "Spanish lake," his actions were totally designed to enrich himself, his men, and his investors. He attacked everything in sight, including the *Cacafuego,* a treasure ship. When he completed his voyage, the booty was so incredible that Queen Elizabeth protected him from an irate Spain, in the process taking her share of the spoils.[23] To the English, Drake was a patriot; to the Spanish, he was a pirate. The Sea Hawks and their Dutch rivals, the Sea Beggars, were happy to act as privateers in wartime; peacetime saw them hunting Spanish ships with equal pleasure.

The long Anglo-Spanish war came to an end in 1603, unfortunately for the English privateers. They were left with the choice of returning to piracy or finding another means of raiding Spain. King James I, wanting to keep his newfound peace with Spain, detested the effects on diplomacy of pirate raids on the Spanish. The solution for the Sea Hawks was to seek a haven beyond the scrutiny of the government. The Earl of Warwick, one of the leading privateers, found one in the Grand Duke of Tuscany. The duke was no friend of Spain and granted commissions to those who wanted to raid Spanish commerce. Armed with his piece of paper, Warwick was in business again. He also invested in the Virginia Company, for he saw the settlement at Jamestown as a convenient and out-of-the-way base for piracy. Other men simply went to sea and became pirates without the slightest cover of legality.[24]

Government officers did more than merely wink at such misconduct. Robert Cecil, Earl of Salisbury and secretary to Elizabeth and James I, financed his own pirate, Richard Gifford, who managed to get in trouble nearly every time he captured a ship. Gifford operated in the Mediterranean, where he preyed on Italian and French shipping. When he was captured, Cecil used his influence to free Gifford from his captors. As long as Gifford returned a profit, Cecil helped him. He never seemed to be embarrassed by the fact that the same Italian diplomats who urged him to stop English piracy represented the states he was robbing. He even entered into a partnership with Charles Howard, the Earl of Nottingham and Lord High Admiral. Their ship, the *Lioness,* was sent out to chase pirates, but instead captured the *Greyhound* of Middleburg and caused a diplomatic incident. Once again, Cecil resolved the problem and pocketed the profits. Undaunted by the trouble they had created, the partners then used two ships of the Royal Navy for piracy, even though they were commissioned as part of a fleet ordered to combat pirates in Ireland. Because the government paid the costs of fitting out the vessels, the profits of the two men were substantial.[25]

Cecil is typical of the entrepreneurs who profited from their positions at a time when men saw government as a path to fortune. Their aspirations went beyond the salary the job brought; they wanted to make real money while in government. Bribes were an obvious source of supplemental income; there were also opportunities for monopolies, use of the state's resources, and sale of inside information. Private business and government business were not seen as antagonistic, but as complementary means to ensure the economic well-being of a family dynasty.[26]

Cecil was by no means the most distinguished dabbler in piracy. In 1633 Charles I sent the *Seahorse* to the Red Sea to capture Spanish ships. On sighting a heavily laden Indian ship, captain and crew abandoned their plans and snapped up the prize. The East India Company was furious, because the Mughal government held it liable for the ship and its cargo. The company petitioned the king, who heard the complaints, uttered soothing words, and pocketed his share of the profits.[27]

There was a final form of official piracy that flourished in the New World, especially in the Caribbean. Spain grimly shielded the South American mainland and the Greater Antilles, while the English, the French, and the Dutch grasped at any island that lay undefended. Each then attempted to defend its territory against all rivals. Controlling by far the largest area, Spain simply could not protect every colony. Strategic and economic centers were fortified, and the all-important treasure that fueled the Spanish state was carried in fast-sailing frigates. Thus the core of Spain's empire, encapsulated in a stultifying cocoon, warily regarded the world. The remainder of the empire had to rely on local resources until help arrived, if it did, from the laggard Spanish bureaucracy.[28]

During the late sixteenth and early seventeenth centuries the situation for the Spanish remained bleak, but that of the newly established rivals was no better. If Spain's enemies settled too close to Spanish possessions or vital interests, they discovered that Spanish swords still had very sharp edges. After forty years of raiding, the French decided to create a colony on the Florida peninsula, from which they could raid Spanish ships sailing through the Florida strait. In 1564 Fort Carolina was founded on the Saint Johns River; a year later Pedro Menendez and his forces swept through the settlement killing everyone in sight and then hunting down the survivors at their leisure. The English fared no better when they colonized Providence Island off the Honduran coast. Founded in 1638 by a group of investors, including the ubiquitous Earl of

Warwick, the settlement quickly turned from farming to raiding the Spanish colonies. Providence Island was simply too close to important Spanish interests to be tolerated, so in 1640 an invasion force was sent to capture the island. Although this first fleet failed to seize its objective, the following year a better-led armada captured the colony and imprisoned the survivors.[29]

We have seen that there were limits to Spain's ability to police the Caribbean. The newcomers found those limits in the Lesser Antilles. The English and the French took Saint Christopher in 1624 and routed a Spanish invasion force in 1629. The English occupied Barbados in 1627 and Nevis the following year, while the Dutch captured Curaçao in 1634 and the French took Guadeloupe a year later. The Spanish refused to acknowledge these rival bases and harassed them when they could, but the tide had turned against them.

While all of the colonizing efforts and many of the raids carried out during this era had the approval of the governments involved, few received any financing. Dutch, English, and French policy-makers sought empire, but did not have the resources to achieve this goal. It was left to entrepreneurs to carry out state policy by private means. The primary attraction in the Caribbean was Spanish wealth; the Spanish colonists, then, had to pay for the imperial ambitions of their enemies. In wartime legal privateering could be organized. In peacetime simple piracy financed the invaders' raids, and once their colonies were established, they too profited from the booty of the corsairs. Piracy, which had helped to create the new empires, now defended and financed their operations.

Thus the Spanish faced a new and terrible enemy at the heart of their New World empire. Many nationalities were represented among the buccaneers, but the English, Dutch, and French were the most numerous. While not deeply patriotic, the pirates retained some residual loyalty—particularly if association with their mother country facilitated access to supplies and to aid in attacking Spanish targets.

The colony of Jamaica illustrates the relationship between pirates and empires. The English had seized Jamaica from Spain in 1655, although their situation there remained perilous for the first few years owing to a bitterly fought guerrilla war. At the Restoration of

Charles II in 1660, Jamaica feared further Spanish attacks. The new government wanted peace with Spain and the opportunity to trade in Spanish dominions. To further this policy, Lord Windsor was sent to the West Indies with instructions to make local treaties with the Spanish. No Spanish governor was empowered to make such agreements, and when Madrid heard the proposals they were quickly rebuffed. Not waiting for further instructions, Windsor simply gathered the buccaneers together, gave them commissions as privateers, and sent them to attack Spanish towns and shipping. Port Royale, Jamaica, became their base and in the process acquired a protective screen of ships and men, as well as the means of plundering the Spanish. English finances could not have funded such a fleet, and Windsor had acquired it at the cost of a few pieces of paper. The citizens of Port Royale profited from supplies and services sold to the pirates, and the merchants acquired many highly desirable cargoes at very little cost. The only losers were the Spanish, who regarded all buccaneers as pirates, regardless of the piece of paper they carried to justify their actions.

Even after the Treaty of Madrid was signed in 1670 guaranteeing the peace between England and Spain, the buccaneers continued to be supported (sometimes covertly, sometimes openly) by the Jamaicans.[30] From the English point of view their policy was an expedient one of providing a defense by private means when the public coffers were incapable of furnishing it. The French and Dutch colonists in the Caribbean, relying on their own buccaneers to help defend them, similarly enjoyed the profits of the association.[31] Even national governments used them during the imperial war of the 1690s: England and France both employed buccaneers to supplement the fleets they sent to the West Indies. And when the French sent a fleet in 1696, at a time when the English were weak, Secretary of State James Vernon warned the buccaneers of its coming.[32] This ancient technique of conducting public policy with private means is directly comparable to the use of pirate fleets by the medieval monarchy. There would be few other such instances after King William's War of 1688–1697, however, for the new states would be set on another course: they would prefer to exercise the state's growing monopoly of violence.

Commercial piracy is difficult to define, although it has two broad categories. The first is associated with merchants who invested in piracy just like their counterparts in government; these individuals, however, relied on their own resources. The second category is identified with communities that practiced piracy as a major economic enterprise. Even though the traditional sea peoples come immediately to mind, the difference lies in the relation of these communities to the growing international market. The expansion of European trade and empire meant a rising volume of ships and more frequent travel to a larger number of ports. The new states could not adequately control or police such a vast augmentation of the old trading networks. Moreover, the merchants of the fledgling imperial powers could not afford to insinuate themselves gently. They had to use every possible means to carve out a place in the sun, and if government officials disregarded the law, the merchant communities followed suit.

Some of the merchants, such as Sir John Watts of London, had learned the joys of commerce raiding in wartime and merely continued the practice after peace was declared.[33] Then there was Robert Renegar, an Englishman involved in the Iberian trade. During one of the many tense periods in Anglo-Spanish relations, the Spanish government seized the property of many English merchants. Renegar should have returned to England, filed a complaint, and requested a letter of reprisal. He did leave Spain, but only went far enough to capture a galleon loaded with an official gold shipment from the New World—plus a considerable amount of smuggled gold. The Spanish were outraged at Renegar's piracy, for he had not the least mantle of legality. But he did have approximately 7 million marevedis of gold, more than enough to buy favor in Whitehall.[34]

The major trading companies used every means possible to establish their monopolies. For years the Dutch West India Company traded and pillaged in the Americas. At the same time it spied on the Spanish convoy system, probing its schedules and weaknesses. In 1628, after careful preparations, the company sent out a fleet under the leadership of Piet Heyn. It struck just as the treasure fleet was approaching Havana. Only one ship from the Spanish convoy managed to struggle into port. Heyn's men looted the fleet and set sail for home. Ironically they had to outrun the pirates of Dunkirk before displaying the treasure before the company leadership. The loot provided a profit of 7 million guilders and the greatest dividend the company's investors ever received.[35]

In Asian waters the targets were Portuguese, and local merchant-men and the Dutch and English East India companies accorded them the same care and kindness the Portuguese had demonstrated toward local shipping when they entered the Orient. The English raids managed to set a new standard for rapacity. The voyages of James Lancaster and Henry Middleton especially hardened the Indian view that all pirates were English.[36] Although they lacked the deadly image of the conquistadors, English merchants looted and pillaged with similar greed.

Another form of commercial piracy flourished on the geographic peripheries of empire. As the newly ambitious imperial states gradually acquired colonies of their own and consolidated their positions in the New World, they created local communities of merchants who faced some stark economic facts. They were caught in a system that forced them to trade low-priced agricultural products for high-priced manufactured goods in addition to paying various duties and fees. The consequence for many merchants was an unfavorable balance of trade and a chronic lack of hard money. Solutions to these dilemmas had to be found in the context of immature local economies susceptible to the slightest shift in the emerging world economy. As a result merchants sought any means to make money, and the pirates provided one way of doing so. On occasion colonial merchants sponsored pirate voyages much as their cosmopolitan brothers did, but most of the time they preferred to give the buccaneers sanctuary and trade with them. Once in port the pirates exchanged their goods, spent their booty, reequipped their ships, and purchased services of all kinds before returning to sea. The townsmen acquired all sorts of cargoes, mostly Spanish commodities, but because they prized "pieces of eight" and other forms of cash just as much as the pirates, they did everything possible to separate the pirates from their money. Port Royale,

Jamaica, and Petite Guave, Hispaniola, earned a reputation for doing this earlier than other ports; in time New York, Boston, Philadelphia, Newport, and Charleston warmly welcomed the brigands. Infant economies everywhere on the peripheries of empire eagerly sought easy money. When they eventually became established, the colonial merchants found the rough ways of the pirates too high a price to pay and turned against the buccaneers, but for nearly a century they provided sanctuary.

If governments and merchants indulged in piracy throughout the empires, it was not long before other entrepreneurs joined in. These men created a wholly new kind of piracy—the deep-sea *marauders,* Europeans who roamed the world seeking suitable targets. They first appeared in sizable numbers in the Mediterranean in about 1570, expanding after the turn of the century into the Atlantic. They were to find a true home and a new name in the Caribbean, where after 1650 the buccaneers were an important factor. Later they spread far beyond America. The first pulse moved outward from the Caribbean in about 1680, when pirates crossed the Isthmus of Panama or sailed around South America to raid in the Pacific—and eventually a few even crossed the Pacific. A second pulse traveled to the west coast of Africa and on around the Cape of Good Hope into the Indian Ocean. During this so-called Golden Age of piracy two different methods of operation were used: one can be defined as *organized* marauding, the other as *anarchistic* marauding. Many men were involved in both; yet a distinction can be made. Organized pirates remained attached to a port as their base of operation. Anarchistic marauding involved leaving behind the base of operation and wandering for months— even years—at a time.

In early modern times organized marauding flourished in the Mediterranean and the Caribbean, and cropped up to a lesser extent elsewhere. The Mediterranean, as befits its ancient traditions, had a number of piracy centers, notably the ports of the Barbary Coast but equally deadly sea robbers operated out of Segna, Malta, Livorno, Villefranche, and other ports. During the sixteenth century these ports experienced a surge of activity in the aftermath of the battle of

Lepanto. The Hapsburgs and the Ottoman Turks abandoned their policy of unleashing crusade after crusade and substituted a policy that allowed anyone to attack the "infidels." Such an atmosphere of disorder breeds lawlessness and encourages renegades who care for neither cause, only their own prosperity. These men gravitated toward the North African ports of Salé and Marmora, and to the old corsair cities of Tunis and Algiers.[37]

These last two ports had long histories of corsair activities.[38] On the whole, pirates there operated in much the same fashion as had the ancient sea peoples of the Mediterranean. After winter was over their galleys went to sea seeking prizes, but the brigands were always prepared to raid settlements for slaves. In fact, slaving was the activity that brought the greatest profits and struck terror in Catholic and Protestant hearts alike. To keep Christians from remaining in the hands of the ruthless Muslim slavers, an extensive network of Catholic orders and Jewish middlemen sprang up to ransom the captives from the corsairs. To pay the ransoms many states and communities levied a "Turk's rate" as general taxation.[39] Periodically, squadrons of warships went to the Barbary Coast to sink the corsair ships and free their prisoners. Lest such actions be regarded as Muslim depravity, it should be remembered that the Christians did exactly the same thing. The Knights of Saint John on Malta supported themselves by capturing, ransoming, or selling Muslims, and there were slave markets in other Christian ports such as Livorno.[40] Dealing in slaves was an odious but widespread activity and an old Mediterranean tradition.

During the second half of the sixteenth century changes occurred in the Mediterranean that would affect the operations of the Barbary corsairs; afterward, they would be less like the traditional sea peoples. The English and Dutch brought their new round-hulled, squared-sailed ships into the Mediterranean to seek out markets in eastern ports. Their nimble craft allowed them to stay at sea in weather that drove galleys to seek the safety of harbors, and their armament proved devastating in combat. Such advantages led some captains to abandon trade for pillage. Others who were already hardened brigands drifted into the Mediterranean and ended their journey in the Barbary port cities. The mere fact that they sailed with the Muslims made them anathema to other Christians; but they, like many who followed in their wake, had left behind their own societies. Nothing was safe from the new marauders, not even the gigantic argosies of the Venetians and the Genoese.[41] Algiers, Tunis, Marmora, Livorno, Villefranche, and Salé became entry ports for pillaged goods, and the merchants followed to acquire bargains. Gifford, Cecil's pirate, took his captures to Tunis, then returned to Livorno to contact the agents of English merchants.[42] These merchants even sold armaments to the pirates, as an English fleet discovered when it entered Salé in 1684 and captured an English merchantman.[43] Corsair influence on the towns varied with the strength of the local government. The community probably most affected was Salé, which was administered by a council of admirals. Elsewhere the pirates had less authority, and in Algiers the new pirates were absorbed into the old corsair community.[44]

Some of the new pirates preferred not to cooperate so closely with the Barbary corsairs. They settled in Marmora or Salé, still in North Africa but without the long traditions of the corsair ports. The most outstanding of these men was Henry Mainwaring. After an Oxford and Inner Temple education he went off to fight in the Low Countries, but in 1612 he bought the *Resistance* and went to Marmora. His leadership qualities soon attracted other crews to his flag until eventually he led a disciplined fleet. In one six-week period he took Spanish ships and cargoes valued at 500,000 crowns. Such wealth attracted a great deal of attention. The Grand Duke of Savoy allowed Mainwaring to use the port of Villefranche, the Grand Duke of Tuscany wanted him to join his fleet of pirates/privateers, and the Spanish preferred to see him dead. When the Spanish navy tried to seize him at sea, his ships won the battle; so the government fell back on the expedient of offering him 20,000 ducats to find another career. Finally, it was the English government, embarrassed by his success and desirous of peace with Spain, that persuaded him to retire. In 1618, two years after returning to England, he was knighted and went on to have a distinguished career in the Royal Navy.[45]

By the early seventeenth century northern Europeans no longer drifted into the Barbary ports in such large numbers. But the corsairs had had time to learn the new marine technology, and from this knowledge developed fast new ships that allowed them to expand their range from the Mediterranean into the Atlantic. They now raided Iceland, Ireland, and the Azores, and even sailed into the Thames, bringing fear to an ever greater number of Christians.[46]

It was in the West Indies that the new breed of pirates found their true home. More and more men there cut their contacts with European society and set out to wander across the seas of the world. Year after year, and at an accelerating rate during the seventeenth century, free and unfree immigrants arrived in the Caribbean. Many of them cared very little for their new life and fled to the myriad islands of the Antilles or settled in isolated areas on the vast shoreline of the American sea. Some were slaves or indentured servants who tired of their bondage and escaped to the freedom of tropical jungles. Others were sailors and soldiers who sought release from discipline in the New World. Marginal people in their own societies, they had little or no status and stood at the bottom of a steep-sided social pyramid. While their leaving might cause some inconvenience to their masters, another muscular back was always available as a replacement.

After they escaped, many settled down to hunting the cattle that roamed free on some of the islands (particularly Hispaniola), where the animals had been left to provide food for ships and the local communities. Gathered together in ragged, self-governing bands, the cow killers honed their sharpshooting skills while hunting. They cooked their meat over a boucan, a practice that led to the distinctive name *boucaniers* and in time to *buccaneers*. For many it was the good life, impossible to duplicate in Europe: enough to eat, independence, freedom from masters. Gradually some individuals drifted into piracy, for it was always difficult to pass up an easy target sailing close to the coast. A practice that started as a few men in a canoe waiting to catch an unwary coastal freighter, gradually grew to large ships with over a hundred in the crew, and finally to whole fleets. Success brought more and more recruits flocking to the red flag (which prior to the skull and crossbones was the pirate banner), until thousands of men could be mustered for an attack.

The availability of so many men made it possible to contemplate more lucrative targets in the Spanish colonies, for any ship that carried treasure had to collect it first in one of the port towns. As the number of buccaneers grew, so did the threat to every Spanish town or village anywhere near the coast. Marshaled by leaders such as Sir Henry Morgan or Laurent de Graff, the ragged bands from the sea captured even Cartagena, Porto Bello, Vera Cruz, and Panama. After each attack they gathered up the loot, killed or delivered up their hostages, and set sail for Petite Guave or Port Royale. There they traded in their booty and caroused before dispersing to hunt in smaller bands or to settle in out-of-the-way islands and await the next call for a raid.[47]

From the ranks of these men came the anarchistic marauders. The life of one such individual can be traced in the deposition of Robert Dangerfield, taken September 27, 1684, when he was thirty-two years old.[48]

Dangerfield's voyage began at Point Negril, Jamaica, when a 26-ton barque arrived. It was captained by Jeremy Revelle, who announced that he intended to go on a voyage of "purchase" against the Spanish. Dangerfield and thirty-five others agreed to join him, and off they went. They spotted a ship and chased it into the harbor, where they found two pirate ships led by a Captain Mitchell and a Captain Laurence. Laurence ordered his men (who were no doubt more numerous) to seize Dangerfield and the rest of his shipmates, disarming all of them and throwing a few overboard. The rest were taken ashore briefly, but when two sails appeared on the horizon Laurence relented and asked them to join with him in taking the ships. Weapons and ship restored, Dangerfield and his mates set sail with the rest, only to discover that the ships were a Spanish prize carrying the notorious Captain van Horne, with whom Revelle did not want to tangle; so he used the cover of darkness to sneak away.

The crew now discussed its next destination. The majority voted in favor of Guinea in Africa, whereas the minority of Revelle and three others favored Campeche Bay in Mexico. It was dangerous, even for a captain, to lose an election among pirates. The minority were put ashore on a deserted island ten miles from the Spanish Main with nothing but a canoe and a turtle net. (As harsh as this sounds, the losers were actually well off compared to others who were simply sent off with the shirts on their backs.[49]) The winners, who had now elected Dr. John Graham, a physician, as their captain, turned north to catch the Gulf Stream out of the Caribbean. Just off Point Comfort they stopped two small colonial ships and persuaded three young men to join them. They avoided the port cities and sighted nothing until, northeast of Boston, they captured a French fishing barque and two French shallops. At this point an argument arose between Graham and the master, John Wright. Most of the crew sided with Wright, so Graham and seven others were given the French barque and sent on their way.

After electing Joseph Anderson the new captain, they set off for Guinea. On the way they stopped at the Cape Verde Islands where they raided three towns, kidnapped as many people as they could (their preference was for priests, who always brought a good price), and ransomed them for supplies and money. They also picked up a consort, a pink that had left Newfoundland with a mixed French-English crew captained by Thomas Scuder. Anderson's crew decided to abandon their decrepit ship and join their new companions, so they burned their ship and went aboard the pink where Anderson took over as captain, with Wright as master. At Gambia they paid a call on the governor of the English factory, or trading post, who informed them that a 250-ton, fourteen-cannon French ship was nearby. Undeterred by the superiority of the target, they set out immediately to capture it. After a three-day search they found their prey and attacked. The issue was settled when they boarded the ship and overwhelmed the French, who were put on a ship's boat and shoved out into the Atlantic. Anderson's crew now had a much larger ship loaded with ivory, brandy, claret, canary wine, arms and ammunition, trade goods, and eighteen slaves. They returned to Gambia, gave their now-unwanted pink to the governor, sold him the slaves and some other goods, and set out in the newly named *Resolution*. After leaving Gambia again, Dangerfield and his companions followed the coast to Accra, stopping now and then to buy supplies and gold. Along this coast they fell in with a slaver, a Captain Strong, who commanded a sixty-ton ship from London and agreed to accompany them. Leaving Accra, they sailed straight south to the Portuguese island of Principe, where the governor rather ill-advisedly refused to let them have wood and water. The pirates immediately captured the town, held it for ransom, burned a Portuguese ship, and got their wood and water.

Their next stop was the River Gabon, where they met a Captain Williamson of London with an eight-man crew and a thirty-ton ship. While they cleaned and refitted the *Resolution,* he went upriver to trade, partly on their behalf. Later, leaving the Gabon behind, they coasted on and off Cape Lopez looking for prey, before deciding to turn north again to the Cape Verde Islands. Yet another quarrel occurred—this time between Captain Anderson and Wright the master. Wright won, so Anderson with four others took their shares of the loot and joined Captain Strong in the consort. The remainder of the crew decided to go back to the Americas. At the Portuguese island of Anaboa they asked for water; when it was refused, the pirates attacked. The townspeople bravely burned their town, leaving only the church untouched before they retreated. If they thought the pirates would not desecrate the church, they were quite wrong; it promptly went up in smoke. After filling the *Resolution*'s water casks, Wright set out to cross the Atlantic. As chance would have it, his path crossed that of a 250-ton Dutch ship. At this point the pirates' luck left them: they failed miserably when they tried to capture the Dutch ship. The Dutch sailed away and the *Resolution* set a course for the Carolinas. This area, notably Charleston, usually welcomed pirates, so they considered it a safe haven.[50] They arrived in bad weather, and while struggling to get into Saint Helena Sound just south of Charleston, the *Resolution* struck a sandbar and was wrecked. Eight of the forty-four pirates and seven of the fourteen slaves on board drowned. While recovering from this ordeal in the home of a local Indian family, Dangerfield and eleven others were arrested and put in jail.

This account is typical. The marauders wandered the seas, dividing and coalescing like amoebas. They lived in small self-contained democracies that usually operated by majority vote, with the minority asked (or forced) to leave in order to keep the remaining crew in happy consensus. The marauders raided fishing vessels, towns, ships—virtually anything ashore or afloat—in search of supplies or loot. Every so often they would return to a safe port to sell their goods and enjoy themselves. Shortly thereafter they would go back to sea again. Many men remained at sea for years, or retired to small settlements in out-of-the-way places, or else crossed into non-European societies. In this sense they were marginal men freed from societal conventions, living beyond restraint except for the few rules they set for themselves. Few ever returned home again; the sea, hunger, thirst, disease, and fighting all took their toll and most of the survivors preferred the free life of the pirate to the restrictive conventions of European society.

By the end of the seventeenth century the deep-sea marauders were increasing in number and extending their range. As we shall see, changing values, prosperity, and defense needs made piracy less and less attractive to officials and merchants, who gradually withdrew their sponsorship. The field was left to the marauders, who continued to cluster around the periphery of empire. By the 1680s some of the buccaneers began to leave the Caribbean to seek greener pastures. They crossed the Isthmus of Panama to the Pacific and raided the undefended rear of the Spanish Empire in America. When the possibilities there were exhausted, they returned to the Caribbean or, in the case of three ships, made incredible voyages across the Pacific to the Spice Islands. In time they found their way into the Indian Ocean, where two streams of buccaneering conjoined. For, while these pirates had crossed the Pacific, others had left the Caribbean for West Africa and the Indian Ocean. Once the two streams flowed together, marauding became a worldwide phenomenon. With the Indian Ocean promising the greatest prizes, the pirates settled on Madagascar and Saint Marie Island. From these new bases they were close to all the major shipping routes to the east. The pirates were now prevalent in so many areas that they were perceived as a critical problem, one that could not be ignored. Demands for action against them rose in frequency and in shrillness, and in England the career of William Kidd became inextricably intertwined with this movement.

TWO

From Pirate to Friend of the Junto

William Kidd emerged from the buccaneering heart of the Caribbean. His
origins are uncertain, which is not sur-
prising because few commoners in the seventeenth century left
much of a record. Even after Kidd became famous, neither he nor
anyone else thought to chronicle his youth. Paul Lorrain, the ordinary (or pastor) of Newgate prison, in 1701 recorded only that his
prisoner was a Scot about fifty-six years old. This estimate supports
the tradition associated with Kidd's early life, which affirms that he
was born in Greenock, Scotland, in about 1645, into the family of a
Presbyterian minister.[1] The tale agrees with Lorrain's account and
provides the ironic twist that the famous pirate was born into a rigid
Calvinist family.

Kidd obviously did not follow in his father's footsteps, but went
to sea instead. The sea would be an attractive prospect to someone
born in Greenock, because it is a port on the Firth of Clyde and a
young boy raised there would have seen ships come and go along the
estuary, with the green hills of Argyll as a backdrop. What perils
and adventures he experienced are unknown, for it is not until
1689, when he was about forty-four years old, that he appears in the
records. By that time he had found his way to the Caribbean, where
he was a member of a buccaneering crew.

It is not surprising that Kidd was drawn to the Caribbean. The
possibility of making a fortune while sailing in tropical waters must
have been alluring to a young man. As Lord Vaughan, the governor

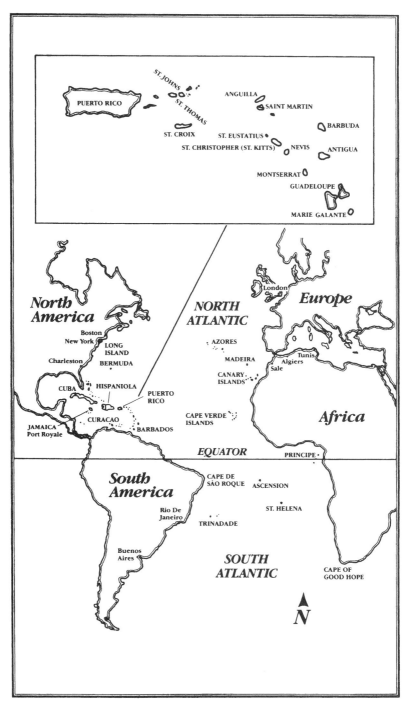

The Atlantic Ocean

of Jamaica, wrote, "These Indyes are so Vast and Rich, And this kind of rapine so sweet, that it is one of the hardest things in the World to draw those from it which have used it for long."[2] We can only surmise that Kidd, in search of plunder, roamed the Caribbean on small ships manned by hardy men dressed in salt-rimmed, decaying clothing, their unkempt hair shoved under wide-brimmed hats. It was a hard school of seamanship—one that only the rugged could survive.

By 1689 Kidd was a member of a French-English crew at anchor near Saint Christopher. The majority of the buccaneers there came from the British Isles, with the French and the Dutch well represented. Because of the animosity all over the Caribbean at this time between the French and the English, it is not surprising that Kidd and the other non-French members of his crew stole the ship and sailed it to the English colony of Nevis.

Sometimes the various nationalities sailed together amicably in mixed crews; yet tensions did arise. For example, the French disliked the way the Dutch and English desecrated Catholic churches in the Spanish colonies.[3] On occasion bloody fighting ensued. A crew of French and Irish on the *Prophet Daniel* differed over their booty and had a terrible struggle in the confined space of the ship. When the fight was over, the Irish stood with dripping swords and control of the ship and its loot.[4]

In 1688 William of Orange and his wife, Mary Stuart, succeeded to the English throne vacated by James II, whose penchants for Catholicism and for a powerful monarchy had cost him the loyalty of his people. As soon as King William had settled onto his throne, he brought England into the war he was fighting against France. This contest engulfed Europe and spread across a large part of the world before it ended nine years later. The peace that followed turned out to be only a period of truce; the war started again in 1702 and lasted until 1713. These conflicts marked the beginning of the century-long struggle between France and England over which nation would be the dominant imperial power. In the Caribbean Spain was thrust into the background as the belligerents confronted each other. Neither side had sufficient naval power for the conflict, so the buccaneers were called upon once again. For some time they had been discouraged, even attacked, because the colonists favored the regular income derived from sugar and the profits of a clandestine but growing trade with the Spanish colonies. Now the buccaneers were asked to remember their patriotism and if that was not enough (usually it was not), they could get a commission from the king against the enemy. Armed with the proper papers, they swarmed out of port.[5]

When Kidd's newly seized ship arrived in Nevis, it was renamed the *Blessed William* (a twenty-gun ship) and given a crew of eighty or ninety men, most of whom were buccaneers happy to serve on what was now a privateer. Kidd became captain, either elected by the men or perhaps appointed by the governor, because the *Blessed William* now joined a small squadron of ships created by Governor Christopher Codrington of Nevis to defend the English colonies against the French. Both Codrington and the crew would have looked for experienced leadership to command a ship of war, so Kidd must have developed such qualities in his previous adventures. He came under the orders of Captain Thomas Hewetson of the Royal Navy ship *Lion*. With the addition of the new vessel Hewetson had three ships and two sloops under his command, and Codrington ordered him to attack the French island of Mariegalante and plunder it for the "adventurers" or privateers in the fleet.[6] Codrington wanted to keep his expenses down, and the best way to do so was to let the men pillage the French in lieu of wages.

Hewetson's squadron arrived at Mariegalante on December 30, 1689. Within five days they chased the French into the hills, destroyed the only town, fired every sugar plantation, and took what they pleased back to their ships. The buccaneers doubtless enjoyed this familiar work. The fleet returned to Nevis, only to be sent out again on a rescue mission. Another English expedition, commanded by Sir Thomas Thornbill, had been sent to capture the island of Saint Martins; but Thornbill quickly found himself trapped by superior forces when French ships with troop reinforcements cut off his retreat. Hewetson arrived to discover that there were five French ships to his three; but as he had the wind in his favor, he ordered his captains to attack. Each side formed a line of battle, and they passed each other in a classic line encounter with cannons and small arms blazing. Then the lines wheeled around and repeated the fusillade, after which Hewetson withdrew to consider the situation. His smallest ship had only twelve cannon and every time the English sailed past the French they risked far greater damage than they could inflict. His captains agreed that they could only succeed if they could board the French ships and take advantage of their superior numbers. The buccaneers preferred to board in any case, as too much cannon fire might damage their potential prize and they were at their best in hand-to-hand combat. After the council of war broke up, Hewetson returned to face the French— only to discover that he had lost the wind and could not dictate the nature of the battle. So once again the two lines passed with all guns blazing. As they turned away, the English recaptured the wind and quickly turned to board the French, but the French would have none of it. By this time Hewetson's ships were close to the shore, where Thornbill's forces waited to be rescued. The English ships maneuvered closer to pick them up, but before they could do so the French reappeared, so once again the two lines of ships roared past each other. Stymied in his rescue attempt, Hewetson called another council of war. As it was nearly sunset, they decided to sail away from the island and reappear at dawn. Just as they were about to leave, they discovered the French ships anchoring in such a way as to cut off Thornbill's retreat. Hewetson ordered his ships to attack the French, who promptly slipped their anchors and sailed out to sea; but instead of fighting they sailed toward Anguilla, allowing the English to effect the rescue and return to Nevis.[7]

As the *Blessed William* lay at anchor, William Kidd had reason to reflect on his good fortune. He had £2,000 of booty in the hold and the good will of those in authority. Hewetson was later to recall that Kidd "fought as well as any man I ever saw" and was a "mighty man."[8] His crew was not quite so pleased. Kidd collected the plaudits, whereas the men had risked their lives in a line-of-battle action while under the "no prey, no pay" dictum. They preferred the campaign on Mariegalante, where they had gotten to fight, burn, rape, and, above all, loot. Fighting a line-of-battle engagement was against their inclinations and their self-interest. Kidd had bullied them into it, and they did not like his "ill behavior." The men were ready to return to the freedom of buccaneering. They may have approached Kidd with their decision, but if so, he refused to listen. He should have, because on the night of February 2, after he had gone ashore, disaster struck. The men decided to abandon Kidd—a rather furious Kidd, because he lost his ship and his £2,000 in a single stroke. It was a sudden and bitter end to a successful first campaign.[9]

Governor Codrington, pleased with Kidd's performance, sent messages to other islands to seize the *Blessed William*. The crew, no fools, steered clear of the English colonies. Kidd was now high and dry—and penniless; governors, however, particularly those leading successful campaigns, had the power to restore good spirits and even sizable fortunes. A recently captured French vessel, renamed the *Antigua,* was presented to Kidd as a reward for his services against the French.[10] If Kidd had been hitherto unaware of the power of patronage, he was quick to learn the lesson. His career thereafter became a search for the patronage of influential men who could further his quest for wealth and prestige. Such individuals were not hard to find, because the political system thrived on patronage. Every position—menial or great—was in someone's control, and all the associated salaries, fees, and privileges could be used to further the career of relatives, friends, and protégés. The more patronage, the greater power to make or break careers and to build factions or buy loyalty. Patronage was the heart and soul of politics, and Kidd reaped the benefits. In time he would discover there also were dangers.

Revenge was foremost among Kidd's motives after he had assembled a new and, he hoped, more loyal crew. Codrington gave him permission to hunt down his old ship even though the search would result in his leaving the Caribbean. During the war many buccaneers abandoned their old hunting grounds because of the pressure put on them by the government to fight in the war and the rising number of powerful navy ships on both sides. The Spanish too had become more adept at defending important targets and had sent out well-armed barca-longas (fast-sailing galleys) to hunt the pirates. By the 1680s the escalation of violence and the declining numbers of easy targets in the Caribbean made Africa and the Indian Ocean far more appealing. Naval ships rarely ventured there, and defenses against piracy were virtually nonexistent.

The *Blessed William,* now commanded by William Mason, needed supplies and a safe place to be refitted before the crew could decide where to go next. As usual, it was the Spanish who were to pay for the supplies. Mason and his crew captured two Spanish ships and raided a town on the island of Blanquilla, acquiring foodstuffs, slaves, money from ransoms, and two thousand pieces of eight from other booty.[11] Having acquired enough loot, they decided to leave the Caribbean for their refitting. New York City, like other mainland ports, had a reputation as a hospitable place where the pirates could sell their cargo and prepare for a long voyage, with no questions asked. Kidd somehow learned of this decision and set off in pursuit. Although he never caught up with the ship, some of the crew, such as Mason, Samuel Burgess, and Robert Culliford, continued to cross his path for the next decade.

The destination of the *Blessed William* was a province in turmoil, brought about by the Glorious Revolution in England. New York became an English colony in 1664 after an English expedition ended the administration of Peter Stuyvesant and the Dutch West India Company. The settlement came under the control of James, Duke of York (the future James II), as his proprietary colony. He installed a governor, who ruled with a hand-picked council but without the guidance of an assembly. The result was the growth of a court party dominated by the New York City merchant community. The governors needed the backing of this group, as they had to support an expensive garrison; in return, the city acquired a number of local monopolies. The people of Long Island and of the Albany region resented these developments but could do little to protest. In time the colony also became increasingly English—especially its institutions, which alienated the majority Dutch population and generated still more friction.

The situation was exacerbated after 1685, when simultaneous but separate events caused a great deal of apprehension: first, the French started to act aggressively on New York's northern frontier; second, the colony was included in the Dominion of New England and governed from Boston; and, third, the regime of Governor Thomas Dongan proved to be particularly rapacious. Thus when word arrived that James II had fled to France, the long-suffering colonists overthrew the government. The insurgents were largely Dutch, and their leaders were either the victims of the old regime or those who had failed to find a place in the court party, no matter how substantial their fortunes. Jacob Leisler, a leading merchant and a captain of the militia, emerged as the new leader of the colony, but his administration was frustrated by the unwillingness of Albany and Long Island to accept his regime. Both went their own way until forced into the fold. Meanwhile the court party was dispersed; some members went to jail, others into exile, and others retired to the country. The court party knew that ultimate disposition of the colony's politics would be made in England, and they concentrated on denouncing Leisler in every letter they wrote. Leisler hoped to have his actions endorsed, but his pretensions to the governorship proved misguided.[12]

The *Blessed William* arrived in New York during the insurrection, sometime in May 1690. The crew sold its cargo, including slaves, and used the profits to supply and refit the ship. That done, they accepted a commission from Leisler to attack French shipping in the Gulf of Saint Lawrence, where they snapped up six prizes, one of which they renamed the *Jacob*. Returning to New York in September, they sold the *Blessed William* and transferred to the *Jacob*. After their prizes were condemned (made legal) by a court, they left for Rhode Island and finally set sail for the Indian Ocean at the end of December 1690.[13] It is impossible to tell exactly when Kidd arrived, although he was on the scene by March 1691, apparently just missing his old colleagues. He did arrive, however, in time to play a role in the final scenes of Leisler's rebellion.

The government of William and Mary sided with the old court party and the growing number of people alienated by Leisler's intemperate administration. The new governor, Colonel Henry Sloughter, appointed September 25, 1689, was given sufficient military force to deal with Leisler. Unfortunately, it took him a very long time to reach his seat of government. He was bedeviled by delays, and when he finally left England the ship in which he was traveling sighted Bermuda one day and ran aground on it the next. So it was not until March 18, 1691, that Sloughter finally sailed into New York harbor.[14] He arrived to discover a very tense situation. Because of Sloughter's unscheduled visit to Bermuda, the troops sent with him on other ships arrived two months before he did. Their leader, Colonel Richard Ingoldsby, asked Leisler to surrender; but instead of complying, Leisler shut himself up in Fort

James, which sat at the tip of the island, and told Ingoldsby that he lacked authority in New York. Many of Leisler's adherents flocked to the fort while Ingoldsby maneuvered his soldiers into position and negotiated with the court party, who came out of hiding ready for the kill. Ingoldsby, with no idea that Sloughter would be delayed for as long as he was, avoided attacking the fort. The tension inherent in the standoff grew until on March 17 there was an exchange of fire, resulting in a number of dead and wounded. By this time Kidd had decided to join the new government. He used the *Antigua* to carry guns and ammunition for Ingoldsby, who was preparing to assault the fort. The next day Sloughter's ship, the *Archangel,* hove into view and Ingoldsby dispatched Kidd to carry a delegation apprising Sloughter of the situation. By placing himself and his ship at the service of the incoming government, Kidd was siding with the winners and putting himself in line for future patronage. Sloughter quickly got Leisler out of the fort, then presided over a trial that was in actuality an orgy of revenge. The court party was not satisfied until Leisler and Jacob Milborne, his second in command, were hanged and beheaded and their chief adherents jailed or driven into exile.[15]

Kidd did not have to wait long for his reward. On the governor's recommendation the new provincial assembly voted him £150 in New York money for his aid in bringing about Leisler's downfall.[16] He was also involved in a suspect Admiralty Court proceeding, which was part of the ongoing retribution of the old court party. We have seen that after William Mason and the crew of the *Blessed William* seized the six French ships, they returned them to New York, where they were condemned in Leisler's Admiralty Court and sold to loyal supporters of the insurrection. Sloughter, no doubt with the advice and consent of the court party, commissioned a new Admiralty Court to examine the activities of Leisler's privateers. Kidd presented a libel against the *Pierre,* one of the captured French ships, stating that Leisler's administration had no authority to appoint an Admiralty Court and that this French vessel had to be properly condemned as a prize before it could be sold. As expected, Kidd won the case: the ship was condemned and sold to Frederick Philipse for £500.[17] Kidd, in getting a portion of this sale, had managed to profit from the activities of his old crew. He had benefited once again from being a man of the moment with friends in high places.

Not surprisingly, Kidd decided to remain in New York. His decision may well have been precipitated by meeting Sarah Bradley Cox Oort. Recently widowed for the second time (the marriage license she and Kidd obtained was dated May 16, 1691, just days after John Oort died), the new Mrs. Kidd brought a sizable estate to the marriage.[18] Momentarily the rough-and-tumble life of the West Indies paled at the prospect of domestic tranquillity, political favoritism, and a substantial income. Had these been sufficient, Kidd would have faded into the background as just another sea captain.

Kidd, however, had arrived in New York at a very bad time. The war in Europe affected the colonies almost immediately. New York felt its sting as early as 1686, when a French expedition swept into the upper part of the region. In 1690 a second French attack destroyed Schenectady. The only royal garrison in North America was stationed in New York City and Albany, but it was undermanned and ineffective. Any attempt to guard the north meant recruiting locally and building new fortifications. Some refused to join the levies going up the Hudson, and most New Yorkers resented the taxes that spiraled higher and higher. As a result, colonists started to leave New York and new migrants refused to go there, further weakening the colony.[19]

The colony's economy was in worse shape than its defenses. The English economy suffered serious distortions due to the extraordinary burdens of the war. Only massive borrowing and the creation of the Bank of England kept the government afloat. Even though these financial misalignments affected trade, the greatest threat to the vital export economy came from the highly effective French *guerre du course,* or war on trade. France was well placed geographically to interdict the trade routes of the North Atlantic and had a superb group of privateers, who exacted a heavy toll on allied commerce. Battered by these two forces, the English economy of the 1690s sank into depression.[20]

The colonial economies, dependent on the trade routes of the Atlantic, quickly followed suit. In New York ships were laid up, and the merchants had time in which to bewail the decline in commerce. There were only two growth areas in the local economy, both related to piracy. The first relied on pirates coming to New York to refit and reprovision their ships. The merchants sold them supplies and bought their loot—whether it was slaves, sugar, salt, logwood, or any other valuable commodity. These were usually sold cheaply, for the pirates had little overhead.

The men of the *Blessed William* provide a good example of this trade. After serving Leisler and acquiring the *Jacob,* they left for the Indian Ocean. The first season, the *Jacob* cruised the west coast of India with scant success. During a stop at the Nicobar islands the crew argued and decided to split up. Mason and Culliford took a number of the men and sought their fortunes elsewhere. Henry Coates took command of the *Jacob* and caught the monsoons back to Madagascar, where the men rested and bought food. On their second voyage they went to the Red Sea, which proved to be a lucky choice. This time they returned to Madagascar flush with loot. Each man had approximately £800, and most of them decided it was time to retire to a less vigorous life. New York immediately recommended itself as a quiet and safe haven. So in 1693 the *Jacob* rounded Long Island, checked the political climate, and dropped anchor in the harbor. It was a welcome sight to the alehouse keepers, prostitutes, and merchants.[21]

The second aspect of the New York piracy business comprised a remarkable piece of entrepreneurship. If the pirates used Madagascar as a base, why not supply them there? New York merchants knew Madagascar already because they went there to acquire slaves. It was far away, but it did avoid conflict with the Royal African Company's monopoly of West Africa, and the lack of competition meant cheaper slaves. At the same time that they were acquiring slaves, they could supply the pirates with liquor, guns, gunpowder, and clothing in exchange for expensive textiles, drugs, spices, jewels, gold, and currency. Anyone who wanted to retire could buy passage for a hundred pieces of eight and the cost of his own food and drink during the voyage. When the ships returned to New York, most of the expensive luxury goods were transferred to other vessels and sent to ports such as Hamburg in Germany, which were conveniently removed from the scrutiny of the customs agents. The risks in such long and arduous voyages were great, as were the profits. Some of the old pirates even entered the trade. Kidd's ex-crewmate Samuel Burgess returned with Coates in 1693, bought a house, and entered the employ of Frederick Philipse, New York's wealthiest merchant, who sent him back to Madagascar to trade with his old colleagues. Thus New York City quietly profited from piracy.[22]

Needless to say, all of this activity was highly illegal. Accessories to piracy were subject to severe punishment. Local officials and royal appointees had to have the will to act, however. In New York neither did. It was not a matter of averting their gaze from criminal activity; government officials actually aided and abetted the wrong-doers. Governor Benjamin Fletcher replaced Henry Sloughter, who had died within a year of arriving in New York. Fletcher was an impecunious, morally bankrupt soldier, and his council consisted of the merchants who traded with the pirates. Money in any form warmed Fletcher's heart; he never refused a present or a bribe, no matter how small. On occasion he did rather well. When the *Jacob* returned, the crew paid £100 each for a pass guaranteeing them protection, then as a sign of their regard they gave Fletcher their ship. He quickly sold it for a tidy £800 profit.[23] Later, when the government asked him to explain himself, he dismissed his complicity by claiming that all he did was grant the brigands safe-conduct passes in order to get them out of the pirating business and make them law-abiding subjects. If some of them returned to piracy, that was their mistake, not his crime. Besides, they were a real asset, according to Fletcher, for "their Treasure was Spanish money, [and] they enrich the charter governments."[24] Under Fletcher's administration the piracy business flourished.

Encouraged by such a lack of oversight, New York became notorious as a pirate haven and the center for supplying the Indian Ocean pirates. Its streets and alehouses were filled with buccaneers, and its citizens were kept awake by their lewd activities with prostitutes.[25] "Turkey" and "Araby" gold and strange coins of all kinds added to the city's diverse currency. In a depressed economy this influx was highly welcome, and while New York was not quite as outrageous as Port Royale in its heyday, it enjoyed a similar reputation. It resembled any of the out-of-the-way places on the periphery of imperial control that enjoyed a living from sea robbery. Along with a few other colonial ports, though, it had developed a new variation, that of trading with pirates in a distant place where they had no access to supplies, but could remain in a corner of the world far removed from the authorities.[26]

Kidd meanwhile took on the role of a man of affairs, making the transition from buccaneer to burgher—although not quite a sedate burgher, because the *Antigua* was still his, and he appears to have kept up his old skills. Captain John Evans of the Royal Navy ship *Richmond* noted in his log on May 27, 1694, that Captain Kidd, a "privateer," left New York harbor in his brigantine.[27] As the records of New York's Admiralty Court are sparse, we know nothing of what prizes he brought in (if he did capture anything, it was probably French fishing ships). Of course he could still rely on his wife's estate for a living. The couple must have been reasonably prosperous because they moved into a fine house at 119–121 Pearl Street and purchased a pew in Trinity Church, the new Anglican church much favored by Governor Fletcher. Some of Mrs. Kidd's property was sold in 1694 to pay for these acquisitions.[28]

Having learned the benefits of patronage, Kidd kept on good terms with the local political leaders. He was particularly close to Robert Livingston and James Graham. Fellow Scots, Livingston was a rising entrepreneur and politician and Graham was the provincial attorney general. In 1693 Livingston bought Kidd's property on Dock Street in order to build a new private dock, and a year later Kidd did him a great favor. Like almost all the merchants in New York, Livingston engaged in illegal trade—in his case trading with the enemy, slightly more odious than trading with pirates. He sent his ship, the *Orange,* to trade with the French buccaneers on Hispaniola. His captain, Cornelius Jacobs, claimed he was forced into port by bad weather, where the French took his cargo of flour, butter, candles, tar, bread, and pork, allowing him only a quarter of its value. However, Chidley Brooke, the customs collector, noted that his return cargo of salt, linen, cash, and bills of exchange was worth £596 more than the value of the cargo he claimed the French took from him. Brooke took the case to the grand jury, which ruled that there was insufficient evidence to convict Livingston of trading with the enemy. The foreman of the grand jury was William Kidd.[29] In time Livingston would return the favor.

For a time Kidd lived in his new house, cultivated powerful friends, enjoyed his new daughters, and displayed every sign of success; but it was not enough. By 1695 disenchantment crept in and the life of the prosperous burgher paled. If Kidd needed a reminder of his exciting past, he only had to walk the streets of New York. There stalked, or more likely staggered, buccaneers, images of his former self. Some of his old crewmates were also there. Samuel Burgess and John Browne had returned with the men of the *Jacob* to spend their £800 shares of the booty. These men were direct testimony to the fortunes pirates were acquiring in the Indian Ocean. They also reminded Kidd of his earlier life of wandering and freedom on the seas. Many buccaneers who tried to retire found it difficult to give up their old ways. Browne remained in New York until his money was gone. Faced then with the choice of being an ordinary sailor or a pirate, he chose the latter.[30] Kidd considered the different choices before him and in the end he too opted for the adventurous life.

He decided to go to England on a trading voyage and while there solicit a royal commission as a privateer. Why he chose to pursue this path is obscure. It seems likely that after he obtained a cargo bound for London, a dangerous voyage in 1695 because of the French privateers, he determined he would try to parlay his background and connections into a letter of marque. His friend James Graham was a protégé of Sir William Blathwayt, the Secretary of War and a master of imperial patronage. Graham wrote a letter of introduction to Blathwayt praising Kidd's bravery, experience, and skill. With this ticket to the world of imperial patronage in his pocket, Kidd said farewell to his family and set off to make his fortune in London.[31]

As the *Antigua* joined the bustling traffic of the Thames, Kidd's optimism and resolve must have flagged. His experience had been acquired in the small port cities of the colonies and their provincial societies. As he wended his way past ship after ship and dock after dock, the vast metropolis spread outward from the river. It was already a great entrepôt attracting trade from every corner of the world—as well as the ambitious and the foolhardy, who hoped to profit from it. Much of the damage of the Great Fire of 1666 had been repaired and Christopher Wren's churches poked above the crowded alleyways and streets. West of the city, apart from the turmoil, stood Westminster and Whitehall, the seat of the government. In the city and in Westminster men fought for very high stakes; each was a world of sharp teeth and long claws. For someone used to the pleasant streets and gardens of New York City, London presented a vast, strange, and callous environment. Kidd was a veritable innocent abroad, and if he was to win his prize, he would need help. It came to him in the form of Robert Livingston, who had preceded him to London. After settling into the home of Mrs. Hawkins (a distant relative) in the maritime community of Wapping, Kidd set out to find his friend.

Livingston had arrived in London July 25, 1695, after a terrifying voyage.[32] A savage winter storm had smashed his ship's rudder, leaving the hapless crew and passengers to drift for weeks with steadily diminishing supplies of food and water. Livingston had ample time to revive his Calvinist beliefs before wind and current brought the ship to Portugal. The remainder of the trip was anticlimactic, and it was a weary and travel-worn Livingston who alighted in London. The reason for this agonizing journey was nothing less than saving his fortune.

When Livingston had landed in Boston in 1673, he possessed nothing but ambition, as his father had been a poor Scots minister. Within a year he left for Albany, where his knowledge of Dutch (acquired during a stay in the Netherlands) held promise that he might be able to enter the fur trade. Albany was a difficult market, however, as the fur trade was in the hands of a few Dutch "handlaers." Undaunted, Livingston made the commitment to stay in Albany. A tough, shrewd entrepreneur, he proceeded to make a series of moves that transformed him into a leading merchant of the colony. Perhaps the most important was marrying Alida van Rensselaer, daughter of the patroon of Rensselaerwyck and a relative of nearly all the major Dutch families. Overcoming a chilly welcome from his new relatives, he entered trade with them and then gravitated to the commercial world of New York City. His second important decision was to align himself with Governor Thomas

Dongan. He became quartermaster to the royal garrison stationed in New York, a position that could be profitable in times of peace. But soon afterward, Leisler and his followers seized the government and Livingston fled into exile. When royal government was restored, he rushed back—only to discover that confusion reigned in the government's accounts and that Governor Benjamin Fletcher was more concerned with building his own fortune than with repairing Livingston's. The two men grew to hate each other, as Livingston harped on the money due him and Fletcher ignored his pleas. Some years later, when Livingston appeared at a meeting uncharacteristically wearing a sword, Fletcher insultingly tweaked his nose and asked him to step outside, but Livingston cared more for his money than for his honor, so he remained indoors. Concerned over his debts and an ongoing dispute with his London suppliers, he decided on the dangerous winter voyage to London.[33]

Kidd came to rely on Livingston because even though Livingston was a neophyte at the English court, Kidd was an ignoramus. He discovered early on that he had little chance of acquiring a privateering commission, no matter how strong his connections. The English and Dutch fleets had suffered a humiliating defeat in 1690 at the hands of the French at Beachy Head. Then in 1693 the French captured many ships of the Smyrna fleet, a large convoy destined for the Levant, and dispersed the remainder. When the allies finally turned the tide, the French commenced an all-out *guerre du course.* The Lords of the Admiralty struggled to overcome the French while defending their rear from critics at home. Parliament censured two admirals and sought other scapegoats. In time, money and new ships solved some of the problems, but the greatest challenge lay in finding enough sailors to meet the demands of both war and trade.[34] The navy needed unprecedented numbers of men at the same time that the merchants insisted on their share of ablebodied mariners and on increasingly large convoys for protection. The lords, working with the merchants, assigned mariners for each fishing fleet and trade route, sometimes doling out the men ship by ship. There were never enough seamen to meet the demand, and the Admiralty saw no reason to make the problem worse by issuing letters of marque to privateers.[35] Some of London's leading merchants petitioned again and again for commissions for their ships, citing England's losses to

French privateers. Had many commissions been granted, sailors in hope of a protected berth and prize money would have flocked to sign up. Compared to the harsh discipline and low pay of the Royal Navy, privateering was a sailor's heaven. Thus the Admiralty rarely authorized letters of marque and stopped altogether in 1695 until the government, responding to pressure from shipowners and merchants (notably the East India Company) forced their lordships to issue them. Even then very few commissions were granted, because the Admiralty imposed strict rules and required bonds for each ship. Only the powerful succeeded in acquiring the prize.[36] Kidd, who hardly qualified as powerful, saw his hopes of becoming a privateer dashed. If he did not want to return to the humdrum and tedium of the burgher's life, Robert Livingston, who had entered the dangerous world of English politics, was his final hope.

The political settlement that accompanied the Glorious Revolution of 1688 resolved many of the vexing problems that had afflicted the reigns of Charles II and James II. Politicians were groping toward the attributes of parliamentary democracy (modern party politics, a cabinet system, a thoroughly controlled monarchy), but attainment lay in the future. Politics at the turn of the century had a certain fluidity that presented opportunities and dangers to the aspiring politician: the king's favor meant the warmth of office, the comfort of salary and pension, and the blessing of a title; a fall from favor meant the loss of these delights and banishment to Parliament. Of course Parliament, particularly the House of Commons, could and did destroy ministerial careers, often on very weak pretexts. If, however, the aspiring politician could garner enough seats in the Commons to be held at his bidding, master the intricate power games, and arouse the Commons by oratory, he could still acquire power and office. This path was a difficult one, because it meant keeping the confidence of the king and Parliament. More than a few failed because of the lack of discipline in the Commons.

Two factions, the Whigs and the Tories, competed for supremacy in the House of Commons. The Whigs had fought for the gains made by representative government in 1688. They sought a strong and vigorous Parliament and a controlled executive. The Tories preferred a strong monarchy, but one controlled by Tories. Other issues divided them—the most important during this period being the war with France and its cost. King William's War, or the Nine Years War, brought unprecedented demands on manpower and on government finances. At the start of the war King William preferred not to align himself with either faction, hoping that a mixed ministry could supply the wherewithal to continue the war. As the costs of the war increased, the Tories gave less and less support to royal policy. They favored recalling the English army from the Continent so that a small army and the militia could defend the nation behind the barrier of an expanded Royal Navy. The Whigs, on the other hand, supported the war effort and asserted that every soldier fighting in the Low Countries was defending England better than if he were fighting in the fields of Kent.

With the expansion of the war William desperately needed money, making inevitable a rapprochement with the Whigs. Using their influence in London mercantile and financial circles, the Whigs raised the first million-pound loan and followed that a year later with a 1.2 million-pound loan plus a charter for the Bank of England. The Tories opposed the bank, arguing that only republics had banks. They lost the debate, because the potential benefits of a central bank triumphed over antirepublicanism. As money poured into the treasury, the Anglo-Dutch alliance started to turn the tide of French victories. King William relied more and more on the Whigs, who reaped their reward in 1694 in a shower of offices and titles. The Whigs lost no time in replacing every possible Tory officeholder with a loyal Whig. By the time the parliamentary session of 1695 convened, there was open warfare between the two factions. The Whigs pressed their advantage, persecuting particularly Tory officeholders involved in corrupt practices. They even purged Sir John Trenchard, speaker of the House of Commons. The Tories retreated to lick their wounds. They knew the Whig heyday could not last forever, for in a corrupt age the peccadilloes of their leaders would sooner or later bring the Whigs down.[37]

The Whig leaders were a disparate group. Dissolute and hard-working by turn, they embodied the best and worst of the age. Their private lives would not recommend them to a modern electorate, but in an age of class privilege and deference they thrived. The most assiduous politician of the group was Thomas Lord Wharton, later Marquis Wharton. His strict Puritan family background repressed his life-style until he went to London, where he quickly earned a reputation as a notable voluptuary. As befits an ardent womanizer and fluid liar, he wielded his sword like a master. Yet he was not known as a killer, usually attempting to disarm his opponents instead. Debauched in private life, as a loyal Whig he yielded to no one. He dominated the politics of Buckinghamshire and had enough influence elsewhere to nominate between twenty and thirty members of the Commons. With his impressive memory he never forgot a face or a failed promise, and could rub elbows at an alehouse as well as any ward boss today. He also recruited new members of the House of Lords, a practice that called upon his intimate knowledge of every degeneracy in London. As in politics, where he was a formidable opponent, he hated to lose in horse racing, where he kept the finest stable of his day.[38]

His rival in love of luxury was the vain Charles Montague, first Earl of Halifax. Born into a distinguished family, he managed to overcome the misfortune in an age of primogeniture of being the youngest son of a youngest son. With such a birthright a life in the clergy seemed inevitable, but at Cambridge his precocity in poetry and science brought him to the attention of the powerful. A seat was found for him in the Commons, where he proved an exceptional debater. But his real talent lay in understanding the complexities of state finances, so at the comparatively early age of thirty-seven he became the First Lord of the Treasury and Chancellor of the Exchequer. His accomplishments, although they made him arrogant and vain, allowed him to live lavishly and cultivate the arts.[39]

The third dissolute member of this group, Henry Sidney, first Earl of Romney, combined exceptional good looks with the talents of a master of intrigue. His pursuit of women never ceased. As a young man, he was thrown out of the Duke of York's household because he seemed too close a friend of the Duchess, and he went to his grave pursued by children whom he would neither recognize nor provide for. Long before it became politically expedient to do so, he knew Prince William well—and remained in his favor. He helped to manage the negotiations that brought William and Mary to

England and received an abundance of gifts and lands when they assumed their joint throne. King William was realistic about Sidney's abilities as an administrator; even though he gave him high offices, they were his for only a short time. Sidney remained a master manipulator—but one who operated behind the scenes.[40]

The remaining members of the Junto, as the Whig leadership was known, were less dissipated. John, Lord Somers, succeeded in politics because of ability: he was an outstanding lawyer, a fine writer, a noted orator, a patron of the arts, and a consummate politician. His probity and knowledge of the law recommended him to King William, who in 1693 made him Lord Keeper of the Great Seal—with control over all judicial appointments. Among the Whigs he came closest to being a leader.[41] Edward Russell, the first Earl of Orford and sometime Admiral of the Fleet and Treasurer of the Navy, had a very different character. Equally at home on the quarterdeck fighting a battle or in Parliament belaboring his enemies (who were rather numerous because of his wicked temper and vindictive nature), he was also well known for taking good care of the men on his ships. His successes at sea brought him high office and he proved to be a brilliant administrator. He kept the English fleet operating in the Mediterranean during the Royal Navy's first extended commitment beyond home waters, while on land he succeeded in managing the complexities of the Admiralty and the Navy Board where others had failed. He took full advantage of whatever office or command he filled; his accounts were not such as to pass close scrutiny. As a result, his enemies never had to look far for damning evidence.[42]

The final member of the Junto stood somewhat apart from his fellows. Charles Talbot, first Duke of Shrewsbury, was widely known as the King of Hearts. Gifted, handsome, a linguist, his virtues and sweet temperament brought him many friendships and wide esteem. Of all the Whig leaders King William admired him most and tried constantly to get him to accept, and remain in, high office. At the king's urging he reluctantly became secretary of state. Once in office, he discovered that his health declined as his responsibilities grew. Shrewsbury simply could not manage the day-to-day grind, so he went to his country estate for longer and longer periods, leaving his surrogate, Sir James Vernon, to handle the burdens of office. He badgered the king to be relieved of his duties, but King William refused until Shrewsbury's disability became a real handicap. In the end Shrewsbury escaped from office by taking an extended tour of the Continent.[43]

The Whig leadership's support of the war and creation of a cohesive bloc in the Commons brought the party to power after 1693. As their newly minted titles indicate, they enjoyed all the prizes of victory. Above all they controlled the granting of offices and favors, so anyone who desired preferment in 1695 had to seek them out.

Unfortunately for Kidd and Livingston, their letters of introduction to Sir William Blathwayt were next to useless. As secretary for war and member of the Lords of Trade and Plantations, Blathwayt dominated imperial patronage. At every opportunity he put his own friends in office and tirelessly sought to control the political development of the colonies. It was quite natural that the two neophytes should seek him out, but Blathwayt was away with King William on a campaign in the Low Countries during the summer of 1695. Furthermore, the Whigs were no friends of his. Livingston, on the way to London, learned of Blathwayt's liabilities as a sponsor and changed his plans.[44] If he had to be a friend of the Whigs to get his money, he would be a friend of the Whigs. By sheer good luck he met William Carter, who introduced him to Richard Coote, the Earl of Bellomont, a member of Parliament and a zealous Whig. For the next five years the careers of Kidd, Livingston, and Bellomont would be closely tied.

Bellomont had two outstanding characteristics: he was an extremely loyal Whig and he was always in need of money. While it was still dangerous to do so, he went to Holland in the spring of 1687 and entered the service of Prince William and Princess Mary. William gave him command of a regiment of English troops and later made him steward of Princess Mary's household. When King James tried to stop the exodus of English politicians to Holland, he ordered Bellomont to Ireland, where he was a member of the Irish peerage; but Bellomont ignored the order and remained in Holland. Thus when Romney came to negotiate with William and Mary, and then later when Shrewsbury arrived to invite them to England, Bellomont was highly visible. He parlayed his advantage sufficiently to catch the attention of the Whig leadership, so that in 1690 they nominated him for a safe seat in the Commons, to which he was elected. Somers, Shrewsbury, Sunderland, and even John Locke took an interest in his career. Bellomont enthusiastically joined in attacking the Tories in the House of Commons, a course that got him into trouble in 1693, when in a speech he savaged Lord Coningsby for his outrageous financial dealings in Ireland. Unfortunately for Bellomont, Coningsby was a royal favorite, and when Coningsby was forced out of office, Bellomont lost his sinecure in Queen Mary's household.[45]

Removal from favor exacerbated Bellomont's unhappy financial position. One of his earliest surviving letters in 1661 relates his difficulties over a £50 debt. Nothing less than a return to royal favor and a new office would help, and he importuned Shrewsbury to do something—anything—for him. Shrewsbury first pleaded with the king to give Bellomont forfeited land in Ireland because of his "necessitous" condition.[46] Nothing much came of this, but Shrewsbury's efforts did ultimately revive Bellomont's fortunes. For on June 14, 1695, the king assented to Bellomont's nomination as governor of the Massachusetts Bay Colony. By June 27 Bellomont had a memorandum before the Lords of Trade and Plantations complaining about the small salary that went with his proposed office and the degree to which it was controlled by the legislature.[47] So a month later, in July 1695, Shrewsbury renewed his efforts on Bellomont's behalf, asking the king to aid "that poor gentleman" by turning out Benjamin Fletcher and making Bellomont governor of New York as well as of Massachusetts Bay. This move, although it made little sense politically or geographically, would at last provide Bellomont with enough money. Shrewsbury warned the king to be wary in discussing this proposal with Blathwayt, who was a "particular friend" of Fletcher and would be prone to "partiality, which is perhaps no fault towards a friend." The second governorship was within Bellomont's grasp if Fletcher could be removed from New York.[48]

Livingston, one of the few people in London who knew much about New York, now had the opportunity he needed to gain the assistance of the Whigs. But there was a price to be paid. Bellomont had only been proposed as governor of Massachusetts Bay after a bruising battle in the House of Commons. The Tories, notably Lord Cutts, wanted the governorship for Joseph Dudley, a native of Massachusetts Bay and a man with considerable experience in colonial affairs. Unfortunately for Dudley, many politicians in Massachusetts hated him, and the provincial agents in London, Constantine Phipps and Sir Henry Ashurst, received orders to block the appointment. Ashurst cast about for a way to ruin Dudley's reputation—and thus his chances. He found the perfect tool in Jacob Leisler, Jr., and Abraham Governeur, who were in England seeking to overturn the convictions and attainders of Jacob Leisler and his followers. In 1691, while acting as chief justice in New York, Dudley had presided over the trials of Jacob Leisler and Jacob Milborne, whose subsequent executions were mourned by many in New York who believed that Leisler had done nothing more than defend the colony in time of war. The younger Leisler traveled to England to clear his father's name and regain his estate, which was attainted when he was hung for treason. Dudley proved all too vulnerable to criticism, because the trial had been an act of vengeance, not of justice. Ashurst adroitly brought the whole affair to the Commons, knowing that only Parliament could reverse the attainder. Against desperate efforts on the part of Dudley's friends, Ashurst successfully managed the reversal of the attainder and the discrediting of Dudley, leaving no obstacle to Bellomont's appointment. But Bellomont was now tied to the followers of Leisler; indeed, Ashurst provided him with a list of those who should be removed from power in New York and the names of good Leislerians to put into their places. Livingston, who had been forced into exile by Jacob Leisler, and Kidd, who had aided in his downfall, had to side with the friend of their old enemy or give up hope of success. Ambition creates strange bedfellows: they quickly decided to cooperate with Bellomont, regardless of his friends.[49]

Livingston first met Bellomont on August 10, 1695. They shared both strong Calvinist beliefs and a firm desire to oust Benjamin Fletcher. No doubt the latter dominated their conversation. The following day, a Sunday, Livingston met with an interesting group: Kidd; Phillip French, a New York City merchant in London on business; Giles Shelley, captain of the *Nassau* of New York; and William Carter, Bellomont's friend who had brought Livingston and Bellomont together. That afternoon they went up the Thames to Chelsea, then a parklike suburb of London. They walked and then dined, all the while discussing how to get rid of Fletcher.[50]

As a protégé of Blathwayt, Fletcher had a powerful sponsor. If questions were raised about his administration, it might be possible to have him recalled. But an attack on a sitting governor had to be launched in the Lords of Trade and Plantations, where Blathwayt had considerable influence. Even in his absence, Blathwayt's nephew John Povey looked after his interests from a position as secretary to the lords. The plotters lacked any viable alternative—and they did have allies on the board, because there as elsewhere the Whigs had found places for their friends.

The charges lodged against Fletcher concerned his interference with elections and his financial peccadilloes. Surprisingly, his close relations with pirates were not brought up—probably because pirates were not yet a major issue. Within a year they would be, and afterward Fletcher would spend a great deal of time defending himself from charges of collusion with pirates. Carter and Livingston's guests did agree to testify about Fletcher's finances and electioneering, and a few mariners from Shelley's and Kidd's crews later joined them. Each appeared in the chambers of the Lords of Trade and Plantations to confront the bewigged power brokers of the empire. The colonial rustics gave their testimony, which was duly written into the record. After due deliberation their lordships recommended Fletcher's recall to answer the charges against him. Accordingly, on September 11, 1695, an Order in Council was issued, followed by a letter from Shrewsbury reassuring Fletcher that although he remained high in the king's regard, he nonetheless had to return to England.[51] What benefits Shelley and French aspired to, beyond the favor of Bellomont (whose path to office was now clear), are unknown. Kidd still wanted his privateering commission, and after the dinner in Chelsea he accompanied Livingston to his rented quarters, just behind the exchange, remaining there for the night. He and Livingston had some private business, concerning a proposed partnership with the Junto that promised future wealth and patronage.[52]

The origins of the scheme are unclear because each partner blamed the other when it went awry. Kidd's version claimed that

Livingston told Bellomont about the pirates in New York, a number of whom had gone to the East Indies. The buccaneers were expected to return to New York, where they would anticipate a friendly welcome. What if they were to receive a surprise in the form of a powerful ship? With visions of pirate treasure floating before them, Livingston and Bellomont approached Kidd to accept command of the vessel. Kidd said he refused; but when they threatened to hold his ship, the *Antigua,* in London, he relented and agreed because he feared the political power of the Whig lords. Bellomont, for his part, placed the blame squarely on Kidd who, he reported, concocted the plan and convinced Livingston of its viability. Livingston then presented it to Bellomont with assurances of Kidd's good character. Bellomont mentioned their scheme to the king, who ignored it. Soon Livingston approached Bellomont again and added that he and Kidd would put up one-fifth of the costs. Bellomont returned with the revised scheme to King William, who this time approved it, stating that he was willing to grant private individuals full possession of all the goods they recovered. The king was unwilling, however, to spend government money to further the plan. Armed with the king's approval, Bellomont sought financial backers. When none could be found, he turned to the Whig lords, who joined him out of patriotism. Another version of the origins of the scheme has the East India Company proposing the plan to the government. The king agreed but, since he could not use the overworked navy, he pledged £3,000 of his own money. The Junto then took over and chose Kidd to lead the expedition because of his knowledge of pirates. Livingston remained quiet about the whole subject. Had he commented, his remarks would no doubt have been as self-serving and misleading as those of the other principals. The chief actors were hardly as passive as each would have it, and the East India Company did not officially protest piracy until considerably later.[53]

It seems likely that Kidd and Livingston developed the plan and that Bellomont readily accepted it and helped in its formulation. Livingston admitted spending a great deal of time during October putting the details together.[54] He and Kidd knew better than anyone in London about the growing piracy business in New York City. Kidd certainly could relate the particulars of the return in

1693 of his old mates on the *Jacob*. To attack and capture one or more pirate ships meant a handsome profit. Kidd had come to London for a different purpose, and he probably harbored doubts about the enterprise; but on the promise of a strong ship and sufficient men and with the influence of powerful men behind him, he succumbed. Once the partners were agreed, Bellomont became the key: only he had the contacts to get the necessary commission.

Accompanied by Livingston, Bellomont visited Shrewsbury, Somers, Orford, and Romney to get their approval and invite them to enter the partnership. To some of the Whig lords, already partners in a scheme to mine gold and silver, the new proposal was merely another speculative enterprise.[55] The Whig lords had precedent for their participation in the plan and enough greed to push it through. They remained in the background, providing political muscle when needed. They were represented on the various documents by servants, whose names appeared in their stead. Nor was Kidd brought forward until the plot was well advanced. Only then did Orford and Romney discuss the venture with him.[56]

The initial agreement, signed October 10, 1695, included only the three original partners—Bellomont, Livingston, and Kidd. Its premise was that Kidd wanted to capture the pirates who had left the colonies for the Red Sea and elsewhere. The partnership agreed to help him. Bellomont consented to obtain the necessary commission from the king or the Lords of the Admiralty, a grant from the government to keep all prizes in their hands without threat of litigation, and to meet four fifths of the cost of the venture. His share of the investment was to be divided into five parts, an indication of the hidden partners. Kidd and Livingston were responsible for the other fifth. As a sign of their mutual good faith, all three agreed to raise a total of £2,000 by November 6. Kidd had the responsibility of recruiting one hundred seamen under a "no purchase, no pay" agreement, meaning that the only pay they received would come from the value of what they captured. The remaining clauses dealt with the further division of the spoils among the partners, including an incentive clause for Kidd promising him the gift of the ship he used if he returned with more than £100,000. If he returned empty-handed, he and Livingston were to keep the ship after they had compensated the partners. Kidd was to sail "speedily" to where the pirates were located, capture them, and without interfering in any way with the spoils, return to Boston, where Bellomont would reside as governor of Massachusetts Bay. Although not mentioned in the contract, Bellomont was to be allowed to have the cargo declared a prize in the local courts, thereby avoiding England altogether; then presumably he could distribute the profits to the Whig lords. To ensure fulfillment of the agreement, Kidd posted a £20,000 performance bond and the other two partners posted £10,000 each.[57]

Another partner had to be added immediately because Bellomont could not pay his share of the £2,000 investment. He borrowed from Sir Edward Harrison, as would Orford and Shrewsbury. Harrison was one of London's leading merchants, with investments in many trades including the Americas and the East Indies. Unlike the other partners, he played an activist role in monitoring the project and corresponding with Livingston. Bellomont showed his gratitude to Harrison by developing an intense dislike for him. He felt their agreement was too one-sided and accused Harrison of having "used me not well" and of getting him in a "terrible hard Presbyterian grip." He later plotted to have Harrison cut out of the deal.[58]

The remainder of the agreement took time and stealth to complete. The partners made application to the Admiralty for a privateering commission, which was duly granted on December 11, 1695—but only to seek out enemy commerce. The next step, a special grant to hunt pirates, led to complications. A Mr. Russell, presumably Edward Russell, submitted their request for the commission. The Lords of the Admiralty appeared perplexed and asked Sir Charles Hedges, Chief Judge of the Admiralty Court, if commissions to take pirates were legal. Hedges' answer has not survived, but in fact such commissions had been granted as recently as 1687, when Sir Robert Holmes received a special warrant to hunt pirates.[59] Because the Admiralty was reluctant, the partners resolved the issue by going elsewhere. They obtained a patent under the Great Seal, the same office that granted the Lords of the Admiralty their powers. A warrant for the patent went forward on January 20, 1696, stating that because Thomas Tew, John Ireland, Thomas Wake, William Mayes, and other pirates from New England and New York preyed on normal commerce, Kidd could hunt them down. Six days later the patent was issued by the Lord Keeper of the Great Seal—none other than John, Lord Somers, a full partner in Kidd's venture.[60] With the two commissions obtained, the venture was well under way, and by early February 1696 Kidd's new ship, the *Adventure Galley,* was fitted out and all the bills were paid. The original three partners reconfirmed and sealed their agreement.[61]

One further document was required. If a merchant knew that his cargo or parts of it were in the hands of another party, he could sue for its recovery. After all, he was the owner of record and was entitled to the return of his goods. This legality put a damper on pirate hunting. Even the Royal Navy lacked enthusiasm for fighting tough pirate crews without reward. The solution was to get a special commission, exempting those who captured pirates from any action of recovery, thereby allowing ship and cargo to be condemned without challenge. Once again, Sir Robert Holmes's commission set a precedent, in that he was allowed to keep what he captured.

The second version of the partners' agreement recognized the need for this power by stating that the person who acquired such authority would get one-tenth of all the profits. Such a grant could only come from King William, and after a long delay Shrewsbury made the approach.[62] After discussing the matter with the king, he sent him a secret letter and warrant to avoid the ubiquitous Blathwayt, who was once again on campaign with the king. He even slandered Blathwayt by intimating that many of the colonial governors he had appointed connived at piracy. Shrewsbury stated that he, Bellomont, Somers, Romney, and Russell had invested £6,000 in a ship to hunt down pirates. If they were to profit, they needed to avoid the Admiralty procedures and the Admiralty shares of the prizes. As a private inducement, Shrewsbury asked the king to reserve a share of the profits for himself. The king signed the warrant on August 24, 1696, and reserved a share that was later set at 10 percent. For reasons unknown, perhaps bureaucratic infighting (for by this time the Whigs were beginning to lose power), the grant did not pass the Great Seal until May 27, 1697. It conferred on the partners (now listed as Bellomont, Harrison, and four other surrogates for the lords) the right to keep all booty taken by Kidd after April 30, 1696, free of the normal legal channels and free of the obligation to divide the spoils with the Admiralty.[63] The partners had pulled off a considerable bureaucratic coup: Kidd now had a royal sponsor for his voyage, and the partners, secure in the knowledge that they were doing the public business, could enjoy their profits without regard to other jurisdictions.

By the time the final commission passed the seals, Kidd had left London far behind. Once again patronage had come his way: he was now allied with the most powerful men in England. The rewards for success danced before him; the dangers of failure did not warrant dwelling upon.

THREE

Voyage to Madagascar

While his partners shepherded the paperwork through the bureaucracy, Captain William Kidd returned to the world he knew best. He prowled the docks seeking a ship and men to carry out the proposed venture. Edward Harrison joined him in the search. The source of much of the financing for the voyage and a person who knew the London wharfs better than Kidd, Harrison was Kidd's adviser and companion. From this time on Harrison served as manager of the partnership in recognition of his investment and his experience, and as a way of insulating the Junto from the petty details and complications of the coming voyage.[1]

The acquisition of an appropriate ship was the first goal of the partners, and their selection was conditioned by the nature of the opposition. Even though pirates captured ships any way they could, they preferred certain techniques to others. Most favored was surprise, preferably by a ruse that allowed intact capture of the victim. If surprise proved impossible, speed could overhaul the victim. Terror was also a weapon. As the pirates approached a ship, every man of the large crew would crowd the deck and rigging, screaming and threatening the other crew with death and dismemberment in hopes of cowing them into submission. If surprise and threats failed, cannon would soften the opposition preparatory to boarding, whereupon pirate numbers and fighting experience almost always carried the day. Many captains simply surrendered if they could not outrun the hunters; they knew, as did the pirates, that they did not carry enough sailors to defend their vessels. During this era every improvement in hull design, sails, and rigging allowed shipowners to cut their costs by reducing crew size until most cargo ships carried crews of less than thirty men. Arms too were inadequate. Merchant vessels from flyboats to pinks carried few cannon, and the captains often kept even those few in the hold until the ship entered a danger zone. Small arms remained under lock and key until the captain decided to arm his men. The merchant captains were well aware that inasmuch as their men had no interest in the cargo, they were unlikely to defend it with their lives. In fact, sometimes their most trusted men were lured to a pirate crew by promises of booty, leaving the ship dangerously undermanned if the pirates returned the ship after having looted it.[2]

There were exceptions to these generalities. Large cargo ships such as East Indiamen carried enough men and cannon to fight off any pirates—as did ships carrying large amounts of treasure. National and religious rivalries influenced the outcome of a fight: the Spanish and the English fought each other tenaciously regardless of the odds, and in wartime the English and the French did the same. But even in wartime some captains preferred not to fight, and French privateers developed a highly efficient system whereby the owners of ships could keep the cargo by paying a "fee" or ransom. The English government disliked these transactions, but the merchants preferred to pay up rather than lose their merchandise.[3]

Given these circumstances, the ship chosen for Kidd's venture would have to be big enough to carry a substantial number of men and strong enough to withstand a cannonade, yet it could not be too large. Kidd, like the pirates, could not count on port facilities. Every ship grew an ever-thickening forest of weeds and barnacles on its bottom. In time this miniature inverted forest reduced the ship's speed and affected its sailing qualities. In tropical waters there was the additional danger of the teredo worm, which burrowed holes in the hull that could, if not cared for, cause the ship's bottom to drop out. To fight these dangers, the ship required periodic cleaning, or *careening*. It was dragged onto a steeply rising beach, where first one side of the hull and then the other was exposed by tilting it over at low tide. After the growth had been scraped from the bottom, a protective coating of pitch was smeared on before a high tide floated the ship out to sea again. Only relatively small ships were treated in this fashion; larger ships needed different facilities, preferably those of a dockyard. So Kidd's choice was limited by the likelihood that such specialized facilities would not be available to him.

The ship the partners decided on was the *Adventure Galley,* launched in December 1695 at Castle Yard, Deptford. It was described at the time of its registration as a ship of 287 tons and thirty-four guns, although the remainder of its dimensions have gone unrecorded. Unique in that it was a hybrid sailing ship with oars, the *Adventure Galley* may have been modeled after the galley-frigates developed as patrol craft by the Royal Navy in the latter half of the seventeenth century. The combination of oars and sails meant that in any weather and in tight quarters these hybrids were formidable fighting ships designed for speed and mobility. The *Charles Galley,* another ship of this kind, was painted by Willem van de Velde the Younger and drawn by Captain Jeremy Roch; the portrayals are of a powerful, three-masted ship with a line of oar ports on the lower deck. When Roch put three men on each oar, the *Charles* could do three miles an hour. The *Adventure Galley,* with this kind of capability, was perfectly suited to the task of hunting pirates.[4]

Manning the ship presented few problems. Kidd's privateering commission allowed him to hire seventy men, only half of whom could be experienced mariners. A privateering berth attracted sailors because it held out the promise of quick money, and anything was better than the discipline of the Royal Navy. All privateers went out on a "no prey—no pay" basis: if they failed to capture anything, they returned home empty-handed. So the partners had little difficulty in hiring a crew. Later the claim was made that all were reliable family men, but this characterization seems unlikely. The venture called for hard men ready to fight.[5]

When the crew had been assembled, the men of the *Adventure Galley* entered into a standard contract, not unlike the less formal agreements of the buccaneers.[6] Once the total value of any captured booty had been calculated and the expenses of the voyage deducted, the remainder was divided among the participants. For his time and trouble Kidd was allocated thirty-five shares; the other officers also got more than a single share. Full shares went to experienced mariners, whereas landsmen and boys were worth only a fraction of a share (rarely less than one-half). All plunder must be handed over: if someone stole for his own benefit, he lost his share. The agreement also contained a system of "workman's compensation." The loss of an eye, leg, or arm brought 600 pieces of eight in compensation; loss of a finger or toe, only 100. The heirs of a dead man collected £20, even if there was no "purchase" from the voyage. All of these obligations had to be met before the general division of the booty occurred. Such obligations were taken quite seriously. At least one group of pirates compensated their wounded, only to discover they had nothing left.[7]

These clauses ensured that during an engagement men would not hold back waiting for their mates to spring into action. Cowardice meant loss of a share, as did drunkenness during an attack. The determination of "drunkenness" involved drawing a fine line, for the technique of dulling fear by way of the bottle is as old as warfare. The Royal Navy routinely issued rum before battle. If the drinking got out of hand, however, an attack might fail. On one occasion a group of pirates took three days to capture a ship because there were never enough sober men available.[8] Disobedience, mutiny, and riot were subject to a corporal punishment to be agreed upon by the captain and a majority of the crew. This democratic method of assessing punishment was the great distinction between privateersmen and the Royal Navy, where the captain was omnipotent and dispensed punishment as he saw fit. The method of the privateersmen reflected the old maritime traditions where the captain and his seasoned mariners consulted over how to handle the ship or mete out punishment.[9] The experience of the crew and the captain were equally valued. With the vast expansion of the navy, the merchant marine, and privateering, thousands of landsmen were drawn into shiphandling, causing a decline of the esteem in which old craft habits were held and a rise in the authority of the captains.[10]

Other clauses in the agreement signed by Kidd's crew dealt with details. The first man to "spot a prize" collected 100 pieces of eight; assignment to a prize ship that sailed for home did not mean loss of rights to booty collected later; money and treasure were apportioned immediately, whereas cargo had to wait for division until it was evaluated by a court; when a sailor obtained his weapons from Kidd (the basic kit comprised a gun, a pistol, a cartridge box, and a cutlass) he was charged £6 out of the first allocation of booty. Finally, Kidd promised to use care in managing the ship and to "make the voyage" (that is, make them rich). As each man joined the crew, he signed this agreement, thereby committing himself to no prey, no pay.

By late February 1696 Kidd was ready. He received his sailing orders from Bellomont, who urged him to sail speedily, carry out his commission, and keep Harrison informed of his progress.[11] No destination is mentioned in the orders, but all the evidence points to the Indian Ocean, after a brief visit to New York to obtain more men and to visit Kidd's family. When Kidd arrived in New York, his venture was advertised as a Red Sea voyage. His later correspondence shows the same understanding of the final destination.[12] It was certainly more sensible to go where pirates congregated than to seek them elsewhere. New York was a possible location, but hardly one that Kidd could consider seriously. Whatever influence he had there would vanish if he stayed in the harbor attacking the merchants' best customers. In addition, no one could guarantee that the pirates would return to New York. Bellomont also ordered Kidd to meet him at the site of his new government post when Kidd's mission was complete, but if he was able to join other ships coming back to England he should go there.[13] All of this points to Kidd's destination being somewhere other than the northeast coast of America.

At the end of February Kidd prepared to leave London. One can imagine Harrison, Livingston, Shelley, Colonel Hewetson, Kidd's relatives, and perhaps even Bellomont at dockside to wish him well. His departure was watched by others who did not wish him well. While he was preparing the *Adventure Galley* and collecting his crew, Kidd earned a reputation for his "rodomandations," or extravagant and arrogant boasts. Around the docks he lorded it over his peers and bragged about his commission and his sponsors. A captain of one of the royal yachts, who took a dislike to Kidd's braggadocio, ordered his crew to pay particular attention to the *Adventure Galley*. They were to note whether or not Kidd rendered all the appropriate honors as he passed the captain's yacht; if he did not, the crew was to fire on him.[14] As a privateer Kidd was permitted to fly the royal jack and pendant, but he still had to defer to the navy. In the arena of naval status there was no more sensitive point of dignity than who was first to dip colors and fire a salute. National prestige and personal dignity required that all ships defer to naval vessels, and navy captains jealously guarded their prerogatives.[15]

After Kidd untangled his ship from the crowded docks and slipped down the Thames, the *Adventure Galley* passed the royal yacht without the slightest sign of recognition. After a warning shot rang out, the *Adventure Galley*'s flags still fluttered on high. Kidd's crew, well aware of the insult, caught the spirit of the occasion. They climbed up into the yards and rendered an often used, if rude, mariner's salute; once in position, they "clapp their Backsides in unison."[16] The object of their derision could do nothing but fume and complain to the Admiralty. Their lordships did not view lightly slurs to royal yachts, so when Kidd repeated the insult shortly afterward to another royal ship at the mouth of the River Medway, they ordered Captain Have Munden to board the *Adventure Galley,* remove all its sailors, then anchor the offending vessel at Sheerness.[17] Kidd's detractors had the last laugh and thoroughly deflated his ego.

This action did more than wound his pride—it threatened his whole enterprise. The navy had been placed on alert six days earlier because of a threatened French invasion. No protections against impressment were honored as the navy desperately tried to man and victual every ship.[18] If the fleet put to sea, the likelihood of the crew's returning to the *Adventure Galley* would be slim. Staring across the anchorage at the *Duchess,* where his men languished, Kidd could only pray that the French fleet never left the harbor. His prayers were answered. The invasion rumor proved to be a scare, allowing Kidd to appeal to his patron, the Earl of Orford, for the return of his crew. Later, to the displeasure of the *Duchess'* captain, he received orders to return the men to Kidd.[19] It is highly unlikely that he returned all of the original crew, because this would have been an excellent opportunity to get rid of some of his own problem seamen while keeping some of Kidd's experienced mariners.

It was not until April 10 that the *Adventure Galley* anchored at the Downs to drop off the Thames pilot. After a brief stay the course was set for Plymouth, a last stop that allowed Kidd to make final preparations before the long transatlantic leg of the voyage.[20] Bound for New York to visit his family and to recruit the rest of his crew, Kidd returned to his element. At sea, in command of a powerful ship, his own deck beneath his feet again, the world had a benign and pleasant aspect. As England slipped farther and farther behind in his wake, he could reflect on his good fortune. Months before he had sailed east in command of a merchant sloop with little hope of acquiring a privateering commission. Now he was retracing his route on a mission sponsored and financed by some of the most important men in England. Kidd had every reason to strut on his quarterdeck. (He might also have speculated now and then about the future, because in order to make his fortune all he had to do was defeat some of the fiercest pirates afloat.)

As the *Adventure Galley* left England behind and headed into the North Atlantic, the crew would learn the qualities and idiosyncrasies of their new ship. Kidd chose to take the northern route, rather than the longer and more usual course that went first to the south and then to the west to make a landfall in the West Indies. In April the northern route was feasible, with only the spring surge of ice floes to worry about. This course also proved profitable. Toward the end of May the lookouts spotted a French "banker," a fishing ship, loaded with salt and fishing tackle for a season's fishing on the Grand Banks. The banker, no match for a privateer, quickly submitted.[21] It was just as well that the *Adventure Galley* had sighted such a harmless vessel, for with so few men to sail the ship and fire the guns, Kidd would have had difficulty fighting a more powerful enemy. He needed approximately a hundred sailors to fire a broadside, plus enough men to sail the ship. The precious seventy men allowed him by the Admiralty were just not enough. He needed at least twice as many sailors, and New York was a good place to find them.

In New York City Kidd enjoyed a reunion with his wife and daughters before devoting himself to the life of a man of affairs. The townspeople probably learned in short order that he had associated with the greatest men in England and was now a privateer in partnership with them. If nothing else, such bragging attracted men to him—and that was the primary business at hand. A broadsheet advertising Kidd's commission and his desire to recruit more crew members circulated through the city and into the countryside.[22] New York remained in the grip of a depression: nothing had changed since he left port in 1695. As the war continued, its inevitable results were declining trade and increasing unemployment. French attacks along the northern frontier meant that Governor Benjamin Fletcher had to send hundreds of militiamen up the Hudson River to defend the Albany region. Many of these men died during the harsh winters from inadequate shelter, disease, and wretched food, causing Fletcher to scour the colony for men. Unwilling to bear the risks, they fled to surrounding colonies. In a desperate attempt to halt the flow, Fletcher issued a proclamation forbidding further migration.[23] The news that a privateer was "fitting out" fell upon welcoming ears, and men flocked from as far away as New Jersey and Philadelphia to sign the ship's articles. When an additional 90 crew members had signed, the recruiting stopped, for the *Adventure Galley* could hold only about 150 men.

What sort of man joined a venture destined for the Red Sea—a long and perilous voyage with danger his constant companion? Samuel Johnson said that "no man will be a sailor who has contrivance enough to get himself into a jail, for being in a ship is being in a jail with the chance of being drowned . . . A man in jail has more room, better food, and commonly better company."[24] Many may have been like the pirate described by Andrew Barker: "He was a mad rascal, would swear well, drink stiffe, stick foot, and like a good cocke, he would never out of their damnable pit."[25]

These characterizations probably describe many of the men who volunteered for Kidd's voyage, but it is difficult to say more. Mariners rarely owned enough property to appear on tax lists, usually were at sea when the infrequent censuses were compiled, and like most ordinary people left few letters and journals to mark the passing of their days. Kidd did record the names of all who sailed with him. Of the 152 men it is possible to identify a few by occupation; 21 were mariners, 3 were carpenters, and others had assorted occupations such as surgeon, cook, laborer, joiner, cordwainer, gunsmith, jeweler, and baker.[26] The crew was much like other pirate/privateering crews that have been studied, composed mostly of young mariners who left commerce and fishing to try their luck in risky ventures.[27] The landsmen had similar motives but came from more diverse backgrounds. Patrick Dremer, Micijah Evans, and Samuel Kennels, Philadelphia laborers, traveled to New York to put their marks on the crew list; Isaac Deenes of Burlington, New Jersey, left his bakery; Saunders Douglas, servant of New York City vintner Michael Hawden, was put on board by his master, who was to get half of his share; Edward Grayham, a New York City carpenter, left his job behind, as did shoemakers John Burton and William Wakeman.[28] These men signed on along with the sailors, but were obliged to serve with the promise of only a fraction of a share until they proved themselves. Among the youngest crew members were three apprentices, Robert Lamley, William Jenkins, and Richard Barlycorne. Lamley was about twelve and served his apprenticeship with Abeel Owen, the cook; Jenkins, fourteen, was apprenticed to George Bollen, chief mate; and Barlycorne, fourteen, had been recruited by Kidd as his apprentice when he was in the Carolinas during a voyage. Kidd also agreed to take his own young brother-in-law Samuel Bradley with him. The ethnic composition of the crew apparently was overwhelmingly English. Family names are not always a sure guide to nationality, but they indicate slightly more than a hundred men as having English backgrounds. The next largest group was the twenty-five Dutchmen, with the rest made up of seven Scots, two Frenchmen, two Welshmen, and one African. Some names (Clexfelders, for instance) remain a complete puzzle.[29]

A few of the men left other traces that tell us something about their lives. Darby Mullins was born about 1661 in a rural area sixteen miles from Londonderry, Ireland.[30] He followed the plow until he fell victim to kidnappers specializing in hale and hearty young men who could be shipped to the colonies as servants. Mullins' first voyage was the long and arduous trip to the West Indies. Upon arrival in Jamaica, the captain sold him to a planter for enough to pay the captain's costs, plus profit; for this Mullins had the pleasure of working for four years. After surviving the heat and disease of his first year, he became that desirable individual, the seasoned planter. He served his time, and when he was freed he became an odd-jobber and waterman in Port Royale. He kept this up until 1692, when an earthquake destroyed the city; he then moved to the new town of Kingston and built an alehouse. This business must have failed, for a few years later he and his family boarded the *Charity* and sailed to New York. After two years of working around the docks, he went on a long voyage to the Madeiras. During his absence his wife became ill, and shortly after his return she died. He sold his house and moved aboard a twenty-ton ship, which he used to carry wood for the New York City market. When Kidd posted his call for men, Mullins decided it was time to take a chance and make his fortune.

Edward Buckmaster started out as a sailor, but by 1689 he kept a tavern in the dock area of New York City.[31] A restless spirit, he took part in the agitation against the Leisler regime. His tavern provided shelter to anti-Leisler conspirators, and for this the authorities dragged him to jail. After his release he continued to agitate and was arrested again for "rioting" against a new tax. Thus he was on the same side as Kidd when Governor Sloughter arrived in 1691. After the restoration of royal government he dropped from sight except for a court appearance to testify against some Leislerians. One can only assume that, like the other artisans who joined the crew, he believed the potential profits of the upcoming voyage to be greater than continued business in a depressed economy.

Benjamin Franks added a distinct note of diversity to the crew.[32] At forty-six he was older than most and was a member of an important Jewish mercantile family, the Franks, who traded to the West Indies, North America, and India. He, however, represented a failing branch of the family. A jeweler by trade, he set up a business in Port Royale, Jamaica, where he suffered reverses climaxed by the earthquake of 1692. Burdened with losses totaling £12,000, he left Jamaica for North America (a notable branch of the Franks family lived in Philadelphia and another had settled in

New York). By 1696 Franks was in New York, seeking a place on the *Adventure Galley* because he wanted to go to Asia. India had become the leading world supplier of jewels, particularly diamonds. The chief European entrepôt for diamonds was London, where many Sephardic Jews (who controlled much of the jewelry business) had settled after escaping Iberian intolerance. The London branch of the Franks family, with other Jewish families, traded inside the East India Company's monopoly; thus their activities centered on Surat and Bombay. Benjamin Franks asked Kidd if he could sign on until the ship got to Surat, where he planned to reenter his old trade and reestablish his fortune.

The crew of the *Adventure Galley* was not made up wholly of amateurs. Kidd knew that his success depended on men who knew how to sail and fight, so he recruited men such as Frans Cordyne, who left a Dutch privateer in the harbor to go to the Red Sea.[33] To get more men of this sort, Kidd even welcomed an old shipmate from the *Blessed William.* John Browne typified the restlessness of those pirates who found it difficult to enter another trade when their money ran low. Browne had lived on his loot after the *Jacob* returned from the Red Sea in 1693, but like so many former pirates he went back to the sea when his money was spent. Kidd's privateering voyage offered Browne another chance at plunder, and he offered Kidd actual experience in the Indian Ocean and Red Sea.[34]

As the time for departure neared, a number of the men sought to finance their voyages and provide for their families. Cordyne must have left the privateer on which he was serving for lack of prizes, because he went to Joseph Blydenburgh, a local merchant, and purchased waistcoats, breeches, shirts, stockings, knives, handkerchiefs, and rum. He borrowed money on the promise that when he returned—and he vowed to return—he would give Blydenburgh one-third of his share of any money, plate, bullion, Negroes, gold, jewels, and silks acquired on the voyage. The three laborers from Philadelphia (Dremer, Evans, and Kennels) also had to be outfitted in this fashion. To make sure they returned, Blydenburgh had each take out a £1,500 bond as a guarantee of his intent.[35] John Burton and William Wakeman, New York City cordwainers, borrowed £60 and £40 respectively and promised on their return to repay 150 percent of what they had borrowed.[36] Such loans and outfitting agreements were common among pirates and privateers who could not collect wages prior to a voyage but who needed to provide for their own needs and those of their families.[37] For instance, when Tom Green joined the pirate ship *Pelican* on cruise in the Indian Ocean, his fellow seaman Joseph Jones outfitted him for a quarter of his share of the plunder.[38] It is easy to understand why a pirate might do this when he could keep an eye on his crewmate and get his money; one can only speculate on why reputable merchants in New York underwrote these loans. Perhaps the economic depression had left them without solid investments—or perhaps the city's reputation for outrageous financial speculation has an ancient history.

Governor Fletcher's dyspeptic view of Kidd's crew as "men of desperate fortunes and necessitous of getting vast treasure" coincides with what we know of them.[39] Unlike the ventures of the Elizabethan Sea Hawks, who always included a sprinkling of gentlemen, the only "gentleman" on this trip was English Smith, who in 1695 had a taxable estate of £5.[40] The dash and glamour had long since faded from piracy and privateering, and men drifted into it as a way of making money. Kidd, Browne, and their crewmate Samuel Burgess all moved in and out of regular commerce as it suited their circumstances. They and other mariners were increasingly joined by landsmen in their ventures, as the demand for seamen accelerated with increasing international commerce and larger and more frequent wars. The *Adventure Galley* carried a crew that reflected the changing circumstances of the late seventeenth century. Many of the men were young sailors or laborers who had few attachments; the remainder were men in search of a future who hoped this voyage would make their fortunes. These men were more likely to be married (indeed, there were two father-son combinations on board) and more apt to return home. When the war against the pirates started to accelerate after 1713, some pirate ships refused to recruit married men, preferring those who had no ties to the land. These were the men who continued the tradition of the wandering marauders.

Thus Kidd's crew contained the two strains in European piracy: those who saw it as another opportunity to make money and intended to return home at the end of the voyage, and those who went to sea to escape and preferred never to return to settled society. Fletcher's final remarks regarding Kidd's venture were sobering: "It is generally believed here, they will have money 'par fas et nefas' [one way or the other] if he miss of the design intended for which he has commission twill not be in Kidd's power to govern such a load of men under no pay."[41]

During August of 1696 the hold of the *Adventure Galley* slowly filled with barrels, boxes, and sacks containing all the necessities for the long voyage to the Indian Ocean. As the crew came aboard, their chests joined the growing piles of material being sorted and positioned. Care had to be given to assure proper access and trim—it would not do to overload the stern and have the bow floating high. When the crew was fully assembled, a New York City magistrate came on board to read Kidd's commission and articles with due solemnity.[42] Toward the end of August the pace quickened. The wind and weather systems needed to get to the Red Sea waited for no ship. By leaving in September the crew avoided the thunderous winter storms of the North Atlantic, and if all went well they should be in the South Atlantic during the Southern Hemisphere summer. After rounding the Cape of Good Hope, they could plot their course depending on where they wanted to stop for supplies before catching the southwest monsoons that started in April.[43] The voyage would be subject to a ruthless calculus. The *Adventure Galley*, like most privateers, had roughly two tons' capacity for every man on board, which put a strict limit on the amount of food and water the ship could carry. In order to arrive in the Indian Ocean with as many of the men as possible fit for service, Kidd would have to shape a course that would get them there quickly. The most dangerous part of the voyage lay in the South Atlantic, where land would be out of sight for many weeks. Should contrary winds or the doldrums delay them too long, or should a storm disable the ship, the men would quickly eat and drink their way through the limited supplies on board. Bad luck or miscalculation could rapidly ruin the whole venture.

During the first week of September activity around the ship hit fever pitch, for the departure was to be on the sixth. Those who lived in New York made protracted farewells to neighbors, friends, and family. Those who came from elsewhere used the alehouses to enjoy a last drunken spree. Not that the ship lacked liquor: sailors loathed nothing more than a "drink-water" voyage, so they would have a daily ration of beer for as long as it lasted.[44] But inasmuch as the supply of alcohol on board was limited, it was only prudent to drink while quantities were plentiful. Like the other mariners, Kidd started his farewells as the days shrunk to hours. He had been away for over a year and would now be gone for at least two more years, unhappy circumstances for his wife and daughters. On September 6 he left his house on Pearl Street and walked toward the harbor. The last farewells passed across the water as the *Adventure Galley* pulled away from the dock and moved into the great harbor, accompanied by a colonial brigantine and HMS *Richmond*, the navy vessel stationed in New York.

For five years the *Richmond,* under the command of Captain John Evans, had remained on station to protect New York from privateers and pirates. Evans was something of a joke, for he guarded New York as pirate ships came to the city to disgorge their booty and as the *Jacob* returned full of loot and was turned over to Governor Fletcher. The governor found nothing strange in all of this, and the merchants certainly never looked askance at their gold. Captain Evans closed his eyes to everything—and probably profited from his blindness. His ship went into winter quarters in October and did not stir until March at the earliest. Meanwhile, his men went to work in the community and he himself ran an alehouse and a bakery. Evans typified the navy of his day. Captains used their ships for trade to supplement low wages and, like Evans, saw nothing wrong with this. The full flowering of the professional navy lay ahead in the eighteenth century.[45]

The three ships made a brave sight as they moved down the East River and fired salutes to Fort William, sitting above the city at the end of Manhattan Island. The dull thuds of the fort's reply rolled across the bay as the trio trimmed their sails and pointed their bows toward Staten Island before heading for Sandy Hook. There they parted company, for the *Richmond* was venturing out on one of its few patrols while the brigantine and the *Adventure Galley* left the harbor behind and headed for the heaving waves of the Atlantic. It was at this point that many of the landsmen felt the first tremors of seasickness and wished they had stayed at home.

The two ships, for the time being together, were bound for Madeira. This was a voyage familiar to many sailors, for the American colonists already had a taste for the islands' sweet wines. This first leg of the voyage allowed the men to learn the ship and gave Kidd time to organize the crew and get to know his officers. The men were organized along the lines of a navy ship. There were two watches—the larboard watch led by Henry Mead, and the starboard by Robert Bradinham. James Emott, friend and confidant of Kidd, referred to Mead as a captain, which suggests he may have been added to the crew for his knowledge of the Indian Ocean. Bradinham doubled as the ship's surgeon. The other officers were John Walker, the quartermaster, and George Bollen, the mate. They would drill the many landsmen on board until they could handle the sails and haul the ropes. When not practicing sail handling, they learned from William Moore, the gunner, the delicate art of heaving ponderous cannon across a pitching deck.[46] These exercises ceased when a sail lifted above the horizon, which in wartime could mean a warship, a prize, or a friend. The first ship sighted was a disabled brigantine from Barbados. They could offer the captain little but good luck, because the merchantman had lost a mast in a storm and could only hope to slip into an English port before a French privateer sighted it. The *Adventure Galley* and its companion continued on their way using the prevailing westerly trade winds to take them to Madeira.

Later the lookouts spotted another ship; as soon as it caught sight of the privateersman, it put up every inch of canvas and took heel. Kidd now had a chance to test his men, and the landsmen learned the art of constant sail trimming during a chase. Buoyed by the hope of booty, the men kept after the other ship for three days as the *Adventure Galley* strained under full sail. They gained on the ship, until finally it gave up the race and hove to while the privateersman came alongside with cannon run out, just in case. The hunted ship turned out to be a Portuguese merchantman headed for Madeira and therefore no legal prize, because England and Portugal were at peace.[47] Disappointed, the men could do nothing but look forward to a visit to Madeira. They finally arrived in early

October; their stay lasted only one day, for all they required was fresh water, food, and some of the island wine.

Having crossed the Atlantic, Kidd now steered south. On this voyage the straightest distance between two points was not a straight line. The course depended upon the wind system and therefore wandered considerably. Sailing directly south from New York would have been very time-consuming, as the prevailing winds and the Gulf Stream would have necessitated a fight for every mile. And at that time of the year hurricanes made the western Atlantic a very dangerous place. So it was quicker and safer to cross the ocean and then continue on the course pioneered by Vasco da Gama nearly two centuries earlier.[48] Da Gama, instead of following in the path of the Portuguese explorers, who fought north-flowing wind and current as they inched their way down the West African coast, had steered south past the Cape Verde Islands until he was opposite Sierra Leone, where he turned west and south. After cutting across the trade winds, da Gama entered the doldrums, that vast vacuum between wind systems. Every breeze and passing squall had to be used to advantage to gain a passage to the south, as the currents tended to push ships to the west. Relief came near the equator when the southeast trade winds started to dominate. The critical juncture came on the approach to Cape São Roque in northeastern Brazil. If one were sent too far west and ended up north of the cape, the prevailing wind and current carried the unwary toward the West Indies; only constant tacking to the south could save the voyage. If the ship went south of the cape, then the course was steady south and slightly east, taking advantage of the southeasterly and easterly winds that dominate the South Atlantic system. Finally, somewhere after thirty degrees south latitude, the winds turn west to northwest late in the year and an easy run to the Cape of Good Hope is possible. As the *Adventure Galley* left Madeira steering south, it was only at the beginning of da Gama's famous voyage.

On its way south the ship passed the Canary Islands without stopping and continued on to the Cape Verde Islands, the last European outpost before the vast reaches of the South Atlantic. These islands lay exposed to the depredations of pirates and privateers, but the islanders clung tenaciously to their land and thrived on the trade in provisions.[49] Boa Vista was the first stop for the *Adventure Galley*, and four days were spent loading salt for preserving the crew's food. The ship next sailed to the nearby island of Santiago, where it lay at anchor for eight days taking on water, wood, and provisions while the men prepared the ship for the long voyage ahead. Leaving the islands behind, the crew began its race to see how far they could get before the supplies ran out.

Some hundred miles south of the Cape Verde Islands Kidd had to start steering south and west. If he remained too far east, he might be caught in the Gulf of Guinea, under the shoulder of Africa. As the ship approached the equator, the trade winds diminished to fitful breezes and then to the calm of the doldrums. There was not much to be done except to take advantage of every breeze or squall. For the rest, the ship continued to drift closer to the equator as the heat grew ever more oppressive. For the 152 souls on board there was no place to escape. During the day the deck was littered with bodies taking advantage of every bit of shade, moving only as the sun did. At night the men remained on deck rather than face the fetid heat below. There was little to do but smoke their long pipes and talk, while fighting the growing legions of lice and cockroaches.

For Owen, the cook, it was easy to keep the stove lit in these calm waters and cook the daily meals of salted beef or pork, with peas accompanied by hardtack. Each mess of seven men would send one of its number to collect its portion of food, which would then be ladled out to give each man his share.[50] If a mess had money, the men bought extra supplies to enhance the basic meal. Strong beer was in special demand, for without it the men had to drink the water that increasingly acquired a life of its own in this tropical zone and had to be strained through the teeth. Messes that were too poor or unprepared for the voyage and relied only on the cook's daily fare probably felt the pinch of hunger, and as the voyage went on some of them sold their clothes for food.[51] They could also fish, for in the calm of the doldrums it was possible to catch tuna, bonita, and shark. Mariners hated sharks and often caught and mutilated them before letting them go. The only part they ate was the tail.[52] If the sailors had a net, they might go after turtle, a favored fresh food in the tropics. Because it was abundant, hunters sought it avidly, especially the English who developed more of a taste for it than did other Europeans. Turtle meat carried a certain danger, however. When it was introduced into digestive systems used to salt pork and hardtack, it tended, in the pungent words of "Rambling" Jack Cremer, to reduce men to a "shitty condition." For the hungry such an aftermath mattered little.[53]

The heat, broken only by an occasional downpour, did nothing to relieve the men's dispositions. Officers needed to watch for flaring tempers and fights, which could get out of hand and seriously divide the crew. Yet they did occur, for sailors had to be tough to survive their harsh existence at sea, condemned as they were to sleeping mostly on deck or on top of the cargo, hauling in sails in terrifying seas, and doing all the backbreaking work of running a ship. It was not a job for the faint of heart. Nor can it be assumed that the landsmen who had signed on for this voyage were weaklings and cowards. Men had to be allowed to fight enough to get the anger out of their systems, but not long enough to endanger life or limb. They would be asked to make up and forget their quarrel, and then separated as far as possible. If two opponents refused to reconcile, they often were put ashore at the first landfall to fight a duel to the death.[54] Such fights could not be allowed in the close confines of the ship; Kidd and his officers could only keep peace as best they could. Kidd was a large, aggressive man and needed all of his bulk to cow the crew. Later in the voyage he would need all of his assertiveness to maintain order.

The enervating climate and lack of activity also could turn the crew against the officers. Why suffer all the way to India, when the ship could move quickly to the rich hunting grounds of West Africa or the West Indies? The nearer targets offered a tempting prospect to many men, but mutiny never threatened Kidd at this point in the voyage. Perhaps there was sufficient alcohol to blunt tempers, for on some voyages it ran "as freely as ditchwater."[55]

The voyage did not pass without its lighter moments. Mariners enjoyed ceremonies that placated their superstitious natures while providing an occasion for drinking and ribald behavior. These celebrations marked progress past important geographic features— whether a dangerous reef, the Florida Straits, the Rock of Gibraltar, or the equator.[56] On the appointed day a King of Misrule and his court, all outrageously dressed, would appear, ready to "baptize" anyone who had not previously passed the great boundary—in this case, the equator. Even the ship, if it had not crossed before, was threatened with having its bowsprit cut off if the captain or the supercargo did not pay a bribe to protect it. Then the "court" held session, starting with the officers and passengers (if any), asking everyone on board whether they had passed this way before. To the court nothing was more upsetting than people who had already made the crossing, because they were exempt from further proceedings. Those who had not made the crossing either paid up, usually a bottle of liquor or a small sum of money, or received a dunking. The punishment might vary from baptism in a barrel to a more thrilling ride sitting on a plank that was hauled to the top of the mainsail spar and then dropped into the water far below. The half-drowned sufferer would undergo two or three repetitions before his ordeal was over. Those so baptized might get a new name based on a geographic feature that captured the feelings of the crew toward them. An unpopular officer on one ship found himself named the Isle of Rats; a sharp-witted passenger became the Devil's Riptide; a female passenger of questionable morals became the Bay of Heats. Once each had a new name, the proceedings came to an end with a water fight that spread to all parts of the ship. Then followed a feast and an extravagant drinking bout. This elaborate ceremony not only helped pass the time, but acted as a safety valve to vent the frustrations of shipboard life. It also acted as a rite of passage for the young boys and landsmen on the ship: after their "baptism" they were admitted to full membership in the brotherhood of the sea.[57]

Crossing the equator was one of the few breaks in the routine of sailing the vast expanses of the South Atlantic. Few ships traveled this route alone. The East India companies sent their ships out in convoys, and they were expected to sail together at all times. As the preferred vessels for these voyages were sizable ships, frequently over 800 tons, they made an impressive sight as they sailed in line day and night.[58] Such a display guaranteed safe passage because few pirates or privateers would attack these large, well-armed ships. In addition to these fleets there were occasional interlopers on the Indies trades and slavers heading for Madagascar. Kidd's men looked at the lonely reaches of the ocean as day after day slipped by, with nothing to do but trim the sails to catch the trade winds that came increasingly from the west. If they were following the classic India route, the *Adventure Galley* would start to turn east at about thirty degrees south to a new heading designed to take them to the Cape of Good Hope.

By early December 1696 the ship was two months out from the Cape Verde Islands and wallowing in heavy fog. The morning of December 12 broke fair and clear, and as the lookouts scanned the horizon they were surprised to discover a sail behind them. Even more astonishing was the way the newcomer spread more and more canvas and started to overtake them; most merchantmen would not bear down on a strange ship in these waters. Then, just as suddenly as the first ship had appeared, three other ships climbed over the horizon and headed toward the *Adventure Galley*. In the vast wastes of the South Atlantic the crew had managed to cross paths with a Royal Navy squadron led by Commodore Thomas Warren.[59]

This meeting is even more amazing given the experience of the squadron before the encounter. Five navy ships had been assigned to escort the 1696 East Indies fleet on its outward-bound voyage. After a great deal of preparation the *Windsor, Tiger, Kingfisher, Vulture,* and *Advice* left England on May 19, accompanied by six frigates bound for the West Indies, five East India Company ships, and a host of merchantmen bound for the West Indies, Virginia, Guinea, and the Canary Islands. In all, ninety-three ships stood down the English Channel in a huge convoy. As they forged south, various components left the main fleet until by the middle of June only Warren's five ships and the company vessels remained on their steady course southward.[60] The farther south they went, the more restless the company captains became as they fretted over the dilatory ways of the navy. The ships plowed along slowly, with frequent dinners exchanged between the navy and the company officers. When the sailing master on the *Windsor* died, leaving Warren without an experienced guide, the company men chafed even more; and when the first case of scurvy appeared, their irritation turned to anxiety.[61] The company had ordered them to avoid the Dutch colony at the Cape of Good Hope and sail directly to the Comoro Islands to resupply; they were also supposed to remain with the navy as long as possible. With scurvy haunting their crews, the captains had a real dilemma.

Scurvy often started to appear after six weeks without fresh food, and the convoy had avoided all the islands where foodstuffs were available. Deprived of ascorbic acid, the men became listless and dejected, lost their appetites, developed blotches on their bodies, and finally experienced the telltale rotting gums and falling teeth.[62] All too soon they became feverish and gradually weaker until they died. On ships that followed the ritual of flying the skull and crossbones to signal a death on board, the flag flew constantly. Captains in the East Indies trades knew the symptoms of scurvy well—and knew the horrible toll the disease could take. The governor of the Dutch factory, or trading post, at the Cape of Good Hope wrote letters home about the cause and consequences of the disease. In 1696 the Indies fleet arrived from Holland with 273 men dead and 606 sick out of a total complement of 950. What proved devastating for the Dutch was their course to the Indies, which required them—coming and going—to sail north around the British Isles, considerably lengthening their journey. One of their ships, the *Vosmaer,* with 225 aboard, limped into Table Bay with 94 dead and only 4 fit for duty. Those who studied the problem urged shorter voyages and various concoctions of boiled fruits and wine, but it was not until the mid-eighteenth century that ships commonly carried fruit juice, and the end of the century before the Admiralty made it mandatory on navy ships.[63]

On July 5 the first death occurred on the *Sampson,* one of the company ships. Within the week the company captains assembled to decide on a course of action. After a great deal of grumbling about the navy, each man was left to make his own decision. On July 14 the *Charles* and the *Dorrill* tacked to the east and left the fleet. By the middle of August the company men could no longer conceal their disgust at the slow progress of the navy, nor their rising concern over the sick and dead on board. Because of the growing casualty list it was clear that they would have to stop at the cape, and they had to get there quickly. On August 12 the *Sceptre,* the *Sampson,* and the *Chambers* turned out of the line and steered in succession past the *Windsor*'s stern to fire a nine-gun salute; after a seven-gun reply they steered southeast away from the detested navy.[64]

Bereft of their counsel, Warren found matters getting distinctly worse. His orders were to sail to Saint Helena to await the East Indies return fleet and accompany it back to England. But Warren could not find the island. Lying at 15°58′ south latitude and 5°43′ west longitude, Saint Helena had long been an important stopping place for homeward-bound ships. Now the squadron blundered on week after week, steering first north and then west and then south. As a result of these changes in course the *Kingfisher* was left behind. The captains consulted constantly, to no avail. On September 13 they sighted land, but it turned out to be Trinadade Island, which lies at 20°30′ south latitude and 29°20′ west longitude. It was not unknown for ships to get lost, but the navy should have done better. After trying unsuccessfully to land on Trinadade, Warren finally admitted defeat and decided to sail for Rio de Janeiro to get relief for his desperately sick crew. He had lost sixty-eight men, and most of his remaining crew was down with scurvy and flux.[65]

After reaching Rio in late August, Warren allowed his men to recuperate until early November. Meanwhile the *Adventure Galley* had left Madeira in early October and sailed south. Leaving Rio on November 16, Warren's squadron proceeded in a southeasterly direction until, on December 12, Kidd hove into view at 33°50′. Kidd must have been startled to find his ship surrounded by navy vessels in the middle of the South Atlantic, and as he discovered the way the squadron had blundered around he must have cursed his luck. All he could do was report to Warren, identify himself, and display his commission. His concern was not about validating his mission, but about keeping his crew. The squadron had left England shorthanded. Warren had raided the East India ships for mariners before he sailed, but was forced to give them back. When strange sails were sighted five days after he left port, he raided the convoy for men, but even after the ships proved friendly he did not bother to return the sailors.[66] Subsequently all the ships in the squadron suffered the ravages of scurvy, so that when it met Kidd the squadron was short three hundred men. The *Adventure Galley* was a welcome sight. When Warren asked Kidd to accompany him to the cape, Kidd could do little but agree. So Kidd joined in the constant visiting and dining that slowed the squadron's progress. Once again he was reportedly full of "Rhodamantadoe and Vain glory." He asked Warren for a mainsail that he needed and when it could not be supplied, he announced he would get it from the next ship he sighted.[67] But the navy captains kept looking at the *Adventure Galley* and thinking of all the healthy men on board. They knew, and Kidd knew, that the navy had the right to half his men. If it took this many, Kidd's voyage was jeopardized. But Warren was not greedy; all he wanted was thirty men—a blow to Kidd, but by no means a fatal one.

The tension on the *Adventure Galley* grew as the days went by and the men waited for the inevitable. Then on December 19, after a week with the squadron, Kidd returned from yet another evening carouse with the navy to find that the wind had died away. In no time the oars poked through the ports as the men willingly pulled their ship away from the squadron. By the time morning broke the *Adventure Galley* had gone, and when the weather grew brisker Warren had to attend to his ships. A week later he sighted a sail he thought was the *Adventure Galley,* but his ship could not catch it in the heavy weather. Kidd had made his escape.[68]

This chance contact proved very damaging to Kidd's reputation with the navy. Warren hated to see much-needed men slip through his fingers, and the episode probably did nothing to boost his opinion of Kidd's character. He and his captains had already come to suspect Kidd before he "skulked" away. He apparently confessed to them, perhaps during a drinking bout, that he did not care what ships he captured; and from his behavior they came to believe he was a pirate. When Warren and his men arrived in Cape Colony, they quickly spread this opinion to the Dutch administration and the five English East India ships anchored in the bay. The merchantmen immediately surmised that the *Loyal Russell,* a small slaver from Barbados anchored at the cape, was in consortship with Kidd; but that theory could not be proved—and it seems unlikely. Yet Kidd was suspected by all at the cape of being a pirate, and the rumor spread.[69] Allan Catchpoole, a passenger aboard one of the company ships, wrote to his employer, Thomas Bowrey, that Kidd, "an old emminant West India privateer," lay off the coast in a "pretty frigate" in need of liquor and sails and was ready to go anywhere for gain.[70] The merchantmen in the harbor were now like chickens in a coop while the fox roamed about outside.

They had little to worry about because Kidd quickly bypassed the cape. He could hardly enter the harbor when it was Warren's destination, so he had to stay out at sea. Like the other ships, however, he had scurvy on board and needed to make a landfall quickly. The African coast to the east of the Cape of Good Hope offered few landing places, so he pressed on through the turbulent waters where the South Atlantic current collides with the Alqulas current. He headed straight for Tulear on the island of Madagascar and landed there on January 27, 1697. As the first leg of the voyage was over, he viewed for the first time the Great Red Island—the pirate redoubt in the Indian Ocean.

FOUR

The Pirates' Last Frontier

The *Adventure Galley* arrived at Tulear none too soon. The crew were riddled with disease as they sailed past the cape, and Tulear still lay nearly two thousand miles to the northeast. The inhospitable African coast, lacking good harbors and willing suppliers, drove them on. So the lookouts, as they sailed toward the Mozambique Channel, watched for a landfall that would bring relief to the long-suffering seamen. As soon as they reached Tulear, fresh food would revive men sick with scurvy and the most diseased could be taken ashore to succor their ravaged bodies.

Torn from Africa many millions of years ago, Madagascar now lies some two hundred fifty miles off the southeast coast of the continent. Slightly smaller than the state of California, it is a land of high plateaus, steep escarpments, and arid plains. The eastern edge of the island has a perpetually shrouded mountainous spine that catches the water-laden trade winds after their long sweep across the Indian Ocean. From December to May cyclones spawned in the ocean's vast reaches crash into the mountains, causing torrential downpours and floods. It is during this season that the rain-bearing clouds pass over the mountains and spread rain across the broad southern part of the island. The rest of the year the south is a semiarid grassland and the home of large cattle herds. The people of the east coast and the central plateau use the abundant rains to grow rice, which along with beef is a food staple for the local population. Most of the inhabitants are descended from Indonesians who arrived

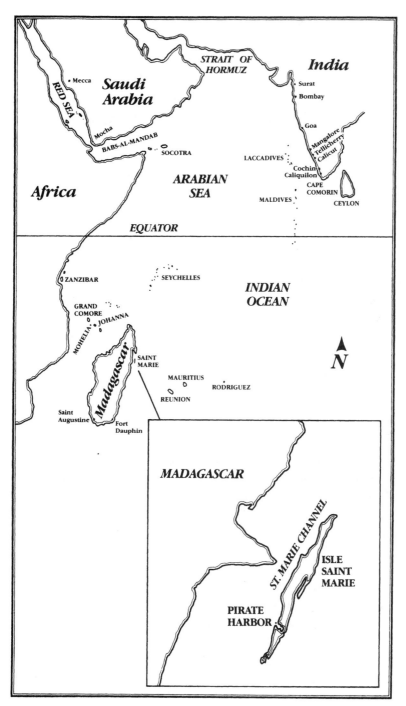

The Indian Ocean

on Madagascar by using the dominant eastern trade winds. Africans also made the journey, but they came across the Mozambique Channel. Whatever their origins, the inhabitants lived in relative isolation for centuries before the Arab expansion down the east coast of Africa crossed to the island during the ninth century. The Arabs had little impact on the island, however, because they carried on only a limited slave trade.[1]

Europeans first sighted Madagascar in 1500 when a violent storm swept Diogo Dias wide of the Cape of Good Hope and he coasted along the east coast of the island after the storm dissipated, before crossing back to Africa. Subsequently ships of other European nations touched at the Isle of Saint Laurence, as the Portuguese named it, until the local name *Madagascar* became the accepted designation. European merchants regarded the island as strategically important because it stood athwart the trade routes to the east and thus promised to be an important way station on the route to Asia. Colonizing the island proved difficult. The English made their attempt in 1644 when a group headed by the noted merchants Sir William Courteen and Thomas Kynnaston tried to establish a colony at Saint Augustine Bay. Touted as more healthful and more bountiful than Virginia, Madagascar failed to live up to its billing. As it was the dry season, the colonists could not grow anything; their survival was further imperiled when natives stole their cattle and attacked them. After eighty colonists died, the remaining sixty abandoned the colony and sailed for India. Although the island was still described in glowing terms by its advocates, the English never again attempted to settle there.[2] The French made the most persistent efforts, but lack of supplies and a vigorous defense by the inhabitants destroyed the colony at Fort Dauphin in 1674.[3]

The European intrusion onto the island in the seventeenth century precipitated a new round of conflict among the tribal states. This combat raged intermittently for over a century before five more or less stable kingdoms emerged. One factor in their creation was the introduction by the Europeans of guns and gunpowder. Given the local demand for a higher military technology, weapons quickly became the favored trade goods; in return, the Europeans accepted war victims as slaves. Because the island lay outside the mainstream of the African slave trade, the price of slaves remained low, a feature that attracted the interest of merchants willing to risk a long voyage for the sake of cheap slaves to sell on the voracious American market. By the 1660s English merchants were making the voyage, and in 1675 a ship from as far away as Boston came to trade. This Madagascar slave trade never rivaled that of West Africa, but it did persist from this time forward.[4] What it lacked was local organization to shorten the ships' turnaround time and to reduce the risks. The pirates stepped in to provide this organization.

Expanding their operations beyond the Caribbean, the buccaneers reached the Indian Ocean about 1685. Some arrived from the east after surviving a remarkable voyage across the Pacific. The *Nicholas* in 1684 and the *Cygnet* in 1686 sought the manilla galleon during its lonely voyage to Acapulco, but both ships failed to find their objective. Unprepared for the long voyage across the Pacific, the crews of the two ships were decimated by scurvy; each day was marked by yet another body tossed over the side with minimum ceremony. The seamen managed to find the Spanish settlement of Guam and refresh themselves before continuing on to China and the Spice Islands; there the crews divided and sought their fortunes separately.[5] Some of the buccaneers, steering clear of the dangerous transpacific voyage, arrived in the Indian Ocean by the more conventional South Atlantic route. And by 1690 any ship's company rounding the Cape of Good Hope had a new danger to worry about.

Because there were few alternatives, Madagascar became the home port for pirates cruising in the Indian Ocean. In Asia the great East India companies built trading factories in the major port cities. Neither the companies nor the local Asian merchants were likely to give the pirates a warm welcome, and only on occasion would the pirates find relief in Asian ports. Unlike the situation in the Americas, it was not in everyone's self-interest to deal with the rovers. Few merchants needed their booty and the governments did not need their martial skills. Madagascar, however, had neither local merchants nor company servants to interfere with the buccaneers. The island had other attractions: a number of fine harbors and supplies of beef and rice. The local rulers also came to appreciate the martial skills the pirates brought with them.

During their struggles to survive or to conquer, the tribal leaders always could use men accustomed to fighting with guns, who could also train the local men in the use of firearms. So the buccaneers went to war and were paid in friendship and slaves. Because of their knowledge of local conditions they rapidly became intermediaries in the slave trade. Merchants who desired to enter the trade were advised that an incoming ship could expect to find someone ready to assist. That someone was invariably a pirate.[6]

Some of the men who resided on Madagascar were remarkable and colorful characters, none more so than Abraham Samuel, self-proclaimed "Tolinor Rex," the king of Fort Dauphin. In about 1696 Samuel came to the Indian Ocean as quartermaster of the pirate ship *John and Rebecca*. He was reported to be a slave who had escaped from the French colony of Martinique and joined Captain John Hoar's crew before it left the Caribbean and headed for the Indian Ocean. After raiding in the Arabian Sea and the Persian Gulf, the pirates took a 300-ton ship near Surat and retired, in February 1697, to the island of Saint Marie off the east coast of Madagascar. There the local natives attacked, killing thirty men before the remainder escaped. Samuel survived, and he and the rest of the crew fled south to Fort Dauphin, the abandoned French settlement at the southeastern tip of Madagascar. There their ship foundered and sank, perhaps owing to faulty ship handling in the dangerous entry to the harbor. As Samuel pondered his next move, a princess, or in some accounts the queen mother, identified him as her child, based on marks on his body that were identical with those of a child she had borne to a Frenchman during the occupancy of Fort Dauphin. The child had been removed by his father upon the collapse of the colony. Suddenly Samuel found himself declared a prince and heir to the unoccupied throne of the kingdom. One suspects his "mother" recognized him as a means of continuing her influence in local affairs. Samuel remained suspicious of his "relatives" and his subjects, for he retained twenty of his old mates as bodyguards.

Slavers and buccaneers flocked to Fort Dauphin to trade with "King Samuel," who accepted their gifts and protected them while they were in port. But the slavers had to take care, for the king preferred his old compatriots. For example, the *Prophet Daniel* of

New York arrived in September 1699 to buy slaves, only to discover that Samuel was at his country house twenty-five miles in the interior. After the captain and a few men had gone to find Samuel, Captain Evan Jones piloted his decrepit *Beckford Galley* into port and quickly looted the *Prophet Daniel* for supplies. As a favor, he gave the *Prophet Daniel* to Samuel, who then sold it to four pirates for 1,100 pieces of eight and gave them a bill of sale signed by Abraham Samuel, King of Fort Dauphin, Tollannare, Farrawe, Fanquest, Fownzahira. This document did the owners little good. When they arrived at Saint Thomas in the Virgin Islands with Captain Rupert Billingsley of His Majesty's ship *Queensborough* hot on their heels, they did not pause to show Billingsley their bill of sale, but abandoned the ship and fled ashore.[7] In 1699 a Dutch slaver visited Fort Dauphin to do business with the king, who was reported to have 300 warriors with him plus his buccaneer bodyguard. When the captain heard a rumor that Samuel planned to steal his ship and leave the island, he quickly sailed away under cover of darkness. A year later Captain Littleton of the Royal Navy entertained Samuel and two of his queens on board his ship and reported that he was "loved" by his people. By 1706, when another Dutch ship visited Fort Dauphin, King Samuel was gone, either dead at the hand of a rival or else successful in returning to the sea.[8]

The harbors of Madagascar contained a number of men similar to Samuel. Whereas some were merely slavers, others became local leaders and managed private armies of as many as five hundred men.[9] While they created a unique era in Madagascar's history, they were only an offshoot of the buccaneer raids in the Indian Ocean.

It was nearly a decade after the pirates entered the Indian Ocean before they caused a major uproar in India. The man behind the spectacular action that ensued was Henry Avery—at least that is the name he used at the time. Like so many of the pirates, his life is a blank until he emerged from the ranks of faceless sailors to captain a pirate ship. Avery was second mate of the *Charles*, a ship hired by a consortium led by Sir James Houblon, to raid the Spanish colonies. After waiting eight months for a squadron of ships to assemble in England, the *Charles* sailed for the port of Coruna, where it waited a further four months. The crew grew restless, for during these long months the men were never paid. Finally a number of them conspired to relieve their condition by stealing a ship and leaving the squadron. On May 7, 1694, Avery and his followers took the *Charles* and sailed away to go "on account." He was quoted as saying, "I am a Man of Fortune, and must seek my Fortune," and his men were described as "true Cocks of the Game, and old Sportsmen."[10]

Avery headed south along the coast of West Africa, stopping at various islands to rob ships of supplies. On the Guinea coast he lured a group of native men aboard under the guise of trade, then seized their gold and carried them away as slaves. Near the island of Principe they came in contact with two Danish ships, and after a hard fight captured both. Some of the Danish crewmen joined with them and the rest were sent ashore. They burned the larger of the two ships and kept the smaller one because of their increasing numbers. Later they destroyed this vessel also, when the men assigned to it could never agree on anything. The wanton destruction of valuable ships for which they no longer had a need was one of the pirate activities that astounded shipowners. To them it was monstrous and inexplicable unless the buccaneers were totally depraved. From the pirates' point of view, they were simply getting rid of an unwanted object. With all his men installed on the *Fancy* (the renamed *Charles*), by now a very overcrowded ship, Avery continued to steer south, rounding the Cape of Good Hope and finally landing on Madagascar in desperate need of supplies. After obtaining water and wood and buying cows and other provisions, the crew continued on to the island of Johanna, in the Comoros chain, where they put the sick men ashore and prepared to get everything needed for the last leg of the journey to the Red Sea. William May, one of the sick men, had the not-so-unusual experience of being addressed in fluent English by one of the "negroes." After recovering from his surprise, May learned that the man had been taken from the island by an English ship and had lived for a time in Bethnal Green, a London suburb, before returning home. May got another jolt when he saw the *Fancy* quickly leave the bay, abandoning him. The reason for the hasty departure was the appearance of three large East Indiamen that swept into harbor. Leonard Edgecomb, one of the Indiamen captains, threatened to take May to Bombay where he would see him dance in the air, but May's English-speaking friend protected him. [11]

Eight weeks later the *Fancy* returned, not out of friendship for May, but to get the supplies the crew needed for the long voyage before them. Avery now did a remarkable thing. On February 28, 1695, he issued a proclamation announcing that although he had one hundred fifty men on a forty-six-gun ship, he did not intend to attack English shipping during his voyage. The English could obtain his protection by flying flags in a particular way so that he would recognize them. By denying any intention of attacking English ships and taking only "country" ships, Avery shared a common belief that it was acceptable to steal from the "moors," and that if he did so the East India Company would leave him alone. [12] As we shall see, the opposite was the case. As news of this remarkable letter circulated, it brought consternation to the company because it was commonly believed that all pirates were English and that the company conspired with the pirates against local trade. This conspiracy theory had received an edifying and quite satisfactory proof in Avery's memo, and the company's servants went apoplectic with rage at this false accusation.

The intended target of the *Fancy* was the pilgrim fleet that sailed annually from Surat to Mocha. This famous fleet took Muslim pilgrims from India to Mocha, where they rested before continuing on to Mecca. The fleet enjoyed a special status in the Mughal Empire. As an act of piety the emperor sent his own ships with the fleet, so that even the lowliest of the faithful could make their pilgrimages. But the faithful shared the voyage with many merchants who were more concerned with the riches they could earn by taking cloth and spices to Arabia, there to trade for coffee and gold. On the return voyage the fleet was the richest prize in Asia and a magnet to every buccaneer. [13] As the *Fancy* got into position to intercept the fleet, Avery discovered that other vultures had the same idea. The first to appear were the *Portsmouth Adventure* (Captain Joseph Faro) from Rhode Island and the *Dolphin* (Captain Want) out of Philadelphia. Both ships carried about sixty men so that the pirate squadron now totaled about two hundred fifty. Three days later their strength was doubled when the *Pearl* (Captain William Maze) from Rhode Island, the *Amity* (Captain Thomas Tew) from New York, and the *Susannah* (Captain Wake), out of Boston, joined them. By this time Avery and his men must have thought that every mariner in America was a pirate.[14]

At the throat of the Red Sea all shipping passes through the strait of Babs-al-Mandab, and this is where the squadron awaited the pilgrim fleet. The ships traversed the strait during the night and nearly escaped from danger until a straggler gave them away and the chase was on. For five days Avery pressed across the Arabian Sea, burning the *Dolphin* along the way because it was such a poor sailor. Finally, off Cape Saint John they sighted the *Fath Mahmamadi*, a ship belonging to Abd-ul-Ghafur, the most prominent Gujarati trader of the day, who now lost his ship and its cargo valued at £50,000 to £60,000 in gold and silver. More was to come, for a few days later the pirates happened upon the *Ganj-i-Sawai*. Captained by Muhammad Ibrahim, this formidable target was the largest of the imperial ships, with forty cannon and four hundred rifles. Unfortunately for Captain Ibrahim, at the beginning of the fight one of the Muslim cannons burst and a shot from the *Fancy* smashed into the mainmast, sapping the fighting spirit of the men on board; against a bunch of rapacious brigands they needed all the courage they could muster. After about two hours of fighting Captain Ibrahim fled belowdecks as the pirates boarded his ship. One report asserts that in desperation he armed some recently acquired slave girls and sent them out to fight—a sight to cause a sensation among the pirates. Shortly thereafter all resistance on the renamed *Gunsway* collapsed. For days the ships drifted together while the men looted and raped their way from deck to deck.[15] The *Gunsway* carried 500,000 rials plus the money of the passengers which, when it was divided, amounted to £1,000 for each man who had a full share. The men of the *Pearl* subsequently lost their shares when they traded gold for silver with the men of the *Fancy*. When Avery's men examined the gold coins they discovered that the edges of the coins had been clipped, lessening their value, so they immediately repossessed the silver at gunpoint.[16]

After stopping at a few places on the Indian coast, Avery readied the ships to catch the northeast monsoon. While they waited for the winds, a number of men decided to remain where they were rather than chance discovery when they returned to America, so only about a hundred returned to England. After a stop at Johanna to careen and resupply, they sailed to Providence Island in the West Indies, where they paid Governor Nicholas Trott twenty pieces of eight apiece for permission to come ashore. Trott did not sell his favor cheaply: once the men had his protection they made him a present of the *Fancy* and ivory tusks worth £1,000. The company divided into two parts, one going to Carolina and the other to England via Dublin. Inevitably some of the men were caught, in one case because a maid in a Rochester tavern discovered £1,045 sewn into a cloak. Ordinary mariners never carried this much money, so when any of them displayed a lot of cash it always aroused suspicion. With one man captured the hunt was on for others, especially for Avery, but he evaded the chase and vanished into legend.[17] In India he left a legacy of fear and hatred toward the pirates as Kidd prepared to sail in his wake.

After the *Adventure Galley*'s arrival at Tulear on January 27, 1697, her water casks were filled and fresh food brought aboard to end the monotony of vile water and salty food. The sick men gradually recovered ashore, where many of the crew joined them to escape the crowded conditions on board. While the ship lay at anchor, another vessel sailed into nearby Saint Augustine Bay, and in due course a party set out to determine its identity. It was the *Loyal Russell,* a sloop from Barbados, come to Madagascar to buy slaves. Earlier it had visited the Cape Colony, where Warren and the merchant captains at anchor suspected it of being in consortship with Kidd. There is no evidence of such a partnership, but their meeting was fortunate for Kidd because he could acquire information about the ships at the cape and also learn that Warren was spreading the word that he was a pirate. The man who relayed this information to Kidd promptly sickened and died in Kidd's cabin. While the most immediate needs of his men were met at Tulear, Kidd desperately needed sails and other equipment unavailable there. As he left port he may have hoped to meet one of the

East Indiamen that had waited in harbor at the cape until after the *Loyal Russell* left—in which case he perhaps could beg, borrow, or steal what he needed.[18]

Near the end of February Kidd left Tulear with the *Loyal Russell* and sailed north toward the Comoro Islands. Strung across the northern end of the Mozambique Channel, at the verge of the Arabian Sea, the Comoros made a convenient rest stop on the way to India. For vessels that did not, or could not, stop at the cape, the islands were the last place to buy fresh victuals. Johanna (modern Anjouan) was noted for the availability of fresh fruits and vegetables and a friendly welcome. It had the additional benefit of being a good place to wait until the southwest monsoon asserted itself and permitted the voyage to India.[19]

As the *Adventure Galley* sailed up the channel toward the islands, two sails rose over the horizon. On investigation they turned out to be the *Sidney*, an East India Company ship, and the *Scarborough*, an interloper in the India trade. If Kidd did plan to acquire naval supplies by bullying a merchantman, these were not the ships with which to start; they were heavily armed and easily his match as long as they remained alert. Shortly after the three ships came to anchor in Johanna Road, Kidd threatened Captain Gifford of the *Sidney*. As senior captain of the Indies fleet, Gifford flew a commodore's flag, but as Kidd hoisted the king's jack and pendant, he asserted his superiority and wanted Gifford to lower his flag. Just then two more East Indiamen, the *East India Merchant* and the *Madras Merchant*, sailed around Saddle Island and prepared to anchor, but hesitated because the *Adventure Galley* and the *Loyal Russell* lay alongside their companions. Captain John Clerke of the *East India Merchant*, who had delayed his departure from the cape for fear of Kidd, now was unpleasantly surprised to find him at Johanna. Captain Gifford quickly defused the situation by signaling that all was well, as Kidd was no match for four of them. Kidd thereafter kept to business and maintained correct, if cool, relations with the others. The merchant captains told him frankly that they suspected him and warned him to mind his manners while in port. They refused his invitations to join him on board his ship and disbelieved him when he indicated that he intended to go to Saint Marie because his men, mingling with theirs ashore, told them that Kidd desperately needed sails and stores and hoped to catch one of the Indiamen alone in order to obtain what he needed. Such reports did nothing to endear Kidd to them. Ashore Kidd also found hard hearts, for he had little money, and business on Johanna was strictly cash and carry. He tried to pass a bill of exchange drawn on King William, but it was quickly refused. On April 2, after filling his water tanks, he left Johanna Road still accompanied by the *Loyal Russell*. Needless to say, the sight of his hull vanishing over the horizon was a relief to the ships in the harbor.[20]

Before going any farther, Kidd had to careen the *Adventure Galley*. So he set his course for the nearby island of Mohilla, where he could do the job in peace. He shipped his guns onto the *Loyal Russell* and then used the sloop to tilt his ship onto first one side and then the other, while the men scraped off the accumulated marine growth, caulked the seams, and recoated the bottom. With that laborious task completed they righted the ship, slipped it back into deep water, and reshipped the guns.

By the time the job was finished, thirty men lay buried in the sandy soil of Mohilla. They died not from overwork, but from some deadly disease. Whether it was brought over from the *Loyal Russell* or was picked up locally we cannot know, but it killed a fifth of Kidd's men in five weeks.[21] The crew was learning the deadly reality of sailing in tropical waters. Even after the rigors of scurvy and shipboard disease, a host of infectious diseases and parasites waited to strike the men down. One hundred fifty years later Royal Navy ships, patrolling Mozambique Channel to suppress the slave trade, confronted the same problems.[22] Not until modern times and the development of antibiotics did conditions in the tropics change for the better. Kidd's men could only watch their companions sicken and die and hope that they would avoid the same fate, but their only weapons were prodigious superstitious practices. For sick mariners in the tropics, little could be done. One of their number summarized their feelings:

> Many are the miseries that poor seamen endure at sea when they are sick, having small means to comfort themselves with, for there they cannot run and fetch what meat and drink they think will do them good. There they want both fresh meat and drink of all sorts, with both fruits and roots, which the sick on land do not lack to give

themselves comfort with, and we having no other thing to eat and drink, to restore health, and comfort ourselves with, unless we can eat a piece of a hard biscuit cake, or a piece of old salt beef or pork, and maybe both stinking and rotten, having lain in pickle one year or two and nothing to drink but a little fresh water, many times both stinking and dirty, and yet cannot get half of it.

And when he is dead, he is quickly buried, saving his friends and acquaintance that trouble to go to the church and have his passing bell rung . . . [instead, they only] sew him up in an old blanket or piece of old canvas, and tie to his feet two or three cannon bullets, and so to heave him overboard, . . . being made meat for the fishes of the sea.[23]

Kidd now faced another problem besides his pressing need for naval supplies, for if he intended to fight his ship, he needed a crew of about 150 men. A handful from the small crew of the *Loyal Russell* joined him; but he needed many more seamen. New recruits might be available on Johanna, and after five weeks Kidd returned there to look into that possibility and see to his supplies. Fortune smiled on him, for he recruited five men who had stolen the pinnace of the *East India Merchant* and run away, most likely with the intention of joining Kidd and thereby improving their fortunes. He also managed to attract an unknown number of French and English sailors, who loaned him money so that he could buy supplies for his ship. One would have to assume that any European mariner stranded on Johanna with money to lend was a pirate who had already made a profitable voyage.[24] These men would also add to the hard core of experienced men on the ship. By the time Kidd completed his resupplying it was the end of April 1697. The southwest monsoon flowed north, driving everything toward the Arabian Sea, including the *Adventure Galley*.

It is safe to assume that by the time the peak of the volcanic mountain on Grand Comoro vanished over the horizon Kidd had developed a plan of action. Unfortunately, none of his post facto statements bothered to explain what it might have been. Indeed, when he wrote a narrative of his voyage he omitted this period entirely.[25] If he had intended to fulfill the original plan for his voyage, he would have returned to Madagascar, preferably Isle Saint Marie, before proceeding any farther. In New York and among his crewmen he would have easily discovered the importance of these two islands to the buccaneers, and presumably he knew a great deal about them. If he had gone to Saint Marie, for instance, he would have found the pirate Captain John Hoar and his hundred men; they had arrived during February with a three-hundred-ton prize and remained until July. Then in June the *Resolution,* under Captain Richard Shivers with ninety men, joined them. So a trip to Saint Marie would have netted a nice haul of pirates.[26] But it appears Kidd never entertained that possibility.

Kidd's options were quite limited, as he had a large performance bond hanging over his head. To return empty-handed meant financial ruin as well as the enmity of Bellomont, now governor of New York, and of the ministry in England. What sort of "Presbyterian grip" might Harrison use on him if he failed? Hardly comforting thoughts for a simple mariner. Of far more immediate concern were his own men. There was now a substantial core of old pirates in the crew and among the others a number who had signed up for a "Red Sea voyage," which meant a readiness to commit piracy. None had yet made a single penny on the voyage, and some of them had sold clothing in order to buy food.[27] Certainly they did not expect to go home empty-handed. There were still close to 150 men on board; if, on occasion, he recalled the episode on the *Blessed William* when his men abandoned him, he may have had a sleepless night or two.

He decided to go to the Red Sea. The pilgrim fleet was already famous as a rich flotilla with few defenses. What if he were able to capture even one of the opulent ships and then vanish? One of the crew reported much later that Kidd hoped to "make his voyage" at Mocha and ballast his ship with gold and silver, and another quoted him as saying "Come boys, I will make money enough out of that fleet."[28] If this is true, he probably thought that he could loot a ship and then turn it over to those who wanted to stay in the East, while he returned home with a few of the men—the fewer the better. He could then use the loot and his political connections to keep the whole affair quiet. It could be accomplished in New York where Bellomont, impoverished Bellomont, could settle the accounts and protect him if need be. If something did go wrong, he would be on home ground with a ship of his own close at hand. It seems an unlikely plan because there were far too many witnesses, but then many other pirates had already returned to New York (and other colonies) and had been protected because of the loot they brought. Why could it not work for him? It was certainly a better plot than attacking armed and dangerous pirates.

The *Adventure Galley* ran north under the influence of the monsoon, passed Zanzibar, Mombassa, Melindi, and Lamu and moved on toward the Horn of Africa. When Kidd rounded the horn and turned due west into the Gulf of Aden, he was all but announcing he had turned pirate. He could still argue that he was there to *look* for pirates, but his actions would quickly undermine that excuse. The Gulf of Aden narrows dramatically at its western end into the strait of Babs-al-Mandab, known to the pirates as the Babs. On the northwest side of the straits the Arabian peninsula thrusts out a headland that reappears a short distance offshore as Perim Island, while less than twenty miles to the southeast the promontory of Ras Sijan, on the African shore, is protected by large sandbars and a group of small islands known as the Brothers. All southbound shipping keeps close to Perim Island in order to avoid the shoals, making the strait an ideal place to intercept vessels leaving the Red Sea. When he arrived at the strait Kidd anchored his ship in the harbor on the south side of Perim Island. Men were posted on what today is called Signal Hill, on the west end of the harbor, to watch the strait while John Walker, the quartermaster, took the ship's pinnace to scout the harbor at Mocha fifty miles to the north. Walker sighted seventeen ships at anchor making preparations to leave, pleasant news to the men waiting at the Babs. He made two other reconnaissance voyages as most of the men settled down to wait for the fleet.[29]

It was August, the wrong time of year to sit around waiting in Arabia, and the men suffered from the terrible heat. They were driven out from below and forced to live day and night on deck in hope of capturing any stray breezes that might pass. Some crewmen became ill from the intense heat; their only relief would come from setting out to sea and that had to await the fleet. They sat around, smoked their pipes and fantasized on the fortunes soon to come their way. Meanwhile two men stayed atop Signal Hill, with flags at the

An accurate depiction of a ship being careened while some of the crew
lounge in a tent made of sails. *(From the Special Collections of the University
of California at San Diego)*

Sir James Vernon, as painted by Sir Godfrey Kneller in 1677. Vernon was at the beginning of his career, still a secretary to the Duke of Monmouth before becoming secretary to the Duke of Shrewsbury. *(Courtesy of the National Portrait Gallery, London)*

Richard Coote, Earl of Bellomont, in an uncharacteristic military pose. Coote was a vice admiral and Governor-General of Massachusetts Bay, New York, and New Hampshire. *(Courtesy of Harvard University, Fine Arts Library)*

Several citizens aid the pirates in their inquiries. The buccaneers are using various modes of torture to gain information. (*Courtesy of the Henry E. Huntington Library and Art Gallery*)

A mock Admiralty Court. The judge sits in a tree as the buccaneers below ridicule the institutions of justice. *(From the Special Collections of the University of California at San Diego)*

The island of Ascension, as drawn in 1704 by Captain Francis Stoves of the East Indiaman *Rochester*. The letter *E* designates the anchorage of the ship's boats when landing on the island; nearby was a rock where messages could be left for other ships. The beach at *F* was the best place to catch turtles. The cross at *G* was placed there by the Portuguese, but by the time this drawing was made it had fallen down. (*Courtesy of the British Library*)

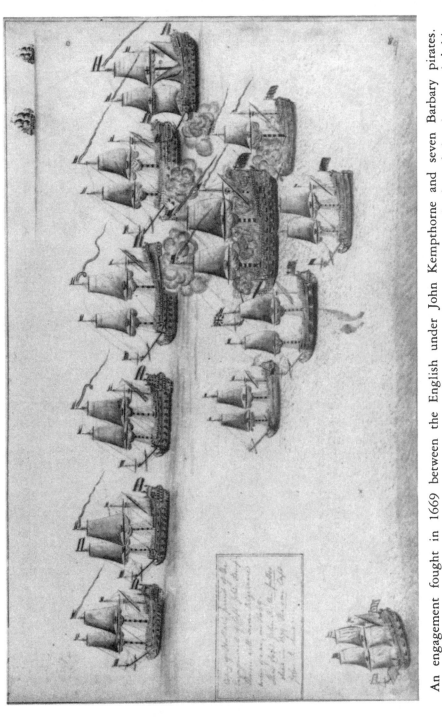

An engagement fought in 1669 between the English under John Kempthorne and seven Barbary pirates. Kempthorne's son, one of many mariners who made watercolor drawings in their logbooks and elsewhere, copied this from a print. (*Courtesy of the British Library*)

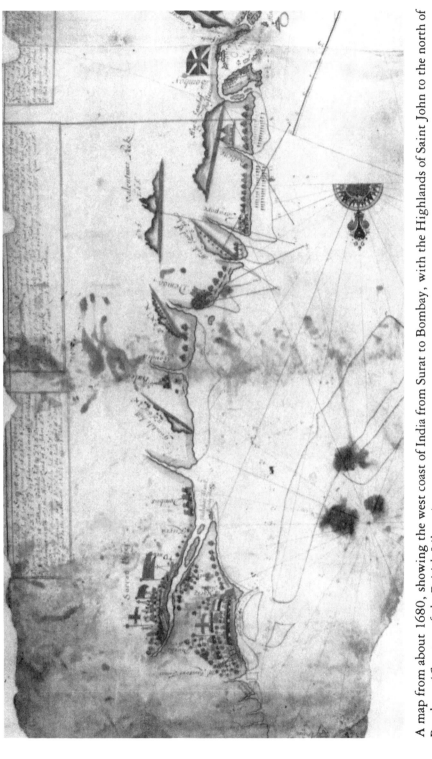

A map from about 1680, showing the west coast of India from Surat to Bombay, with the Highlands of Saint John to the north of Bombay. (*Courtesy of the British Library*)

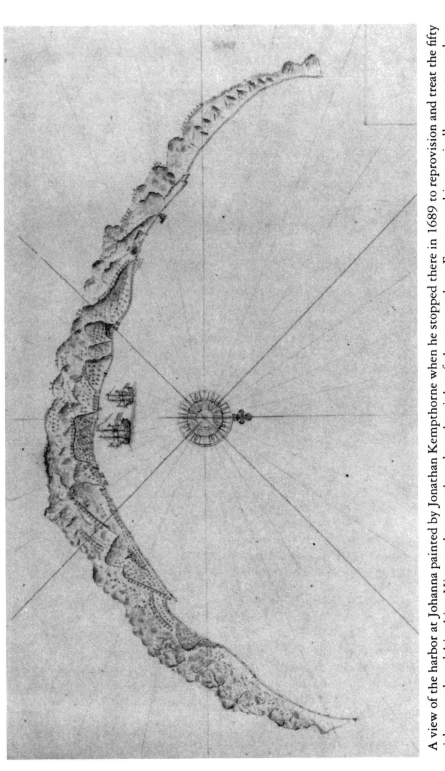

A view of the harbor at Johanna painted by Jonathan Kempthorne when he stopped there in 1689 to reprovision and treat the fifty sick men aboard his ship. His vessels are anchored to the right of the town where European ships typically came to anchor. *(Courtesy of the British Library)*

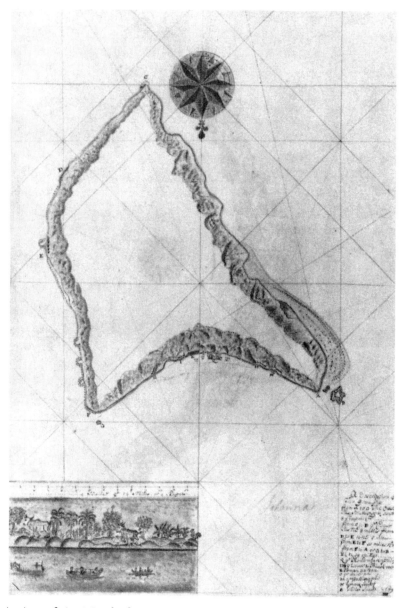

A view of the island of Johanna as painted by Jonathan Kempthorne in 1689, showing the pirate anchorage on the northern side of the island *(at bottom)*. The cartouche shows Europeans and local inhabitants rowing along the coast, with beasts and trees in the background. *(Courtesy of the British Library)*

ready to alert the ship in the small harbor below them. Two weeks passed before they sighted the first ship.[30]

If Kidd had hoped to escape detection, he was disappointed. Walker had been sighted, and other reports had reached Mocha because earlier, as Kidd sailed toward the Babs, he stopped at a town called Motta to replenish his badly depleted water supply. When the inhabitants had refused to make a deal, forty men had gone ashore to take what they wanted, including a number of natives who were ransomed for cows and sheep. On another raid for food they had killed some of the residents who resisted. News of these raids had spread north to where the pilgrim fleet waited.[31]

The pilgrim fleet finally left Mocha on August 11, 1697, under the protection of three European ships. The *Ganj-i-sawai,* or *Gunsway,* had already cleared port some time earlier, so the most famous Indian ship of the day escaped the trap. The three convoy ships assigned to the fleet were there as a result of the uproar after the capture of the *Gunsway* by Avery and his men. An enraged Emperor Aurangzeb ordered the Dutch, French, and English East India companies to protect Indian shipping, especially the pilgrim fleet. The English company agreed reluctantly because it had so few ships in Indian waters at the time, but in the end the *Sceptre,* a thirty-six-gun ship, sailed to Mocha.

The *Sceptre,* it will be remembered, had come out to India in convoy with Warren. It had left him early because of the slow pace and so was gone long before Warren intercepted Kidd. The first mate of the *Sceptre* was a rather remarkable seaman named Edward Barlow.[32] His is perhaps the finest sea journal written by a mariner during the seventeenth century. Not only is it rich in detail, it is also illustrated with Barlow's own watercolors of the ships he sailed in and the ports he visited during his long career. He had gone to sea as a boy and gradually worked his way up to the position of first mate on the *Sceptre.* When he arrived in India, Barlow had a stroke of good fortune when his captain died and the company placed him in command for the voyage to Mocha. An ambitious young man, Barlow wanted to have a successful voyage even though this was his first trip to the Red Sea. Arriving in Mocha, he exchanged his cargo of sugar, pepper, knives, scissors, lead, and iron for Mocha's chief commodity, its famous coffee, and for some spices, dyes, and ivory.[33]

All was going well until rumors reached Mocha that a ship was lurking at the Babs. Barlow's voyage suddenly became a far more serious endeavor. He knew the story of the *Gunsway*, and the last thing he wanted was to raise the ire of his employers by losing more pilgrims to the pirates. He also knew that he could not count on the two Dutch ships assigned to the convoy. It was widely assumed in India that all pirates were English, and the French and the Dutch did everything they could to confirm that opinion. When the Dutch East India Company captured some English pirates, they happily returned them to the English with a great deal of fanfare.[34] If another English pirate looted a pilgrim ship, the Dutch ships would be glad to rush to Surat with the news—anything to hurt the competition. So Barlow had his career in his own hands.

Barlow did meet with the Dutch captains on August 10 to formulate a strategy. Their main concern was to keep the fleet together—a notoriously difficult task given the different sailing qualities of the ships—and to prevent attack. They agreed to stay upwind of the fleet, ready to run downwind to aid anyone in trouble. The next morning the merchant ships and convoys raised anchor and, before turning into the Red Sea, slowly sailed around the shoals that protected the Mocha Road. The surface of the sea was littered with dead and dying locusts blown in from Africa—hardly a happy omen with which to leave port. Bunched together, the ships steered south and slipped past the Babs during the night of August 14 in hopes of escaping the pirates.

When the sun rose the next morning, it revealed one too many ships in the convoy. The extra vessel was the *Adventure Galley*, moving fast on a slight wind, under topsail only, and in lieu of the usual king's jack and pendant flying from the masthead was the bloodred banner that betokened pirates. Barlow's heavily loaded ship was the only vessel close to the *Adventure Galley* as the Dutch lagged far behind, intending to stay out of the action. Barlow waited until the *Adventure Galley* sailed past him before firing a few of his guns and raising the East India Company's flag. Kidd and his men were taken quite by surprise, because Walker had reported only seventeen ships in the harbor at Mocha and had mentioned nothing about the three European ships now visible in the morning sun. Kidd had rejected Walker's advice to attack at night, but he must have had second thoughts in the light of day. Weak, fitful winds hampered the European convoys so the advantage lay with Kidd, who could use his oars to good effect. He picked out a large Malabar ship and steered toward it, hoping to capture it and escape before the other ships could stop him. As he ranged alongside, his cannon fired into the ship, which desperately tried to steer away while returning his fire.

Barlow refused to become a scapegoat. After identifying his antagonist as the *Adventure Galley,* and having no doubt about its intentions once the sound of cannon fire rolled across the water, he determined to thwart the attack. While he lacked the oars of a galley, he did not lack strong backs and ship's boats. So in a flurry of activity he had the boats lowered into the water, and after picking up a towline the men started to pull the *Sceptre* forward. Urged on by the frantic Barlow, the boat crews slowly pulled toward the *Adventure Galley.* Long before it was in range Barlow started to fire his guns, and to make an even more impressive display he sent his men into the rigging to shout threats and curses at the pirates. As Barlow approached, Kidd lost his nerve. Barlow thought he did so because he mistook the *Sceptre* for a navy ship, which seems doubtful, but then Kidd must have been puzzled by Barlow's actions. Would a merchantman chase a pirate ship? Caught between an evasive victim and Barlow, Kidd raised his sails, put out his oars, and moved out of range, waiting to see Barlow's next move. Barlow kept on coming and twice more pulled toward him in a direct challenge, with cannon firing and men yelling. Because of the size of the *Sceptre,* with its thirty-six guns, Kidd edged away each time Barlow pulled toward him. He probably considered fighting his tormentor, but a lucky shot could disable his ship, leaving him at the mercy of the three European vessels. In the late afternoon Kidd finally gave in to his doubts and sailed away. The next morning he was no longer in sight, and Barlow was quick to offer the opinion that only his bravado had saved the fleet and the East India Company's reputation. The Dutch, of course, put out a very different story, hinting at dark conspiracies between Kidd and Barlow.[35]

Unfortunately virtue and bravery went unrewarded. Although

the company officers appreciated Barlow's actions, they removed him as captain some months later. Barlow, to the company's loss, had failed to onload sufficient pepper during a trip down the Indian coast, and then got into a dispute about his men's wages. So, while he was not "sottish," the company deemed him "deficient in government" and replaced him. Barlow had enough insight to write, "I always being reckoned rather too mild than too harsh to bear command over a parcel of seamen, for they are troublesome and unruly at times."[36] It rankled that he had been ousted, and he thought that it had been done "for self interest, they put another man commander over my head: I not having money enough to buy their good will and few friends to stand by me." But he had the last laugh. In his journal he noted with satisfaction that the *Sceptre* was wrecked on its next voyage because of unskillful handling by the captain.[37]

Kidd's plan for a quick strike and subsequent vanishing act lay in ruins. While he remained out of sight, he did not leave the vicinity of the convoy because he still hoped to catch a stray ship. But his water supply continued to diminish rapidly, so he could not dawdle with the slow-moving and by now thoroughly alarmed fleet. In the old maritime tradition he called the crew together for a consultation. He proposed two alternatives; they could either hang around the edge of the fleet hoping for a straggler or they could use their superior speed to sail ahead of it to the highlands of Saint John. The first choice seemed a poor one because of the shortage of water and the fact that the fleet was unlikely to have laggards. The second option seemed more promising. Ships commonly used the highlands of Saint John on the northwest coast of India as a convenient landfall and then turned north for Surat. Whether he knew it or not, Avery had captured the *Gunsway* off the highlands, so it was indeed a good place to await local shipping. The men decided on the second alternative. The *Adventure Galley* left the fleet behind and headed for India.

As the Indian coast drew near, the mood on the ship was tense. The men grumbled about the shortage of water to Walker, the quartermaster, who in turn went to Kidd. Once again the crew was called together to consider the situation. The choices this time were to turn toward the nearest supply of water or continue to the highlands. After discussing the alternatives, they decided to stay on the present course and get water when they arrived. But the shortage of water and the constant heat did nothing to improve morale. A few men were quite sick and several had various ailments. Some members of the crew privately considered their own predicament. The men who thought they had signed on for a privateering voyage and had continued to hold this belief now recognized that they were on a pirate ship—a pirate ship bound for the coast of India, where the likelihood of making a quick strike and fleeing home undetected was far less. These men wanted to leave the ship rather than continue. The condition of the *Adventure Galley* was also a cause for concern, for it was now "leaky and rotten" and the men pumped water daily to keep down the water level in the bilge.[38] So they sailed on with short supplies, an unhappy crew, and a deteriorating ship. It was hardly the formula for success.

So far Kidd had not actually committed piracy. Although he had threatened ships at Johanna and again at the Babs, he had not yet taken any. He quickly crossed the line when he came to the Malabar coast. The *Adventure Galley* arrived far to the south of its intended landfall, the highlands of Saint John. Shortly thereafter a small local trader from Bombay, flying English colors, came into sight. Kidd's men put a shot across its bow, and it hove to and was quickly overtaken. Captain Thomas Parker went aboard his captor's ship. For the next few hours Kidd and Walker interviewed him on local conditions and probably discovered, to their dismay, that they were already considered pirates. Captain John Clerke had gone directly from Johanna to Bombay, arriving in June. At the request of the East India Company he had written a report on Kidd's meeting with Warren in the South Atlantic and his actions at Johanna. This report was sent to all the company factories, so that by the time Kidd arrived in late August many had reason to suspect him.[39]

While the three men talked, some of Kidd's restless deckhands went aboard Parker's ship. There they seized some of his men, tied their wrists behind their backs, and hoisted them aloft on ropes.

While their shoulders slowly pulled out of the sockets, the unfortunates were beaten with naked cutlasses for the pleasure of the pirates and to ascertain whether there was hidden wealth on board. One hundred pieces of eight were located, only enough to give each mess of seven men two pieces of eight to buy supplies. A greater prize was Captain Parker who, because he knew the coast well, was forced to remain aboard the *Adventure Galley* as pilot; one of his Portuguese sailors was retained as a "linguistor," or translator. Food and pieces of eight were transferred before the trader continued its voyage. With these actions Kidd became in actuality the pirate he was reputed to be.[40]

The need for water on board the *Adventure Galley* by this time was critical. Kidd steered south and after passing Bombay sailed boldly into the port of Carwar on September 3. Thomas Pattle and John Harvey, the East India Company agents who resided there, could do nothing to stop the crew from filling their water casks and buying wood for the ship's stove. They did attempt to find out everything they could about the ship and Kidd's plans. While Pattle and Harvey questioned the men who came ashore, Captain Charles Perrin and William Mason went out to talk to Kidd.

When Mason climbed over the rail of the ship, he encountered old crewmates, for he had served with Kidd and other members of the crew of the *Blessed William:* he had commanded the *Jacob* when it left New York with Kidd's old West Indian crew. Unlike John Browne, who now served under Kidd, Mason had not returned with the *Jacob.* During the ship's cruise along the west coast of India a dispute had split the crew. Mason and eighteen others left the ship at Mangalore and offered their services to the East India Company.[41] The fact that the company would hire old buccaneers reveals just how desperately it needed experienced European mariners.

The company did take advantage of Mason's knowledge of pirates, having in fact used him once before to negotiate with them. In November 1696 the *Resolution,* under Captain Dirck Chivers, sailed into Calicut and fired a broadside into one ship. In the confusion Chivers seized this ship and three others, including one of the company's, before cutting the anchor cables of all the other ships in port to send them onto the beach.[42] Indian shipowners and merchants were outraged and threw the local representative of the

East India Company into jail. Rightly or wrongly all pirates at this time were identified as English, so the company suffered every time there was a pirate attack. Mason, sent out to negotiate, returned with the pirates' demands: pay £10,000 or all the ships would burn. The local governor thought this outrageous, as did the company representatives, so Mason returned to the *Resolution*. He told the pirates of the governor's fury and the dilemma of the company with its trade stopped, its representatives in jail, and worse to come. They remained deaf to his entreaties, even when he asked them to consider the plight of their countrymen ashore. Their reply was that "they acknowledged no countrymen, they had sold their country and were sure to be hanged if taken. They would take no Quarter, but do all the mischief they could."[43] This creed was a familiar one to Mason, but one he had turned his back on. The hard core of the pirate community recognized no allegiance except to the other members of their own group and expected no hand in friendship from the world they had left behind. They reduced their demands to 40,000 rupees and sent Mason back with the warning that if these terms were not met, one of the ships would burn. Mason continued to shuttle back and forth, but in fact the local governor was stalling. He had sent a message to the local Malabar pirates asking for help but before it arrived two ships had burned. When ten "grabs" (local sailing vessels) anchored one night, the pirates retreated, leaving their two prizes behind but taking the unfortunate Mason. Later he transferred to a local ship and was deposited on the beach just north of Calicut. Before he got home some locals, upset by the pirates, stripped him naked and roughed him up. So it was understandable if Mason was apprehensive as he now boarded the *Adventure Galley*.[44]

Kidd related to Mason that he had been at Madagascar, Johanna, and the Babs looking unsuccessfully for pirates, and was now going to try his luck on the Indian coast. He said nothing about the capture of Parker's ship or about Parker, who was confined below decks. As it was, Mason and Perrin learned a great deal about the ship and its activities during their visit, and this knowledge was supplemented with information from a few of the crew who managed to jump ship before it left port. One of these was Benjamin Franks, who finally realized his ambition of getting to India.

Franks typified those men who were extremely unhappy with the turn of events on the ship. A group of them who tried to get away on a ship's boat while the *Adventure Galley* was at Carwar were captured, returned to the ship, and whipped. About ten men did manage to escape, and from them the company acquired a detailed picture of conditions on board the *Adventure Galley*. The ship was leaky and rotten; there were supplies aboard for only one more month; and, most important, morale was plummeting. Dissatisfaction was rife and Kidd maintained discipline with freely used punishment. In this wretched atmosphere men fought one another, thereby increasing the level of violence. In what would have been an ironic twist, some of the old hands took Mason aside while he was aboard and tried to get him to become their captain. He refused to return to his old trade, but carried back their complaints. In his report to the company the local representative wrote:

> Kidd carries a very different command from what other pirates use to do, his commission having heretofore procured respect and awe, and this being added to by his own strength, being a very lusty man, fighting with his men on any little occasion, often calling for his pistols and threatening any one that durst speak of anything contrary to his mind to knock out their brains, causing them to dread him, and are very desirous to put off their yoak.[45]

Confronted with a desperate situation, Kidd had to do something quickly, and it appears he set out to make a big strike as fast as possible.

Kidd had learned that a large "Moor's ship" was expected soon. This knowledge caused the company great concern, for it belonged to Abd-ul-Ghafur, who even after the loss of the *Fath Mahmamadi* to Avery was still the most powerful Gujarati merchant of the day. Ghafur was no friend of the English. In 1691 he had lost a ship to pirates and immediately demanded from the governor of Surat and Emperor Aurangzeb that the English East India Company reimburse him for his losses, even though he had no evidence that the pirates were English. The government, however, sided with Ghafur and ordered all the English in Surat confined to their factory and their trade stopped until they paid £100,000 to Ghafur. The company had refused until it could be proved that the pirates were

English. Fortunately, evidence emerged that the guilty party was a Danish ship, but the company's men remained locked up from August until December. For a brief period in 1692 Ghafur had succeeded in having them confined once again, on the usual premise that all pirates really were English pirates. Thus the company remained very anxious about any act of piracy committed against Ghafur. With Kidd on the high seas hunting one of Ghafur's ships, alarm bells sounded up and down the Malabar coast.[46]

Instead of a prosperous merchantman, Kidd found himself confronted by two Portuguese men-of-war carrying twenty-two and forty-four guns, sent by the viceroy of Goa to destroy him. It was the morning on September 12, 1697, when the two ships intercepted the *Adventure Galley.* Kidd turned tail and ran. The smaller of the two ships outsailed her larger companion while overtaking the *Adventure Galley.* Unfortunately, speed and ambition overrode good tactics: Kidd merely waited for the distance between the two ships to grow and then turned and bore down on the smaller tormentor. Morale problems were forgotten as his men willingly joined in the attack, and the Portuguese captain suddenly found himself confronted by a much more powerful vessel. The fight was extremely lopsided, as the *Adventure Galley* simply stood off and pounded the smaller ship with cannon fire until the second Portuguese ship came to the rescue. The *Adventure Galley* then bore away, while the second Portuguese ship shepherded its crippled companion to Carwar. Kidd was later to brag of this triumph that "no Portuguese will ever attack the King's colours again."[47]

Having finally seen action at the cost of nine or ten wounded men, Kidd continued to cruise down the Malabar coast. His next stop was Calicut, where he arrived on October 4. Firing cannon salutes to announce his presence, he sailed in boldly. Thomas Pennynge, the company's representative, was suspicious of this strange ship and sent a boat out to investigate; but Walker cut it off and returned to shore with it, not allowing anyone to get too close to the *Adventure Galley.* Walker bore a disingenuous note from Kidd, declaring that he simply could not understand why everyone was afraid of him. He carried a royal commission to hunt pirates and wanted only to carry out his mission; to that end he needed supplies, for which he would pay. Pennynge considered this "impudence" but could do nothing to oppose Kidd. He waited and watched until Kidd had sailed away, then sent another report north to company headquarters in Bombay, where an already large dossier on Kidd continued to grow. All of the information was negative in content.[48]

Just after leaving Calicut, Kidd's ship met the *Thankfull,* under Captain Charles Perrin, who got a nasty surprise when he sighted the *Adventure Galley* with French colors streaming at the masthead. Kidd was trying an old ruse often used by privateers, which involved sailing under a foreign flag until a merchantman was lured close by. For their part the merchant captains also carried sets of false flags and commissions, hoping that if they sighted an enemy ship they could run up the correct colors, get out the right ship's papers, and outfox the privateers. But if the privateer revealed its true colors at the last moment, the merchantman might be left with a false identification and thus become an easy victim. In this case Captain Perrin saw through the ruse and kept his English flags flying instead of unfurling French colors. Kidd, dropping his French flags at the last moment, ran up the king's jack and pendant and ordered Perrin on board. Perrin was closely questioned about the whereabouts of the "Moor's ship," Ghafur's vessel, but knew nothing about it, so he and his ship were freed.[49]

Before continuing the search for the elusive ship, the *Adventure Galley* sailed away from the coast toward the Laccadive Islands. The ship may have been careened at this time. Some of the men later commented on the use of myrrh for pitch on the ship's bottom, a rather extravagant way of protecting the timber, but another indication of the shortage of supplies on board. Typically the men avoided the hard labor involved by forcing local men to work for them. In fact, harsh treatment of the locals characterized the pirates' entire stay. They used local boats for firewood and raped a number of the native women. In revenge the ship's cooper had his throat slit, an act that elicited a savage response from the crew, who attacked a village, killing and maiming the inhabitants before retreating to the ship. Such retaliation was common when the pirates called at these islands, making them very unwelcome visitors indeed.[50] Kidd never admitted to this particular stopover: he claimed to have gone to the island of Saint Marie to refit. Given the pattern of the monsoon winds, however, the story is evidently one of the many lies he told in his narrative to cover his tracks. In this case his secret was immediately revealed, because the islanders went to the mainland to complain about the behavior of the pirates.[51]

In the great weather cycle that dominates the Indian Ocean, the southwest monsoons weaken in September; sometime in October the winds reverse and instead of waterborne clouds from the sea the dry northeastern winds from the Himalayas dominate the skies. With these winds a southerly passage along the coast became easier for Kidd and his men. Close to the tip of India the East India Company ship *Loyal Captain,* under Captain How, crossed the path of the *Adventure Galley.* How knew about Kidd from talking to Captain Gifford and feared the worst. When summoned on board the *Adventure Galley,* he went quickly, hoping to keep the pirates from his ship. Kidd maintained his policy of not harming company ships. His men, desperate for prize money, now disagreed with this approach. They did not wait for Kidd to call a meeting but rallied themselves; two-thirds of them voted to seize the ship alongside. Kidd refused to give them arms and raged at them not to leave the ship. Captain How helped him by swearing he carried nothing but sugar. Kidd bullied and cajoled to prevent his men from doing the one thing he felt would surely end any hopes they had of remaining out of trouble with the company. His fuming gradually convinced them to let Captain How leave the ship. When How did get away, he sailed off fast, before Kidd could lose the argument with his crew.[52]

Aboard the *Adventure Galley* emotions ran high. The men had very little prize money, while they continued to pay for supplies. Those who had already gone over the side had made their decision to abandon a pirate ship; those who remained had no illusions about the ship and its purpose, so why avoid company ships? The crew had already committed an act of piracy and had badly smashed a Portuguese ship: Kidd deluded himself if he thought these deeds could be covered up. The men correctly assumed that the company knew all about them and would only put them in danger. With all these factors in their favor, there must not have been a natural leader among the men—or at least no one with a large following—or surely Kidd would have been directly challenged early on.

Finally the heat, illness, lack of supplies, and frustration with Kidd resulted in a challenge to his authority from William Moore, the ship's gunner, on October 30. The ship lay close to a Dutch vessel and the men became restless once again about the lack of action. Moore was on deck grinding a chisel, chatting with a few men about the means of taking the nearby ship when Kidd came up and denounced him, calling him a "lousie dog." To which Moore replied, "If I am a lousie dog, you have made me so; you have brought me to ruin and many more." Kidd turned away from him, muttering "Have I ruined you, ye Dog?" and then reached down, picked up a bucket, whirled it, and smashed it down on Moore's head. Moore crumpled to the deck saying, "Farewell, farewell, Captain Kidd has given me my last." This only elicited a final "You're a villain" from Kidd. Bradinham, the surgeon, rushed to the wounded man and had him carried below, where he died the next day of a fractured skull. Kidd showed little remorse, saying later, "for I have good Friends in England, that will bring me off for that."[53] Kidd's predicament was now very dangerous. The next challenger would arm himself in light of Moore's death. Kidd needed a prize and soon.

Four days later, on November 3, the *Adventure Galley* sailed into Tellicherry, but fate once again played tricks on Kidd. As he crept into the harbor, he discovered two East India Company ships—the all-too-familiar *Sceptre* and the only slightly less familiar *East India Merchant*. Captain Clerke of the *Merchant* had just died, but Barlow was still captain of the *Sceptre*. For fifteen minutes the ships lay close to one another before a shot rang out from a shore battery that was urged on by Pennynge, the company's agent from Calicut, who had come south with Barlow. That was enough for Kidd: he immediately turned his vessel around, as he did so sending up French colors to replace the English flags he flew and firing a few shots before he headed back to sea. Once again reports went north to Bombay with information on Kidd's voyage.[54]

Relief for Kidd finally appeared in the form of the *Rupparell*, a large "Moorish" ship, but not Ghafur's long-awaited merchantman. Flying French colors, the *Adventure Galley* approached, playing cat and mouse with the *Rupparell's* captain. The victim was actually a Dutch-owned vessel with a mixed crew of Dutch and local "lascars," or sailors, who carried on a limited trade in drugs, cloth, sugar, and coral. After firing a few shots to convince the victim to stop, Kidd waited for her captain to come aboard, hoping that his accustomed ruse of wearing French flags would work. When Captain Michael Dickers came into the great cabin, he was confronted by one of the French pirates from Johanna, a Monsieur le Roy, playing at captain. In hopes of saving his ship Dickers presented a French pass; as soon as he did, Kidd cried: "By God have I catched you? You are a free prize."[55] Dickers had fallen victim to the old stratagem: Kidd could claim to be acting legally because his commission allowed him to seize French ships, while his men finally got their big prize. His ship gone, Dickers and two of his men joined the pirates. The Dutch now had additional reasons to assure the Mughal government that all pirates were indeed English.

The crew gave the *Rupparell* the rather derisory name of the *Maiden,* signifying that at long last they had a valuable prize. Shortly they renamed the ship *November,* after the month in which they had captured it. Their prize carried very little portable wealth, so Kidd needed to sell its cargo as quickly as possible to keep the men happy. They went to Caliquilon, a little-used port just north of Anjengo, where they sold the cargo to Gillam Gandaman, a renegade East India Company employee. Unfortunately for the company, Gandaman's activities only fed rumors that Kidd actually was in league with the company to ruin local merchants. The money from the sale of the goods went back onto the ship, where the anxious crew awaited their shares. The men trooped one by one into Kidd's great cabin as Walker called off their names and their shares. Name and share confirmed, each man took off his hat—not in deference to Kidd, but to use it as a pouch as he swept the money from the table and trooped back onto the deck to count his gains. Supplies such as tobacco and sugar were divided up by the mess groups to sweeten the men's dispositions. At last, after a year and a half of suffering, the men had something tangible. The newly named *November* was attached to the *Adventure Galley* by a towline and a small number of trusted men were put on board. As soon as they could, the men left Caliquilon to resume hunting.

A month passed without incident until toward the end of December 1697, when a small ketch was captured which carried sugar and coffee sufficient to resupply the messes. There was no patina of legality as there had been with the *November:* the ship was stopped and robbed, and that was piracy. About two weeks later a Portuguese ship carrying rice, iron, butter, and cloth was victimized. Although each of these prizes eased Kidd's supply problems, they were hardly the stuff of pirates' dreams. The men could only keep sailing in hope of the long-sought big prize.[56]

Finally on January 30, 1698, they got their wish. The *Quedah Merchant* had started its voyage in Surat, with a cargo of cloth bound for the Spice Islands. It was a four-hundred-ton ship and the value of its cargo was estimated at 200,000 to 400,000 rupees. A very significant part of the cloth (about five hundred bales) belonged to an umbraw, or secretary of state, at the mughal's court. Entrusted with the safety of the ship was an English captain named John Wright. The first part of his voyage had gone peacefully as the crew sailed to Bengal, sold their goods, and loaded a return cargo of silk, muslin, calico, sugar, opium, iron, and saltpeter. Sailing without escort, the *Quedah* rounded Cape Comorin at the southern tip of India and started north. It was just off the port of Cochin that the *Adventure Galley* and the *November,* once again flying French colors, intercepted the cargo ship. Wright put up his set of French flags, and when the summons came for him to board the *Adventure Galley* he sent a Frenchman, one of his gunners, over with a French pass. When the gunner failed to convince Monsieur le Roy that he was the captain, Wright was sent for. Once he arrived, his ship was claimed as a prize. When Kidd boarded the *Quedah,* Coji Babba, one of seven Armenians sailing on the ship as supercargoes, or merchants, approached him with an offer of 20,000 rupees to set the ship free. Kidd spurned this amount as insufficient. The money on board quickly changed hands. Then Kidd, needing to get rid of the cargo, retraced his route to Caliquilon, where he sold the bulk of it. One approximation of the value was £7,000 to £8,000, but all such estimates are doubtful. Once again the men lined up outside the great cabin and went in with their hats at the ready to pick up 200 rupees each, plus rights to the many bales of goods that remained in the hold.[57] With this sort of money the men could get down to some serious gambling, thereby easing the tension on board and allowing Kidd to sleep a little easier at night.

By now it was early February. Every week that passed brought the ship closer to the time when the great monsoon cycle would revolve once again. Now the northeast winds would die to a whisper, ushering in the rainy season and the southwest monsoon. If the ships did not leave the coast soon, the men would have no choice but to remain until the following October. That was out of the question because the *Adventure Galley* was in poor condition: her pumps worked every day in order to keep the ship afloat; water seeped in relentlessly; and cables were secured around the hull to help keep it together. Time on the Malabar coast was limited.[58]

Kidd continued to cruise south looking for potential prizes. He took another small Portuguese ship, which he retained as an escort. By now Kidd had a small flotilla. He had kept the *Quedah*, which was towed by the *Adventure Galley;* and the *November* towed the new Portuguese ship. One evening they sighted a group of five ships bearing down on them, but darkness intervened. Kidd shortened sail and waited for morning to see who they were. When the sun rose, only the largest of the ships remained close by. It proved to be the East India Company ship *Dorrill.* Her companions were two Dutch ships, a Portuguese ship, and the *Blessing,* a small company ship. They were traveling together for protection and none was ready to fight. The crew of the *Dorrill* had already battled a pirate ship, and the two Dutch ships were under orders not to fight unless attacked. In the morning light the *Dorrill* seemed large and menacing and the other large ships appeared ready to come to its aid, so Kidd turned away from them. The *Rupparell* even dropped the tow of the Portuguese ship, leaving the stripped hulk for the *Dorrill.*[59]

Kidd's final action on the coast came a few days later when he met the *Sedgewick,* another East India Company ship. For the next three days he chased this vessel, rowing after it most of the time because the wind failed. Captain Lockyer Watts managed to stay ahead of his attackers by letting his ship's boats tow the *Sedgewick.* In the end, Watts managed to remain just beyond reach and made his getaway. His luck ran out during his return voyage when the pirate ship *Resolution* caught him after a nine-hour rowing match.[60]

Chasing the *Sedgewick* was a change of policy for Kidd, for to this point he had avoided taking company ships. Either he failed to identify it, which seems unlikely as it flew the company's distinctive flag, or else he decided that the *Dorrill* meant to attack him. His failure to capture the *Sedgewick* also indicates that the *Adventure Galley* simply was no longer a seaworthy ship, and if Kidd could not catch a fully loaded merchantman, he might as well leave the Malabar coast. Furthermore, each passing day brought the change of the monsoon that much closer.

Preparations to leave started shortly after this incident. The pirates captured another "moorish" ketch and stripped it of food and water before allowing Captain Wright and the long-suffering Thomas Parker to board it and depart the pirate fleet. Parker's services were no longer needed, now that they planned to abandon the coast. Dickers, the original captain of the *Rupparell*, took over as master for the voyage across the Indian Ocean. Kidd also moved most of the lascars from the ketch to the *Adventure Galley*. His men did not want to pump constantly during the long voyage ahead of them, and if the *Adventure Galley* was to survive the trip, it had to be pumped out day and night. It was just this sort of nasty hard work that caused pirate crews to keep slaves on board. In this case, the lascars could serve. They *could* do such work and at other times could wash the men's clothes, light their pipes, and, if they were women, provide sexual services.[61]

After this sorting out of the crews of the various ships, the little flotilla of the *Quedah* (now commanded by the mate, George Bollen), the *November,* and the *Adventure Galley* set off toward the pirate stronghold on the island of Saint Marie.

Only a few sources of relief lay in their path. One was the island of Mauritius, a small speck in the middle of the Indian Ocean that received more than a few distressed visitors—including pirates. It was a temporary shelter at best, as conditions on the island were quite desperate. The governors of the Dutch colony spent most of their time pleading with their superiors to remove the colonists from the island and end their misery. Europeans had brought about an ecological disaster. They destroyed the "hard-fleshed" dodo bird and threatened every other living thing by inadvertently introducing rats—which, through their explosive population growth, overran the island, eating everything they could reach. The Dutch finally transferred the colonists, leaving behind a shattered ecology visited only by mariners seeking refuge in the vast ocean waste.[62] Kidd avoided the island, and as each day passed, his ships lumbered toward a landfall on Madagascar.

This voyage was a test of Kidd's seamanship because he was engaged in a deadly race. His only true fighting ship, the *Adventure Galley,* required continual pumping to stay afloat. Her hull planks were worm-eaten and loose from too many months at sea, causing water to seep in relentlessly even as eight men pumped. So the ship wallowed along to the mournful clank of the pumps. As long as the monsoon winds held steady the crew was safe, but cyclones were a new worry. Like their counterparts in the Northern Hemisphere, the hurricanes, they brought awesome winds and high seas. One day at the edge of a cyclone and the *Adventure Galley* would go to the bottom, as its seams would tear apart and create a flood no amount of pumping could stem. It was time to pray—and to look anxiously for a landfall.

FIVE

Life in a Pirate Settlement

In the popular image, pirate headquarters are located on sun-drenched islands with long palm-fringed beaches, adjacent to a harbor and port town. Saint Marie is a little different. Ten miles from the northeastern coast of Madagascar, it is a long, narrow island with a bulge in the middle. Toward the southern end, on the western or leeward side of the island near modern Ambodifototra, there is a very good harbor. It was this harbor that attracted pirates. Certainly it could not have been the climate, which is basically very hot and very humid. October is the best month; after that the weather gets worse and worse until in March, just the season when the *Adventure Galley* was approaching, the temperature averages about 80° F, and rainfall during the month is about 23 inches. Ships approaching the island usually did so at this time through a sea sizzling with rain and accompanied by a low, deeply clouded sky. Canoes would suddenly appear and vanish in the dim light, and landfalls were equally sudden and unexpected.[1] The pirate settlement on the island was by all accounts a ramshackle affair. It consisted of a few houses, a low palisade, and a couple of cannon.[2] Yet the greater the distance from the island, the more formidable it became. Worried by the increasing piracy in the Indian Ocean, the government in England collected testimony about the "fort," which magnified it into a substantial structure bristling with cannon and filled with hundreds of villains who, it was feared, would create a "settled government."[3] Just before Kidd arrived this supposed fort was overwhelmed by local natives, who drove away the resident Europeans. Kidd would not find it abandoned because of its value as a rendezvous. Shortly after this attack the pirates made their peace with the residents and returned to the harbor.

If the weather remained appalling year round and the accommodations were slight, what was the attraction? The harbor was one of the few anchorages along the eastern edge of Madagascar, which is characterized by steep escarpments. It had the additional virtue of a small island at its mouth that narrowed the approaches and made Saint Marie easy to defend. The island's resident population was also small, making it somewhat safer than Madagascar, where the pirates confronted large and powerful tribes who were uncomfortable neighbors. Saint Marie's proximity to Madagascar made it convenient when a ship was seeking food or other supplies up and down the coast. These virtues made it the favorite pirate base. Merchants soon followed. A regular trade sprang up and was so successful that resident factors, or traders, came to the island. The activities of Adam Baldridge illustrate this phenomenon.

Baldridge arrived at the island of Saint Marie in January 1691, ready to settle down on the island. He and his apprentice John King joined local residents in making war on their enemies. Four months later Baldridge was well supplied with cattle and slaves. He built a house with slave labor and attracted a number of natives, who came to live under his protection.[4] Baldridge was not a fully independent agent, for he was employed by Frederick Philipse of New York City. Philipse was a remarkable entrepreneur who seized any opportunity to make money. The Madagascar slave trade and the ancillary pirate trade appealed to him as a potentially rich venture. He had sent ships to Madagascar for some years before he employed Baldridge, an old buccaneer, to trade for slaves, thereby shortening the turnaround time of his ships and also providing Baldridge an opportunity to do business with his old comrades.[5] Philipse even hired retired pirates to sail to Madagascar. One of them was Samuel Burgess, who had sailed with Kidd on the *Blessed William,* gone to the East Indies on the *Jacob,* and then settled in New York with his fortune. Philipse recruited him as a merchant captain, then sent him back to Saint Marie to trade.[6]

Philipse loaded his ships with clothing, liquor, naval supplies, arms, and ammunition. These commodities found ready markets on Madagascar. The hard life at sea combined with the constant exposure to salt water quickly ruined the clothes of any mariner. Whenever anyone died at sea, his clothes were quickly auctioned off at the mast by his comrades. In the tropics mildew and other fungi hastened the process of decay and caused the men to use the silk, brocades, and cotton fabrics they stole to make their own clothing. They delighted in such brilliant costumes because in Europe the use of luxury fabrics was confined by law to the upper classes. On the peripheries of empire they could indulge themselves and flaunt sumptuary legislation. While it may have been splendid to look at, such clothing could not withstand the hard use it received; so there was a ready market for old canvas and wool in good condition. (Besides, when a man went home, silk shirts, brocade pants, and other fripperies brought the local constable around for a little chat.)[7] Naval supplies were also in demand, because rigging and sails succumbed to rot and storm damage just as clothing did. Without enough on hand, a ship was useless. The pirates accordingly searched any vessel they captured for usable sails, spars, and rope. One group of buccaneers in the Pacific simply beached their ship when they could no longer manage it, and started to walk. Members of another crew confronted by a similar situation were quite ingenious. They took their captured silks and made them into sails. They might not wear as well as canvas sails, but they certainly caused a sensation when they appeared at sea as a gorgeous apparition. Liquor and armaments too, from Philipse's cargoes, found ready customers among the buccaneers and natives.[8]

When one of Philipse's ships arrived, Baldridge would offload the cargo and set to work to organize the return load. Philipse insisted that Baldridge return a full cargo of slaves, because they remained the most consistent item of trade.[9] While Baldridge saw to this part of the cargo first, he never neglected the pirate trade. Once the pirates returned to Saint Marie, which quickly became a more popular haunt because of Baldridge, the men started drinking and Baldridge began to relieve them of their booty. Whether they had gold, silver, jewels, or currency, he could quote a price for whatever they needed, making sure never to go too high for fear of enraging his customers. He was even reported to give credit to those men who did not "make their voyage" or who had lost their shares in the interminable shipboard games of chance.[10] He also acquired the best of their spices, drugs, and exotic textiles, particularly if the men were going to remain in the Indian Ocean for another voyage. For those who wanted to return home, he arranged passage. The standard price was 100 pieces of eight for transportation plus the cost of food.[11]

When everything was ready, Baldridge put the cargo, the slaves, supplies of beef and rice to sustain them, plus the retiring pirates on board the ship and then sat back to wait for his next customer. After they left Madagascar, the ships represented themselves as slavers and used the normal way stations along the route. Samuel Burgess stopped at Saint Helena when Warren and his squadron were at anchor awaiting the East India return fleet. Burgess convinced Warren that he was an innocent slaver homeward bound, so Warren gave him a pass certifying his status as a legal merchantman.[12] Leaving Saint Helena behind, the ship proceeded to Ascension Island and then to the West Indies and North America. The paying passengers debarked at convenient places along the way.

By the time the ships got to New York, very little of the cargo remained. The slaves either stayed in the city or were sent to the Chesapeake tobacco colonies. Gold, silver, currency, and jewels went to Europe to pay for costly manufactured goods. The expensive Asian commodities also went to Europe, where there was a larger market and higher prices than in the colonies. Philipse had this trade equally well organized. In 1698, when the *New York Merchant* returned from Madagascar, another of Philipse's ships, the *Frederick*, met it off the Delaware Capes. The *Frederick* took on board all of the cargo except the slaves, who remained on the *New York Merchant* to be carried to New York City while the rest of the cargo proceeded to Europe. Because a colonial vessel loaded with East India goods might raise questions, the *Frederick* went north around the British Isles to Hamburg, where Philipse's agents got the cargo ashore before the local British consul could seize it. This was truly an incredible piece of entrepreneurship—New York to Madagascar to New York and finally to Hamburg before the profits returned to

New York. Much could and did go wrong over such vast distances, but that the system existed at all is a testament to Philipse's skill and daring.[13]

Baldridge continued to act as Philipse's agent on Saint Marie until 1697. In July of that year Baldridge bought an interest in the brigantine *Swift* and left to trade along the coast of Madagascar. While he was away the natives rose up against the intruders, killed about thirty men, and destroyed or stole all of Baldridge's store of goods. Luckily for Baldridge, he met a ship that warned him not to return to Saint Marie. He took this advice and returned to New York to lead a more peaceful life.[14] Shortly afterward, Edward Welsh took over as the resident trader and supplier of slaves. Merchants quickly directed their ship captains to contact him on arrival. Thus little changed with Baldridge's departure, and the island remained a popular haunt for pirates.[15]

Kidd arrived at the island at the beginning of April 1698, in company with the *Rupparell;* the *Quedah,* now renamed the *Adventure Prize,* did not arrive until some time in May. The two ships rounded the northern tip of the island and used the southward-running current to approach the harbor. They advanced with great care because the harbor was treacherous and because those on board did not know who might be there. Ilot Madame lies at the mouth of the harbor commanding all approaches and leaving only one feasible and very narrow entrance.[16] As the *Adventure Galley* approached the northern channel, the men could see a ship at anchor with its guns trained to control the entrance. Soon they were approached by a canoe filled with well-armed and raffish-looking Europeans. The men climbed aboard and greeted Kidd, with whom they were acquainted. Not only did they know him, but they also knew he sailed with a commission to capture pirates. Kidd quickly reassured them that "he was as bad as they."[17] The statement was not difficult to prove, so they took Kidd with them to reassure their captain—who was also familiar with Kidd because he was yet another former shipmate from the *Blessed William.* As Kidd clambered on board the *Resolution,* he was greeted by none other than Robert Culliford.

Those pirates who managed to survive their harsh life at sea lived in a small world. As men changed from ship to ship and moved around the world, they were likely to encounter fellow crewmen of bygone voyages. While the oceans seemed limitless, pirates congregated where trading ships converged or where the main trade routes were close at hand. The fact that Avery was joined by four other ships while waiting for the pilgrim fleet attests to this phenomenon. Pirates also wanted to remain in contact with those merchants with whom they could do business, a policy that meant convenient rendezvous points such as Saint Marie or Port Royale. There the men might switch ships or rejoin old comrades. Terms such as "brethren of the coast" or "pirate fraternity" are apt, for these men were tied by bonds of shared experience and a common past. But Culliford needed to be reassured, because he thought Kidd meant to hang them all. Kidd swore to Culliford that he would do nothing to harm him, indeed, "I would have my soul fry in Hell-fire" before he would do so. Reassured, Culliford returned to the *Adventure Galley* and piloted it into the small harbor. That done, Kidd and Culliford had time to drink the rum punch known as "bumboe" and reminisce.[18]

Culliford had first come to the Indian Ocean with Kidd's old crew in 1691, but along with William Mason he had left the *Jacob* at Mangalore.[19] Like Mason he entered the service of the East India Company as a gunner and served without incident until 1696, when he joined a mutiny and seized the *Josiah*. The mutineers decided to go "on account" and sailed to the Nicobar Islands in the Bay of Bengal. While they were ashore getting water, they received a stunning setback: a passing ship boarded the *Josiah*, repossessed it, and left the mutineers on the beach. Sometime later another ship happened along, took them on board, and returned them to Bombay. A supposedly repentant Culliford was allowed to return to the East India Company's service, a further indication of the company's desperate need for European sailors, who were cut down in frightful numbers by disease. Not much later Culliford joined a gang on his new ship, the *Mocha*, that succeeded in killing the captain and taking over the ship, renaming it the *Resolution*. Along with the *Charming Mary*, also known as the *Soldado*, they went to the strait of Malacca. There they captured four ships, including a Portuguese merchantman reportedly carrying 100 pounds of gold. Afterward they retired to the Maldive Islands in the Indian Ocean to refit and, like Kidd, ended up burning and looting the local villages.

Having done so well in the strait of Malacca, they returned; this time they caught another heavily laden Portuguese ship on its way to Macao. During a watering expedition Ralph Stout, captain of the *Resolution*, was killed and the men elected Culliford to fill his post. When they returned to sea in June 1697, the assembled crew voted to go to China. They started to sail through the strait of Malacca but met the East India Company ship *Dorrill*, outward bound for China. For three days they pursued it. When they finally came alongside, the *Dorrill* surprised them with cannonball into the *Resolution*'s mainmast. Culliford was compelled to pull away, leaving the *Dorrill* to sail on. After this encounter the crew of the *Dorrill* refused to go farther, forcing the captain to return to India, where they met Kidd. Because of the damage to his mainmast Culliford also had to abandon plans for China and retreat out of the strait. But as he did so, his luck changed. The crew sighted and captured two Javanese ships and a 300-ton Chinese merchantman, more than enough to compensate for the loss of the *Dorrill*. In order to better pick over the Chinese ship, they retreated to Cape Negrais in southern Burma, where they established a base. Culliford knew they could not stay there indefinitely, because his men continued to capture local ships for supplies and ultimately that would bring some form of retribution. He ordered a retreat to Saint Marie, where they could rest and refit in peace. The appearance of Kidd, preceded by rumors of his commission, disturbed that peace; but once assured that Kidd was again one of the brethren, Culliford and his men could rest easy.

Now it was time to relax, drink, and above all count their gains. When the *Adventure Prize* arrived and the whole of Kidd's crew reassembled, the men insisted on making the final division of their loot. Once again they trooped into the great cabin of the *Adventure Galley*, scooped up their money in their hats, and this time acquired also three to four bales of cloth (mostly calico, muslin, and silk) as their share of the loot.[20] That done, they could drag the bales to Welsh's house and sell them for liquor and supplies. Some of the men resented the fact that Kidd received forty shares in order to compensate his investors. On an ordinary pirate ship he would only get two or three shares, certainly nowhere near forty. But Kidd insisted on keeping to the original agreement they had all signed. The most disgruntled men went aboard the *November* and looted it down to the keel, then sank it in the harbor. Still no one attacked Kidd, which is testimony either to his skill as a bully or to the precautions he took. He later described one occasion when he was forewarned of an attack and secured himself in his cabin by barricading the door with bales of cloth and preparing "40 small armes besides Pistols ready charged."[21] These episodes must have passed quickly; Kidd was on the island for nearly six months, and if someone had wanted to kill him there would have been ample opportunity. So while some got upset about the division of the booty, the rest of the men took their shares and enjoyed the good life on Saint Marie, what little there was of it. For although it was a tropical paradise (albeit somewhat damp), it lacked the more refined pleasures of a Port Royale.

Sailors had a well-earned reputation for "playing the king" for a week until they ran out of money. Deprived at sea for so long, many indulged in gargantuan drinking bouts, where treats were lavished on hangers-on and prostitutes were tipped lavishly until the money was gone and the sober, if bleary-eyed, men returned to sea. It was hard to play king on Saint Marie. The men could get liquor from Welsh with which to drink themselves stupid, and slave women were available, but that was about all the island offered. The only other alternatives were gambling and fighting; sometimes the two went together. Many men admitted to acquiring fortunes, the greater part of which were won at play. Gerrard van Horn, a New Yorker, won 1,300 pieces of eight on a single roll of the dice and reportedly returned home with £3,000, while another man did the same to the tune of 3,400 pieces of eight.[22] With big-time winners there were also heavy losers. On at least one occasion seven men who had nothing at the end of a voyage because of gambling losses were objects of pity to their crewmates, who—when they went ashore at the end of their voyage—gave their mates the ship to try again. Other losers could be dangerous. When Raveneau de Lussan, a lucky gambler, crossed Nicaragua on his way back to the Caribbean in 1683, he carried 30,000 pieces of eight. The losers among his companions resented his luck and went ahead of him, the better to ambush and rob him. Informed of their plan, de Lussan divided his fortune among his friends so that he would not lose everything. They all managed to escape the thieves and then de Lussan only had to worry about getting his money back from his friends.[23] Some men refused to go home empty-handed, and if one story is to be believed they went to extremes to "make their voyage." Fourteen men on Madagascar who belonged to different crews, all of whom felt they had too little booty, made a pact to fight for everything they jointly owned. They made one pile, then divided into two groups to fight for it. As their crewmates stood and watched, the two sides fought until all the members of one group lay dead and only two men from the "winning" side remained standing to collect the loot.[24] Such were the grim turns pleasure took on the island.

Whether from gambling or theft, the amount of money some of the men took home from the Indian Ocean was substantial. The pirates struck it rich when they preyed on the relatively unprotected shipping of the East. Many trades were carried on in very large vessels that sailed infrequently, therefore carrying large amounts of goods and money. Unfortunately, the amounts of loot reported by the pirates often were more than a little exaggerated. But there are a few solid estimates of individual fortunes that date from this period. When Captain Mathew Lowth captured Samuel Burgess at the Cape of Good Hope in 1699, he arrested him for trading with pirates and seized all the pirates on board who had bought passage with Burgess. He later tallied the money carried by these men. Four of them had sailed with Kidd: Humphrey Viele had £1,100; Stephen Smith, £500; Richard Roper, £400; and John Smith, £400. The largest fortune on board belonged to Hugh Banks, who was returning home with £1,500. The grand total for all twenty-eight men aboard was £11,140, a very handsome sum. John Eldridge, who made it as far as the Delaware River before being captured, carried 1,600 pieces of eight, 249 pieces of silver plate, 20 Arab gold coins, 1 gold box, 200 broken pieces of coin, 2 pounds of amber beads, 10 pieces of muslin, 1 piece of flowered satin, 30 pounds of spices, 1 African boy, and various oddments. Samuel Bradish, who was caught in New York, had 2,005 pieces of eight worth £942 in New York money.[25]

Contrast these sums with the wages that Samuel Burgess' crew received for their voyage to Madagascar. The common seamen made less than £2 New York money per month; the doctor, £2.10 plus 1 slave and 12 pennies for every slave who arrived in New York; the first mate, £3.10 per month plus a slave; and the second mate and the boatswain, each £2.8 per month.[26] Thus, for the lucky survivors piracy was often a profitable occupation, offering far more money than normal mariner's wages.

The moral choice might not be all that difficult either, because for over a century piracy accompanied European expansion and was condoned by the states involved. A century of oversight certainly clouded the issues for a mariner, particularly if he had a family to feed and his likely victims were "moors." Certainly he expected few questions about how he had made his money when he returned to one of the port cities in the colonies, where currency of any kind was always welcome.

Thus for many of the men the only question to ponder was when they should go home. The temptation of yet another voyage where an even greater fortune might come their way frequently kept them "on account" for longer than their original plans. Home was never that difficult to get to once they did decide to return. Ships came out every year—during 1698 four ships left New York alone, so men retiring from the business rarely had to wait long to find a berth.[27]

The regularity of trading vessels also made it possible for married men to remain in touch with their families. Letters to the men on the islands were entrusted to the captains or to friends in the crew, then on the return voyage the same seamen carried the replies. When Samuel Burgess was captured at the Cape of Good Hope, he had a number of domestic letters in his sea chest. Ede Wilday wrote to her husband, Richard Wilday, who went out with Kidd, about their family and the high price of food in New York. Sarah Horne, wife of Richard Horne, who also served with Kidd, sent news that per his instructions she had placed their son as an apprentice to Isaac Taylor. She asked him to write because "wee here abundance of flying news concerning you wherfor I should bee very glad to here from you." Denis Holdren and his wife also asked to be remembered to him.[28] An "abundance of flying news" indicates how regularly the ships traveled to Madagascar. Henry Crosley wrote to his brother that, contrary to early reports, he now learned that the brother was still alive and pleaded with him to come home. His wife and children had moved to live with friends on Long Island, and if he returned Crosley would help them "for I am Shuer that yor Life cannott be soe Comfortable theare, as it would be with yor owne flesh and blood."[29] Some of these pleas to come home went unanswered.

Many men died during the voyage, but others just did not plan an early return. Abraham Sasnoya wrote to his wife: "This is to acquaint you that I am now in the eastingyes and I doe think that our vioage will bee to or 10 years but I am of an honist mind to you still, . . . soo having no mor at present but my love to you and to our Child your ever tru and Constant husband till death us depart."[30] Evan Jones wrote to his wife, Frances, that he had endured great hardship but was now captain of a ship. As a result he was going out on another voyage and she should not expect to hear from him for about five years.[31] One can only marvel at the long-suffering wives who endured at home awaiting the return of their husbands while left with the burdens of providing for and rearing children. In a world where women usually became the legal wards of their husbands, who then conducted their affairs and certainly controlled the finances and made the major decisions, the wives of the pirates (and, one suspects, of many seamen) had far greater authority over the finances of the family and made many of the important decisions. Their lives were far different from those of their rural sisters.

Not heedless of the difficulties of their families, many of the men made arrangements for them. When Gabriel Loffe and Martin Skines received their shares from Kidd on Saint Marie, they arranged to put some of their cloth bales into their sea chests and sent them home with a New York ship trading at Saint Marie.[32] Thomas Pringle sent his wife 200 pieces of eight on another ship and later admonished her to save the money.[33] The men also wrote wills and asked friends to carry back their shares in the event of their death. Culliford wrote to a Mrs. Whaley, wife of one of his crew, stating that her husband's will left everything to her and that Captain Shelley of New York would bring his possessions to her.[34] But many wives had to press their cases. Elizabeth Breho of Newport,

Long Island, wrote to Elias Rowse demanding her husband's money because she had learned of his death and knew Rowse held all his estate. Nearly a year later Rowse replied that he had sent the money home with John Dodd, who lived in New York City.[35] Some wives issued letters of attorney to ship captains in hopes they could collect for them. Ann Cantrell, ex-wife of John Reed, who died during his voyage, sent a package of legal documents trying to claim his estate. She was probably overoptimistic in her claims. Merchants also pursued men out "on account." Richard Laurence gave his power of attorney to Samuel Burgess to collect debts owed him by men on the *Resolution*. This continuing web of obligation implies that some of the men never left society completely behind and that they hoped to return home. Piracy for them was an interlude in an otherwise normal life, although they hoped it would be a profitable interlude.

Not all of the men exhibited domestic virtue, however. For many, living on Saint Marie meant leaving behind a society bound up in hierarchy and order, where rules repressed them and social mobility was a joke. Even the more fluid societies of the colonies had elites of merchants and planters who expected deference and imposed sumptuary laws just as they did in Europe. Everyone dressed to his or her station in life, so that a glance was enough to place an individual in the social hierarchy.[36] Laws and hierarchy did not exist on board ship or in the pirate settlements. The rules were informal and agreed upon by a democratic system that gave the men a voice in their affairs. Life in these egalitarian surroundings was attractive to many men who were willing to suffer its hardships in order to enjoy the good times that outdid any others they had experienced. Samuel Burgess returned to Madagascar to live after having been a pirate, slaver, merchant captain, privateer, and condemned man. The island simply offered him more freedom than any other place.

For some of the men their new freedom extended to sexual relations. European societies denounced homosexuality and treated it harshly. The Royal Navy periodically conducted savage antibuggery campaigns to repress homosexual practices among men who might often be confined at sea for years. On shipboard or in the renegade settlements, pirates could more openly engage in homosexual alliances. Louis Le Golif complained of the prevalence of homosexuality on the island of Tortuga, where he had to fight two duels to keep his most ardent suitors at bay. Some men bought "pretty boys" as companions, some had consorts; Culliford, for instance, had a "great consort," John Swann, who lived with him. Not all their shipmates or fellow settlers appreciated their behavior. On one pirate ship, when a young man admitted a homosexual relationship, he was put in irons and maltreated.[37] In general, though, life in the pirate settlements offered greater latitude of individual behavior than anywhere else.

When the authorities came into contact with the pirates, they were often shocked by their democratic tendencies. The Dutch governor of the stopover colony of Mauritius commented after meeting a pirate crew, "Every man had as much say as the captain and each man carried his own weapons in his blanket."[38] These customs were unnerving to anyone accustomed to the hierarchical nature of European society, where guns normally were confined to the upper classes and democracy was unknown. Whole communities of men who lived by consensus appeared very threatening, particularly when those communities lay in such close proximity to the sailing routes to the East. The English government held hearings, and the authorities in the Dutch colony at the Cape of Good Hope investigated the pirate communities. Their reports magnified the size of the settlements and the numbers of men who lived in them, raising the alarm level in England and finally catching the attention of the Royal Navy.[39] But this was in the future. Meanwhile Kidd and his men could enjoy the pleasures available on Saint Marie.

The crew of the *Adventure Galley* had to make a decision. Should they go home, or should they stay on Saint Marie and return to the Indian Ocean with Culliford? Most of them were still disgruntled by the number of shares Kidd had reserved for himself, but other than stripping and burning the *November,* they accepted their lot. Of the approximately 117 men who remained in the crew, nearly 100 decided to remain "on account," for as Edward Buckmaster reported, "Kidd made no good voyage." Having come this far, the men decided it was easier to stay on and hope for a rich voyage with Culliford. In early June 1698 the men transferred their belongings into the *Resolution* as Culliford prepared to leave the island. Kidd gave him four great cannon to strengthen the firepower of his ship, and after his men had given messages to friends going home and Culliford had completed his other preparations, the *Resolution* carefully moved out of the small harbor and set sail for Johanna.[40]

Kidd had to ponder his own situation. If he stayed on in the Indian Ocean, he would surely be branded a pirate and lose everything he had gained since his days in the West Indies. Any thoughts he might have had along those lines were foreclosed after his men left to join Culliford, for he no longer commanded enough crew to fight. Kidd could only hope to return to New York, satisfy his investors, and return to his family. The sooner he returned and explained events during his cruise, the better chance he had of remaining free. It no doubt pleased him to have the vast majority of his crew leave with Culliford because it meant that fewer witnesses would return home with him. By the time he left the island in 1698 his crew consisted of about twenty men and boys and a few slaves.[41]

In the months Kidd had to wait before the winds were right, he had ample time to decide upon and prepare a good story. He would claim thereafter that his crew had forced him into every illegal deed he committed. Not only did they coerce him into piracy, but they frequently threatened his life. The two ships he captured—and he only admitted to two—were legal prizes. These claims, combined with other fabrications, made up his basic "narrative." Among the fabrications were lapses such as never admitting he had gone to the Babs to raid the pilgrim fleet and pretending that his men refused his orders to attack Culliford. He also accused his men of going to Welsh's fort and breaking into his chest to steal all his money and his journal. He is the only one who claims this happened, so the story is suspect, particularly because it was one that benefited Kidd. In his original commission he had been enjoined to keep a journal of his proceedings. With that journal destroyed, there was no official record of his travels, thus one of the major pieces of evidence against him no longer existed. Destroying journals and logs too was a favored pirate practice, especially when the men mutinied and took over a ship.[42] By the time Kidd left the island, he and the mariners who accompanied him had agreed on a basic story. That story was their protection against the authorities; their ability to make it believable was all that stood between them and the gibbet.

The return trip to New York would again test Kidd's seamanship. When the men left for the *Resolution,* they took with them the "moors" who had been pumping the *Adventure Galley.* Without them that ship could never remain afloat. It was pushed up on the beach and burned so that the iron fittings could be recovered. Now there were three wrecks littering the harbor.[43] Kidd was left with the Indian-built, ungainly *Adventure Prize* in which to sail home. It was certainly a commodious carrier for the bales of cloth that remained, but its Indian design would cause a sensation in any American port. It was the equivalent of shouting, "I have been robbing ships in the Red Sea." But that was a problem for the future, not one Kidd had to deal with as he prepared to set sail for America.

SIX

Revenge of the Company

The staff of the East India Company who lived in Surat came to hate William Kidd. The thirteen men normally gathered each day to relate news, celebrate deals, and enjoy a small part of England away from the exotic, alien city around them. After April 1698 their topics of conversation diminished to one—the disaster Kidd had caused.

The *Quedah Merchant* was no ordinary ship, not even one of Abd-ul-Ghafur's. Instead it was leased out to Muklis Khan, a leading member of the emperor's own court, and to his friends at the court. The cries of outrage over the loss of this investment emanated directly from Aurangzeb's palace and retribution came quickly.[1] The streets of Surat filled with outraged mobs infuriated at the taking of yet another ship by the "hatmen," as the pirates were known. Fortunately for members of the company's staff, their pleasant two-story building, a gift of the emperor in happier days, was surrounded by a high wall that protected them until soldiers from the local garrison arrived.[2] The soldiers intervened to hold back the mobs but quickly became their jailers as well as their protectors. "Firmans," or imperial orders, arrived in Surat, stopping the company's trade as well as that of the Dutch and French and demanding both compensation for the investors in the *Quedah Merchant* and better convoying for Indian ships. This struck a hard blow to the English company already beset by declining trade and powerful rivals at home and in Asia. Beset on all sides, the company's leaders in India and London determined to restore its reputation and its fortunes. To do so it would see William Kidd hanged and order restored to the Indian Ocean.

Yet this was not a simple vendetta between Kidd and the East India Company. Kidd was entrapped in a larger movement that would find him a convenient symbol for a much broader problem. By the end of the seventeenth century England was no longer a brash, thrusting, new power, but an established and ever more formidable imperial state. English merchants had created trades throughout the world, making London an entrepôt of ever greater importance. As the merchant community expanded, it looked upon the world with different eyes: it prized order and regularity because they enhanced profits; disorder interrupted the regular flow of trade. This movement coincided with a similar movement in political life. The pressures of war in Europe caused England to expand the administrative apparatus of the state. Like the merchant community, the members of the government would also prize routine and discipline. From these twin streams would flow a potent movement that would turn on the forces of disorder, and on none more than the pirates.

Kidd never allowed for the relentless malevolence of the East India Company. The company's ill will stemmed from the fact that while it was the most powerful economic institution in England, it had recently fallen on hard times. Its influence was based on its past spectacular economic performance and on its political connections. After the company had acquired a new charter in 1657, it had entered a period of high prosperity, especially during the 1680s. From 1678 to 1688 the mean annual value of its imports from Asia was £416,828. The profits from sales of these goods allowed the company to declare incredible dividends. During that same decade it announced dividends of 20 percent three times, 25 percent four times, 50 percent three times, and in 1682 one of these 50 percent dividends was followed by an unheard-of 100 percent stock bonus. Buoyed by such a performance, the company's stock climbed steadily, rising 450 percent between 1681 and 1691.[3] The company had all the appearances of a moneymaking machine and used its position to cultivate political friendships. Sir Josiah Childe, who led the East India Company during this vibrant period, bought influence with the monarchy and the Tories. Loans and gifts of stock endeared him to the king, and smaller gifts to politicians kept them happy.[4]

Such was Childe's confidence at this time that he ignored political advice and went to war against the Mughal Empire. Even though Emperor Aurangzeb was campaigning against rebels in southern India, he still had vast resources at hand; men and equipment were marshaled and sent against the upstart company. A short campaign in 1689 dealt a crushing defeat to the English, forcing Childe to sue for peace. After paying suitable compensation, the company was allowed to resume its trade. This reverse, however, inaugurated a new era of hardship.[5]

On the home front during the 1690s the company faced the problems of trade depression, French privateering successes, and credit distortions that accompanied King William's War. From 1689 to 1699 its mean annual imports slumped to £134,893, whereas during the decade 1678 to 1688 the company had shipped an average of £416,828. In 1689 it could only manage to export goods worth £8,253 and the following year it did little better, exporting £10,239; these were its worst years since the Restoration in 1660. In 1682 it had shipped £746,535 worth of goods on twenty-two ships. Not until 1699 did it come close to this record, when £567,587 was spent on goods for India. The price of the company's stock plummeted from a high of £500 in 1685 to £158 in 1691.[6] All in all, a sorry record for the once-great cornucopia.

In politics its fortunes were no better. William and Mary bore no animosity toward the company; however, the Whig ascendancy signaled serious problems. On one front the company was attacked by a combination of English textile manufacturers who resented the wide variety of Indian fabrics the company imported. While economic depression was more to blame than the company for the declining demand for cloth, the company was a far easier target. In 1696 a bill was introduced into Parliament to restrain the wearing of cloth from India. The company fought the bill, but the delay in its passage only outraged the suffering textile workers, who rioted on a number of occasions—with the East India Company a favored target. Only the intervention of the Lord Mayor and the sheriffs kept one mob from looting the company's headquarters on Leadenhall Street. On another occasion George Bohun, governor of the company, shot down two rioters while defending his home. Parliament responded to the arguments inside its walls, and to the shouts from without, by finally passing a bill in 1701 that restricted the wearing and use of certain kinds of Asian cloth. Although unhappy over the decision, the leadership of the company simply stressed the importation of different cloths until the clamor diminished.[7]

Of far greater concern was the attack on the company's charter that granted it a monopoly of the Asian trade. Childe had forced a number of merchants out of the company as he acquired control. Many of these men, such as Sir Thomas Papillon, continued to trade with India but were now considered interlopers by the company, which prosecuted them whenever it could to protect its monopoly. Papillon and others found solace among the Whigs, and as their star rose so did their hopes; they wanted nothing less than to overthrow the company by depriving it of its charter.[8] This goal set the stage for a great battle in 1693 when the charter had to be renewed. The interlopers found that the company retained its fighting instincts and its ability to pay prodigious bribes. Some £200,000 in cash left the company's treasury and was widely believed to have found a home in politicians' pockets. The bribes assured parliamentary approval of a new charter, but only for five years, the briefest period ever granted to the company. By granting this short-term monopoly the leaders of Parliament placated the interlopers and their allies, besides opening the way to another (for them) profitable struggle. By 1698 the company's enemies were prepared, and this time the company lost. Parliament allowed it to continue operating but in competition with the New East India Company, controlled by the interloping faction.[9]

In India the company suffered through equally bad times, for the most part caused by the pirates. Until 1691 the explosion of piracy into the East had caused few problems. In that year, however, a pirate sailed into the mouth of the Hoogli River at Surat and captured a very large ship belonging to Abd-ul-Ghafur. A leader among the Gujarati merchants, Ghafur already disliked the company; with this episode he was transformed into its most prominent foe. Learning of the loss of his ship, he went immediately to the governor of Surat and demanded that the governor and the emperor compel the English East India Company to reimburse him for his loss, even though there was no evidence that the "hatmen" were English. On August 27, 1691, a firman confined the English to their factory and stopped their trade until they reimbursed Ghafur 700,000 rupees valued at £78,750. The company refused to pay until it was known that the pirates were indeed English. Fortunately, the guilty parties proved to be Danish; but the English remained confined until December 2. In 1692 Ghafur succeeded in having them confined once again—on the premise that because all pirates were actually English, any act of piracy should be the company's responsibility. The awkward truth was that most of the pirates *were* English, so the company could do very little to fight Ghafur and his allies.[10]

The company's servants had a few years' respite until 1695, when the forlorn *Ganj-i-Sawai* limped into Surat after Avery and his men had looted it to the keel. As rumors about the killing of holy pilgrims and the violation of women spread through the city, angry crowds turned violent and besieged the English in their compound. Local troops arrived and saved them from death. Governor Ahmanat Khan arrested President Samuel Annesley and sixty-three other company employees and put them in jail for eleven months. Only the intervention of Issa Cooly, an Armenian friend of the company, kept the emperor from sending an army to wipe out all of the English factories in India.[11]

Ahmanat Khan freed the English on June 27, 1696, but stopped all their trade until they would agree to provide protection for Indian shipping. He made the same demand of the Dutch and the French (to get still more bribes), but they, like the English, refused until their losses overcame their resolve. The French gave in first. The others followed, with the English agreeing to protect the "Superstitious pilgrimage to Mecca," thus setting up the meeting between Kidd and Barlow in 1697.[12] Trade conditions remained abominable for the English, as they had only a small store of goods and very little bullion, the lifeblood of their commerce. Their competitors gave them no help either. The Dutch East India Company happily amplified the rumor that all pirates were English and ordered their officials to send any captured English pirates to Surat for delivery to the governor. The English interlopers circulated stories that blamed the company for piracy and proclaimed that it had lost its trading monopoly in England.[13] Meanwhile pirates continued to terrorize local trade: Ghafur lost another ship in the Persian Gulf, the company's own local brokers lost ships at the Babs, a pirate ship threatened Tellicherry, five pirates cruised the Red Sea, and Dirck Chivers from New York seized three ships at Calicut. As the toll mounted, captains refused to leave port because of the risks. Then in quick order the company lost the *Josiah,* the *Gingerlee,* and the *Mocha Frigate* to mutinous crews. Company employees felt that their options were financial ruin or having their throats cut by outraged Muslims.[14] And then came William Kidd.

Before Kidd even arrived at the Red Sea, the company's leaders in Bombay and Surat knew all about him from those captains who had heard Warren's report at the Cape of Good Hope and then met Kidd at Johanna. Captain John Clerke wrote a long report about him, which was delivered to the company in June 1697, and all the company factories were alerted to his coming. When he did appear on the Malabar coast, every scrap of information about him was collected and transmitted to Sir John Gayer, the high-ranking governor of the company, who lived in Bombay. Three men who deserted his ship (Jonathan Tredway, Nicholas Anderson, and Benjamin Franks) faced arduous examinations that were put into reports then rushed overland to London.[15] Gayer continued to write lurid descriptions of the progress of Kidd's voyage, managing to transform him into a shipborne Attila the Hun.[16] Kidd came to personify all of the unknown and unnamed pirates who tormented the company.

It was the capture of the *Quedah Merchant* that caused the company to come to grief once again. The Armenians and Muslims on board reported that Captain Wright refused to fight when Kidd attacked, and that Kidd had shown them a commission from the King of England granting him the right to take the *Quedah.* There were even stories that Wright rendezvoused with Kidd by prior arrangement.[17] Samuel Annesley, the company's president at Surat, could do little but wait for the inevitable. He absolutely refused to post the pardon for all pirates that had recently been issued in England as a means of getting pirates to surrender and leave the Indian Ocean. Any such pardon would have been misinterpreted by the company's all-too-numerous enemies. The Armenian merchants on the *Quedah* went to the emperor's court to report to Muklis Khan about his losses, and while the English waited for the wrath of Aurangzeb to fall on them, news of Kidd and other depredations by pirates roused the populace and sent Annesley and his fellow employees into retreat behind the walls of the factory. [18]

The emperor issued orders in December 1698, once again commanding all the European companies to compensate the victims of piracy, and to guarantee the safety of all Muslim trade. If they did not comply, the whole European community would be expelled. This imperial edict was promulgated by Ahmanat Khan, who intended that its full force would fall on the English, unless the bribe to avoid it was really huge. He demanded that they pay their annual customs dues immediately, questioned and then beat their Muslim brokers, sent 500 soldiers to watch over them, and stopped their trade. Town criers went through the city beating drums and announcing that no one could contact the English or sell them food. Their chief broker was threatened with being flayed alive. And their old nemesis Abd-ul-Ghafur advised the governor to throw them out. One horror story after another spilled over the little band of entrapped Englishmen. The French and the Dutch quickly convinced the governor that they had little to do with piracy, and after paying suitable bribes they were let go. But the English had no relief. [19]

Annesley pleaded with Gayer to permit him to make a deal with Ahmanat Khan, but Gayer, safely out of trouble in Bombay, refused because to give in would open the way to many other demands. In a wholly gratuitous comment Gayer also informed the company servants in Surat that they had not yet suffered enough and that masters were ill served by servants who would not expose their lives to protect their estates. Annesley, threatened with death, unable to buy food, and well aware of the beatings suffered by anyone who dealt with the company, had a very different view of the role of servants. [20] Fearing Annesley's weakness, Gayer rushed to

Surat to put iron into his spine. Sitting safely on board a ship at Swally Hole, he ordered that the prisoners do nothing because the Royal Navy was on the way; in actuality the navy would arrive long after the crisis, as Gayer knew it would.[21]

The reality of the company's position in Surat finally seeped into Gayer's consciousness, and fearing for the company's future, he relented enough to tell Annesley to make a deal with the governor. If Ahmanat Khan allowed them to load all of their goods at Surat and sail away, Gayer would send a ship (an old and slow one) down the Malabar coast in search of pirates. This was an unacceptable offer in Khan's eyes, and while Gayer postured, refusing even to meet Ahmanat Khan, Annesley faced reality. He called his fellow prisoners together and put it to them that there was little they could do but meet the demands of the government. Few around the table could dispute his conclusion, and a surrender was quickly arranged. The English went free immediately and were allowed to trade, but few would deal with them. Although his decision had been made some time in the past, Gayer chose this moment to remove Annesley from office.[22]

The company had to compensate some of those who had shipped goods on the *Quedah,* particularly Muklis Khan, and undertake the difficult task of convoying ships from Surat to the Spice Islands. The French and Dutch had previously agreed to convoy ships on far easier routes going to Mocha and Persia. Ahmanat Khan graciously accepted a sum of money for his continued beneficence.[23] But good fortune did not smile on the company for long. The very next Mocha convoy, under the protection of the Dutch, was attacked by pirates. Abd-ul-Ghafur lost yet another ship, and three others also vanished over the horizon as prizes. Emperor Aurangzeb had remained unconvinced of the honesty of the English East India Company and joined the many at his court who assumed that all pirates were English; thus the company was blamed for this attack. In December 1701 the grand wazir, Asad Khan, ordered all the company's factories closed and its trade privileges stopped. The Surat factory was taken and plundered, to compensate Ghafur, and the other factories were overrun or besieged. Sir John Gayer remained safely behind the defenses of the Bombay factory, imprisoned and unable to act. The company teetered on the brink.[24]

Thus Kidd came to be identified with the most disastrous years in the company's history. What made him even more important to the company was its failure to capture and hang Avery. In July 1696 a report to the government in England had outlined his activities and demanded a royal proclamation ordering the arrest of Avery and his men. The Privy Council approved the proclamation but refused to offer a reward, so the company reluctantly agreed to pay £500. The proclamation was duly issued and stern orders sent to the governors of the American colonies.[25] In fact, Avery and his men found it very easy to get help in the colonies, and as they dispersed a number of them headed for home in England. While a hue and cry went up for Avery, he managed to escape his pursuers and vanish.[26] Six of his men were captured and brought to justice—a trial that was to prove more than a little embarrassing for the company and the government.

The leadership of the company looked forward to the trial of Avery's men so that it could trumpet the expected results in India. The six men were brought to the bar at the Old Bailey on October 19, 1696, for piracy on the *Ganj-i-Sawai*. Dr. Newton, the king's learned counsel, described to the jury how that act had poisoned relations with the "Great Mogul." So that they should have no doubt about the consequences, he stated:

> For suffer Pirates, and the Commerce of the World must cease, which this nation has so deservedly a share in, and reaps such advantage by: And if they shall go away unpunished, when it was known whose subjects they are, the Consequences may be, to involve the Nations concerned in War and Blood, to the Destruction of the innocent English in those Countries, the total loss of the Indian Trade, and thereby, the impoverishment of this Kingdom.[27]

John Dann and Philip Middleton from Avery's crew provided the testimony needed to convict the men, and the jury left to deliberate its decision. When the jurors returned, they stunned the courtroom—and the members of the company's leadership gathered to witness the trial—by declaring the men not guilty. The leaders of the company were mortified. They had brought to trial six men whose conviction seemed certain and was plainly necessary to convince the moghul that they detested pirates. The men were not allowed to go free, but were confined until a new trial could be held.

When the court reheard the case on October 31 of the same year, the luckless Dr. Newton no longer led the prosecution. (The company had tried to put in its own lawyers, but had been rebuffed.) In Newton's place sat a stellar cast of legal talent led by Sir Charles Hedges, Chief Judge of the High Court of Admiralty. As the new trial got under way, Hedges reminded the audience that "Piracy is only a Sea-Term for Robbery" and the "King of England hath . . . an undoubted Jurisdiction, and Power, . . . for the Punishment of all Piracies and Robberies at Sea, in the most remote Parts of the World." He may have been implying that the earlier jury let the men go because their crime was committed so far from England. Just before the second trial began, potential jurors were warned that it was dangerous to let the malefactors go free unless there were very clear reasons for doing so. Otherwise:

> Since Foreigners look upon Decrees of our Courts of Justice as the Sense and Judgement of the whole Nation, our Enemies will be glad to find an Occasion to say, that such Miscreants as are out of the Protection of all Laws, and Civil Government, are abetted by those who contend for the Sovereignty of the Seas. The barbarous Nations will reproach us as being a Harbour, Receptacle, and a Nest of Pirates.[28]

And, he continued, if justice be denied, the only path left to foreigners would be to take reprisal on English ships.

This impressive summary undoubtedly recited the real issues as far as the leadership of the company was concerned, but they could only regard the jury with suspicion and hope. When the sheriff announced the jury for the trial and it became apparent that some of the previous jurors were among them, Lord Chief Justice Holt thundered, "If you have returned any of the former Jury, you have not done well; for that Verdict was a Dishonour to the Justice of the Nation." He need not have worried, for with so many warnings before them and the evidence so clearly against the pirates, the jury found them guilty. Justice Holt thanked the jury fulsomely: "You have done very much to regain the Honour of the Nation and the

City." The death sentence was pronounced with due solemnity, while at Leadenhall Street the decision was a cause of rejoicing. Avery might have slipped away, but all the same there was good news to report to India.

The verdict actually did little to help the men in India. What the company really needed was the hanging of a major figure. And while the majority of the pirates remained faceless, one did not. Kidd had originated in New York, was known in London, and was now on his way back to New York. He had form and shape, a past and a future, and impressive value as a symbol of all the afflictions besetting the company, afflictions it no longer had any intention of enduring.

The company, with its long experience at lobbying, contrived a campaign against the pirates. Depositions and examinations were collected and forwarded to the Lords of Trade, the Admiralty, the Privy Council, and anyone else in power. Witnesses "lately returned from India," attended by members of the company, were ushered into meeting rooms to testify as expert witnesses. Three persistent themes were discernible in this campaign. One was the danger presented by the pirate "fortress" on Saint Marie and the need to eradicate it. The few rude shacks on the island were transformed into a fort bristling with forty to fifty cannon defended by fifteen hundred hardened renegades and seventeen ships. A second line of attack was on the active support given the pirates by the American colonists. The company tried to create the impression that the colonists were solely responsible for the extension of piracy into the East, and if their trade on Madagascar could be stopped, piracy in the Indian Ocean would end. This claim too was an exaggeration, for while the merchants did help the pirates, they also found willing customers in India such as those Kidd had met at Caliquilon. Their third theme was Kidd himself. The company, and others, kept his name before the government at all times. In 1698, when the government decided to take some action by issuing a new proclamation of pardon, only Kidd and Avery were specifically denied its benefits. Kidd came to symbolize all pirates, and he was hunted with an intensity rarely seen before.[29]

By this time the political stakes surrounding Kidd had also been raised, for the Whig Junto saw its power slipping away. As the campaign mounted, members of the Junto felt the first chill of concern. Somers wrote to Shrewsbury that he feared that the Old East India Company would make the most of the "Kidd business." He met with Romney, Orford, and Harrison to discuss the problem; they agreed that they should admit to sponsoring Kidd, for which "we hope there can be no crime, though perhaps we may appear somewhat ridiculous."[30] The East India Company had suffered too long at the hands of the Whigs, and as the Tories returned to power they joined the company in mutually satisfying plots. A good friend, the company could also be a malignant enemy. A web spun by people and forces far distant from Madagascar was entangling Kidd as powerful men used him to further their own plans. He became a catalyst to create the proper atmosphere for government action.[31]

The East India Company was not the only commercial enterprise concerned about piracy. While English merchants had enjoyed the profits of brigandage in the early seventeenth century, they came to relish the profits derived from regular, disciplined trade. Ships coming and going safely from port to port were the source of profits closest to the hearts of the commercial community. By 1700 the volume of that trade had grown considerably, which in turn led to important changes. Enterprises expanded, and more trades came to be dominated by fewer men.[32]

The last decade of the century also witnessed a financial revolution that made London an important rival to the capital market in Amsterdam. These trends brought on a certain hardening, for as men came to deal with larger endeavors they resented unpleasant surprises generated by unruly elements in the market. They even turned away from free-market ideologies toward those that buttressed a more controlled and disciplined economy.[33] London had become an entrepôt where men who profited from its growth wanted trade organized along systematic, predictable lines and looked to the government to ensure an appropriate framework of law. When the government did not adequately match their expectations, they organized in new ways to try to get it to work for them. Sir Josiah Childe had concentrated on gaining the ear of the king in order to influence policy; but the larger merchant community could not count on such access, particularly when the state was becoming ever more complicated. Issues of importance to merchants came before a number of branches of government, and in order to know where and when they should try to intervene, the traders organized into lobbies.

In 1670 a group of men involved in the sugar trade joined together to look out for the interests of sugar planters and merchants. Calling themselves the "committee for the concern of Barbados," they appointed a secretary to attend the meetings of Parliament and the offices of state, and held weekly meetings at the Cardinal's Cap in Cornhill.[34] They came together primarily to represent their interests when Parliament moved to raise taxes on sugar. The threat of new taxes frequently catalyzed the formation of such groups, and by the 1690s most of the merchant community was organized for this or other reasons. Some lobbies were structured by commodity, such as sugar or tobacco; others by geographic unit, such as the trade to New England, New York, or Carolina.[35] During the Nine Years War these groups became closely involved with the government as the need for convoys and other protective measures grew. With greater and greater frequency the agents of the committees came before the Admiralty, the Customs Board, the Lords of Trade and Plantations, or Parliament to discuss a variety of issues relative to trade, the empire, and, often enough, the problem of piracy.[36]

At the end of the war in 1697 the relationship between the bureaucracy and the merchants continued, for by that time it was advantageous for both parties. Information on appointments to office, new policy initiatives, and questions about trade and politics in distant places kept communications open.[37] The merchants overstepped their bounds, however, when they asked to have a permanent representative attend the meetings of the Admiralty so that information could flow more quickly to the various committees. This extraordinary request was rebuffed by the Lords of the Admiralty because state secrets were not commonly shared with merchants.[38] The activities of the merchants represent the birth of modern business lobbying; while not yet the "iron triangle" of today, the merchants had created the means to make their opinions known. All the same, the merchant lobbies faced a very old tradition of relative inaction and ineffectiveness against piracy. England had never led the attack on sea robbery, and if the East India

Company and its allies were to succeed in their campaign against this evil, they would need to convince the government to attack the problem.

Since the rise of early modern piracy the government had done very little to control its spread; if anything, it had often been a participant. Only the most inept pirates ended their lives on the gallows during the late sixteenth and early seventeenth centuries. The nadir of English concern and ability to curb piracy came during the reign of James I. Taking no special pride in the Royal Navy and abhorring the expenses generated by the fleet, James sold some of his ships and let most of the others rot at the docks. The resulting growth of piracy in and around English waters caused the Dutch to request permission to send their ships into English waters to attack the brigands. Bereft of means to do the job, James acquiesced.[39] When, on occasion, a Royal Navy ship did receive orders to go on patrol, the captain often found himself in the same situation as Captain John Chudleigh of the pinnace *Desire*. Chudleigh sailed into Falmouth and discovered a 400-ton pirate ship at anchor. Confronted by this far more powerful ship, he decided to ignore it. As he put it to his superiors, "You cannot but commiserate a man that is employed in service without the hopeful means to do it."[40] Given the weakness of the navy, merchants applied for and received commissions to apprehend pirates when they sailed to dangerous areas. Communities also were given permission—and on some occasions they were ordered—to attack pirates.[41] If by some chance a pirate was apprehended, the courts and the law suffered from organizational weaknesses just as the navy did.

While the common law was one of England's glories, it was not a convenient tool for prosecuting pirates. In the common law system magistrates presented the evidence in a case to local jurymen, who then made a judgment based upon their knowledge of the case and the evidence. But some juries balked at deciding questions on matters that took place outside their own county and therefore refused to make decisions on piracy. During the fourteenth century the central government created the Admiral's Court, which had civil law procedures and thus was better adapted to maritime disputes. The merchant community was pleased, because England's growing trade with the Continent engendered more mercantile disputes and foreign merchants preferred to deal with civil law procedures rather than the unfamiliar common law.

The civil law had a weakness when it came to felonies at sea, however. A conviction that carried the death penalty must rest upon a confession of at least two eyewitnesses to an overt act. Because "dead men tell no tales" was often a policy among free-booters, convictions of even the most notorious pirates were hard to obtain. Even if witnesses existed, they would in all likelihood be sailors who earned their living at sea and hence often failed to appear in court when needed. The common lawyers used this weakness to fight the encroachment of an alternative legal system. They also called attention to the lack of juries in Admiralty Courts, thus denying trial by peers, a hallowed English tradition. For the next three centuries common and civil lawyers fought over jurisdiction in these matters, spurred on by faith in "their" system and mindful always of their own pocketbooks.[42]

As the problem of piracy grew, a compromise had to be fashioned, and in 1536 a new statute created the first piracy law. This statute declared England to be an empire, thus bringing pi-racy, no matter where it was committed, within the purview of the monarch's justice. Piracy was put under the jurisdiction of the High Court of Admiralty, but it was no longer triable by civil law rules. The preamble to the statute, referring to the difficulty in acquiring convictions in civil law courts because of the rule requiring a confes-sion or "indifferent" witnesses, proposed a solution. Once the Ad-miralty lawyers decided that a case existed, the Lord High Admiral issued a commission to a special common law court of oyer and terminer, which had common law procedures and common law juries.[43] This central court operated in London, so every malefactor had to be brought there for trial. The government later created the vice admirals of the coast, new offices designed to bring law and order to maritime disputes in the outer port towns. The vice admi-rals were permitted to call these special courts into session, thereby extending the system into every coastal county. Unfortunately, the men who held the offices frequently were as likely as the Lord High Admiral to profit from piracy.[44] While the law had improved, the men who ran the system had not.

When all else failed, as it usually did in the sixteenth and early seventeenth centuries, the final means available to the government to halt piratical actions was the royal proclamation. If frequency of use is a sure guide to inadequacy (if not downright failure), the proclamations of pardon were hardly worth the paper they were printed on. The first Tudor proclamation on piracy was issued on November 17, 1490, and others followed in 1498, 1519, 1549, 1558, then four during the 1560s, four in the 1570s, and others in 1591, 1599, 1602, and 1603.[45] These were often issued to placate foreign governments pestered by English pirates, or to stop men from entering the service of a foreign prince who was engaged in piracy. More often than not they promised the pirates a pardon if they would stop what they were doing and return to England. As we have seen, Sir Henry Mainwaring returned with such protection. The Stuarts were equally active in promising pardons, and they had the usual effect. The proclamations provided employment for clerks, but had little impact on the continued growth and geographic expansion of piracy.[46]

Prior to 1670 the government had a sorry record in controlling pirates. When it did choose to act, it sought to do so in ways that would cost very little money. It favored permitting merchants or communities rather than the navy to hunt pirates. In other words, the government preferred to conduct public policy using private means. But the steady increase in buccaneering provided a major challenge to this way of doing business because the buccaneers interfered with England's commercial and foreign policy goals, particularly after the Treaty of Madrid in 1670, in which England promised Spain that it would do something about the problem.

England carried out this clause of the treaty sporadically and without a decisive order. The problem was that England's major rivals, the Dutch and the French, also had colonies in the Caribbean, and as England also went to war with them the buccaneers provided protection against more than just the Spanish. Kidd, for instance, first made his reputation fighting the French.[47] So the government often lacked the will to move resolutely. Instead, governors were sent out with orders to act against the pirates, but without means to do so. Governor Thomas Vaughan of Jamaica accurately described the major problem: "These Indyes are so vast and Rich, And this kind of rapine so sweet, that it is one of the hardest things in the World to draw those from it which have used it for so long."[48]

The other difficulties the governors confronted were the lack of naval vessels to pursue freebooters; the ease with which the pirates could move from the colonies of one nation to another, thereby removing themselves from English control; and the muddled legal situation surrounding trials for piracy. This was not a situation the government could shirk, for as time passed the number of merchants in the colonies who wanted the profits of steady trade grew in number, and they attracted powerful allies in England such as the Royal African Company, which monopolized the slave trade to the colonies. The pressure to do something would only continue to grow.

The last thing the government wanted was to spend money, so many of the "new" policies were distressingly familiar. Proclamations, duly authorized by royal assent, continued to be issued. They also offered each man who would retire thirty acres of land on Jamaica, hardly an enticing offer to men used to the sea, who knew sugarcane best in the form of rum.[49] The major effort to control the buccaneers came in the legal arena, where the government struggled to make the colonies responsible for the trial and execution of pirates. Because of the tangled legal situation this was not as easy as first imagined by policymakers in England. The common law courts were established early in the colonies and in the absence of any other type of jurisdiction assumed broad powers. The colonists simply could not support, nor did they need, the cumbersome and luxuriant legal apparatus of England. As a result they relied on and preferred their own legal systems and resented the intrusion of novel jurisdictions such as the civil law courts with their different procedures and lack of juries.[50] This did not bode well for expansion of the Admiralty Courts. Commissions for Vice Admiralty Courts were issued sporadically; their procedures varied widely owing to lack of expertise with the new rules. Jamaica had a Vice Admiralty Court very early, as it was needed to condemn prizes captured by English ships in wartime. But trials for piracy occurred in the common law courts where all criminal trials were held and where the all-important jury held sway. The legality of the trials was questionable because under English statute pirates should have been tried in a special court of oyer and terminer. For a time the East India Company was also given vice admiralty jurisdiction, but because the great pirate onslaught had not yet begun, it functioned infrequently.[51] The alternative, sending the men to England for trial, seldom happened. If a pirate was tried, it was with any means at hand. In one case in India the East India Company used a court-martial. All too often the men got off scot-free, as local jurors recoiled from hanging a man for something many of them did not view as a crime.[52] Thus the government had legal problems to clear up if the colonies were to take charge of trying and hanging pirates.

The first step came in 1673, when an Order in Council mandated that all piracy trials be held in the Admiralty Courts. This directive involved slowly extending Admiralty Court jurisdiction to all of the colonies, but before this became a reality, problems arose in Jamaica. When Governor Thomas Vaughan, acting in his capacity as vice admiral, tried and condemned John Deane for piracy, Dr. Richard Lloyd, the chief judge of the Admiralty, disapproved of the trial. He claimed it was not in accord with civil law procedures; furthermore, Vaughan had no power to hold such a court unless he had a special commission of oyer and terminer from London.[53] Deane's conviction was overturned and a new trial ordered; meanwhile, the problem of the special commission received a thorough review. In late 1677 a special commission was finally approved for Jamaica and piracy trials could proceed. But it was also decided that the system would be far less cumbersome if the Jamaican assembly passed a law that would cover all contingencies. The matter was first broached by the ministry in 1677; however, it was not until 1681 that an act, "For the Restraining and Punishing of Privateers and Pirates," finally passed the Jamaican assembly. This statute approved trials in the Admiralty Courts under the procedures and penalties of 28 Henry 8 c. 15. Inasmuch as the government appointed the judges of the Admiralty Courts, there would be a royal official overseeing the trial of pirates who would be harder on wrongdoers than local juries. At least that was the theory.[54]

The man who presided over the campaign against the pirates on Jamaica was the next governor, Thomas Lynch. Committed to using every means at his disposal, Lynch in 1684 corresponded with the notorious buccaneer leader Laurent de Graff to try to get him to surrender. If de Graff would retire to Jamaica,

Lynch promised him a pardon with no questions asked. By luring away the best leaders Lynch hoped to curtail the buccaneers' activities.[55] But in the end he would be his own worst enemy. His problems started with the first Royal Navy captains sent over to protect commerce, who acted in a very high-handed manner. They pressed men into service on their ships, while in port they punished some men to the point of death; they insulted local captains; and they picked fights with the Spanish merchants who came to Port Royale to trade. Local mobs attacked them for the captains' insolent ways, amid growing pressure on Lynch to do something about their behavior. As a vice admiral, Governor Lynch believed he should be able to order the captains to do as he saw fit, but they would take orders only from the distant Admiralty. Frustrated, Lynch wrote to England asking to have his powers as vice admiral defined. Did he or did he not have the right to issue orders to navy captains, and did he have the power to try them in a court-martial? If he did not have power over them, his only recourse would be to arrest them and return them to England; for otherwise they could operate as independent powers beyond the law.[56]

The Lords of Trade and Plantations received Lynch's complaints in December 1683 and sent them out for legal opinion. When the opinion was returned, it raised such doubts about the powers of the vice admirals that the lords felt called upon to send the whole issue to the Crown's top legal officials. Their report was a bombshell. It was not confined to Lynch's complaints, but went beyond them to invalidate the Admiralty Courts and the antipiracy law passed in Jamaica. The legal officers declared that Admiralty Courts as presently structured in the colonies only had jurisdiction over the lesser maritime offenses such as wrecks, charter-party disputes, mariners' wage disputes, and trade laws in general; they had no authority over capital crimes. Nor could those courts be given this power specifically in new commissions, because the English piracy law of 1536 "doth not extend to the plantations." That law mandated trials by special commission of the High Court of Admiralty in London and in no other jurisdiction.[57] This decision was a terrible blow to the government's policy. It had taken four years to persuade the Jamaican assembly to pass a piracy law, and the Lords of Trade had just sent a copy to all the colonies, with orders to pass it in the local legislature.[58] Now the basis of a legal attack on the pirates lay in ruins.

The report did contain the suggestion that the Vice Admiralty Courts could operate under a local law granting them power to conduct piracy trials under the civil law rules that had prevailed in England before the Henrician statute passed in 1536. In other words, the colonies would have to operate under trial procedures found unworkable in England prior to 1536 and do so without civil lawyers, who were about as common in America as Catholics in Massachusetts Bay. The only good news in the report was that the governors in the colonies did have the right to fit out ships to capture pirates. If successful, they would then have to send them— and the witnesses against them—to London for trial. This was hardly an efficient way to run an empire.

In the early 1680s the government moved to restructure the old policy in light of the law officers' opinion. The attorney general prepared new commissions for vice admirals and their courts, and an accompanying model law to be passed by colonial assemblies incorporating the pre-1536 civil law rules in piracy cases. These documents were approved and sent to the colonies, where they met with little enthusiasm.[59] It was not simply that they had no love for the civil law, they also lacked basic enthusiasm for the task. The buccaneers continued to leave the Caribbean and seek safe havens elsewhere, finding them in the North American colonies where the cheap goods they sold were welcomed almost as warmly as the gold and silver currency they carried. As merchants, tapsters, carpenters, sailmakers, and prostitutes greeted them, the colonial governments turned their backs and ignored the problem or, like Governor Benjamin Fletcher in New York, decided to profit from it. In the end a number of the colonial legislatures passed piracy laws, but varied them to suit local tastes. Most of them did not have the death penalty and not many bothered with the civil law. Few pirates were ever tried under these laws, and fewer still were convicted.[60]

The legislation that perhaps most revealingly shows the government's reluctance to act appeared in 1682. In that year Parliament tried to halt the spread of piracy by forcing its victims to fight back. Sailors often declined combat when pirates attacked, for they had no stake in the cargo or the ship. Why risk their lives when they got nothing for it except cuts, bruises, and perhaps a quick trip to the bottom of the ocean, wrapped in a sheet with a cannonball at their feet for company? The pirates were aware of these sentiments and usually did not harm the mariners (particularly if they were of the same nationality) or loot their sea chests. As a rule, only the captains and supercargoes, who knew the location of money on board, received the unpleasant attentions of the sea robbers. Parliament decided to order all mariners who served on ships over 200 tons, with at least twenty cannon, to fight when attacked. Failure to do so would be punished by the loss of wages and bonuses.[61] The burden of fighting the pirates was placed squarely on the backs of ordinary seamen.

As the 1680s drew to a close, the English government still lacked a coherent and viable policy. It continued its old way of doing business by making someone else responsible for solving the problem. This situation might have continued were it not for long-term trends that came to fruition at just this time.

While the "rise of the state" is a commonplace of the early modern era, there was a distinct and decisive surge in the size, power, and authority of the state in England in the late seventeenth century.[62] The chief engine driving this process was the demands of war. From 1689 to 1713 England remained at war with France, with the exception of a truce from 1697 to 1702. These wars spilled far beyond Europe as the two chief combatants fought for the spoils of empire. European wars became world wars, and as such made unprecedented demands upon the governments.

As always in wartime, the executive departments benefited the most. The Treasury and the tax collections agencies associated with it—customs and excise—grew as Parliament passed new taxes to pay for the unparalleled costs of the war. The offices spending money—the Admiralty, Navy Office, Army, and Ordnance—similarly flourished. The men who controlled these new bureaucracies differed from their predecessors. Social position still opened the way to office, but training and diligence could bring rapid advancement in the more complicated new system. What emerged was the beginning of modern bureaucracy. Increasingly professional in their attitudes, the new bureaucrats demanded a steady flow of statistics, censuses, and detailed information of all sorts so that their offices could better serve the state in making policy. The nature of their ambition can be seen in the plans advocated by Sir Charles Hedges for the State Paper Office:

> My aime is to make that office which is the repository of the Papers of State, as useful as I can to His Majesty, and the Publick, by putting it into So good Order, that We may find precedents of publick affairs and Transactions of State, without difficulty which in the present Condition it is, can not be done, but that it should be made easy is, in my opinion, a thing of great importance.[63]

The institutions for making policy were also undergoing change. At the center of power the government came to be controlled by a smaller and smaller body of men. The unwieldy Privy Council had long ago given way to a compact group of ministers who could meet with the monarch to make policy. When King William left the country for long periods to campaign in Europe after 1689, he appointed a small group of lords justices to act on his behalf. These men were the holders of the traditionally great offices of state as well as those of increasing importance. The trend in government was toward frequent meetings of a few of the most important ministers; while it was not yet cabinet government, the tide was running in that direction. Even though the House of Commons was at the height of its powers in the 1690s—it investigated the spending of any office it chose to, impeached ministers, and in general oversaw every action of the government—the long-term trend was toward a more controlled and disciplined body, with the cabinet giving broad guidance.[64] What this movement produced was a concert of interests: the merchants liked order and regularity in mercantile affairs, the new bureaucrats desired governmental efficiency, and the politicians wanted disciplined restraint after the tumults of the seventeenth century. The so-called Venetian oligarchy lay just over the horizon.

The structure of diplomacy and international law also blossomed. As the nation-states grew in size and power, their relationships became more formal, if not more pacific. Under William III the English appointed representatives to eighty governments, an unprecedented number. While many of them went to the warren of petty German states, thereby teaching generations of diplomats the true meaning of boredom, England had diplomats in all the major courts from Moscow across the arc of northern Europe and back to Constantinople. A splendid embassy was even sent to the court of Emperor Aurangzeb.[65] The seventeenth century marked a growing regard for law as a mediator between princes, whose relationships grew more and more densely thicketed with expanded trade, complicated alliances, multiple imperial systems, and ever larger state structures. Hugo Grotius, John Selden, and others provided the intellectual basis for the new international system, while the burgeoning diplomatic corps worked out the day-to-day problems. This activity did not create international order, but it did bring some stability to the affairs of nations. For instance, the English previously had treated anyone not in alliance with their country as an enemy who could accordingly be plundered and robbed at sea. As the century wore on, the concept of noncombatant neutrals developed, although the problem of contraband carried by neutrals in wartime remained.

The web of rules, laws, treaties, and diplomacy slowly but surely curbed the private use of violence. The nation-states brought an end to overly powerful subjects who operated as independent entities without regard for issues of national policy. The renaissance bravado displayed by Drake, Hawkins, and Mainwaring, which could bring governments to the point of war or cost states prestige and money, withered during the seventeenth century. Instead, governments moved to control the actions of their domineering subjects and stripped them of their private armies and mighty ships. In the new regime of baroque order the government controlled the national army and navy and no longer feared the use of private force. The level of violence on the international scene by no means diminished, as the nearly constant warfare between 1689 and 1713 testifies, but now the states monopolized force for their own goals. Only the pirates remained on the periphery of empire with ships, forts, settlements, and men outside the new system, endangering powerful interest groups.

The English government moved on a broad front to bring order to the empire. First, in 1696, the long moribund Lords of Trade and Plantations gave way to the Board of Trade, a smaller but far more active body staffed by at least some men who actually knew something about the colonies. The new board immediately began systematically to acquire data, interview experts, and generally push itself into colonial administration.[66] At the same time the board was created, Parliament passed a new law, "an Act for preventing Frauds and regulating Abuses in the Plantation Trade," designed to control illicit trade in the colonies. The customs commissioners sent platoons of officers to the colonies to enforce the new act. They were aided in their efforts by a revised system of Vice Admiralty Courts placed in nearly all the colonies, with power to oversee trade and maritime affairs. This flurry of activity finally resulted in an administrative apparatus capable of carrying out English policy in the plantations.[67]

There was also a determined attack on governors who cooperated with pirates or who overlooked trading with them. Governor Nicholas Trott, who negotiated with Avery and his men, was recalled and interrogated and then dropped from office. Governor William Markham of Pennsylvania, who befriended anyone with ample gold in his pockets, lost his office, even though William Penn, proprietor of the colony, tried to keep him. The most notorious of all the governors was Benjamin Fletcher of New York. As New York City gained a reputation as the chief supplier of pirates on Madagascar, Fletcher became the focus of concern. He was recalled with a promise that he still had royal approval, but when he returned to England he faced a long series of hearings to clear his name. Although he managed to avoid formal charges, his career came to an abrupt end. The king also sent a circular letter to other governors warning them to obey the laws if they did not want to lose their offices.[68]

The officials being sent out to the colonies were also a new breed. Among the most vigorous was Jeremiah Basse. When he set out to take up his office as governor of New Jersey, he was captured by pirates on the way—a first-hand experience that generated a lasting enmity on his part.[69] Within a few years the government succeeded in mounting a campaign against lax administration in the colonies. New institutions and new personnel, plus threats and orders to those already in office in the plantations, finally brought real substance into the campaign against piracy.

The drive to bring order extended to policies relating to commissions for privateering and reprisal. Both were subject to abuse, reprisal more so because it validated the raiding of commerce in peacetime. As the relations of the new states grew more complicated, such abuses became intolerable. When the Spanish invaded the island of New Providence, they expelled the English and seized £20,000 worth of English property. The victims, petitioning for relief, were told to take their records to the Admiralty Court, which could approve them, then pursue their losses through diplomatic channels.[70]

Owners of ships taken at sea received similar treatment. During the 1670s Captain Rowland Simpson and Captain Edmund Cooke both lost ships—one to the Spanish, the other to the French. Their cases were discussed and adjudicated for years while they pleaded for a commission of reprisal to recoup their losses. Instead, the English ambassadors in Madrid and Paris pressed for legal redress.[71] The English government preferred this course to allowing aggrieved parties to go out on their own to raid Spanish shipping, a course that would in all likelihood cause bigger problems. When the English were found to be the guilty parties, diplomacy was also used to gain reparations. Governor Lynch of Jamaica, for instance, was ordered to cooperate fully with a Spanish judge sent there to investigate the buccaneers' raid on Vera Cruz. He was even told to divulge the secret pact between the pirate leader van Horne, who led the raid, and the governor of the Spanish island of Santo Domingo.[72] The diplomats rarely produced results that pleased the victims, but they did stop the endless rounds of reprisals that so often led to further piracy and to heightened tension between states. As a method of compensation, reprisal was passing from the scene.

After 1688, with the onset of King William's War, privateering entered a new phase. None of the combatants was willing to forgo raiding commerce during wartime, but the Admiralty was reluctant to license large numbers of privateers because of the enormous demand for trained sailors to man the navy, merchant, and fishing fleets. The French enthusiastically embraced the *guerre du course* when the weight of the allied fleet kept their navy bottled up in port. In fact, the government started a policy of leasing navy ships to *armateurs*, or groups of investors. With expansion, however, came tighter regulation under the *conseil de prise*.[73]

England too brought privateering under tighter regulation. A statute passed in 1692 regulated the manner in which prizes were declared (only in appropriate courts) and the division of the prize money among the Crown, the shipowners, the officers, and the men. Many of the customary practices of petty looting were prohibited in order to put the entire system on a legal footing. This law accompanied a raft of new administrative rules issued by the Privy Council and the Admiralty. Owners now had to post substantial bonds for good behavior, and twenty-two instructions defined such conduct. Privateering had become a regulated enterprise. Abuses still existed, especially in the gray areas of enemy cargoes on neutral shipping, but the thrust of the new policy was to limit the targets of opportunity to enemy shipping properly captured and brought before the Admiralty Courts before any division of the loot occurred.[74] These rules clarified the often-blurred lines between piracy and privateering. It was now much easier to identify the privateers; for anyone who lacked the required passes, certificates, regulations, bonds, and even flags, was a pirate.

The need for an effective antipiracy law remained, and that had to be tackled in England. When the issue returned once again, it proved to be just as thorny a problem as it had been in the past. In 1696 the newly appointed Board of Trade tackled the matter. The members prepared an elaborate report for the lords justices, but in it they expressed doubts about the possibilities of getting a new law. A few days after they submitted their report, Sir Charles Hedges, chief judge of the Admiralty, was called in for consultation. Hedges was one of the leading civil lawyers of his generation and an astute politician to boot. He was to parlay his legal training and administrative abilities into the position of secretary of state. He was, in other words, one of the new men in government.[75]

When Hedges met with the board, he advised them that the newly created colonial Admiralty Courts could not try pirates unless the particular colony had passed a law modeled on the piracy law of Jamaica. So the board followed his advice and ordered the governors to pass such a law and act vigorously against the pirates. Some of the colonies did, but the proprietary and charter colonies—

those that were not actually royal colonies by this time—balked. They felt that these orders infringed on their prerogatives and control over justice in the colonies. Even those colonies that passed the Jamaican statute usually neglected to make the death penalty mandatory.[76] With failure threatening the new initiatives, the issue of a uniform law emerged yet again.

Hedges had discussed a uniform antipiracy law when he visited the board on November 24, 1697, but put the idea aside because he and the members of the board believed Parliament would never pass such legislation. Within the year the steady drumbeat of petitions concerning piracy and reports of further depredations caused Hedges to change his mind and urge a new law. More important, Parliament became increasingly concerned about the problem. With the war at an end it had time to turn to other problems.[77] By early March 1698 the board reminded Secretary of State James Vernon that a new uniform law was needed and followed this with a report to the House of Commons on March 22. The report stated that the board had failed to get the colonies to pass the appropriate legislation and that the proprietary colonies were particularly recalcitrant. By this time the board was aware that the Vice Admiralty Courts recently created in the colonies did not have the power to try pirates.[78] Vernon ordered the board to confer with the attorney general and the solicitor general and then draft a bill.

In the end, Hedges took over the task of writing a statute that would apply throughout the empire. Wasting no time, he returned a week later with a draft bill, which then started a long round of consideration by various legal officers and interested parties.[79] It was not until December 1699 that the House of Commons ordered a bill to be brought in, and three months more before a committee was appointed. Included on the committee were all the merchants sitting in the house, hardly a group of disinterested legislators. In the midst of a report by this committee the news arrived that Kidd had been captured. The house stopped its proceedings to order that Kidd be returned to England and that he not be tried until Parliament's next meeting. By the end of March 1700, spurred on by Kidd's capture, the law passed both houses and the empire had its first meaningful legislation on piracy.[80]

The preamble to the "Act for the More Effectual Suppression of

Piracy" stated that "idle and profligate" persons were increasingly turning to piracy because of the trouble and expense of returning captured pirates to England for trial. To change this, the law provided for a seven-person court of officials, or of naval officers, who could assemble anywhere to try pirates. The statute detailed the operations of the court but the essential fact was that it had to operate on the basis of civil law.

Unlike the statutes passed in most of the colonies, this law did provide for the death penalty and ordered that those found guilty be put to death on or near the sea. In a victory for those who advocated taking a hard line with the colonists who traded with pirates, those who aided and abetted the freebooters would suffer the same penalties. There were a number of clauses dealing with other aspects of the problem. To encourage mariners to resist when their ship was attacked, they were to be awarded a percentage of the cargo they saved; and those who revealed a plot by some of the men to take over their ship were also to receive a reward. Those who joined the pirates forfeited their wages. The law ended with a warning to the proprietary and charter colonies that had fought the imposition of new laws and courts. If they interfered with the operation of the new courts mandated by this statute, their charters would be revoked.[81]

The government did not stop with passage of this bill. The new Admiralty Courts would need to be guided in how to proceed with the new law, which meant training officials of the colonies in the new procedures. To that end, James Larkin was ordered out to the colonies to install and instruct the new courts wherever he could.[82] But the Board of Trade also decided to give the governors in the colonies an option: if one of them felt he could not get a conviction in his province, he could send the malefactors and the evidence relating to the case to England for trial. This provision would produce a small flood of pirates in the next few years, as governors sent men home to England for fear of local courts and also to curry favor with the ministry in England.[83]

While activity in the area of administrative control, the law, and the courts was vital, these policies had to be matched with muscle in the form of the Royal Navy. The navy had started during the administration of Oliver Cromwell to recover from the neglect of the early seventeenth century, a recovery that was advanced by Charles II. The king and his brother James, Duke of York and Lord High Admiral, lavished money and attention on the navy. William Pepys, the famed diarist, provided the expertise to build a proper administration for the proliferation of ships and men. By 1675 the navy was strong enough to send an expedition to North Africa, two ships to Jamaica, two to Newfoundland, and one to Barbados. Even though the navy was still a small peacetime service, it was on duty to protect commerce in distant ports.[84] By 1685 twenty-five ships were in pay and thus were manned and available for service; six were off North Africa; there was one each at Barbados, the Leeward Islands, Virginia, Newfoundland, and two at Jamaica. Besides these ships on station, the navy was reaching far beyond its normal range. One ship had been dispatched to the west coast of Africa and another sent to cruise in the Indian Ocean.[85] The navy continued to grow during the rest of the decade, but the advent of war in 1688 transformed it in many ways. When the conflict started, there were 88 ships ready to meet the French navy; at the height of the war in June 1696, there were 234 ships with a total complement of 45,906 men and officers.[86] The peerless Royal Navy extended its power over very large areas. The main battle fleet assigned to guard England contained 151 warships and 20 fireships. Squadrons patrolled the Mediterranean and the West Indies; ships remained on station at Barbados, Jamaica, the Leewards, Virginia, New York, and New England, while other ships held station off the Irish coast and the Shetland Islands to provide protection for vessels struggling to make it home; and others sailed with convoys.[87] In size and mission the navy had been transformed.

The navy's role in wartime was time honored—to seek out and destroy the enemy, to blockade ports, and to secure English commerce. The last activity expanded enormously during the war. At the beginning, large-scale fleet actions dominated the war at sea and the combined Anglo-Dutch fleet suffered defeat at the hands of the French. In time the initiative swung toward the allies, and the French government switched to the *guerre du course*. The French privateers then captured hundreds of allied ships, and the privateering war forced a change in allied tactics.[88] Early in the war the government in England paid little attention to protection of commerce. The French raids were not particularly damaging, and there was a widespread belief that merchants were profiting from the war. Then in 1693 came the disaster of the Smyrna convoy.

For two years the French had kept English shipping bound for the Mediterranean in port because of the danger of sailing south along the French coast. To protect them the Admiralty organized a vast convoy with hundreds of ships protected by the channel fleet. After accompanying the convoy close to the northern coast of Spain, the fleet returned to its station in the channel while a smaller squadron continued south with the merchantmen. Meanwhile a large French fleet had slipped ahead of the English and a few days after the main channel fleet retired, they struck. The remaining Royal Navy ships could do little to protect the large number of merchantmen that were captured, driven ashore, or dispersed. It was a calamity for the Levant merchants, many of whom were ruined, and their trade took a long time to recover after the war. Their howls of outrage forced the Admiralty and the government to take protection of commerce more seriously.[89]

Convoying, never an easy task, required continuous cooperation of the Admiralty, the Board of Trade, the fishermen, and the merchant community. Each had different schedules, depending on wind patterns, crop harvesting, trade patterns, and fishing habits. The Admiralty wrestled with these problems plus the individual avarice of some merchants who ordered their captains to leave a convoy early, to beat the competition into port to get higher prices. Those merchant groups that had not already organized now did so. Thus when advice was needed, merchants representing the sugar, coal, naval supplies, fish, and tobacco interests trooped before the Admiralty to bargain for convoys and even to assign a few experienced mariners, still in short supply, to each ship.[90] Until the war's end this arrangement proceeded in its awkward way. But what about peacetime? As it turned out, no matter how awkward the relationship each side needed the other. The navy preferred to keep as many ships as possible in pay and the merchants preferred the security of the convoys, particularly when each month brought new complaints about pirates.[91] In 1697 the Admiralty prepared for a larger peacetime navy than ever before as the ministry accepted the arguments of the merchants and the navy.

After 1697 the navy changed character to meet a different set of challenges. Laid up in the docks were the first rates, the fearful leviathans at the heart of the battle line. The only slightly less formidable second rates also stretched their anchor ropes. Of the line of battleships, only the third rates remained in service—and there were only thirteen of them. The navy consisted mostly of fourth, fifth, and sixth rates, the fastest-growing categories of ships during King William's reign. When he came to the throne, there were 49 of them; when he left, there were 108. In contrast, the large ships of the line increased only from 59 to 68. The smaller, more agile vessels were simply best suited for convoy duty, hunting pirates, and stalking smugglers. The enlarged size of the peacetime fleet was made possible by the war years. In order to pay for the war, more and more new taxes were levied, particularly excise taxes on goods. At the end of the war most of these taxes were continued, thus helping the government to pay its debts, but also enabling it to continue to grow and take over more and more services. The service the merchants wanted most was protection of commerce.[92]

This boring job did not always reveal the navy's best side. While it had grown and had become more efficient, the navy was still not a thoroughly professional body; certainly it had not yet attained the standard it would reach during the Napoleonic wars. Tedious patrol duty in the colonies managed to bring out the worst in some captains. Many of them assigned to the West Indies could not overlook the opportunities for profiting from the slave trade, where merchants were happy to have them involved because of the buccaneers. At one point during Queen Anne's War all of the Royal Navy ships in the West Indies were carrying slaves to the Spanish colonies. On occasion they embezzled goods from ships they stopped, whether or not they had sufficient cause to intercept the ship in the first place.[93] The officers suffered from the inefficiency of a supply system that left them short of food and pay, but their way of dealing with it hardly met the standards of a modern navy or, for that matter, those of the Admiralty, which prosecuted the worst offenders.[94]

The real victims of this system were the sailors who suffered the most from it, so much so that there were fears that one particular navy ship might turn pirate. One plot, discovered just in time, caused James Vernon, the secretary of state, to write a remarkable passage in a letter:

It is a melancholy reflection to find the fleet infected with this kind of debauchery, which nobody knows how far it may spread. One may see what has led them to it,—the long want of pay, and the abuses in the manner of it, the ill example set by the officers, who have defrauded the men of the shares they should have had of prizes, cheating and embezzling themselves, and allowing nobody else, at least not the poor sailors, to be the better for it; the corruption and neglect of the governors in the West Indies, in receiving pirates under their protection, and sharing with them in the plunder. How the discipline of the navy will be restored is another question, and without it our security is gone, and our sea walls are undermined.[95]

Vernon's dejected ruminations reflected on the imperfect state of the navy.

The navy, even when this inefficient, could still take action in the colonies in ways that pointed to the future. Two events illustrate the trend. The East India Company not only sought changes in legal institutions, it also wanted the exercise of naval power in the wake of Kidd's raid. With the war at an end in 1697, this was a propitious moment to ask for a display of force, and King William assented. Having been able to find Saint Helena after stopping at the Cape of Good Hope and then managing to return to England, Thomas Warren was given command of this squadron, no doubt because of his experience. The government was particularly concerned that the lair at Saint Marie be destroyed to prevent the pirates from creating, as Vernon put it, "a formed Government of Robbers there."[96] Warren carried with him an offer of pardon to any pirate who willingly surrendered, but he died during the voyage and never got to Saint Marie. His mission hardly qualified as a success, but it did show the flag in Indian waters and two of the ships even convoyed the pilgrim fleet to Mocha in 1698, earning the English some good will.[97]

The second event of note occurred in Chesapeake Bay. Captain

John Aldred of the *Essex Prize* patrolled the Chesapeake, and during the summer of 1699 suddenly found that he was opposed by the pirate ship *Providence Galley,* a twenty-six-gun ship with 130 men. Aldred's vessel was no match for the pirates, and he had to use all of his skill to stay away from his opponent.[98] A year later the results were very different. The *Essex Prize,* still on station, was now accompanied by the larger *Shoreham,* commanded by Captain William Passenger. When a large pirate ship, the *La Paix,* was sighted at Linhaven Bay, Aldred left his ship to go aboard the *Shoreham.* There the two captains were later joined by Governor William Nicholson of Virginia, who wanted to be in at the kill. The *Shoreham* sighted the pirate ship at 4:00 A.M. when it ran up a red flag, and once within cannon range, Passenger kept blazing away until he had fired 1,671 shot and reduced the pirate ship to a blazing hulk. The fight ended twelve hours after it started, with twenty-six pirates dead, over fifty wounded, and the remaining eighty locked up. Governor Nicholson overruled Passenger, who wanted to try the prisoners immediately, as was possible under the new law; instead, he sent them to England as a sign of the success of the campaign against the pirates.[99] These were the men who would be hanged with Kidd in 1701.

In the period between the beginning of Kidd's voyage and its conclusion, a considerable change had occurred in the policy toward piracy. During the early 1690s the government had managed only to issue a proclamation of pardon, and it excused the meager effort by noting the pressing needs of the war.[100] Then in the middle of the decade the Kidd expedition was mounted to do something about attacking piracy. After 1696 a new imperial law was written, errant officials were recalled, the administration of the colonies was tightened, a naval expedition was sent to the East Indies, protection of commerce by the navy was vastly enhanced, and a considerable campaign was mounted in England to ensure action against the pirates. Thus Kidd sailed home to a very different atmosphere from the one he left. An unwitting catalyst to these changes, Kidd was now in deadly peril as the East India Company urged the ministry to make sure he was brought to justice.

SEVEN

Cat and Mouse

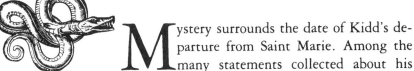**M**ystery surrounds the date of Kidd's departure from Saint Marie. Among the many statements collected about his stay there, none mentions when he left the island. One deposition hints that he left five months after the *Resolution* departed in June 1698, which would place his departure some time in November.[1] A departure at that time of year would have found advantageous winds and would match Kidd's arrival in the West Indies in April 1699. A slow voyage, but understandably so given the sailing qualities of the lumbering *Quedah Merchant.* Kidd must have stared longingly at the remains of the *Adventure Galley* as it sank lower and lower in the mud: he was left with a huge beast of a merchantman, while his former fighting ship slowly became a playground for fish.

Kidd and his small crew slowly prepared the ship for the voyage. Long before, the cannon of the *Adventure Galley* had been placed in the hold of the *Quedah,* partly to give the ship ballast but primarily to save the valuable weapons.[2] Only a few men were left to pilot the ship back across the Atlantic, all of the officers from the *Adventure Galley* having either died or gone with Culliford. Most of the thirteen remaining members of the original crew were young men—the apprentices Robert Lamley and Richard Barlycorne and Kidd's brother-in-law, Samuel Bradley, for instance. As before, the old sailors (such as Kidd's New York neighbor, Edward Buckmaster, and Gabriel Loffe) were supplemented by slaves, who performed most of the real work.[3] Kidd recruited the rest of the crew from men who wanted to leave the island and go back home with their booty.

The most intriguing of these newcomers was James Kelley, alias Sampson Marshall, alias James Gilliam. Kelley typified those who went into buccaneering and stayed on year after year, surviving all sorts of experiences. Like other hard-core freebooters, he preferred the life at sea, to returning to home and hearth. Kelley first left England in 1680, on a slave ship bound for the west coast of Africa. Upon arrival, his ship was captured by pirates, and Kelley decided to throw in his lot with the crew of Captain Yankee, who shortly afterward decided to return to his normal cruising ground in the Caribbean. There Kelley joined the brethren of the coast and spent the next few years moving from ship to ship. During one of the episodes of national friction, he and the English members of the crew threw out their French brethren. Under the leadership of John Cook they seized two French merchantmen, one of which was a sturdy vessel appropriate for a voyage to the South Sea, or Pacific Ocean, the goal of so many buccaneers in the 1680s. But first they went to Virginia to sell their goods and get supplies and men. About twenty men joined them, including William Dampier and Ambrose Cowley, who wrote famous journals about this voyage.[4]

In April 1683 Kelley's ship slipped out of the Chesapeake and crossed the Atlantic to the Cape Verde Islands, where the crew bought supplies and then sailed to the African coast. After taking a stout Danish ship, they traded their own vessel to a slaver in exchange for sixty African women, renamed the Danish ship the *Batchelor's Delight,* and steered for Cape Horn. By February 1684 they were rounding the cape. A terrible storm struck, forcing them farther and farther south until they were below sixty degrees south latitude. The extreme cold killed the young women one by one until all were dead, while the men discovered that by drinking three quarts of brandy a day they could stay warm and alive. Finally they rounded the cape and headed north seeking a rich Spanish prize; but the first ship they met was the *Nicholas,* another buccaneering ship. For a time they cruised in tandem and later joined one of those extraordinary gatherings of buccaneers in which six ships sailed together. Luckily for the Spanish, there was no leader with the qualities of a Henry Morgan; so the men quickly divided, usually on national grounds. The group Kelley went with, led by Edward Davis, achieved very little. They returned to the Caribbean, where Kelley found his way to Jamaica, accepted King William's pardon, and became a privateer. Like the men on Kidd's *Blessed William*, Kelley disliked the life of a king's privateer. He joined a group that seized the sloop *Diamond* and set out for the East Indies. Perhaps because he had been "on account," or a pirate, for ten years, Kelley was elected captain. After resupplying at the Cape Verde Islands the ship rounded the Cape of Good Hope and vanished into the Indian Ocean.

The next few years of Kelley's life are obscure, but it appears that he spent some time on Madagascar living with the natives. He enters the records once again as a sailor on the *Mocha Frigate*, along with Robert Culliford. (It was he who killed Captain Edgecombe when they took the ship.) On board the *Resolution* with Culliford, he used the name Sampson Marshall until they returned to Saint Marie. Loaded with booty, he decided to retire and approached Kidd about returning with him. It was during Kidd's return voyage that Kelley changed names again, becoming James Gilliam. The arduous life at sea paled as he approached the end of his second decade as a buccaneer. It was time to return to his wife and family in London and settle down to enjoy his gains.[5]

Little is known about most of the other new men with Kidd. One was John Harrison, who desired to return to his home on Long Island; another was John Hales, who wanted to retire to London and open a victualing house; and another was the intriguing Edward Davis, an "extraordinary stout man." This is undoubtedly the Edward Davis who captained the *Batchelor's Delight* on its return to the Caribbean. He ultimately fled north to Virginia, where he and his companions were caught rowing across Chesapeake Bay. After a long and tedious legal struggle the men won their freedom and even recovered their treasures, minus £300 used toward founding a new college in Virginia—the present-day William and Mary. After collecting his booty, Davis vanished for a few years until he reappeared in 1697 as a crew member on the *Fidelio*, with Tempest Rogers as captain, bound for the Indian Ocean. One voyage was enough for Davis, who ended up on Saint Marie seeking passage home just as Kidd prepared to depart.[6]

It is difficult to know exactly what kind of welcome Kidd expected by the time he left Saint Marie in November. News traveled constantly between the island and New York. Kidd's friends could correspond with him, and in 1698 they had multiple chances to write as four ships left New York to trade on the island.[7] This precaution was well taken, because of the four ships only one had reached Madagascar by November and that was the *Nassau*, captained by Kidd's friend Giles Shelley, who later denied meeting Kidd while he was there. Two of the other three ships were taken by pirates who needed ships, and the other was seized by an East India merchantman at the Cape of Good Hope.[8] Fortunately, Captain Samuel Burgess of the *Margaret* did not have enough time to throw his papers overboard when he was captured, so we have the opportunity to read Kidd's mail.[9]

James Emott, Kidd's friend and fellow Scot, wrote a long letter, mostly reassuring in tone, but containing disquieting phrases that urged Kidd not to believe rumors about Bellomont's displeasure with him. As Emott put it:

Some flying reports about this towne that his Excelly Should have conncived an ill oppinnion of yo and that it was not Safe for you to Returne here, Upon wch his Lordship did asure me that there was noe Such thing but on the Contrary he ever has a good opinion of Capt. Kidd . . . I mention this more largely lest these false reports should reach you and thereby put you after measures than what you formerly proposed to me.[10]

Emott closed with a warning that if by any "Inadvertancy, necessity or Insolency of your men you have made any false steps," Kidd should return directly to his home port because, "Lett this assure you that there will be efectuall Care taken to Remedy the same."[11] Robert Livingston wrote a more positive letter, also exhorting Kidd to return; and Bellomont sent a similar note, adding that as a sign of his favor Kidd could return to New York rather than going to Boston as his original orders stipulated.[12]

Given the prevailing practice of sending multiple copies of letters in order to avoid the perils of the sea, it is likely that Kidd received these communications. When he arrived in Saint Marie, Carsten Leursen of New York City was there trading, and he could have brought letters and returned with news as well as portions of the booty sent home by the men.[13] The letters must have left Kidd in a state of perplexed anxiety, for while they contained soothing phrases they also hinted at lurking danger. Kidd preferred to believe the assurances as he prepared to leave the island, but he realized he would need to approach the familiar waters of New York with care.

While almost all of those who were later interviewed about Kidd's voyage said something about the journey to the Indian Ocean, none mentioned the trip home. The voyage seems to have been something of an afterthought and lacked exciting events, although sailing the *Quedah Merchant* across the rough seas south of the Cape of Good Hope must have provided some notable moments. Because the appearance of the *Quedah* at the Cape of Good Hope or at the English station at Saint Helena would have attracted the attention of the authorities, the crew was forced to stay at sea during the long voyage north. After rounding the cape the ship benefited from the steady winds and currents that move north along the African coast. There were few breaks in the long, monotonous voyage; the equator could even be crossed without ceremony, for by now everyone had been through that rite of passage. Ascension Island was the only place the ship might have stopped. A lonely outcropping in the middle of the South Atlantic, it attracted mariners for one reason—fresh turtle meat. One of the green turtle groups lives most of its life in Brazilian waters but crosses 2,000 miles of ocean to breed on Ascension. Almost every ship stopped to load the turtles, which were placed on their backs to immobilize them; they were kept alive for fresh food as the voyage continued. So common was the practice of stopping here that a large rock with a hole in it close to where the boats tied up was used as a mailbox by captains who left messages for other ships from whom they had become separated.[14] After the break at Ascension, the ship drifted through the doldrums once again. Finally the glassy sea was ruffled by occasional breezes from the east, which gradually strengthened into the steady benevolent trade winds streaming east to west, pushing everything before them to the New World.

In early April 1699 Kidd made a landfall on Anguilla Island.[15] Barbados was the usual target for ships returning from the East Indies; because it was the most easterly island in the Lesser Antilles, it was often possible to pick up an escort there for the trip to England. All the same, Kidd continued to avoid busy places and headed for the more northerly and more quiet island of Anguilla. By the time he arrived, he desperately needed water and fresh food. He stayed only four hours, long enough to get what he needed before making a rapid exit. Along with the food he acquired some very bad news: the government, at the urging of the East India Company, had sent a general alarm to the West Indies on November 23, 1698, declaring Kidd a pirate, excepting him from any pardon, and ordering an all-out manhunt. By February this news had reached the islands.[16] Kidd now knew that he could expect nothing but trouble if he went near an English colony, and any calculations he had made about his welcome in New York had to be reworked. He still needed supplies—and time to think—so he sailed southwest to the Danish island of Saint Thomas, a safe haven for pirates with goods to sell.

He arrived there on April 6 and immediately asked for permission to enter the harbor, which was granted. But Kidd went on to ask for protection from the Royal Navy, perhaps remembering an earlier occasion when the pirate ship *La Trompeuse* was burned in the harbor by HMS *Francis*.[17] Governor John Laurents preferred not to have a recurrence, so he denied the request; should a Royal Navy ship arrive, there was little Laurents could do to stop it from attacking the ships in the harbor, or for that matter from blockading the port. Kidd persisted and sent another note requesting protection until he could send a message to Bellomont proving he was not a pirate and receive his reply. Laurents would have none of it and denied him again. After two days of getting nowhere, Kidd decided to leave; but before he did, five men asked to be left behind. One was Kidd's brother-in-law, Samuel Bradley, who for two years had suffered from some illness and could bear it no longer. He wanted care on dry land, even if it meant staying among foreigners.[18] Kidd did nothing to stop him, perhaps hoping to keep Bradley out of the trouble he, Kidd, was now in. Leaving Saint Thomas, he steered the *Quedah Merchant* toward the island of Mona, in the channel between Puerto Rico and Hispaniola, where he had arranged to have supplies delivered.[19] Mona was small and not under the immediate control of any government, so it was a safe place to anchor. Once he was there,

Kidd could consider his problems. With alarms set off all over the Caribbean, it was unlikely he could find a haven while he negotiated with Bellomont. His reception at Saint Thomas had convinced him of that, and it was unlikely that he could find protection elsewhere. The Spanish colonies were out, the Dutch too far away, and the French too unreliable. He could remain at one of the out-of-the-way islands such as Mona, but every day he risked detection: the ungainly *Quedah* could hardly be hidden forever from prying eyes. In fact, the governor of Nevis dispatched HMS *Queensborough* for Puerto Rico as soon as he heard that Kidd was in the Antilles. The longer he remained in one place, the more likely it became that he would be detected. To negotiate with Bellomont, he would have to go to New York.[20]

On the way to Mona, Kidd intercepted the sloop of Henry Bolton, an unsavory character who, as collector of customs for the Leeward Islands, had absconded with government money and used it to enter trade as a merchant in Antigua.[21] Bound for Puerto Rico with a load of hogs, he readily agreed to sell twenty of them to Kidd's hungry men. Kidd asked further if Bolton could find buyers for his muslins and calicoes—and could find him a sloop, as the *Quedah* was becoming unseaworthy. Bolton agreed to sail for Curaçao to find buyers for the cloth and to buy Kidd a ship. After Bolton's departure two sloops, one French and the other Dutch, happened by, and some of the cargo changed hands for more supplies. Meanwhile Bolton headed directly south to Curaçao, where he contacted two acquaintances of Kidd, John Stonehouse and Walter Cribble.[22] These may have been former buccaneering companions, but they may also have been previous trading contacts. New York had carried on a steady trade with the Dutch island since the days when both had been part of the Dutch West India Company's New World empire. In 1698 eighteen ships had sailed from New York City to trade on the island for Spanish goods. Any materials sold there could be readily converted into bills of exchange and forwarded to New York.[23] Kidd could protect his own interests by following this procedure, but technically he would thereby violate his contract, which called for no sales from his cargo until he returned. In his current uncertain situation he probably thought very little about the terms of his contract.

Before any potential buyers arrived, the *Quedah* pulled from her anchors during rough weather. Regaining control, the crew steered west and entered the Bay of Savona, where Kidd piloted his ship into the mouth of the River Higuey and lashed it to trees on the riverbank.[24] He was now ensconced on the Spanish island of Hispaniola, where before long ships from Curaçao caught up with him. Slowly but surely the 500-ton *Quedah* was offloaded as one small ship after another pulled alongside and packed its hold with bales of East Indies cloth. Perhaps as many as five ships came to buy cheap goods that would bring a handsome return in the Spanish colonies or even in Europe. Bolton and his associate William Burk purchased the largest number of bales, and after these were loaded on Burk's brigantine, Bolton sold Kidd his sloop, the *Saint Antonio*. The biggest individual haul was made by Burk, who bought 130 bales and sailed with them to Saint Thomas. There he put them in the warehouse of the Brandenburgh Company, a German trading firm that had a form of extraterritoriality and thus was beyond the reach of Governor Laurents.[25] While the overlapping national jurisdictions in the Caribbean might generate conflict between states, they also provided multiple opportunities for sharp traders to find a market or haven where few questions were asked about the source of goods as long as the price was right. The Caribbean was (and still is) a smugglers' paradise.

It is impossible to state with accuracy just how much Kidd and his men profited from selling their cloth goods. The estimates made by others, who probably had little to go on, range from £16,000 to £1,200 plus 2,000 pieces of eight.[26] It is certain that the sellers managed to get rid of bulky goods and acquire more portable forms of wealth. Each man who decided to continue on with Kidd moved his belongings and any goods he had onto the *Antonio* while arrangements were made for the remaining cargo. Bolton, accompanied by eighteen men from various ships, agreed to stay with the *Quedah* for three months—during which time Kidd or his friends would return to get the remaining goods. In the meantime Bolton had Kidd's power of attorney to sell more of the goods if he could.[27] His business finished, Kidd transferred to the *Antonio,* weighed anchor, and set sail through the Mona passage before steering west for the Florida Strait.

Bolton and his crew remained with the *Quedah* a few weeks before the sloops returned from Curaçao. Then, taking what they could of the remaining goods, they abandoned the ship. Bolton went back to Curaçao and subsequently sailed for Africa on a new ship, the *Seahorse;* but he did not get very far. The authorities learned of his trading with Kidd and were on the lookout for him. Captain Legg of HMS *Fowey* caught him and he was sent to England as a "notorious criminal."[28] The *Quedah* ended its long voyage where it lay, in the river. Although it was still a valuable ship, its strange lines would bring only curiosity and trouble to anyone who tried to use it in the Caribbean. Not long after it was abandoned, someone set fire to it. All that remained were charred ribs embedded in the mud, slowly disintegrating as tide and marine creatures destroyed any trace of a ship made famous by Captain Kidd.[29]

The Gulf Stream sweeps through the Florida Strait and flows north, a vast river of warm water that aids mariners sailing north along the American coast. The *Saint Antonio* followed it north with fabulous rumors trailing in its wake. Governor Grey of Barbados reported that the *Antonio* had £400,000 on board and that Kidd had gone to the new and ill-fated Scots colony at Darien. By the time these rumors reached New York, they were greatly inflated. Robert Livingston stated that Kidd had £500,000 in sterling on board. For the pessimists, Captain Thomas Warren announced authoritatively that when he visited Lisbon, the news there was that a Dutch man-of-war had taken Kidd.[30] Needless to say, the colonists preferred to believe the more positive reports. Appetites whetted by these stories promised a warm welcome for Kidd, but he came north slowly, stopping here and there to let men leave the ship and to collect the latest tidings from New York. The news cannot have comforted him, because Bellomont had raised a storm of controversy in his new government.

Bellomont's campaign for office had started in 1695, but he did not set foot in the New World until April 2, 1698. The interim was filled with continual politicking to attach as many governments, and their salaries, to his administration as possible. By the time he left England, he was captain-general and governor of New York, Massachusetts Bay, and New Hampshire. Because the English government was currently worried about New York the most, his first American stop was in New York City. It was there that he could best implement the government's campaign against piracy. But it was also there that Fletcher and his friends still ruled. Because Bellomont had already sided with the Leislerians in order to destroy Joseph Dudley's chance to become governor of Massachusetts Bay, all his potential allies were out of power.[31] To unite the divided colony would have required consummate diplomacy, but this was not one of Bellomont's talents.

The day he arrived, Bellomont arranged to issue a proclamation prohibiting cursing, drinking, lewd conduct, and sabbath breaking. New York was to become a moral bastion, something it had failed to be under Fletcher. Even though the two men met in strained circumstances, Fletcher put on the best show possible. He met Bellomont at dockside with the city's assembled elite, along with the garrison to provide a little pomp and circumstance. The two men managed to remain on polite terms for just over a week before they argued violently; afterward their relationship deteriorated rapidly. Fletcher went to visit Bellomont in his rented house and found Robert Livingston there. His presence reminded Fletcher of Livingston's testimony against him in London, so he decided to pick a fight. Noting that Livingston was carrying a sword (a relatively uncommon practice for merchants), he grabbed his nose and squeezed it hard in a challenge. Livingston, ever the canny Scot, was not about to fight the professional soldier; he contented himself with complaining to Bellomont about Fletcher's behavior. Bellomont forced Fletcher to apologize for his rough ways, but Fletcher had already made his point.[32] Bellomont sneered that Fletcher was "pride without quality . . . no better than an underactor on the stage in Dublin."[33] By May 8 he was writing to the Board of Trade, his letters full of tales about Fletcher's association with pirates.[34] It was the end of a strained, unnatural relationship.

Bellomont moved slowly against the anti-Leislerians who controlled the government. William Nicolls, who had arranged protection for the men on the *Jacob,* was removed from the council, but the council members avoided Bellomont and continued to meet with Fletcher. As a sign of their appreciation Fletcher was provided with a "loyal address," a testimonial signed by the gentlemen, merchants, and inhabitants of the city.[35] When Bellomont finally met with the council on May 18, the meeting was devoted wholly to piracy and the piracy trade. He denounced both, whereas the councilors temporized and excused the two activities. Because many of them, of course, were involved in the trade, they were hardly willing to jump on the bandwagon.[36] The next day Bellomont met with the assembly and delivered a ringing speech, warning that the iniquitous ways of the province were well known in England and that he intended to stamp out the "abomination" of piracy because it was "not only injurious to the Honour of his Majesty, and the English Nation, but also highly prejudicial to the Trade of England, and particularly to the East India Company."[37] It is doubtful that his audience cared much about the East India Company, as their interests lay closer to home. They would wait to see if Bellomont's bite was as sharp as his bark.

Bellomont got his chance when the *Fortune* sailed into port in 1698 after a trading voyage to Madagascar. Stephen de Lancey, leader of the consortium of investors in the ship, warned the captain not to come directly into New York harbor, so he veered away and offloaded most of his cargo on Long Island. When Bellomont got wind of this, he ordered Chidley Brooke, the customs collector, to seize the ship and all its goods. But Brooke was too closely connected with the local merchant community to do any such thing. For four days he offered one excuse after the other, while small boats transferred the cargo into the city. Finally, when Bellomont ordered Brooke in no uncertain terms to do something, Brooke actually managed to seize the last boat bound for the city with £1,000 worth of goods on board. The sheriff and the constables either refused to do anything or could not be found when they were asked to search the city for contraband. The merchants, used to no regulations and easy payoffs, also opposed everything Bellomont did.[38] He considered this "mutiny," and it only spurred him in his campaign. He filled letter after letter with evidence against Fletcher and his cronies. Old pirates were ferreted out and their testimonies duly

An eighteenth-century fantasy depicting Henry Avery and his famous prize. It bears little relation to reality. *(From the Special Collections of the University of California at San Diego)*

Edward Barlow's depiction of his ship, the *Sceptre*. A sturdy merchant-man, it was fearsome enough to chase Kidd away from the pilgrim fleet. *(Courtesy of the National Maritime Museum, Greenwich, England)*

In an incident from the book, Captain Mathew Lowth captures Samuel Burgess at the Cape of Good Hope in 1699. Lowth celebrated by drawing this scene in his logbook. His ship is already in port, while the unsuspecting Burgess pilots his ship into the harbor. *(Courtesy of the India Office, London)*

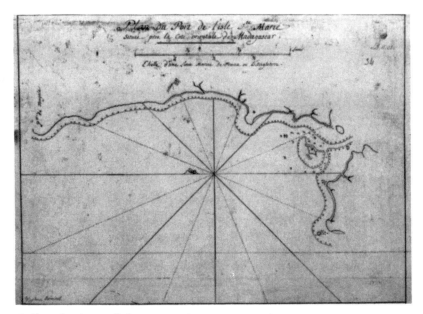

A French chart of the approaches to the harbor at the island of Saint Marie, drawn about 1760. The island at the mouth of the harbor and the narrow entrances made it easy for the pirates to prevent invaders from sailing in. *(Courtesy of the British Library)*

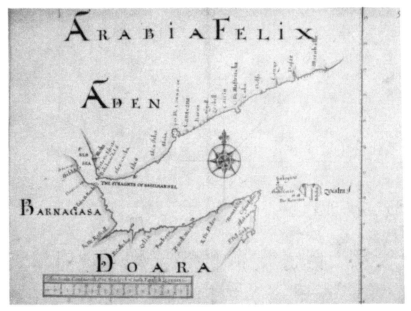

An early-seventeenth-century map depicting the strait of Babs-al-Mandab. Perim Island, where Kidd waited for the pilgrim fleet, is visible at the right side of the strait. *(From a collection of maps compiled by the Earl of Orford and given to the Crown in 1624; courtesy of the British Library)*

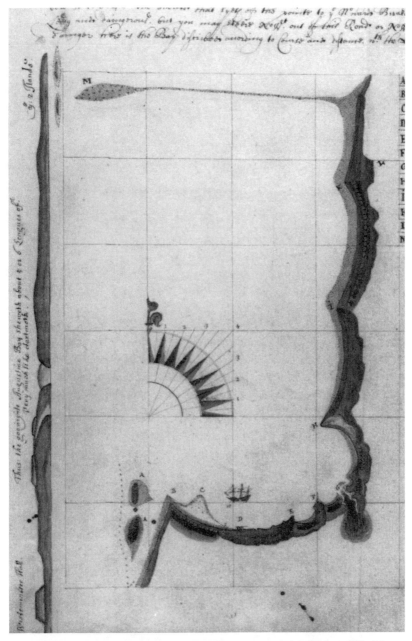

The bay of Saint Augustine, Madagascar, drawn by Charles Wylde in 1642. At the bottom are the land contours sighted upon approaching the harbor. Near the top is a long sandbar that protected the anchorage. The ship at *D* is in the best anchorage, and freshwater streams enter the bay at *G*. (*Courtesy of the University of Minnesota, James Ford Bell Library*)

Captain Jeremy Roch's watercolor of his ship, the *Charles Galley*. The *Adventure Galley* under oars probably looked much the same. (*Courtesy of the National Maritime Museum, Greenwich, England*)

A highly imaginative Dutch view of a tropical harbor, featuring an approaching sea spout. The men lounging about in broad-brimmed hats holding their guns are accurately drawn and could be a group of pirates. (*From the Special Collections of the University of California at San Diego*)

An eighteenth-century sketch of a pirate hanging at Execution Dock. Although not totally accurate, the drawing does give a sense of the public nature of the event. The man on the left bears the silver oar, symbol of the Admiralty. *(Courtesy of the National Maritime Museum, Greenwich, England)*

noted, while every rumor was solicited. Bellomont moved on to Fletcher's other crimes of embezzling public funds, lavishing estates on his friends, and fixing elections. As a parting shot Bellomont asked Fletcher to post a bond for the financial shortages in the colony's accounts before he left for England.

Once Fletcher was out of the way, his friends were vulnerable and Bellomont went after them. Brooke was removed as collector and eight members of the council were abruptly dismissed.[39] The new regime moved quickly against any hint of illicit commerce. When a customs searcher discovered East India goods in the home of Ouzel van Sweeten, officials went to seize them but were imprisoned in the house by an angry mob. Lieutenant Governor Nanfan promptly came to the rescue with soldiers from the garrison, who dispersed the crowd.[40] And so it went with Bellomont in full chase, ousting Fletcher's friends and installing Leislerians in their place. The changeover was symbolized one stormy day when a large crowd accompanied Bellomont to the gallows where the bodies of Leisler and his son-in-law Jacob Milborne were interred. The bodies were removed from the earth, carried to sanctified ground, and reinterred. Well over a thousand people attended the ceremony to witness the vindication of their slain leader.[41]

The anti-Leislerians could do very little against Bellomont in New York, but they could and did appeal to their friends in England to discredit him in the eyes of the government in London. Nicolas Bayard sailed to England to represent New York merchants and to arouse the support of English merchants who traded with New York. He accused Bellomont of engineering a Dutch majority in the Assembly, of undermining the Anglican church, and of allowing illegal trade to continue between the colony and Amsterdam.[42] Bayard and his allies also utterly denied the charges about an organized piracy trade in the colony. They did admit that ships went to Madagascar for slaves and occasionally were offered "India" goods that they bought cheaply and returned to New York; the goods were assumed to have mysteriously swum to the island on their own.[43] These attacks irritated Bellomont and represented a real danger to him because of the changed political kaleidoscope in England.

In London the Whigs were losing power, and the Tories moved to assail the Junto and their placemen such as Bellomont. William Blathwayt, leading figure in imperial affairs, friend of the Tories, and patron of Fletcher, accused Bellomont of laying New York "desolate" and driving out men of substance. One of his correspondents went so far as to suggest, "Id suppose the King will put a Stop to his Career."[44] So the accusations against Bellomont had to be taken seriously. He might end up out of office, with little hope of a place in a Tory regime, faced with a return to Ireland and penury. In desperation he struck back, urging his friends to defend him even as he wrote vigorous denunciations of his accusers. Never one to mince words, he slashed at his critics and continued to rout out their friends in New York.[45] By continuing to keep pressure on those engaged in the piracy trade, he could claim he was only following the government's orders and helping the East India Company, which he knew was an old ally of the Tories. When the four ships set out for Madagascar in June 1698, he tried to halt them; he suspected correctly that they were off to trade with pirates, but the still unreformed council refused to allow him to stop the ships as the trade was not proscribed by law. Bellomont reluctantly acquiesced to its opinion, but was vindicated a short time later when the Board of Trade informed him that the East India Company's new charter added Madagascar to its monopoly, so that all trade there needed company permission.[46] All he had to do was wait for the ships to return, for then he could seize them—a rather pleasant prospect, because he would benefit when they were condemned in his Vice Admiralty Court: he would get a share of the spoils by virtue of his commission, and his cause with the Tories would be advanced. Needless to say, the merchants were equally determined to make sure he failed. So as Kidd crept northward he was approaching a very tense situation with many men on the lookout for returning "Madagascar" ships.

In the spring of 1699, as Bellomont prepared to harvest a large crop of smugglers, the time arrived for him to leave New York. He had lived there for a year without visiting his other governments in New England. As the weather improved, he could no longer put off making an appearance, if for no other reason than to pick up his salary. Just before he left, Bellomont received his first real news about Kidd. The report stated that Kidd's men had forced him to plunder two ships and that they had almost killed him because he refused to turn pirate.[47] Because this story is so close to Kidd's prepared alibi, it may have been spread by Emott after he received a letter from Kidd. In any event, Bellomont went off to Boston uncertain of Kidd's fate and with some concern that he might now be the patron of an actual pirate, an event that would only bring smiles to his enemies' faces and put his career at risk.

If Kidd had hoped to sneak into New York and get a feel for the political climate, he was bitterly disappointed. By the time he finally appeared off Long Island, the whole coast was in an uproar. The first "Madagascar" ship to return in 1699 had been Giles Shelley's *Nassau*. Shelley, who had been in London with Kidd in 1695, was swept into the attack on Fletcher and, as a result, into Kidd's affairs as well. When he returned to New York, Shelley entered the Madagascar trade and by May 1699 was completing his second voyage. His first landfall then was Cape May in New Jersey, where the sloop of Henry Gravenraedt of New York City lay waiting to intercept him. Some of Shelley's passengers went ashore, while Gravenraedt went on ahead bearing messages to Shelley's partners. By this time the New York merchants had built a system of rendezvous to thwart overeager officials. After Stephen de Lancey and John Barbarie, Shelley's partners, received the good news that his cargo consisted of muslins, calicoes, opium, ivory, slaves, 12,000 pieces of eight, and 3,000 Lion dollars, they set out to ensure that none of it got away from them. Shelley was instructed to move to Sandy Hook, at the edge of New York harbor, where de Lancey joined him. Some of the most valuable parts of the cargo were offloaded and brought into the city that night. Afterward Shelley drove his leaky ship ashore at Red Hook on Long Island, where the rest of the cargo followed circuitous paths into the city. Once again rich pirates enjoyed the local hospitality while merchants counted their gains.[48]

Lieutenant Governor John Nanfan, Bellomont's brother-in-law and acting governor in New York, could hardly ignore the jingle of ready cash in the streets. Some of Culliford's men had returned with

Shelley and—unless they were unlucky gamblers—they all had their shares. A rumor circulated in the city that one man had won 2,400 pieces of eight in a single roll of the dice.[49] Nanfan asked Shelley to come to see him, but when Shelley appeared he would admit to nothing more than a slave-trading voyage to Madagascar. There was no evidence against him, so Nanfan could not arrest him, much as he would have liked to do so. The pirates, well protected by locals, were slipped out of the city; the illicit goods were carefully hidden and Nanfan's agents found very little of the cargo.[50] Nanfan could not allow the merchants to frustrate the government, so he finally called Shelley before the council in an attempt to browbeat him. Shelley maintained his composure, and all Nanfan could do was put him under a £5,000 bond for good behavior. Shelley had no trouble raising the money.[51] Nanfan also seized Edward Buckmaster, Kidd's old neighbor, and Otto van Toyle, another resident of the city, and imprisoned them as pirates. Buckmaster provided Nanfan with his first real information about Kidd, a vague report that stated Kidd had made "no good voyage."[52]

Just prior to Shelley's return Joseph Bradish and the crew of the *Adventure* had also arrived on the coast. These men had originally signed on in London for a voyage to Borneo. When the ship stopped for water in the Spice Islands, Captain Thomas Gullock and most of the officers and passengers went ashore to break the monotony of the very long voyage. A number of the crew decided that this moment was the opportune one to take the ship and the cargo, which was mostly precious metals. Those who would not join the mutineers were put on boats and sent ashore with the bad news, while the remaining men elected Bradish captain. The mutineers had plenty of time at sea to count their booty, which came to £1,600 per man plus a share of the goods (Bradish enjoyed two and one-half shares). With this tidy sum for a few minutes' work, the men decided to return home. Their first stop was at Mauritius, where they replenished their supplies. They set off again, not stopping until they reached Ascension Island. Like Kidd, they thought it best to avoid settlements.[53]

By late March they were passing along the sandy coastline of Long Island, where they made their first stop. Bradish's birthplace was Cambridge, Massachusetts, but he did not want to return there with his fortune until he knew what sort of reception he would get. So the ship stopped off Long Island while he made a deal with Colonel Henry Pierson, who agreed to store his booty. The *Adventure* next appeared at Block Island, near Rhode Island, where the crew sighted sloops coming toward them. Fearing the worst, they turned around and headed out to sea, but the 350-ton ship was no match for the swift sloops. As soon as they were alongside, the men on the sloops made it clear that their intentions were dishonorable and that they had come to trade. Crew and booty went over the side into the sloops, and once the *Adventure* had been stripped, it was sunk. Upon reaching land, the men bought horses and promptly dispersed throughout New England. But the alarm had been raised. Before long many of the pirates decorated the jails in Rhode Island, Connecticut, and Massachusetts. Bradish and ten others were captured and jailed, but on June 25 he and a companion escaped. Bellomont, by now in Massachusetts, sent Indians after them; the two were taken in Saco, Maine, and brought back to Boston.[54] Bellomont had arrested his first pirates.

If Bradish and his men created an uproar in New England, the men who left Shelley's ship in New Jersey and New York did the same in the middle colonies. Robert Quary, the new customs collector for Pennsylvania, issued an alarm that Kidd was hovering off the coast and set out to hunt for him, managing to capture two men.[55] Jeremiah Basse, the new governor of the Jerseys and self-proclaimed expert on illegal trade, immediately set out in a sloop when he heard that Shelley was near the coast. He found and arrested six men and seized their chests containing 7,800 rix dollars, 30 pounds of silver, assorted gold coins, jewelry, and silks.[56]

Quary and Basse were typical of the new officials who believed in the antipiracy campaign and disregarded the local inhabitants who loved the easy money the pirates brought with them. Their activities, combined with the alarm sounded by the arrival of Bradish and his men, meant that the coast from Maine to Maryland was thoroughly aroused with reports of pirates galloping across the countryside, pirate ships skulking just over the horizon, and rowboats filled with treasure slipping up every river. Kidd sailed into the middle of this excitement, when every eye on the coast searched for sails and every head dreamed of fortunes.

When the *Saint Antonio* arrived at Whorekills in lower Delaware Bay in early June, it met (perhaps by prearrangement) a sloop from New York City. The ships stayed together for two days while men, bales, and chests transferred out of the *Saint Antonio*. The next stop was Orient Point on the north shore of Long Island. It seems unlikely that Kidd ventured up the East River, thereby passing the city; he probably went around the east end of the island and down Long Island Sound to the harbor at Oyster Pond Bay. Kidd's wife and daughters, accompanied by James Emott, were waiting. After nearly three years and many miles Kidd was reunited with his family and friend.[57]

When the talk finally turned to business, the conversation centered on what sort of response to Kidd Bellomont would make. Did the antipiracy campaign include Kidd, or did the alibi so carefully nurtured since Saint Marie have a chance? It would appear that it did, for in May Bellomont had written to the Board of Trade: "I am in hopes the several reports we have here of Captain Kid's being forced by his men against his will to plunder two Moorish ships may prove true. And 'tis said near 100 of his men revolted from him at Madagascar and were about to kill him because he absolutely refused to turn pirate."[58] So the weathervane of Bellomont's opinion moved in Kidd's favor. But could Bellomont protect him from a government bent on prosecuting pirates? That question could only be answered by his lordship, and Kidd decided he would not confront him. Emott was sent on to Boston while Kidd remained behind with his family.[59]

Late on Tuesday, June 13, 1699, Emott was ushered into Bellomont's presence in Boston. He brought a letter from his friend, and Bellomont heard for the first time the "truth" behind the rumors: Kidd had taken two ships, both of which were legal prizes, and had resisted the efforts of his men to turn pirate. Afterward they had threatened him with murder, robbed him of his papers, and left with Culliford. The new elements of the story were that the *Adventure Galley* was lost, but that Kidd had managed to sail the *Quedah* to a safe and secret berth in the West Indies, where she lay with £30,000 worth of goods in her hold while Kidd brought

£10,000 with him. Emott followed up with a proposal. If Bello-mont would promise to pardon Kidd and a few of his loyal men, he would come to Boston and surrender himself. This offer might have raised a few doubts about Kidd. If everything was as Emott reported, why did Kidd want the guarantee of a pardon? Bellomont could only quiz Emott on every aspect of the voyage until he had satisfied himself that he was dealing with an honest man, or at least a reasonable facsimile thereof. He decided, before proceeding further, to send Emott back to Kidd to obtain some proof of his statements.

While still in Boston Emott contacted Duncan Campbell, a fellow Scot and friend of Kidd, who joined him on his return voyage to meet Kidd near Block Island. While Emott had been negotiating with Bellomont, Kidd had moved to the eastern end of Long Island, where he sailed back and forth near Gardiner's Island. As before, whenever the ship neared land, boats came out to carry away goods and money. Carsten Leursen captained one of the sloops and could confirm for some of the men that the chests they gave him on Madagascar had been safely delivered in New York. Along with the gold, silver, cloth, slaves, and bags of money transferred from one ship to the other, some of the passengers also left. In the case of John Harrison, his parents came to take their son home. The days passed with sporadic activity that broke the suspense of waiting for Emott to return.[60] When the two Scots did arrive, their discussions centered on how to reassure Bellomont. The decision was to turn over to him the two French passes found on the ships captured in the Indian Ocean. With those in hand the two emissaries returned to Boston.

They arrived on June 19 and met immediately with Bellomont, who was suffering a painful gout attack. After the meeting Bellomont was sufficiently recovered to go to the Massachusetts council and discuss the situation. He later asserted that he had done nothing without first consulting the council, but to this point he had carried on negotiations without ever informing the members. Emott and Campbell, testifying to the council about their contact with Kidd, related his story. Bellomont reported on letters from the governor of Rhode Island and from Thomas Paine of Jamestown, Rhode Island, about Kidd's presence in Long Island Sound. His final document was a copy of the Rhode Island proclamation declaring Kidd a pirate, as ordered by the lords justices on November 26. We can only assume that he glossed over the fact that he had never issued such a document in New York and Massachusetts (he had received a similar order but for his own reasons had kept it secret).[61] After these presentations Bellomont asked the council to advise him on his best course. The members agreed that he should continue to negotiate with Kidd and that if all was as Kidd stated it would be appropriate to request a pardon from the king. Bellomont then wrote a letter to Kidd more or less reprising Kidd's story and adding that he knew several persons in New York who could corroborate it if need be. After these reassurances he stated that the council had agreed that Kidd could come "safely" to Boston, where he could get the supplies he needed to make the *Quedah Merchant* seaworthy. His letter ended with promises:

> I make no manner of doubt but to obtaine the King's pardon for you . . . I assure you on my word and honour I will performe nicely what I have now promised tho this I declare before hand that whatever treasure or goods you bring hither I will not meddle with . . . they shall be left with Such trusty as the council will advise until I receive order from England.[62]

The words of a true friend, or a well-baited trap?

When Kidd received this letter, he felt secure enough to turn the *Saint Antonio* toward Boston. He sent a message ahead to Bellomont announcing his intention and took the opportunity to excuse himself for his careful approach, blaming it on the rumors that made him "fearfull" about steering into any harbor. Once again he repeated the core of his alibi and blamed everything on his men. Before closing, Kidd put forth an argument that probably aided him with those who regarded him suspiciously—if he were guilty, why would he come back to Boston when there were so many other places he could go in safety?[63] As a sign of his good intentions he sent Lady Bellomont an enameled box with four jewels in it. By not sending it to his lordship, Kidd helped him keep his promise not to have anything to do with the treasure.[64] Nevertheless, he could be sure that Bellomont's mind never strayed far from that subject.

Bellomont sat waiting in Boston, pondering his next move.

Bradish had just escaped, inflaming the governor's gout and doing nothing for his temper. Every day he sat with the Massachusetts council and conducted business as usual. The council was involved in the tedious but politically important business of choosing justices of the peace for the counties. After spending Friday, June 30, putting the list together, Bellomont and the council agreed to meet on Saturday to finish up. When Saturday arrived, Bellomont sent a message pleading that an indisposition kept him from attending the meeting. The "indisposition" was not his ever-present gout but Kidd, and the astute members of the council could easily put together the strange ship in the harbor and his lordship's illness.

Although later on Bellomont always claimed that he acted only in concert with the council and never spoke to Kidd without witnesses, there are no records of their discussions this Saturday or the following Sunday.[65] We may never know the details, but it is not difficult to guess their topic. Kidd's task was to convince Bellomont of the veracity of his story, while Bellomont pushed him for details and did his own mental calculations on the danger Kidd presented to his career. He was under royal command to capture Kidd; yet to do so meant violating a contract with the Whig lords, whose power was ebbing but still very real and who were also his sponsors. Could he deny and perhaps endanger his patrons by striking a deal with Kidd? Another issue intertwined with this one. The reason he was now in America was his poor financial condition, which had not improved in New York—a source of great concern to him. It cost him £1,500 per year to live in New York City, "this extravagant dear place."[66] Food and housing were far more expensive than he had imagined, and he was haunted by the thought that "I shall have to return home as rich as I came abroad, which gives me many a Melancholy reflection."[67] If he could not get his salary raised, he wanted permission to return to England. At least now he probably had some insight into why Fletcher took presents and bribes. Even though he could have done the same, Bellomont appears to have run a clean administration, which was for him a road to the poorhouse.[68]

Kidd represented a way out of his difficulties. He allegedly had with him £10,000, with another £30,000 in the West Indies. If true, these figures meant that the partnership had made £40,000 from Kidd's voyage. After costs of approximately £6,000 were deducted, the partners would net £34,000, with certainly no more than £5,000 going to Bellomont. Then he would have to relieve Harrison's "Presbyterian grip," thereby further diminishing his share to perhaps less than £1,000.[69] A nice sum—but not much, in view of the high hopes at the beginning of the voyage. Bellomont, however, had an alternative set of figures that came down decisively in his favor. If he arrested Kidd as a pirate, in his role as vice admiral he would get a third of any loot he seized. One-third of £40,000 was £13,000, and none of it could be claimed by Harrison. If he then brought the other partners in for "snacks," or shares, he would keep their favor.[70] By taking this path and arresting Kidd, Bellomont would also fulfill the orders of the increasingly Tory government at home and in so doing protect his position in America. So the rough, weatherbeaten sea captain fought to keep his freedom by arguing his case, while the smooth politician considered the danger to his career and the profits to be made from the desperate man before him.

When their private meetings ended, Bellomont told Kidd to be ready to go before the council on Monday to repeat his story. Until then he was free to visit his friends and give out a few rewards. To Campbell he presented a slave plus some cloth and promised him £500 if he helped Kidd win a pardon. Lady Bellomont received another present, this time a gold bar; but on the advice of her husband she returned it. Robert Livingston by this time had caught up with Kidd and arrived in Boston to protect his interest; after all, he had put up the money for Kidd's £10,000 bond. He must have been disappointed to learn that Kidd had far less than the £500,000 Livingston at one time believed him to have. To assuage the disappointment, Kidd gave him a slave and told him that he had a forty-pound bag of gold that he had kept secretly hidden until he knew how the wind blew.[71] In New York Bellomont's friends and enemies also waited to check the wind. His friends hoped he would be "prudent"; his enemies were ready to denounce him if his anti-piracy campaign proved to have a blind spot.[72] Bellomont had done nothing publicly at this point to declare his intentions, so his options were still open.

At six in the evening on Monday, July 3, Kidd appeared before the council to plead his case. The members heard him out, then asked for a full accounting of his goods. He reeled off bales of calicoes, silks, and muslins; tons of sugar, iron, and saltpeter; anchors; fifty cannon; eighty pounds of silver—and now, for the first time, publicly revealed the forty-pound bag of gold. The councilors could do their sums as well as anyone and came up with a handsome amount. At the end of his presentation the council asked Kidd to prepare a narrative of his voyage for their consideration, plus a written account of his cargo. To be on the safe side, Bellomont sent men aboard the *Saint Antonio* to make sure the cargo remained untouched.[73] The next day Kidd appeared before them again. He came without his narrative, which he had been unable to complete, but with five of his men, who turned in sworn affidavits of their voyage. The councilors sent for him again on July 6, and when he appeared he pleaded that he still needed more time to finish his written account. This time the council insisted and told him to return at five with the document in hand.[74]

While the council negotiated, Bellomont had decided to spring a trap. Clearly the most profitable course was to arrest Kidd, and by this time Bellomont knew he had to act soon or Kidd might escape. He later explained that he felt Kidd looked very guilty in his appearances before the council, and with each appearance his doubts grew. It also appeared to him that the three Scots—Kidd, Campbell, and Livingston—were conspiring to embezzle the cargo. Livingston also threatened him: if Bellomont did not return Livingston's bond for Kidd's good behavior, Kidd would reimburse him from the cargo on the *Quedah*. Livingston denied these statements, but whether or not they were true does not matter, for the real reason lay in Bellomont's accounts.[75] Bellomont called in Lieutenant Governor Stoughton and a few members of the council to show them the orders from England expressly telling him to arrest Kidd—orders he had previously denied receiving, or glossed over. Stoughton and the others responded by telling Bellomont that Kidd had to be arrested, so he issued to the constable a warrant for Kidd's arrest. The constable searched for a while around Boston without finding Kidd until he returned to Bellomont's quarters. There, just ahead of him, Kidd approached the door to keep his appointment with the council. The constable seized Kidd, who wrestled away and rushed inside shouting for Bellomont, with the constable hard on his heels. Inside, the constable subdued Kidd and dragged him, still shouting, to jail. With Kidd's cries ringing in his ears, Bellomont could start to count his profits.[76]

EIGHT

Winners and Losers

nce the unquestioned master of his own ship, Kidd now found himself confined to the small stone prison in Boston. It was a jail that regularly leaked prisoners. Bellomont had fired the jailer who allowed Joseph Bradish to escape, and prevented another attempt when someone nearly succeeded in slipping James Kelley a 5½-foot crowbar. To make sure Kidd stayed put, Bellomont gave the sheriff a substantial raise. So Kidd and his crew shivered away the winter, recalling happier days in the tropics, until the sheriff relented and let them have some warm clothing.[1] Bellomont meanwhile continued to round up as many pirates as he could and went as far as sending a ship to the West Indies to hunt for Kidd's treasure.[2]

Kidd languished in jail. As long as he was at sea in command of the *Saint Antonio* he could determine events, but now he had lost control of his destiny. He was like a cork in the grip of a whirlpool. Forces and men beyond his grasp would determine his fate, and he would be sucked inward and downward to eventual destruction. He discovered the other side of patronage. To date it had always propelled him upward as smiling men rewarded him. Now he would discover that great men in danger would cast down everyone around them without a by-your-leave in order to save themselves. For a while they would still need Kidd, for he could be brought out and displayed like a puppet. But when his usefulness came to an end, he would be discarded to continue his downward plunge.

Just as the rumors about Kidd had preceded his arrival in the

West Indies, so now a similar spate of tales spread throughout London. When a rumor circulated in 1697 to the effect that Kidd was raiding in the Red Sea, Harrison rushed forward to reassure the other investors that Kidd could not possibly have arrived in Asia already.[3] But the awful truth could not be denied when in August 1698 the East India Company received the first letters from India detailing Kidd's activities. As in the colonies, gossip focused on the size of his fortune; the talk was that Kidd was worth £400,000.[4] Calmer heads rejected such an outrageous sum, but every time the amount rose, Kidd's notoriety increased and anxiety about his whereabouts grew. Harrison took careful note of all the rumors and repeated only three. One stated that Kidd had surrendered on Bellomont's terms; the second was the converse and claimed that Kidd had returned to sea because he distrusted Bellomont; and the third was that Kidd proposed giving £20,000 to anyone who could obtain a pardon for him. Harrison's own conclusions were that Kidd was near New York and would be taken there.[5]

Finally, the joyous news of Bellomont's success arrived in England, and by September 1 it was confirmed and quickly spread about. King William was promptly informed and reported to be very pleased. Shortly afterward Sir James Vernon wrote a long follow-up letter giving the king all the details. With such royal concern, certainly Kidd was not regarded as an ordinary felon.[6] The lords justices immediately ordered the Admiralty to dispatch a ship to return Kidd to England—a singular event, for many government officials lacked a naval escort when taking up or leaving office in the colonies. The Admiralty ordered the *Rochester* to sail to Boston so that none could doubt the government's intentions.[7] The ship left England on September 27, 1699, but on November 6 Captain Gerard Elwes turned back after his ship was crippled by a savage winter storm. By November 24 he was in Plymouth, and gossip immediately spread about the reasons why. Doubts were raised about the true condition of the *Rochester,* because some felt it might be part of a devilish Junto plot to keep Kidd away from England. Captain Elwes spent a great deal of time verifying to experts the condition of his ship and his need to return to port. The House of Commons even demanded a report on his activities.[8] In a further effort to dispel the gossip, the government dispatched the *Advice* to Boston; this ship did manage the difficult winter voyage to bring back the infamous pirate.[9]

The extraordinary care taken to assure Kidd's speedy and safe return to England testified to important political events that made him a pawn in a deadly game. During 1696–1697 the Whig Junto was at the height of its influence. They attacked the Tories when ninety of them refused to sign an Association (or Declaration of Loyalty) declaring that King William, not James II, was the true king. The Whigs immediately asked that all nonsignatories be kept from office and preferment. They followed this with other measures, particularly the financing of the ever more expensive war, and reaped their rewards. Montague was made the first Lord of the Treasury, Somers became Lord Chancellor with a barony, and Russell was created the Earl of Orford. During sessions of Parliament these men met daily at one another's homes; if they needed to meet with larger groups, they favored the Rose Tavern. Their very success contributed to a general unhappiness with them and to a weakness in their organization. The spate of honors fell upon so few heads that some loyal Whigs looked askance as the Junto kept rising while others were left behind. Another problem arose when so many individuals accepted peerages and left the House of Commons for the House of Lords, weakening their control over the debates and volatile proceedings of the Commons. In moving to the Lords, they were forsaking the institution that had made their ascendance possible.

As the war marched to its conclusion in 1697, the country's discontent with the government moved into the open. Long years of high wartime taxes were resented and the thought of having to support a large standing army after the war was over made many shudder. The Tories moved to the attack during the summer of 1698, when an election allowed them the opportunity to rouse the country. When the polls closed, fewer Whigs returned to Westminster. The Junto could still manage the Commons, but to do so they needed all their friends and their long experience. Unfortunately for them, some had no stomach for the struggle. Shrewsbury finally convinced the king that he no longer wanted to be the chief secretary of state and was allowed to resign. Montague decided that he had had enough of defending himself from charges of malfeasance at the Treasury and slipped away to the more lucrative, if minor, office of Teller of the Exchequer. Even the feisty Orford wilted when he came under fire for holding the position of First Lord of the Admiralty as well as that of Treasurer of the Navy, and he finally resigned both. The Junto crumbled as each left the ministry, to be replaced with a moderate Tory or a lackluster Whig. The Tories won a signal victory when Sir Robert Harley, fast becoming their best parliamentary leader, proposed to cut the king's hoped-for army from 20,000 to 7,000 men, excluding William's beloved Dutch guards. The Whigs refused to fight hard against this bill, as many of their own followers despised the idea of a standing army. When the bill passed, the king felt betrayed by a ministry unwilling to fight for his program. By 1699 the Junto was a shadow of its former self and the Tories had taken the measure of its weakness. In November Parliament was recalled. The Tories prepared to oust the last of the Junto and take their revenge for all the indignities visited upon them.[10]

The news that Kidd had turned pirate provided the Tories with yet another cudgel with which to beat their foes. At about the time the Board of Trade began ordering colonial governments to hunt Kidd down, the Whigs began to appreciate the danger he posed for them. The Old East India Company knew immediately that it had a fine political issue in the Kidd affair. As Somers put it, the merchants would "make the most malicious use of it they can." The company had no love for the Whigs, who had furthered the cause of the New East India Company, and as a result bore a "mortal grudge" toward the Junto.[11]

Until Kidd appeared in the flesh, the directors of the Old Company were content to build a case against him and to publicize the problem of pirates. In August and September of 1698 they presented various witnesses testifying to conditions on Madagascar, the supplies the pirates received from New York, and the activities of a number of infamous pirates. But the company's leaders never lost sight of Kidd, and in August they produced two prize witnesses. Benjamin Franks and Jonathan Tredway had been rushed back from

India on the *Charles* and on August 22 they testified before the Board of Trade regarding their voyage.[12] The company also carried on a whispering campaign about Kidd's sponsors, whose identities were not yet well known outside the partnership; when the company discovered papers tying the Junto to Kidd, the campaign accelerated. The arrival in London of weekly information on pirates created a growing demand for action. Fortuitously for the company, the *Frederick* of New York was caught in Hamburg trading in East Indies goods, testimony to the way in which the colonies flaunted trade legislation, traded with pirates, and disposed of the loot. The cries for action grew louder. It was hardly the time for the ministry to be identified with pirates.[13]

By November 1698, members of the Junto knew they had to take action. On orders from Shrewsbury, Sir James Vernon urged Harrison to gather all the official documents relating to the venture (apparently none of the partners had copies). Vernon believed the Old East India Company would take the issue to Parliament, where it would be "a handle for clamour."[14] Montague even feared he would be impeached for his participation in the partnership. While the others tried to reassure him, they recognized that they could not leave the issue to the company, whose intentions were to join with the Tories and hound the Junto. Their response was to meet in early December at Powys House (Somers' home) and map strategy. Montague, Orford, and Harrison discussed their problem with Somers and decided that if Harrison were confronted in the Commons about the partnership, he should reveal the participants—even if, as Somers put it, "we may appear somewhat rediculous."[15] All they could do was wait to see if Kidd returned from the wastes of the Indian Ocean. Then, like a nemesis, he sailed into Boston.

By this time only Somers continued to serve in the ministry, but his new office of lord chancellor kept him in the House of Lords, leaving Vernon to represent the Junto's interests in the Commons and the ministry. Vernon was a shrewd, knowledgeable observer and participant in English politics. His career represented the rewards of diligence and self-effacement. His first jobs after graduation from Oxford were in Holland and France, working for various English ministers. By 1671 he was secretary to Charles II's illegitimate son, the Duke of Monmouth. He left the duke in 1678 to become editor of the government's newspaper, the *London Gazette,* a post attached to the office of the secretary of state. His great patron and benefactor proved to be the Duke of Shrewsbury, whose service he first entered in 1688. As the duke's fortunes rose, so did Vernon's. By 1695 he had entered Parliament as a Whig and a ministerial loyalist.

When Shrewsbury returned to office in March 1694, Vernon went with him and gradually became the acting secretary of state (because Shrewsbury's frequent illnesses drove him from London). He carried on a near-daily correspondence with Shrewsbury and acted as his agent with the Junto. On December 5, 1697, in recognition of his performance, he was allowed to control the secretary's seals. When Shrewsbury retired a year later, Vernon was vaulted into the office and put on the Privy Council. He was humbled by the office, as well he might have been, because he lacked the political power normally associated with the secretary. When the assignment was first proposed to him, he demurred. Vernon had lost all his teeth after a bout of "scurvy" and, as he put it, being "without quality, without friends, without an estate, without elocution, and without everything that is proper for it, [it] is [like] dressing up a ridiculous figure to be hooted at."[16] In his darkest moment of introspection he thought he should "fill my pockets with stones and leap overboard under the bridge."[17] Such was the stout shield upon which rested Junto fortunes in the ministry.

Bellomont wrote to Vernon directly about his famed prisoner. Vernon knew immediately that while it was important for Bellomont to have captured Kidd, it would have been better for Kidd to have been swallowed by the sea. The whole board of directors of the Old East India Company trooped to a meeting of the lords justices to make "all the bustle about it they can."[18] They demanded the treasure in Bellomont's hands (estimated at £14,000) to compensate Kidd's victims and to relieve the pressure on the company in India. Until Parliament met, they lacked a stage on which to punish the Junto, and when it did meet, the Old Company's leaders and the Tories wanted to pull down the Junto once and for all. Their arena was the House of Commons.

Saint Stephen's Chapel lay within the precincts of Westminster Palace and had long served as the meeting place for the House of Commons. Sir Christopher Wren had overseen its renovations in 1692 and had provided the Commons with a spacious and handsome chamber with two galleries running along the north and south sides of the chamber. Below the galleries were four tiers of green painted benches, where the active members of the House sat within easy earshot of the whole chamber. Unfortunately, Wren lowered the ceiling of the new chamber and provided it with too few windows. As a result, it was extremely hot and stuffy when the members packed in for big debates.[19] On December 1, 1699, a large crowd gathered to witness an attack upon Somers. The oratory was impassioned enough to keep even the most torpid Tory backwoodsman awake.

The occasion was a debate on the trade of the nation. Arthur Moore, a leading member of the Old East India Company, lost no time in pointing out the despicable way Kidd's partners had encouraged him to steal the goods of honest merchants. Jack Howe, a Tory firebrand given to vituperation whenever he discussed Whigs, followed with a speech denouncing a government that sent its own thieves to graze among upright traders. Sir Charles Musgrave rose to deplore such a horrid turn of events and demanded that the guilty parties be punished. After allowing the wolves their chance to howl and gnash their teeth, the House decided to examine the matter closely and ordered the clerk to place before the House all official documents relating to Kidd's commission, the merchants' complaints against piracy, Kidd's activities, and the government's actions toward him.[20]

Before the next day's parliamentary session Powys House again was the scene of an anxious meeting. Somers, Montague, Orford, Vernon, and others met to determine what papers they needed to place before the Commons and how to shape their case. Somers wanted no delay in admitting openly who stood behind the names on the commission and how much it cost to outfit Kidd. While rumors still circulated about the Junto and Kidd, there had not been an open admission of its role. With candor as their shield, the Whigs returned to battle.[21]

Three days later William Loundes, secretary to the Treasury, brought to the House all of the required records. Sir William Blathwayt added papers submitted by the East India Company, and Vernon added to the substantial pile the accounts of the ministry's actions from the first notice of Kidd's turning pirate until the orders to bring him home. The Tories wanted to reject Vernon's papers, preferring to consider only the legality of the grant; but in the end the members decided to see the whole body of evidence. Howe was quickly on his feet again to rouse the Tories and to move that the original grant to the Junto regarding Kidd be declared illegal. The emerging Tory leader Harley, a bitter foe of the Junto, moved to declare the grant illegal and prejudicial to the trade of the nation. This motion struck directly at Somers who, as Lord Keeper at the time it was issued, had to approve using the Great Seal on the document. Each side of the aisle then sent its orators forward. While the Tories wanted to call the question immediately, the Whigs argued that it was hardly fair to vote without having read all the evidence. In this way they managed to put off the vote for two days, when the House would again sit as a committee of the whole.[22]

At noon on December 6 the Commons met for the climactic debate and vote of censure of the Junto. The Tories concentrated on the illegality of the original grant and generally avoided hyperbole, except for Howe who denounced "ye avarice of ye Great."[23] Because the commission issued to Kidd named the pirates he was to seize and granted him possession of their goods, they charged violation of an Act of Parliament that forbade giving away a felon's property until after he or she was convicted, when the king could claim it. The king was only the trustee for the goods, however, until the merchants who owned them could file claims and have their property returned by legal process. Thus the grant was dishonorable to the king, against the law of nations, contrary to the laws and statutes of the realm, invasive of property, and destructive of trade and commerce. In the words of Edward Seymour, this grant "beggard Ireland, set Scotland in a flame and ruined England."[24]

Although the Tories wanted to fight along this line, the Whigs preferred the larger perspective. Vernon rose to give an account of the whole affair, beginning with Livingston's introduction of Kidd to Bellomont and continuing to Bellomont's arrest of Kidd in Boston. The session continued after daylight faded and suppertime passed. The Whigs also dealt with the legal aspects of the matter: for over two hundred years the Lord Admiral had been granted all pirates' goods as an encouragement to suppress pirates. At the present time the Admiralty was run by a commission and the king reserved certain rights to himself, among them a claim to pirates' loot. This conclusion was brought home to the dominant landed interests in the House, for they were reminded that almost every manor lord had the grant of felons' goods, and if this grant were disallowed, there would be "a great shaking of property." Sir Richard Cocks, a loyal Whig, lauded the Junto for sending a thief to catch a thief. He reminded the dwindling audience that in 1695, because the government did not have the men or ships to send against the pirates, the ministers sent a ship at their own cost and hazard. He ended by stating, "I would rather trust my estate with these gentlemen than with any I know of."[25]

As the debate moved into its ninth hour, more and more of the Tories slipped away, driven either by the need to eat or by a desire not to threaten property rights. When the question was finally called at 9:00 P.M., the Whigs carried the day, 189 to 133, leaving the Tories to eat gall and complain about their missing members. There was an interesting reaction outside Parliament that confirmed the alliance between city financial circles and the Whigs—for the Public Fund, which had been declining for a week, rose by 1.5 percent the next day.[26]

Vernon believed the Whigs had carried the day because the Tory leadership, sure of its numbers, meant to strike a killing blow against Somers. But even its own members had blanched in the heat of the attack on the chancellor and the "willful" dismissal of the facts. They might have agreed to "a gentle censure," but they were not given that choice. Vernon was quietly content, for "a majority of 56 is thought no small matter as this House is constituted."[27] The Whigs might be in retreat, but they still had enough strength to protect their great men from censure. Somers continued to hold office and to retain the king's confidence; Kidd, though, bound for

England, would have to be dealt with before he did permanent damage. As Vernon put it, "parliaments are grown into the habit of finding fault, and some Jonah or other must be thrown overboard, if the storm cannot otherwise be laid . . . Little men are certainly the properest for these purposes."[28] Kidd was a very little man.

Meanwhile the frigate *Advice* beat its way across the Atlantic through gale after gale until on February 2, 1700, Cape Cod came into view. Captain Robert Wynn lost no time anchoring in Boston harbor and paying his respects to Bellomont. Two weeks later Kidd was sent aboard and confined to a small cabin in steerage—a bitterly cold place to be as ice swirled around the ship. By March 11 Wynn passed Cape Cod, outward bound with thirty-two prisoners locked safely below decks. After a voyage of less than a month, wind and weather defeated Wynn's attempts to get the *Advice* into the English Channel, so he put into Lundy's Island and sent letters ahead to London advising the government of his arrival.[29]

By this time Vernon had been joined in his office by the Earl of Jersey, newly appointed secretary of state, who now acted as the senior secretary. A moderate Tory, Jersey was willing to leave the work to Vernon, while making sure that Tory interests were not overlooked. Wynn's letter put Vernon into a state of apprehension; he feared that Kidd might not arrive in London before the end of the parliamentary session. "If this fellow is to lie in prison the whole summer, one cannot tell what lessons he may be taught by winter."[30] Vernon wanted Kidd kept quiet and untutored and if possible brought early before the Commons, then speedily tried and executed. Members of the House told him, however, that it would be impossible to interview Kidd before the Commons went home. He and Orford therefore agreed that the king should be asked to send one of his yachts to the Downs to intercept Kidd before he arrived in London. Kidd could then be brought to the city, where the cabinet could interview him before he went to the Marshalsea, the Admiralty's prison. When the Privy Council met the next day, it took this advice and ordered the Admiralty to send a yacht with an Admiralty marshal and a royal messenger, to make sure Kidd spoke to no one and sent no messages.[31]

The object of all this attention lay sick aboard the *Advice*. The trip had given him ample time to consider his situation; he was kept apart from the crew and the thirty-one other pirates on board and was served by the captain's servant only. By the time the *Advice* sailed into the Thames, Kidd was unfit to face the ordeal before him.[32] Ill though he was, he wrote to Orford and Montague setting out his case. He enclosed a copy of the protest he had written in Boston, which gave a sketchy and highly inaccurate account of his voyage. The most glaring omission was any mention of the Red Sea. Kidd stated that he had gone directly to the coast of India where he had fought the Portuguese, had friendly relations with the East India Company, and taken only two ships, both of which flew French colors. He accused his men of trying to force him to commit piracy but claimed he had managed to resist them until they went over to Culliford at Saint Marie. After they had robbed him and destroyed his records, he had managed to sail home—only to find himself declared a pirate. "I am in hopes your Lordship and the rest of the Honorable gentlemen my owners will so far vindicate me I may have no injustice."[33] If an appeal to justice did not bring them around, he hinted at irregularities in the care of his treasure in Boston and at the fortune awaiting in the West Indies for him to recover for them.

These letters never reached Montague and Orford, for like everything associated with Kidd they were treated with caution and turned over to the Admiralty. No welcome note from his sponsors greeted him. Instead John Cheeke, the Admiralty messenger, seized him and his effects and marched him off between a file of soldiers to the royal yacht, the *Katherine,* where he was kept incommunicado while the ship moved to Greenwich.[34]

Meanwhile Vernon's plan went awry. He had caught King William's attention prior to a cabinet meeting and discussed his efforts to isolate Kidd and have him interviewed by the cabinet; the king had agreed, adding that he thought it best the plan be brought before the Commons. Vernon demurred, mentioning the busy schedule of the House as it attempted to finish its business: the members of the House might see such an attempt as disruptive. King William did not press the issue, but when the Earl of Jersey raised Kidd's near-presence before the cabinet, the king decided the Commons must be told immediately. Vernon was given the job, and on December 12 carried out his orders. As soon as he sat down, George Churchill (brother of the soon-to-be Duke of Marlborough), who had been appointed to the Lords of the Admiralty to serve Tory interests, rose to acknowledge that the Admiralty had ordered a yacht to go after Kidd and that the lords now needed some direction on how to treat their prisoner. Shortly thereafter, perhaps on cue, Harley proposed that no one involved in Kidd's crime be present at the interview. This stipulation was quickly agreed to, with the added proviso that all of Kidd's papers sent by Bellomont were to remain in the Admiralty office. So Vernon's plan to have Kidd interviewed in the more friendly confines of the cabinet, where Somers could listen and interpolate, was undone.[35]

Before this interview the Admiralty wanted to examine the papers sent by Bellomont. Vernon and Jersey turned over the boxes of letters sent on the *Advice,* and what happened subsequently caused many to wonder about Vernon's loyalty to his friends. In the past he had followed a course of openness as the best policy (because in the long run the Tories in the Commons would drag out the truth anyway). But Vernon carried this policy one step too far before the assembled Lords of the Admiralty. When his box was opened and his letter withdrawn, he asked that it be read aloud. Thereupon the members of the board and their clerks were entertained by Bellomont's indiscretions. The letter was full of nasty comments about Sir Edward Harrison, toward whom Bellomont still felt bitter because of the harsh conditions of his loan. Bellomont refused to consign Kidd's treasure to Harrison as requested, because Bellomont would not give the "Ministers the go-by and direct them to a merchant." He also laid claim to one-third of the goods of all the other pirates recently captured, and while the Junto might share in this bounty, Harrison must not. Never one to stop scheming where his purse was concerned, Bellomont went on to propose that the partners acquire a new grant from the king for Kidd's treasure. One indiscretion flowed into another; Bellomont even asked Vernon to solicit a present for him from third parties.[36]

Heedless of Bellomont's privacy, Vernon then asked that the Duke of Shrewsbury's letter be opened and its contents read. Sir David Mitchell, a member of the board, protested that the letter should be sent unopened to the duke, but Vernon insisted—and the Tories were happy to hear more of Bellomont's peccadilloes. This time the letter was short. It commented on the House of Commons; then Bellomont went on to state that he doubted Kidd would be proved a pirate and that the original partners would need a new grant from the king for the treasure. Having established a precedent by reading these two letters, the Admiralty proceeded to inform all the other addressees that letters awaited them and that they should come to the Admiralty office to have them opened. Vernon was not at all contrite about his action, writing Shrewsbury that Bellomont should have been more discreet in his letters.[37] Perhaps Vernon was protecting himself from the political quicksand of the day.

In the days that followed, Bellomont's friends and patrons streamed in, or sent their servants to get their letters. Sir Thomas Littleton, Somers, Sir John Stanley, Mr. Yard (secretary to the lords justices), Mr. Loundes of the Treasury, Mr. van Hulst (the king's Dutch secretary), Sir Henry Ashurst, William Popple (secretary to the Board of Trade), John Locke, Sir William Blathwayt, and even the much maligned Edward Harrison all had their letters read, and then retained by the Admiralty if they dealt with Kidd. Sir Henry Ashurst complained about the extraordinary proceedings and demanded his "privilege as an Englishman," but he too had to read his letter and make it available as evidence.[38] The letter to Harrison was short, if not brusque: Bellomont excused the brevity because of his gout, but Harrison probably knew that Bellomont had written many long letters the same day.[39]

At times Bellomont outdid himself. In his letter to Shrewsbury he stated that Kidd was probably innocent, only to contradict himself in a letter to Sir John Stanley (who handled his private business affairs), in which he pressed Stanley to see that the partners got a new grant for Kidd's goods, because he was certain that Kidd had committed piracy, "but this is under the rose and to you alone."[40] The letter also revealed Bellomont's rapacity:

Try to find if anything be allowed to [me] for [my] pains. There is a quantity of Gold and all ye Jewells now sent home which Kidd had nothing to do with, but they belonged to James Gilliam [James Kelley] . . . I am told that as Vice-Admiral of these Seas I have a right to a 3rd part of them, if the rest of the Lords come in for Snacks I shall be satisfyed, but that Sr Edward Harrison should pretend to a Share of what was not taken by Kidd is very unreasonable.[41]

These private communications went far beyond the Admiralty, for Tory leader Robert Harley had copies of all of them. They might have enhanced Bellomont's reputation for cupidity and thoughtlessness, but they did little else for him.[42] One exception is that even in his most private communications it was obvious that Bellomont acted scrupulously with regard to Kidd's treasure. Somers and Montague regretted the entire episode and lost no time in telling Vernon he had gone too far in his desire to be candid and open. They would rather have had the whole business conducted in a private forum until they knew just how dangerous Kidd's testimony would be for them. Vernon could only reply, "If it be an error, I shall be glad to resign to those that commit none."[43]

Kidd, meanwhile, sank deeper and deeper into melancholy and his health deteriorated dangerously. John Cheeke, the Admiralty marshal, feared for his prisoner's life and urged the board to interview him soon. Of particular concern to Kidd was the loss of all his effects, for Cheeke even made Kidd empty his pockets to get every scrap of paper. Having lost control over the evidence, Kidd was overwhelmed by the imminence of his own death. If he had to die, he wanted to do so by the firing squad, not by the "shameful" rope—but to avoid these alternatives he asked for a knife. His captors denied him the means to self-destruction.[44]

On April 14 the Admiralty Board sent their private barge to whisk Kidd and his guardians from Greenwich to London, where he was transferred to a sedan chair and brought to the Admiralty's brand-new building next to Whitehall Palace. At four in the afternoon the disheveled prisoner met his tormentors in their paneled meeting room. The Earl of Bridgewater presided, with Lord Haversham, Admiral Sir George Rooke, and Sir David Mitchell present. This audience was not one friendly to Whigs; these men owed their allegiance elsewhere. Rooke, for instance, was an old professional and political rival of Orford. Sir Charles Hedges, Chief Judge of the Admiralty, cross-examined Kidd about the circumstances of his piracy. Kidd deviated not at all from his established alibi. When Hedges was finished, a transcript of the testimony was presented to Kidd to sign, then Hedges was asked to leave while the board discussed more delicate, and more political, issues. The members were interested in Kidd's partners, in what was now being referred to as the "Corporation of Pirates." Kidd gave them a "plain account" of his owners and the cost of fitting out. With whom had he discussed the venture? He had never met Somers, met Romney once, met Orford a number of times (including a private meeting), and had been in Shrewsbury's office once. There he had witnessed Bellomont, with Kidd's proposal in his hands, discussing it with Vernon. Vernon admitted to this meeting but hastened to add that he had never spoken to Kidd.

As 11:00 P.M. approached, the board had heard enough. A transcript of the testimony was read to Kidd for his signature; then, as a clerk dripped wax upon the fold, each of the board members brought out his seal to secure it. The secretary was ordered to keep it safe while they went ahead and disposed of Kidd.[45] The House of Commons had requested that he be kept in prison until its next session, so he was held a "close prisoner" and committed to Newgate rather than the Admiralty's own jail, the Marshalsea. He was to be held incommunicado, allowed a physician, and given paper to write only to the Admiralty. His seven-hour ordeal over, Kidd was led away to the pestilential hole known as Newgate. As he passed beneath its ornate gateway, he was cut off from the world.[46]

The next day Vernon bustled to meet Sir George Rooke and find out what had happened—his open, if studied, neutrality put to good use. Rooke gave him the details of Kidd's testimony and the opinion that it would not be satisfactory to the Tories: there was no evidence tying the Junto to piracy, and what had happened during the voyage was none of their doing. Rooke's news was so welcome that Vernon could hardly wait to tell the others that "so good [an] end made of it as the way it is gone."[47] Vernon's glee that his "prudence" and "integrity" had been vindicated received a lukewarm reception from Somers, who regretted that the interview had been conducted by the Admiralty rather than the cabinet, but was mollified by the result. Montague rebuffed Vernon, who preached to him that men allow "ill-grounded" suspicion to create "uneasiness," by answering that often there are reasons for it.[48] Vernon was right in one regard: Kidd's examination by an impartial body took suspicion away from the Junto. A secret cabinet meeting presided over by Somers might be bitterly attacked in the Commons when it met. The object of all this concern was now a state prisoner in Newgate rather than in Marshalsea, where the other pirates brought over with Kidd were confined after having been interviewed.[49] At the next session of the Admiralty Court they would be dealt with and quickly dispatched to their fates. Kidd would have to wait for the political forces that controlled his destiny to do battle before he would learn just how bleak his future was.

Having disposed of Kidd himself, the Admiralty moved to finish the other business that related to him. Having a high regard for the political repercussions of his case, the members decided to obtain legal advice before they acted on the treasure still waiting in the hold of the *Advice*. They asked their own chief judge, Charles Hedges, plus the attorney general and solicitor general to meet with them. With the full board in attendance, the Crown's two chief legal officers were asked two questions. The first was how to dispose of the goods and effects brought over from Boston. Although the Admiralty was free to do whatever it wished, the lawyers' advice was to keep the treasure under the control of the Court of the Admiralty. The second question reveals the extraordinary nature of Kidd's situation. The secretary read the order the board had issued to the keeper of Newgate. It seems the Admiralty had begun to question the legality of keeping Kidd under such close confinement. Was such treatment amenable to law? The answer was that such conditions were formally allowed only in cases where the prisoner had been accused of treason, and then by orders from the King-in-Council. But the attorney general saw no harm in imposing them in this case, and the solicitor agreed that the prisoner would thereby be prevented from escaping. So the board saw no reason to change its policy: its most famous prisoner would have to languish in Newgate as if he were a traitor to the kingdom and not a simple pirate. After the legal officers had withdrawn and they had issued orders relating to their advice, the board continued to ponder its own legal liability. In the end it concluded that in the future the legal officers should write down their opinions for the record.[50]

Only a few pieces of business remained before the board could return to running the peacetime navy. Three days after the meeting the members gathered to check the iron chest containing the treasure. They once again invited Hedges plus Mr. Taylor of the Treasury, Mr. Crowley (their own register), John Cheeke, Captain

Wynn of the *Advice;* and Lieutenant Daniel Hunt was sent by Bellomont to watch over the strongbox. The board took no chances. When the chest was removed from the *Advice,* the ship's hold was cleaned and the bottom searched. The treasure chest was double locked, so Wynn and Hunt brought out their keys, moved forward, and opened it. On top was a pile of original documents relating to the venture, which had escaped the supposed destruction of Kidd's papers on Saint Marie. Beneath lay the bags of silver and gold. The gold was spirited from the chamber to an adjacent room to be weighed by a goldsmith, while the board attempted with little success to interview Dundee and Ventura, Kidd's two slaves. Even a Portuguese interpreter and an "Indian" could not communicate with Dundee, and Ventura offered little beyond the circumstances of his life. Although blameless in the whole affair, the two were confined in the Marshalsea. The goldsmith returned to report that Bellomont's invoices were proper and, if anything, that the gold was worth more rather than less than the estimate. The bags went back in the chest, which remained in the board's chamber until a safe place could be found.[51]

At the first rumor of treasure the Old East India Company entered a claim against it as a means of compensating the *Quedah Merchant's* owners and the company for all the damage caused by Kidd. When Vernon asked the Admiralty to consider this petition, it replied that nothing could be decided until a year after Kidd's conviction (there seems to have been no doubt that he would be convicted), when the legal owners could enter a claim with the king. Thus the company would receive no balm for its wounds, and the legal owners would have to come from India.[52]

Newgate prison, a full five stories tall, towered over the intersection of Holborn and Newgate streets. People crossed the street to avoid the building, for it was a horror even to the hardened sensibilities of that age. Many physicians refused to enter and confront its overcrowded squalor. The government had allocated £10,000 to restore it, but the money was ill spent on a fancy facade that only gilded the garbage can. Newgate was insufferably overcrowded, a situation endured by those who were sent there only because most of them stayed only a very short time before their cases were decided. Penitentiaries did not yet exist as a means of correction; instead the courts settled cases by fines, humiliation, physical punishment, exile, or hanging. Locking prisoners into jail in hope of moral regeneration awaited richer governments less convinced that evil needed to be punished.

Newgate had two types of long-term inhabitants—a few particularly notorious debtors, and prisoners of the state. If the latter were of high status, they stayed in the masters' side, in private rooms where their servants attended them and brought in catered meals. On the common side rested those who relied on the jailers and their stomach-churning food. Kidd was probably kept on the masters' side in the press yard, where the state prisoners were held. Even there, the malodorous air and ever-present deadly fevers would sap the health of the most robust inmate. In the middle of the eighteenth century the government adopted the novel idea of pumping the dreadful stench out through the roof. This innovation did little to alleviate the mephitic air of the interior, and outside it blighted a larger area of the neighborhood.[53]

In this ghastly pit Kidd's health went downhill fast. When the keeper of Newgate reported in early May that Kidd had a fever and was suffering great pain, the Admiralty finally relaxed its severe policies. Not only was he granted clothing, bedding, and better care, but his uncle Mr. Blackborne, a fishmonger, and Mrs. Hawkins, his wife's relative and his former landlady, were allowed to see him in the presence of a keeper. These two relatives had earlier sought the board's permission to visit Kidd, only to be rebuffed. Now, with Kidd's health seriously impaired, the board decided to let them attend to him and also to allow him to see a physician.[54] After the immediate crisis had passed, the visits were stopped. By July the prisoner petitioned for an allowance and for liberty to visit with his friends and go to chapel with his "two negro children." If these privileges were denied him, he was "like to perish in his confinement."[55] The board relented once again, but only to a point. It was willing to allow him 20 shillings per week, visits in the presence of a keeper from his friend Mathew Hawkins, and occasional supervised chapel services in the company of one of the African boys.[56]

With these modest contacts to the outside world established, the months passed a little more quickly. The board continued to monitor his imprisonment, particularly any attempts to visit him. At one point Captain Wynn had to interview his officers because the board heard that one of them had tried to see Kidd. Wynn reported back that his chaplain had tried to visit Kidd, as had Wynn's own servant, who had attended Kidd on the *Advice;* both of them had been rebuffed by the keepers.[57] The Admiralty obviously did not want anyone to get to Kidd before the House of Commons dealt with him, and while their query to Wynn indicates that they investigated any rumors of a meeting, they could not keep interested parties from getting to see him. Money and power could blind a Newgate keeper, and charges leveled at a later date accused the Tories of interviewing Kidd. We know with certainty only that Kidd continued to complain about the severity of his confinement. On December 20, 1700, he pleaded to have the "liberty" of Newgate as did his fellow inmates. Perhaps imbued with the New Year's spirit, the board allowed Kidd to exercise, under guard, but he could talk to no one.[58] So the very special nature of Kidd's circumstances brought him a terrible sentence, discharged in awful conditions; although his health was frequently poor, his constitution, long attuned to the rough life at sea, kept him alive.[59]

All things waited on Parliament, and when it met in the spring of 1701, a Tory-controlled Commons stood ready to punish the Junto. After the election of 1700 the Whigs were diminished in numbers, although they were still determined to protect their reputation and their gains. One of the victors in this election was the Old East India Company. The old and new companies fought a bitter struggle to get their own supporters into the House, and the Old Company prospered along with the Tories. When the Commons met, the Old Company rubbed salt into the wound by having ten of the New Company's men thrown out, by invalidating their election. The Tories also prospered; for when the session started, Sir Robert Harley moved into the speaker's chair, thereby cementing Tory control.[60]

In 1701 Parliament was dominated by concern over the succession to King William and by foreign affairs. Princess Anne's only son had died, raising again the question of the appropriate Protestant succession. While it was easy to agree on the claim of the House of Hanover, the difficulty lay in determining what powers the new government would have. In the end a bill was passed that settled all of the questions. The second issue revolved around the intricate politics of the European powers. The central concern was the succession to the Spanish throne, where King Louis of France sought to ensure French domination. Earlier partition treaties had been agreed to by the powers involved, but when the idiot King of Spain died, he left his throne to one of Louis' grandsons, thereby opening the way to war. King William wanted to take vigorous action against the French; but the Tories profoundly disliked the thought of an expensive new war. In fact, Parliament turned to consider the partition treaties that King William had negotiated largely without the advice of his English ministers, and because the treaties contained clauses contrary to English interests, they were distasteful to many Tories. Even though the Whig ministers had little to do with the treaties at the time they were negotiated, they had provided the necessary legal approval. This assent was seized on by the Tories as a convenient instrument to attack both the Junto and the treaties. This time they would settle for nothing less than impeachment, and the Kidd affair was added to the list of Junto offenses. The pawn was moved onto the board.[61]

The Commons started by demanding that all records pertinent to the case be turned over to Paul Jodrell, clerk of the House. Vernon brought in some original papers, but the bulk were delivered by Josiah Burchett, secretary to the Admiralty.[62] Most of these documents were put on the table in the center of the House so that any member might read them, and no doubt Bellomont's pungent remarks about some of the members titillated the readers. On March 20, 1701, a large and strongly Tory committee was formed to examine the documents and prepare a report. With the Kidd affair revived once again on the floor of the House, other actors appeared. The Old East India Company brought Coji Babba all the way from India to demand his goods lost on the *Quedah Merchant*. If the Admiralty had thought to dismiss the company's claim to the treasure by stating that only the original owners were eligible, here now *was* the original owner demanding compensation for a loss of 440,000 rupees. In addition, Henry Bolton, the receiver of Kidd's goods in the West Indies, had been caught in Jamaica and returned to England. While Bolton was hardly germane to the real issue at hand, he had dealt with part of the reputed treasure, so he was called before the House of Commons to appear along with Coji Babba. The Old Company wanted everyone involved with the stolen goods to testify in order to build its claim. For the Tories the benefit was to keep Kidd alive as a weapon against Somers, their prime target.[63] Having examined all the documents, they now moved to interview the star witness.

On March 27, 1701, Kidd was finally released from his close confinement to keep his appointment in Parliament. Hundreds of people followed the famous pirate as his keepers marched him through the narrow streets toward Whitehall Palace.[64] When he entered Saint Stephen's Chapel he took his place before the bar to await the debate. Coji Babba was there also, but not Bolton, who had managed to raise bail and had immediately fled.[65] The Commons were in no mood to accept this turn of events and took revenge on Edward Whitaker, the Admiralty solicitor, who had approved the bail. He was brought before the House, berated for his "great neglect of duty," and put in the custody of the sergeant-of-arms while his conduct was investigated. Poor, luckless Whitaker was the first casualty of the Kidd affair, for his career was ruined.[66] Upon the report to the Commons of Sir Humphrey Machworth that all of the papers relating to Kidd were in order, the transcript of the private interview, so carefully sealed by the Admiralty board, was opened and the contents read aloud. Then Coji Babba's petition was read. Kidd was ushered into the chamber, where the curious could examine this now-famous villain. Unfortunately we know nothing of what transpired, because detailed records were not kept at the time. One commentary merely records that the interview was "to little purpose."[67] Another states that the questions revolved around Kidd's meetings with the Junto and that Kidd did not deviate from his earlier testimony that he had never met Somers or Shrewsbury but had met Orford and Romney. When the role of Harrison and Bellomont came up, he identified them as managers of the enterprise. Kidd was then ushered out while Bellomont's letters, jibes and all, were read. Kidd was recalled for more testimony, again unrecorded, and again he was ushered out. The House then resolved to have Harrison in attendance the next day and vote on the same question as before—whether or not the original grant was legal.[68]

Kidd wended his way back to Newgate, again with a crowd of the curious following him. It was later charged that shortly after he left Westminster he was taken to Romney's house, which lay close by, where Romney and Somers interviewed him. There is little direct evidence about such a meeting, and in the heat of charge and countercharge it is hard to state that it ever occurred. But if the two men had not had the opportunity to interview Kidd before, a quick chat at this point to congratulate him on his testimony, and perhaps to make promises about the future, might have been worthwhile. At any rate, at the end of the day Kidd found himself back in his cell, his brief tour of the outer world at an end.[69]

The following day the House interviewed Harrison (whose testimony is not recorded) and considered all of the pertinent documents on the origins of the "Corporation of Pirates." The debate went on until eight at night when the question was finally put to the House. As before, the Junto had enough support to fend off the Tories, although the final vote was a close 198 to 185. One member hoped that the vote would "take the edge off many of the fierce men."[70] It did not. The House moved within a month to reconsider the partition treaties, and this time the Tories would not be defeated. Even after an eloquent speech by Somers, the House voted on April 14 to impeach Somers, Orford, and Halifax. In the end the Lords refused to accede to the bills against the Junto and the attack collapsed.[71]

Meanwhile the Commons were not yet finished with Kidd. The day after his appearance, a resolution passed urging the king to proceed in law against Kidd.[72] At about the same time, a rumor to the effect that Kidd wanted to tell the truth in order to save his life was reported to Sir Edward Seymour. A Tory partisan, Seymour arranged for Kidd's second appearance before the House. He tried to interview Kidd before his appearance, but two other members, presumably Whigs, witnessed the attempt and rushed forward to stop him. The veracity of this story is doubtful, but Kidd did make a second appearance on March 31, when he was brought in, heard, and removed. None saw fit to record his testimony; it appears he made no revelations. A report states that afterward Seymour blurted out, "The fellow is a fool as well as a rogue, and I will never credit what he shall say hereafter."[73] On the way back to his cell the keeper accompanying Kidd relented enough to let him visit a tavern at Charing Cross. With his trial imminent and those in power no longer in need of him, Kidd's keeper could let him rest and drink. He probably had a deal with the tavern owner, who hoped to do more business with the famous pirate as an attraction.[74] All that remained for Kidd was his trial.

NINE

The Trial

Kidd's trial started on May 8, 1701, and was over on May 9. In those two days the prisoner was tried and convicted of murder and multiple piracies. Two days of a modern felony trial would hardly allow time for a few pretrial motions, but our system of procedural safeguards lay far in the future. In Kidd's day prosecutors did not go to trial unless they were sure of a conviction, and although they did not always win, they had a very high rate of success. The accused had to conduct his own defense and could use a lawyer only for very limited purposes. The professional lawyer usually worked for the prosecution. Thus Kidd would confront the serried ranks of English justice alone.[1]

The Admiralty lawyers had been preparing the case against Kidd for some time and exercised great care in issues involving their famous prisoner. As the health of the old buccaneer James Kelley failed, the prosecutors feared for his life if he went to trial. Edward Whitaker, the Admiralty solicitor, asked the Lords of the Admiralty for instructions; while he wanted to try Kelley, he hesitated for fear that the Commons or the Old East India Company would see such a move as an attempt to do away with a witness against Kidd. Whitaker refused to act until he had a clear directive. The company did not object to the death of a notorious pirate, so Kelley was brought to trial, convicted, executed, and then at the king's orders, hanged in chains at Gravesend "as a greater terror to others."[2]

After Kelley was disposed of, the Admiralty board continued to interview members of Kidd's crew who had been caught with him or who had been arrested later and returned to London by Admiral John Benbow. The men who arrived with Benbow had a simple story. Having signed on with Kidd "no purchase, no pay," they had merely followed the obey-or-death rule of privateers. After taking ships on Kidd's orders, they had gone to Saint Marie, where Kidd had divided the loot and then abandoned them to return home as they could. Sir Charles Hedges believed this to be strong evidence against Kidd.[3] The court needed two eyewitnesses to obtain a conviction, so two men were to be chosen for their knowledge of events and their willingness to betray shipmates. The Admiralty ordered its legal officials to seek the most "proper" witnesses and after interrogating a number they chose Robert Bradinham and Joseph Palmer. Bradinham had been the ship's surgeon until he defected to Culliford on Saint Marie. He had traveled with Giles Shelley to New York in 1698, but was later arrested and returned to England. Palmer had joined the crew in New York as a mariner and followed exactly the same path. Neither of the men was notably bloodthirsty or a leader, and both apparently had had a clean record until this time. They were typical Admiralty Court witnesses, and for telling all they knew they were promised a royal pardon.[4] By April 30 the prosecutors had met "about perfecting the indictment" with the witnesses and were ready to go to trial. Thomas Bale, the acting Admiralty solicitor, even went so far as to place all of the evidence before the judges, who refused to give him any advice; but before the trial started they had heard the government's case.[5]

Throughout his long confinement Kidd had continued to pepper the Admiralty with requests to have more visitors and the freedom of Newgate, but he met the same unrelenting answer. After his first appearance in Parliament and the subsequent demand that his prosecution proceed immediately, his appeals took on new urgency, for now he needed his friends and writing materials in order to prepare his defense. George Churchill carried this request to the Commons, because the Admiralty refused to make an independent decision. When the reply indicated a willingness to allow him visitors and the materials to prepare a defense, the board ordered the keeper to permit the changes in his imprisonment. Later the Commons relented further and allowed him to be treated like any other prisoner.[6] The concession desired most by Kidd was the return of the papers sent over by Bellomont. With those in hand he could prepare his defense. Once again the Commons was accommodating and ordered its clerk, Paul Jodrell, and the Admiralty's secretary, Josiah Burchett, to supply his demands.[7] Kidd quickly forwarded an itemized list of the documents he needed: his original commissions, the articles between Bellomont and himself, his bond, Bellomont's sailing orders, the orders sent him from the Admiralty, other letters taken from him and essential to his planned defense, and the two French commissions taken from the only prizes he admitted to seizing. Burchett and Jodrell cooperated to find and send to Newgate the papers available to them. Five days after the original request the Admiralty had another, more explicit letter. Missing from the papers sent Kidd were a "blue skinned" book naming his owners and containing his accounts, the instructions sent by the Admiralty relating to his letter of marque, the letter sent by Bellomont as he approached Boston (which had been taken from Kidd's pocket by Captain Wynn), and the vital French passes. The very next day Burchett replied that he knew nothing of these documents and that Jodrell must know where they were because the Commons had taken nearly everything in his possession that related to Kidd. If Kidd had a clue to their whereabouts, he would be happy to accommodate him. But the essential passes were not to be found. It was hardly unusual for records to get lost because the Admiralty lacked a "keeper of the records" until 1809. Nascent bureaucracies had difficulty keeping track of their paperwork during periods of rapid expansion.[8]

In this case it appears that while Burchett controlled the records returned by Bellomont, he did not keep them solely in Admiralty House. When turning in the documents demanded by the Commons, he had to ask seven individuals to return letters to him so that he could give them to the House. Secretary Vernon also had a cache of his own, for it was he who sent Burchett the original articles of agreement between the partners, Kidd's and Livingston's bonds, and "other" papers. So the records sent over with Wynn had been in other hands.

When Burchett failed to find the passes, he carried out a search—even writing to Captain Wynn about them—but to no avail.[9] Yet the passes were in London, for in this century they were found in the records of the Board of Trade. How they got there is unclear; however, at a later time the archives of the board were created from its own records and those of the secretaries of state. The finger points at Vernon, who had access to the papers at the time and kept some of them in his office. Bellomont informed Vernon of the two "commissions" he had secured and sent over on the *Advice,* and both men knew that Kidd would base his defense on the passes. In reality the passes made little difference to the case; still, if Vernon wanted to protect his patron Shrewsbury and the other members of the Junto, he could strip Kidd of any defense by misplacing the evidence. He may have remembered the jury's reluctance to convict Avery's men on similar evidence and decided not to take any chances. Kidd was denied the evidence he believed would prove him innocent.[10] This disappearance of crucial evidence has led a number of modern observers to raise the charge of judicial murder. Even so, Kidd was hardly an innocent man killed by the system.[11]

The trial was scheduled for May 8 in the Old Bailey.[12] This legal arena is synonymous with famous criminal trials, and Kidd's was to be just another legal struggle within its paneled chambers. Kidd was in no mood to appreciate the drama of his trial, and before it started he wrote a remarkable letter:

My Lord

Before I make any answer to ye Indictment read against me, I crave leave to acquaint your Lordship that I took no ships but such as had French passes for my justification.

In confidence that they would and ought to be allowed for my defense, I surrendered my selfe to my Lord Bellomont when I could have secured myself in several parts of ye world.

But my Lord Bellomont haveing sold his share in my ship, and in ye Adventure, thought it his Interest to make me a pirate, whereby he could claim a share of my Cargo, and in order to it, stript me of ye French passes, frightened and wheedled some of my men to misrepresent me, and by his Letters to his friends here Advised them to admit me a pyrate, and to obtain a new Grant of my cargo from ye King.

The more effectually to work my ruin, he has sent over all papers that would either do me little Service, or as he thought, would make against me, but has detained the French passes and some other papers which he knew would acquit me, and baffle his design of making me a pyrate, and my cargo forfeited.

If ye design I was sent upon, be illegal, or of ill consequence to ye trade of ye Nation, my Owners who knew ye Laws, ought to suffer for It, and not I, whom they made ye Tool of their Covetousnesse. Some great men would have me dye for Solving their Hononor, and others to pacify ye Mogull for injuryes done by other men, and not my selfe, and to secure their trade; but my Lord! Whatsoever my fate must be, I shall not Contribute to my own destruction by pleading to this Indictment, till my passes are restored to me. It is not my fault if I admit my selfe a pyrate as I must doe I plead without having those passes to produce.

Let me have my passes, I will plead presently, but without them I will not plead.

I am not afraid to dye, but will not be my own Murderer, and if an English Court of Judicature will take my life for not pleading under my Circumstances, I will think my death will tend very little to the Credit of their Justice. [13]

His view of Bellomont and the other investors is not without insight into their motives, particularly those of Bellomont, whose penury had as much to do with his antipiracy campaign as did policy. Kidd's charge that Bellomont withheld evidence is untrue: he went out of his way to ensure that every scrap of paper went to England so that the Tories could not lay a charge against him. [14] That the "great men" were embarrassed by him and that the East India Company wanted to please the Mughal are charges that do ring true. Many powerful men had a strong desire to see Kidd dead, and he knew it; while he might defy them by not pleading, by this time his fate was sealed. He could hardly continue to hope for a pardon.

The trial started on the appointed day in a courtroom decorated with the symbols of the Admiralty. A short silver oar lay in front of the judges, and above the king's arms was spread a cloth holding three anchors. Before this panoply stood the disheveled pirates.

Kidd was charged with murder and piracy, and Nicholas Churchill, James Howe, Darby Mullins, Abeel Owen, Hugh Parrot, Gabriel Loffe, William Jenkins, Robert Lamley, and Richard Barlycorne were charged with piracy. The trial record reads strangely to someone used to our present-day judicial system. Studied neutrality on the part of the court was uncommon in the seventeenth century, even if the defendant was a powerful man. The judges were activists—in Kidd's case, active on the side of the prosecution. While it might seem that the proceedings were biased against Kidd, by the canons of the day he was given a relatively fair trial, whether or not he had his passes. There is no doubt he was guilty of piracy, although in two of the cases he was tried for, Kidd argued that he did have a legal basis for acting as a privateer.[15]

The trial opened with a grand jury discovering whether or not there was a case against the pirates. The assembled forces of the prosecution filled the benches with those ready to help them. Dr. George Oxenden, leader of the prosecution, had with him Sir William Cowper, king's council and a staunch Whig; Sir Salathiel Lovell, the recorder of the City of London; Dr. Henry Newton, the advocate of the Admiralty; Sir John Hawkes, the solicitor general; and a number of other associates. Oxenden was perhaps the leading civil lawyer of the day. He had specialized in law at Cambridge and thereafter became a notable pluralist, besides serving as a Whig member of Parliament.[16] After reading the king's commission empowering the court to act, a grand jury was empaneled. Oxenden read out the charges against the prisoners, following which the jury left the chamber for a short time before returning with a bill of indictment against the defendants. The prisoners now entered the court for the first time to view the setting for their drama and the array of legal talent brought against them. While the trial record says nothing about the audience, one can assume that the room was packed. Among the crowd was Coji Babba, no doubt accompanied by members of the Old Company who wanted him to see English justice at work. Kidd's former comrade in arms Colonel Hewetson was in attendance, as was a familiar individual from New York, Giles Shelley—with Kidd at the beginning and now at the end.[17]

The clerk of the court turned to the prisoners and asked Kidd to hold up his hand, at which point Kidd brought the proceedings to a standstill by demanding that he be allowed legal counsel. Lawyers for the defense were allowed, but they could speak only to matters of law, not of fact, and were not active participants in court proceedings. Until much later, defense lawyers had no role until after the defendant pleaded guilty or not guilty. Lovell, the recorder, immediately asked why Kidd wanted counsel, to which the accused replied that he wanted to discuss a matter of law relating to the indictment against him. Oxenden pressed him to state what matter of law, and the court clerk blurted out, "How does he know what it is he is charged with? I have not told him." Lovell ignored him, turning to Kidd to question his knowledge of the law. Kidd in turn asked for a delay until he could gather his evidence. Oxenden and Lovell returned to the matter of law that Kidd wanted to raise, so Kidd finally asked to have his counsel, Dr. William Oldys and Mr. Lemmon, heard on this issue.[18] The clerk, outraged that the defendant should call in defense lawyers before he had even made a plea, would have none of it. The court was of the same mind. Kidd switched grounds again by asking for the two French passes. This request met stony faces and only produced an inquiry on how long he had been given to prepare his case. Kidd replied that he had had about two weeks. That was long enough to satisfy the court, so the clerk once again asked him to hold up his hand. Kidd's arm remained at his side as he stubbornly demanded counsel and a delay, for he was "not really prepared." Lovell's immediate rejoinder was, "Nor never will if you could help it." The court rebuffed Kidd's requests and continued to insist that he plead, while he in turn demanded his passes. Lemmon, Kidd's lawyer, entered the fray to reiterate the importance of the evidence, which only brought him a rebuke from the bench. The spectators by now were buzzing at the commotion, and the clerk shouted, "Make silence."

As quiet was restored, the struggle with Kidd continued until, worn down by the implacable hostility of the prosecution, he grudgingly held up his hand. The clerk turned to Nicholas Churchill with the same request, only to be confronted with another balky prisoner. Churchill addressed the court, stating that he had come in under the pardon contained in the 1698 proclamation. Lovell had had enough. "If you were indicted for a felony, and you will not plead, the law takes it in the nature of a confession, and judgement must pass, as if you were proved guilty." Churchill held up his hand. While some of the other prisoners also claimed a pardon as promised in the proclamation, in the end they stood in a row, hands in the air. The clerk returned to Kidd and asked him "Art thou guilty or not guilty?" Kidd was nothing if not stubborn and returned once more to the matter of the passes. Lovell and the clerk were adamant and although Kidd continued to raise questions, they hammered him into submission. In the end he pleaded not guilty. Then came the ritual exchange:

"How wilt thou be tried?"
"By God and my country."
"God send thee a good deliverance."

After his codefendants had gone through the same procedure, Kidd again asked for a delay to prepare his defense, but the court at last could proceed without bothering with him.

Now the full panoply of the law was displayed. On the call "All rise," six judges led by Lord Chief Baron Sir Edward Ward paraded into court and took their places on the dais. There was no longer any pretense that this was an ordinary criminal trial.[19] Nor could the defendants question the seriousness of their situation.

The first trial involved only Kidd, who had to stand trial on the charge of murder of his gunner William Moore, whose skull he had crushed with a wooden bucket. After Kidd pleaded not guilty, the clerk of the court informed all the defendants that if they had any objection to a juror they must challenge him before he took the oath. That done, Kidd immediately insisted on counsel, which the court now granted him, but with a strong reminder to Oldys and Lemmon to stick to matters of law. Oldys then asked for a delay of Kidd's trial for piracy until Edward Davis, who had seen the two passes, and the passes themselves, were produced in court. The judges discussed both requests and ordered Davis to be brought from Newgate as soon as possible. As for the passes, Lemmon accurately claimed that they had been "transmitted from hand to hand" and might be in the Admiralty or the Commons. The judges debated this issue, plus the length of time Kidd had had to get ready for the trial, and whether or not the £50 given to him to prepare was an adequate amount. Justice Ward pushed remorselessly to start the trial, because Kidd's demands related to the charge of piracy, not murder, which was the issue before the court. Ward carried the day, and the court proceeded to a consideration of the first charge. A jury was chosen and three members of the prosecutorial team followed one another in quick succession to sketch out the crime—murder by wooden bucket.

It may seem unusual to have tried Kidd for murder, given the broad authority granted a captain on the high seas. But captains did not have the right to commit murder. For instance, Captain Wildey was tried for the murder of his surgeon, Mr. Pine, who had called one of his passengers, a Mrs. Stanley, a whore. Wildey, apparently a protector of women's virtue, had Pine strung on a sling from the yardarm and dunked into the sea until he died. Another case involved Captain John Rock, who had "hot words" with a Mr. Pink, his passenger. Pink questioned the virtue of Elizabeth Wallis, who it was said "lay" with the captain on the long voyage to Guinea. Captain Rock killed his loose-tongued passenger. In both cases the captains stood trial for murder.[20]

Joseph Palmer appeared as the first witness against Kidd. The prosecutors and Justice Ward quickly took him through the circumstances of the murder. The drumbeat of questions confused Palmer, who had to be reminded to face the jury. When the interrogators were finished, Justice Ward turned the state's witnesses over to Kidd. As was the custom at the time, Kidd had to conduct his own cross-examination and had to compete with members of the court and jury, who interrupted at will. Kidd tried to get Palmer to state that he had struck Moore because the crew was mutinous over his unwillingness to take the *Loyal Captain.* Palmer refused to follow Kidd's lead; then Kidd had to compete with a member of the jury, Justice Powell, and the solicitor, in asking questions before Kidd was cut off and Bradinham called to the stand. Bradinham testified about the death blow and then was asked a leading question. Had he ever discussed this matter with Kidd at a later date? Not surprisingly, he had; he reported that Kidd had said, "I do not care so much for the death of my gunner . . . for I have good friends in England, that will bring me off for that."[21] Ward then told Kidd to direct his questions to the witness. All Kidd asked was whether

Bradinham knew of differences between himself and Moore, to which the answer was no. The prosecution rested. Ward turned to Kidd and asked, "You are charged with murder . . . What have you to say for yourself?" For Kidd also had to conduct his own defense.

His initial statement revolved around a threatened mutiny led by Moore, which caused him to throw the bucket at the gunner. His witnesses, Richard Barlycorne, Abeel Owen, and Hugh Parrot, proved slender reeds on which to build a defense. After discussing the mutiny as a cause of the death blow, Justice Ward got Owen to admit that the supposed mutiny had occurred a month before the murder. One of the jury also interrupted to ask whether Kidd threw the bucket or struck him with it, to which Owen answered that Kidd had taken it by the strap and smashed it onto Moore's skull. Barlycorne, loyal to his master, testified along the lines of Kidd's defense, but the judges and the prosecution picked apart his statement. Then Barlycorne insisted that Moore had been sick for a month and that the blow was not the cause of his death. Bradinham quickly denied this, and Barlycorne looked foolish trying to press the point. Kidd next went after Bradinham by inquiring whether or not he was involved in the mutiny. Justice Ward said that was immaterial and told Kidd to get on with his defense. Hugh Parrot then made a long statement culminating in an admission that he never saw the murder. The court by now was impatient with the proceedings, so Ward asked Kidd if he had any more to say. The reply was no, except for a note of contrition: "I had no design to kill him, I had no malice or spleen against him." Then, a short time later, Kidd added, "It was not designedly done but in my passion, for which I am heartily sorry."

Justice Ward turned to the jury and summarized the case in detail. When a juryman interrupted to correct him, the justice admitted to no error and continued to sum up the testimony of each witness. He concluded by defining manslaughter as killing in the heat of blood, whereas murder was killing without provocation or reasonable cause. If the jury was convinced by the evidence, it must find the defendant guilty of murder; if not, the verdict should be acquittal. No sooner was he finished than Kidd pleaded with him for permission to present character witnesses and testimony regarding his service to the king. It was too late. Ward had made his summary and Kidd had had his chance. The case was in the hands of the jury, who left the courtroom.

With barely a pause the court went on to consider the charge of piracy on the *Quedah Merchant,* and this time all the prisoners were involved. After reading the charge, which included an estimated loss of £3,530 to the owners, the defendants were warned to object to the jurors before they were sworn. Then the "cryer" chanted the traditional "Twelve good men and true, stand together, and hear your evidence." The clerk had just sworn them in when Nicholas Churchill interrupted the proceedings. "My Lord, I beg your opinion, whether I may not plead the King's Pardon." Howe, Mullins, and Churchill claimed to have learned about the proclamation of pardon when they were in Guiana and had returned to East New Jersey, where they surrendered to Governor Jeremiah Basse under the terms of the proclamation. Justice Ward asked for a copy of the proclamation, which Churchill gave him. After reading it, the justices were in agreement that it did not apply to these cases. With the prisoners insisting otherwise, Justice Powell challenged them to prove it. They were well prepared. Not only did they have an affidavit from New Jersey, but Governor Basse himself was in court. The proclamation they pressed on the court had been agreed upon in 1698 and sent to the East Indies with Thomas Warren's squadron. Under its terms three commissioners, plus Warren, were permitted to receive the surrender of the pirates. But Warren was also carrying the special royal ambassador to the Mughal's court, and Ambassador Norris was in a hurry to get to India and negotiate an agreement to end the trade embargo. With the choice of delivering him on time or spending months seeking out pirates, Warren chose to deputize his son to go to Saint Marie and Madagascar and there accept the pardons in the name of the commissioners. The son managed to get twenty-two pirates to surrender, including Culliford and some of his men. Others, such as Churchill and his crewmates, claimed the pardon at a later date. Justice Ward and Dr. Newton, the Admiralty's advocate, interpreted the proclamation narrowly: unless you surrendered to the commissioners, your action had no validity. When the pirates' lawyer Maxon objected to such a strict construction of the terms, Justice Ward remained unyielding. "There are four commissioners named in the proclamation; there is no governor mentioned." With that the prosecution immediately started to declare its case against the defendants.

It should be pointed out that the Admiralty and its legal officials did not always so narrowly define the proclamation. Robert Culliford, being tried at exactly the same time, was pardoned because the Lords of the Admiralty decided his surrender to the younger Warren was valid. They did not insist on relying solely on the four commissioners. But Justice Ward, pressing on, offered little time to debate this issue.[22]

Dr. Newton was about halfway through reading the long charge to the second jury when he was interrupted by the return of the jury considering the murder charge against Kidd. They had retired for about an hour before returning to give their verdict. Once they were arrayed before the court, the clerk asked each of them his name. On completing the roster he asked, "Are you all agreed of your verdict?" The reply was affirmative. The clerk turned to Kidd and ordered him to hold up his right hand before asking the foreman of the jury, "Look upon the Prisoner. Is he guilty of the murder whereof he stands indicted, or not guilty?" The foreman intoned the dreaded word "Guilty," condemning Kidd to death with no appeal, except to the king. These were appalling circumstances for Kidd. In the middle of a trial for his life on the charge of piracy, the judges thought nothing of concluding his first trial and condemning him to death. It is remarkable that he continued at all, but he would go on presenting a spirited defense.

Newton recapitulated the voyage of the *Adventure Galley* up to the capture of the *Quedah Merchant* and then described Kidd's meeting with Culliford on Saint Marie. He ended by hammering home the growing "mischief to the Trading World" that piracy represented. The prosecution called Bradinham to testify once again and went through a long examination of the voyage, which included every episode that Kidd had tried to cover up before the taking of the *Quedah*. Justice Powell intervened to have Bradinham individually identify each of the prisoners as present at that time. The cross-examination was a swirl of questions, because each of the defendants could question the witness. And each, of course, was trying to establish his alibi. Lamley, Jenkins, and Barlycorne wanted to confirm the fact that they were mere servants. The others insisted they had only obeyed their lawful captain. Kidd settled for questioning Bradinham's accuracy and raising the familiar issue of the two French passes. Palmer's examination went along the same lines—with a brief cross-examination, as most of the men refused to question him. Kidd only asked about the passes, which Palmer claimed he had never seen, and concluded with, "It is vain to ask any Questions." At this point Justice Ward taunted him with, "Come, Mr. Kidd, what have you to say in your own Defense?"

Kidd first read into the record his privateering commission to take French ships. He claimed that he had even tried to give back the ships he had captured, but his men had voted against it. Palmer then turned and pointed at Coji Babba, saying, "This man offered you twenty thousand rupees for the ship, and you refused it," and asserted the men were lukewarm about taking the *Quedah*. Before going on to read into the record Kidd's second commission against pirates, Justice Ward pointed out that if they were French ships they should have been condemned by a proper prize court, and that this had not occurred. Ward was right, for Kidd had had condemned the small fishing ship he had captured on the way to New York, but had never tried to do the same with the other two ships. On the other hand, Kidd could claim that prize courts did not exist in the Indian Ocean and that he had acted correctly in returning to the colonies to seek out proper authority. He could also claim that the special grant given to the investors exempted them from prize courts. Strangely, he never developed either argument. Instead Kidd called Edward Davis, whom he expected to verify the existence of the passes. Davis admitted to having seen the passes, although he had never examined them and did not know their relation to any particular ship. After this disappointing testimony Kidd wanted to call character witnesses, to which Justice Ward replied, "If all the defense witnesses were like Davis the prosecution could sit back and relax."

While new witnesses were gathered, the other men conducted their defenses along lines by now familiar. Colonel Basse came to testify for those claiming the pardon, but he too proved a slender reed when he admitted that he did not think he was permitted to take their surrender according to the proclamation. Only Owen made any kind of impression; for not only had he reported himself to obtain the pardon, he had immediately signed onto a Royal Navy vessel. Ward admitted this action might commend Owen to the king's mercy, but it had nothing to do with the case.

Kidd produced his character witnesses, Colonel Hewetson and Captain Bond, who testified to his service in the West Indies. Justice Hatsell remarked that this service was all before 1695. Kidd irrelevantly said that he had kept company with Captain Warren and his squadron and that nothing in the world could make him guilty. This outburst brought the rebuke that he had kept company with Culliford for longer than he had with Warren. For the last time, Kidd demanded his passes—but to no avail, for Ward was ready to close the defense. He brushed aside the issue by saying, rather gratuitously, that Kidd should have raised it at the beginning of the trial.

Justice Ward then set out to "distinguish the Evidence as well as my memory serves me." He speedily summarized the case against the defendants and spent longer examining and criticizing the defense. Each argument that had been raised was dismissed as inadequate except that of the three young servants, because "a Pirate is not to be understood to be under Constraint, but a free Agent." If the jury decided that these men had acted under orders from their masters, then they should find them not guilty. Ward finished the charge and the jury filed out. A half hour later they returned and the clerk proceeded to carry out the ritual, proceeding from prisoner to prisoner while the foreman intoned the verdict. All but the three servants were found guilty. Kidd now lay under two death sentences.

The court immediately proceeded to trial for two more acts of piracy. Only after the indictments were read did the court adjourn until eight o'clock the following morning. The condemned faced a long night in jail before returning for another long day in court.

The second day was a mirror of the first. The two trials for piracy were both like the first one. New juries were picked for each trial, so all the testimony had to be repeated.[23] The defense remained the same but became more and more desultory. Often Palmer and Bradinham were chided, told to tell the truth, or insulted. Kidd and the others had given up and faced the inevitable guilty verdicts. The young servants continued to make clear that they acted as their masters had told them and were rewarded with "not guilty" verdicts. The only change occurred when Michael Churchill, Robert Culliford, John Eldridge, Robert Hickman, James Howe, and Darby Mullins were tried separately for piracy on the *Great Mahomet* and other ships. They were all found guilty; however, Culliford's sentence was set aside. He had come under the proclamation because his case was "particular." That must have been bitter gall to the others who claimed the pardon. The "particular" aspect of Culliford's case was the testimony he was providing against his old shipmate, and Kidd's—Captain Samuel Burgess.[24]

The clerk now proceeded with the final phase of the trials. Each man was asked to hold up his right hand and was reminded that he stood convicted. The clerk intoned, "What hast thou to say for thyself why thou should'st not die according to Law?" Kidd answered, "I have nothing to say, but that I have been sworn against by perjured and wicked People." Every man in turn received his chance and most of them claimed the pardon or said "not guilty." Oxenden uttered the mandatory sentence: "You shall be taken from the Place where you are, and be carried to the Place from whence you came, and from thence to the Place of Execution, and there be severally hang'd by your necks until you be dead. And the Lord have mercy on your souls." Kidd had the last word: "My Lord, It is a very hard sentence. For my part, I am the innocentest Person of them all, only I have been sworn against by Perjured Persons."

On Sunday, May 10, the day after the trials ended, Judge Oxenden had an audience with King William. The king knew the results of the trials, but he had the final say in the fate of the condemned because he could always extend royal clemency. Here was the last chance for anyone to act on Kidd's behalf. No one spoke, however, and as the king studied the list of the condemned, he gave the fateful orders to Oxenden: Kidd, Eldridge, and Mullins were to be hanged, the rest would be kept waiting for the royal favor, and two French pirates left over from the mass hanging of the crew of *La Paix* were to join their shipmates in eternity.[25] With the royal warrant in hand, Oxenden returned to his office. The bureaucratic wheels were set in motion. The Admiralty ordered the hangman, the keepers at Newgate, the sheriff of London, and others to prepare for the solemn ceremony that would be the final act in Kidd's life.[26]

Kidd tried one last desperate gambit. Bitterly disappointed in his erstwhile patrons, he wrote to their chief enemy, Robert Harley, Tory speaker of the House of Commons: "The sense of my present condition (being under condemnation) and the thought of having been imposed on by such as seek by my destruction thereby to fulfill their ambitious desires makes me incapable of expressing my selfe in those terms I ought."[27] Kidd went on to make the same proposal he had already made to Bellomont and Orford. If he were sent to the West Indies, he would recover £100,000 he had hidden there for the benefit of the government. If he failed, he should be "forwith [*sic*] executed." While never spelling out the alternative, he clearly hoped for a pardon. He asked Harley to send a committee to discuss the matter with him. There is no record of such an interview. It is unlikely that Harley had any interest in helping Kidd. From his point of view, Kidd had had his chance to ingratiate himself during his appearances before the Commons and had failed. Once his trial was over, he lost any value he possessed as a weapon against the Junto. Time and opportunity were running out.

If Harley no longer needed him, the Old East India Company did. Coji Babba had come all the way from India to recover the goods he and his partners had lost, and he was not going home until he discussed the issue with Kidd. He applied for, and received, permission from the Admiralty to visit Newgate. He appeared with an interpreter and a member of the company to discuss the loot taken from the *Quedah Merchant.* These discussions went nowhere, for Kidd no longer had control over any part of the booty. Coji Babba would have to file a claim to the portion of Kidd's loot that Bellomont had seized.[28] In doing so, he would have to join a lengthening line. In April, the widows of Henry Mead and William Berk, two of the original crew of the *Adventure Galley,* had interviewed Kidd about their late husbands' estates. They had filed the wills in court and wanted to collect the money Kidd owed them from the sale of goods in the colonies. While Kidd could give them details of the sale, he could help them no further and left them to the mercy of the courts when they disposed of his loot.[29] While the courts quickly disposed of the pirates, the more serious matter of their plunder would not be so easily resolved.

The execution was set for Friday, May 23, 1701. Until that day arrived, the prisoners would see more of Paul Lorrain than anyone else. Lorrain was the ordinary, or pastor, of Newgate, responsible for the spiritual condition of the diverse population of the jail. His was not an easy task. The chapel shared the awful stench of the prison and suffered regular desecration from many of the prisoners who cared little for the comfort dispensed from the pulpit. They did, however, like to use the benches in the chapel while fornicating. The ordinary needed strong lungs to shout over the babel caused by his unruly auditors, who frequently disrupted his best efforts. During his most quickening sermons prisoners were also likely to wander in and relieve themselves in the corners of the chapel. Fortunately, the tobacco smoke hung so thick that the ordinary might not see the offenders. Charity and forbearance were vital qualities.[30]

Lorrain resented the conditions under which he had to work, but he knew how to make a silk purse out of a sow's ear. The reading public in London had already developed a taste for sensational crimes and information about outstanding malefactors. To meet this demand, printers put out broadsheets detailing the activities of the courts and giving extensive coverage to the most outrageous crimes. The ordinaries of Newgate were well placed to supply such information, as they heard the confessions of the criminals. They began to write their own accounts of the trials and the last days of the convicted because, when printed, these would bring a tidy profit as well as allow them to warn the readers of their own spiritual peril. Lorrain brought this practice to a fine art. His *Account* inevitably followed the execution of famous (and not-so-famous) criminals and provided a nice supplement to his income.

Needless to say, success bred competition and professional writers such as Daniel Defoe and George Barrow moved into the market.[31] This spurred a spirited competition to publish the first "account" to reach the public. Lorrain was at a disadvantage because he did, after all, have to attend to the condemned. Nevertheless, he was nothing if not a modern entrepreneur. He fought back with newspaper advertisements warning against "sham papers" and alerting his audience to when his "true account" would appear. While Kidd represented an opportunity to bring a tormented soul into proper condition to meet its maker, such a famous criminal also meant a substantial opportunity for a big sale of his account. Lorrain arranged for a newspaper advertisement.[32]

On the Saturday after they were condemned, Lorrain visited his charges and urged them to repent and examine their lives. The next day he preached to them twice and continued to urge repentance; if that was not enough, he visited them twice a day during the following week. The climax came on Sunday, May 18, when he preached on two occasions before a packed house. No event would slip by if someone at Newgate could make money from it. The attractions at these services were the condemned, who were made to sit in the front pews, facing a coffin draped in black. With a famous criminal, the curious flooded into the chapel, first paying the turnkeys a small fee. The morning service heard Lorrain expound on Ecclesiastes 12:13, "The fear of God makes men truly wise"; and the afternoon heard 2 Corinthians 5:10, "God's judgement is based on close examination of the public acts of the individual sinner."[33]

After the ceremonies Lorrain continued to urge the men to confess, repent, and hope for God's mercy. Mullins and Eldridge succumbed to his blandishments and confessed their sins; Kidd remained unrepentant or, in Lorrain's words, kept a "hard, unmelted heart." It appears that, deep down, Kidd hoped for a reprieve at the last minute. During the week, rumors that such a late reprieve might come circulated through London.[34] It was inevitable that they did because of the highly charged atmosphere surrounding Kidd. Such thoughts were a delusion. Kidd had outlived his usefulness to his patrons, who were tired of his being used as a club to beat them. There was no reason for them to intercede with the king. One last-minute reprieve—for Eldridge—was forthcoming from the king, and only mocked Kidd's hopes.[35]

When execution day arrived, two more services punctuated the condemned men's day. Lorrain was pleased when Kidd repented his sins and forgave the world. Lorrain left for the execution dock at Wapping, ready to see the men through the ordeal ahead of them. In the late afternoon two horse-drawn carts pulled into the prison, accompanied by officials from the Admiralty and the sheriff of London and his men. When the four men mounted the carts, the procession moved out onto Holborn and turned toward Wapping. In the parlance of Newgate, the doomed normally "went west" toward Tyburn; but in the case of the Admiralty Court they turned east toward the city of London and the Thames.[36] The silver oar symbolizing the Lords of the Admiralty led the parade, followed by John Cheeke, marshal of the Admiralty, and the other officials required to witness the execution, who were followed in turn by the carts and their guards. They moved through the city accompanied by children, apprentices, and the curious. People called out to the condemned, offered them liquor, and often abused them. Merchants could see visible evidence of the new policy toward the pirates—an added plus for the Admiralty. Finally the doomed men arrived in Wapping, the end of the trip.

For Kidd the return to Wapping was replete with irony. In 1695, when he had come to London seeking a privateering commission, he had lived there with Mrs. Hawkins. He had left the narrow streets of this suburb, built out of a marsh to serve the growing maritime population of London, to meet with some of the most powerful men in the kingdom, and had returned in triumph with his commission and the favor of the mighty. He had continued to live there until the *Adventure Galley* was ready to go to sea. Now he came back as a condemned man—betrayed, for so he believed, by the same great men. He returned to the same execution dock he had passed in earlier, happier times, never imagining that his last image in life would be Wapping, wretched Wapping.

Large numbers of people flocked to public executions. These were occasions for a display of the majesty of the law and the awful judgments that awaited malefactors. They were also a form of public entertainment. People poured in on foot, in carriages, on horseback, in carts, and in this case on boats. The very poor and the very wealthy and every social group in between came to witness the drama of the last moments of the condemned. If all went well, they would be treated to the edifying spectacle of a convicted felon warning those in attendance against repeating the folly of his sinful ways before they were turned off. On this occasion Kidd's notoriety, plus the continual newspaper coverage of his trial, guaranteed a large crowd. While it is impossible to recapture in detail the composition of the crowd, it would be surprising if a large number of the directors of the Old East India Company did not attend with Coji Babba. The latter could return to India, if not with his goods, at least with the experience of witnessing English justice. When he got home, the company hoped he would relate what he had seen and relieve some of the pressure on its representatives.

This was an age in which dying was an event attended by one's friends and relatives, whether at home in bed or in public at the end of a rope. In fact, the condemned felon hoped they would attend. For the hangman would carry his victim up a ladder and at the proper moment toss him off. Because the drop was not sharp, it was possible to survive and hang there, choking and suffering, for a long time. If this happened, the victim's friends and relatives would rush forward, jump up and grab the dangling body, and pull down on it to break the neck and end the misery. So it would not have been unusual for Kidd's relatives to attend, or old comrades such as Colonel Hewetson, or perhaps even old shipmates such as Robert Culliford, who had just escaped the rope himself.[37]

Lorrain waited at the gibbet with the other ministers, ready to guide the condemned through their last moments on earth. He left Newgate believing that Kidd would make a final confession when he arrived at Wapping, because to that point Kidd still blamed his crew and his sponsors and refused to admit his own guilt. Lorrain hoped that, confronted by the gibbet, Kidd would make a full confession. Kidd had other ideas about the best way to approach his maker—he arrived drunk. If the condemned were not already inebriated before they left Newgate, the crowd along the way treated them to drinks as they passed by. To Lorrain's "unspeakable grief" Kidd was now in an "ill frame of mind" and "much out of order" and therefore unfit for the "great work" before him.[38]

Even when drunk, Kidd claimed his right to a last speech. He proclaimed his confidence in God's mercy even though he was a sinner. He left little doubt that he felt more sinned against than sinning. Those who had given evidence against him were liars and their evidence mere hearsay. In a parting shot at the Junto he denounced those who had promised they would be his friends, only to be the traitorous instruments of his ruin. The crowd would know for whom that jab was intended, which only made the confession more delectable. As for killing Moore, that had been done in a passion after he had been provoked. He did express sorrow about leaving his wife and children, but that was about all he was sorry for as he lashed out at his antagonists. He finished by warning seamen, especially captains, to use caution and prudence in private and public affairs.

This tirade was hardly an appropriate last speech. The condemned were supposed to be filled with repentance and give a fulsome admission of guilt and sinfulness, a final warning to youthful listeners to avoid wicked ways. Instead, Kidd unleashed his bitterness against the men who had raised him up only to cast him down. Lorrain, in his account, merely touches upon Kidd's final speech because it was unedifying and nearly blasphemous, not to mention politically touchy, when it denounced the mighty who might just return to power. The author of the *True Account,* on the other hand, preferred to report the whole speech and titillate his audience. From a religious point of view the condemned Mullins was far more rewarding. He "cheerfully" submitted to the judgment against him and desired all young men to take warning from him. John Dubois and Peter Manquianam remained mute and were attended by a French minister.[39]

The speeches at an end, the ministers sang a penitential psalm and said a prayer with the men. Then the hangman and his helpers moved in to make sure the men's bonds were tight before moving them toward the ladders. Mullins and the Frenchmen, in tears, several times cried out, "Lord have mercy on me, Father have mercy on me, Sweet saviour of the world have mercy on me." At about six o'clock on this spring evening, the four men were turned off. Kidd's journey stopped considerably short of eternity because the rope broke—a rare, but not unknown, occurrence.[40] As Kidd lay stunned and confused upon the ground, the hangman grabbed him and carried him back up the ladder to a new and, he hoped, stronger rope. Lorrain was not about to let this opportunity pass and begged the hangman to let him go to Kidd. He "found him in much better temper than before." As Kidd stood dazedly on the ladder, Lorrain clung to his knees, urging him to repent. Given a second chance, Kidd now sincerely repented with all his heart and in perfect love and charity. At least that is what Lorrain reported. They prayed together one last time before the hangman earned his fee by sending Kidd on a shorter, shattering fall. Thus ended the life of William Kidd, pirate.

TEN

Of Death, Destruction, and Myths

For a time the body dangled in midair as the crowd slowly dispersed. Tom Sherman and Jim Smith came forward to claim the corpse before setting out for Tilbury Point, where a gibbet awaited. After wrapping the body in specially made chains so that it would remain in the semblance of a human and be a "terror to all that saw it," the men took the corpse to the designated spot. The body remained on show to all who passed along the Thames until it had served the needs of the Admiralty, after which it was probably buried at Lyme House, there to molder and disintegrate. The bills for all this ceremony were paid, and there the Kidd affair ended—or so the Admiralty believed.[1] But Kidd's demise would not proceed in such a straightforward and bureaucratic fashion: his story would be transformed into legend.

Few of the crew of the *Adventure Galley* shared the fate of their captain. Samuel Arris and seven others died in jail—not an unusual event in the typhoid-ridden pestholes.[2] The more fortunate escaped with pardons: Churchill, Dawson, Eldridge, Howe, Loffe, Owen, Parrot, Roper, Turner, and Viele all walked away from jail.[3] Samuel Burgess and Robert Culliford also were granted pardons. Culliford immediately vanished, probably into a Royal Navy ship, while Burgess lived another fifteen years before a native king on Madagascar poisoned him when he suspected Burgess of cheating him in a slave trade deal.[4]

Kidd did not live to learn that Bellomont had preceded him to the grave. Bedeviled by gout and frequently ill, Bellomont succumbed on March 5, 1701, leaving an encumbered estate for his wife.[5] Of the Junto leaders, suffice it to say that they were spared the worst of the Tory malevolence and eventually returned to office.[6] Robert Livingston managed to avoid paying anything on the bond he put up for the venture. In 1706, however, Robert Blackham, one of the original partners, had him arrested for nonpayment of his investment in the voyage. In a hurry to leave London and return to business in New York, Livingston had no alternative but to make a deal before leaving England, so in the end he paid up.[7]

Sarah Bradley Cox Oort Kidd, once again a widow, had a difficult time after Kidd's arrest. Bellomont put her in jail and seized all the property she had with her in Boston. He had no reason to keep her; she regained her freedom and started to acquire her property once again, even picking up part of the loot left by Kidd. But as long as the hunt for Kidd's treasure continued, she could not rest, for even her servants came under suspicion. She did not rush into marriage again, as she had done with Kidd, but continued to live quietly with their daughters, Sarah and Elizabeth. In 1703 she married Christopher Rousby, survived him, and finally (in her mid-seventies) died in New Jersey in 1744. In an era when men usually were the ones who married several times, owing to the terrors of childbirth, Mrs. Kidd managed to raise five children and outlive four husbands—a remarkable achievement.[8]

One of Kidd's legacies was a treasure legend. No image is more closely associated with pirates than the habit of burying treasure: on a moonlit beach buccaneers drag ashore a heavy chest, then stagger across the sand to find a convenient spot back from the water where they can safely bury their loot. Sometimes dead bodies accompany the chests, as only one or two men return to the ship in full possession of the secret. This familiar tale is a pleasant fable, but it does not jibe with the facts.

The men who turned to piracy did so because they wanted money. As soon as possible after capturing a prize they insisted on dividing the loot, which they could then gamble with or carry home. The idea of burying booty on a tropical island would have struck them as insane, especially since all the men on board would demand to know the "secret," which would then be no secret. These men robbed, pillaged, and stole for their own benefit; for who would endure the conditions under which they labored unless there was a payoff at the end? If they survived and did not lose their money gambling, they could return home and live extravagantly or else invest in a business and settle down. (Those who did the latter were a very small minority.)[9]

Kidd's "treasure" created a controversy in his own day that has continued into modern times. When he arrived in the West Indies he had a cargo of textiles, gold, silver, and jewels. He traded away the bulk of the cargo in order to get rid of the *Quedah*. He bought the *Saint Antonio* for 3,000 pieces of eight and acquired 4,200 pieces of eight in bills of exchange and 4,000 in gold bars and dust. So he added a total of 8,200 pieces of eight, in portable form, to an unknown amount of goods and treasure that were then collected on his new and smaller ship.[10]

When he arrived in New York he was immediately met by Emott and Mrs. Kidd, so he might have transferred the portion of his fortune that he considered his own. He could not afford to send substantial parts of his cargo to New York City, because his bargaining power with Bellomont depended on the amount of treasure Bellomont would enjoy. On the other hand, a prudent man would plan for some contingencies. He did send away the bills of exchange, for instance, because they never appear in any inventory of the goods taken from him, and the likelihood is that he transferred them when he first arrived in New York waters. Then, as Kidd's ship lingered between Gardiner's Island and Block Island, three sloops came alongside to remove some of his passengers and crew plus their sea chests and share of the cargo. Mrs. Kidd, too, made some precautionary withdrawals. She sent a six-pound bag of pieces of eight with Thomas Way, and an unknown amount departed with Thomas Paine of Jamestown, Rhode Island. Kidd also sent "pounds" of gold with Thomas Clarke, who appears to have taken it to Major Jonathan Selleck in Stamford, Connecticut. Selleck was suspected of receiving £10,000 worth of goods at this time.[11] The greatest amount came into the hands of John Gardiner, proprietor of Gardiner's Island. Kidd landed on the island on two occasions while he waited for his visitors to come and go. He bought food from Gardiner, and at the end of his second visit he left behind five bales of cloth, a chest of "fine" goods, and a box containing fifty-two pounds of gold. The latter may well have been Kidd's ultimate security, in case he had to escape in a hurry. By leaving it with Gardiner he avoided having to return to New York City or any other location where he might have had to confront the law. If things went well with Bellomont, the gold would have been convenient enough to recall quickly. Unfortunately, things did not work out that way.[12]

Once Kidd was taken, Bellomont lost no time in hunting down those who had come in contact with him. Campbell's house in Boston was searched, and 463 ounces of gold and 203 ounces of silver, along with smaller amounts of precious metals and cloth, were removed to safekeeping. John Gardiner refused to tangle with Bellomont, so he sent along eleven bags of gold and silver.[13] Magistrates also tracked down Thomas Clarke, Thomas Paine, and Thomas Way to question them and remove any loot they might have. After Mrs. Kidd had languished in jail for a while, Bellomont released her and—after her strenuous pleading—returned her household goods.[14] After rounding up every bit of the loot he could, even Lady Bellomont's presents, he sent off 1,111 ounces of gold, 2,353 ounces of silver, 41 bales of goods, 52 bags of silver pieces, and various small jewels. Estimated to be worth £14,000, all of this went to England on the *Advice*.[15]

What remained behind cannot be known with any degree of certainty. With so many ships and men slipping about with shares of the booty, we will never know conclusively whether a "treasure" remained behind. If there *was* a substantial amount, it was surely in the hands of some individual and subsequently spent. Robert Livingston introduced the possibility of a hidden treasure by reporting that Kidd had stored a forty-pound bag of gold somewhere between Boston and New York (probably on Gardiner's Island) and that only Kidd could find it.[16] This rumor seems unlikely for a number of reasons. Kidd's men probably would have seen him depart with such a large bag and used the information to gain their freedom. Or perhaps Livingston was describing the fifty-two pounds of gold that Kidd had left with Gardiner. Or this may have been yet another story in Kidd's campaign to gain his freedom. He tried to make a deal with Bellomont, Orford, and Harley to the effect that if he were given a ship he would go to the West Indies to recover the *Quedah* and return with the goods that remained on the ship, which he estimated to be worth at least £75,000.[17] In reality, as we have seen, the *Quedah* was stripped before it was burned. Kidd's last forlorn hope was that by playing on someone's greed he could obtain a ship and somehow get free. Livingston's story has the same quality to it; thus it appears unlikely that there was a forty-pound bag of gold waiting to be uncovered.

In the long run the tale has fed a never-ending stream of rumors about Kidd's treasure. From his own time forward, searches have been conducted from Nova Scotia to the South China Sea in search of his treasure—after all, did he not have £400,000 on board at some time? In the nineteenth century companies were even founded to search in the lower Hudson River valley. Time has not diminished these chimeras, even to our own day.[18]

When the remnants of Kidd's "treasure" arrived in London, the Admiralty locked them up as claimants demanded their share. The City of London, the Old East India Company, and the persistent Coji Babba all filed.[19] The claims of the city and the company had no real basis, and only Babba's suit received attention. Nothing could be done until Kidd was tried, his case disposed of, and his property condemned. Even then, one year had to pass before the court could dispose of his property. On May 5, 1701, a claim was filed on Coji Babba's behalf and shortly thereafter the proctor of the Admiralty Court sent commissions to Bengal, Isfahan (Persia), and Surat to collect evidence. The court waited three years for the documents and when none appeared, Babba's case lapsed.[20]

On November 21, 1704, Kidd's goods were condemned and sold for £6,472.1.0. The difference from the original value came from the charging of certain costs to the "treasure" and the sale of the perishables. Still persistent, Coji Babba filed a claim in Chancery Court for a share of this amount, but with the money safely lodged in the Exchequer he lost once again.[21] Meanwhile the directors of

Greenwich Hospital decided they should press a claim, and after they had received the Admiralty's approval, Queen Anne agreed to turn the money over to them. With this windfall the directors decided to buy the house, park, and gardens of Colonel Sidney of Greenwich, thus making possible the creation of the splendid Greenwich Hospital still visible today on the Thames River.[22]

While Kidd's treasure remained in the firm grip of the courts, his fellow buccaneers continued to seek their fortunes. But the actions taken by the government at the end of the seventeenth century to undermine the buccaneers would finally take effect. Queen Anne's War, or the War of the Spanish Succession, continued until 1713, delaying the full implementation of the tools at the government's disposal to curb piracy. When those resources finally were brought to bear, a bitter and deadly struggle erupted, causing piracy to evolve once again.

During the early eighteenth century European piracy changed to reflect new conditions just as it had in the past. Large numbers of men remained active in the Americas, West Africa, and the Indian Ocean. The men involved were far more deeply alienated from their own societies than at any time in the past. They found themselves increasingly cut off from the people who formerly had supported them. Royal officials unrelentingly opposed them; local governments and merchant communities in the colonies became antagonistic. Even in North America the situation worsened. In New York the loss to pirates and the East India Company of three of the four ships that went to Madagascar in 1698 dimmed the ardor of the New York merchant community.[23] Charleston, South Carolina, remained a hospitable port until the volume of rice exports and the expansion of trade proved an attractive target to the pirates. Before long the local community decided it preferred safe shipping to supplying pirates. The more colonial trade expanded, the more likely it was that the pirates would attack it as the number of other targets diminished; and the more they turned on local trade, the more the tension grew between the buccaneers and their old merchant friends.

Other events fed the growing hostility of the pirates. Word that the men who surrendered upon the proclamation of pardon of 1698 were denied the benefits of that pardon when they turned themselves over to officials spread among the men and bred distrust. One report stated, "They therefore resolve no longer to attend to any offers of forgiveness but in case of attack, to defend themselves on their faithless countrymen who may fall into their hands."[24]

Another contributing factor was the precipitous drop in the pay of mariners at the end of the war. During wartime the wages for mariners had remained high as the navy, privateers, fishing fleets, and commercial carriers competed for men. At war's end the situation changed dramatically. For instance, in 1703 the navy enlisted 53,785 men, but after demobilization in 1715 there were only 13,430; and that number declined to 6,240 in 1717 before recovering to a more stable 16,220 in 1718.[25] Thus 40,000 men found themselves without work in a depressed postwar economy, where they had to compete with the men who lost their jobs in the privateering fleet and in the maritime economy. Vast unemployment allowed shipowners to slash wages, as can be seen in the voyage of the *Hamilton* under Captain Nathaniel Uring. The crew embarked on their voyage in the West Indies earning £4.00 per month, but when Uring arrived in Lisbon and heard that the war was over, he paid off the men and engaged another crew at £1.15 per month. When he arrived in Livorno, Italy, he let these men go and hired a new crew for even lower wages.[26] One can well understand why piracy seemed a real alternative to starvation, and why one pirate would say that the "reasons for going a pirating were to revenge themselves on base Merchants, and cruel commanders of ships."[27]

Within the pirate community changes reflected these trends. Many crews refused to take married men, wanting only those without ties to home and hearth, ready to leave everything behind and even spurn salvation, for they were "going on their Voyage to Hell, wither they were all bound."[28] The level of violence toward captains and fellow mariners increased. In the past captains were often tortured by the pirates if they refused to give information about their cargo, but now they would be put to death if their own men testified that they were harsh masters. If ordinary mariners refused to join a pirate crew, they were abused, tortured, and even killed.[29] As a visible symbol of their alienation, the pirates changed from flying the "bloody flag" to using flags filled with the symbols of passing time and death that often included the familiar skull and crossbones.[30]

The forces of order soon gathered to oppose the pirates and the war was joined. It was not fought in London, where fewer and fewer men appeared for trial as pirates. There were no piracy trials in the High Court of Admiralty from 1704 to 1715, and only a few between 1719 and 1725. From 1725 to 1759 there were none. The court spent far more time completing commissions for the trial of pirates in America, Africa, and Asia.[31] The action spilled all over the empire as the navy and local communities hunted the pirates down. Two episodes illustrate this trend.

In 1721 Captain Chaloner Ogle of the *Swallow* was sent to patrol the west coast of Africa, where pirates had not been reported for two years. As luck would have it, the pirate ship *Royal Fortune* appeared and quickly snatched a few prizes. Ogle took up the chase and captured one of the prizes loaded with pirates before finally locating the pirate ship, flying the English flag and jack plus a black pendant, near Cape Lopus. Ogle remained under French colors to confuse his opponent until he moved into close range. Then he hoisted his true colors and unleashed his broadside. In a two-hour fight he shot down the mainmast and the mizzenmast of the *Royal Fortune* before the pirates finally surrendered. With more than 250 pirates under guard, Ogle returned to the English trading station at Cape Corse, where a trial was called using the rules of the new law. The 75 Africans on board, free or not, were sold into slavery and the Europeans were tried. At the end of the trials 52 were executed, 20 sent to servitude in the Royal African Company, 17 remanded to England for further consideration, and the remainder acquitted and either brought into the navy or abandoned. Such was the quick justice available to the navy.[32]

South Carolina experienced a great deal of trouble from some of the most notorious villains of this period, such as Stede Bonnet and the improbable Edward Teach, known as Blackbeard. These men and their crews terrorized the coast from Virginia to Florida, but regarded Charleston as the choicest port on the coast until the townspeople turned against them. The pirates responded by laying siege to the port, robbing ships at their leisure as they sailed unknowingly into the trap.[33] In 1718 their depredations aroused the colonists to serious action, and Governor Alexander Spotswood of Virginia hired and manned two vessels and sent them out in the company of two navy ships to locate Blackbeard. They found him just before a similar group of Carolinians did, and in a fierce struggle Blackbeard succumbed to twenty-five wounds of various kinds.[34] Not to be outdone, a Carolina expedition of two sloops, under the command of Colonel William Rhett, captured Stede Bonnet and his men.[35] As a finale, Governor Robert Johnson of South Carolina sent out two more ships, which captured the last pirates on the coast.[36] Such vigorous campaigns reveal how definitively the atmosphere had changed. No longer safe havens, the colonies had become deadly hunting grounds, with the colonists the chief hunters.

As if to underline this trend, a spate of funeral sermons marked New England's farewell to piracy. Cotton Mather led the way with four sermons: "Trials of Eight Persons Indicted for Piracy" (1718); "Useful Remarks: An Essay upon Remarkables in the Way of Wicked Men: A Sermon [for] 26 Pirates"; "Trials of Sixteen Persons for Piracy"; and "A Vial Poured upon the Sea" (all 1726). Benjamin Colman contributed "It Is a Fearful Thing to Fall into the Hands of a Living God" (1726). And these were by no means all.[37] Certainly no one in New England could doubt the evils of piracy and the rewards that awaited those who strayed into it; for that matter, given the death and destruction that followed the pirates up and down the coast, neither could any other colonists. One is struck by the numbers of men executed at one time. No longer was it the designated four, so common in the past. Now it was fifty-two or twenty-six men who were executed at one time.[38] What was taking place can only be characterized as an extermination campaign: once and for all, the pirates were to be destroyed.

This assault by the forces of law and order signaled that England had become a mature imperial power able to exercise its authority throughout the empire. It also made clear that the developed economy of the empire no longer nourished marauders. The era of rambunctious groups of disaffected men, roaming the seas in search of plunder, was over by 1730, thus marking the conclusion of the relentless campaign against the buccaneers mounted throughout the empire. Piracy would continue until the present day; but European large-scale piracy, made possible by the expansion of maritime enterprise, was over. The English government wanted to monopolize violence and refused to tolerate threats to law and order. Even the highland Scots, long considered a reservoir of rebellion, were crushed after their uprising in 1745.[39] In the modern era the state intended to destroy rebels and maurauders alike, wherever they threatened security or commerce.

The irony is that the society that destroyed the buccaneers would ultimately make them a staple of popular culture. By the late eighteenth century the pirates would emerge, along with Italian bandits, as the stuff of adventure tales. Heroes and heroines would be placed among a group of pirates who could be either benign good fellows of the sea or sinister ne'er-do-wells capable of any evil. In the nineteenth century the buccaneers became Americans. A young country without a mythic past filled with heroes such as King Arthur, Roland, or Siegfried, the United States reached out to its margins to use frontiersmen, whalers, and buccaneers as suitable characters for a national literature. Washington Irving, Edgar Allan Poe, James Fenimore Cooper, and others found them useful.[40] The exploits of the pirates also provided a middle-class audience with stories of adventure that took place in exotic locations outside the possibilities of their own lives. These streams would merge to make the pirates familiar characters.

Kidd's legend was very much a part of this evolution. That he was no ordinary pirate was signaled by the publications at the time of his death. Besides the various *Accounts,* there were transcripts of his trial, polemical works that came from the ongoing struggle between the Whigs and the Tories, and two ballads: "Captain Kidd's Farewell to the Sea" (sung to the tune of "Coming Down") and later "The Dying Words of Captain Robert [William] Kidd." These were essentially penitential hymns in which Kidd expressed regret for his evil ways. "Dying Words" went into nineteenth-century hymnals, and both songs continued to have a lively secular existence into the vaudeville era of the twentieth century.[41]

Kidd also appeared as a figure in novels. Joseph Ingraham used him in two of his mid-nineteenth century works—*The Spanish Gal-*

leon, or the Pirate of the Mediterranean: A Romance of the Corsair Kidd and *Captain Kyd, or the Wizard of the Sea: A Romance.*[42] Neither of these is particularly interesting, although there are engaging touches, such as Kidd dressed in black velvet and the odd embellishment that his mother was a witch (Hurtel of the Red Hand). The *Spanish Galleon* helped feed one of the most curious episodes in the Kidd legend. During the 1840s and 1850s Kidd was made into a romantic figure who captured and had an affair with the Mughal's daughter. Instead of remaining with the princess, he supposedly killed her and fled with the treasure. Her avenging spirit created storm after storm to batter and sink his ship, but he sailed on to New York City. Just as he approached the harbor, the great mother of all storms smashed down upon him and drove Kidd and his wrecked ship to a watery grave in the lower Hudson River valley. Into this tale are melded parts of Kidd's career, Avery's career, and of course the Flying Dutchman. Although the story is quite fantastic, there were enough realistic elements to cause investors to rush forward and fund a number of companies that had as their sole purpose finding the sunken ship and salvaging Kidd's treasure.[43]

Even today Kidd is associated with the heyday of buccaneering, although he was never so successful as Avery, Chivers, Morgan, van Horne, or many others. His legend, enshrined in song and literature, helps keep alive the memory of a time when the world was younger, when it was possible for a group of men to seize a ship and sail to the end of the world seeking their fortune, while living in a consensual society free of the constraints that dominated their lives at home.

Ultimately the buccaneers' success in expanding their geographic range aroused the forces of order and brought the pirates into collision with the demands of empire. The struggle that ensued was lopsided: the resources mobilized by the rising imperial states far exceeded those of the pirates, even in such out-of-the-way places as Saint Marie Island. As time passed, many others would suffer the same fate when they came into conflict with the needs of the modern state. Pirates were not the last group to be crushed by the modern world; but they passed into legend and won at least a posthumous triumph.

Abbreviations · *Notes* · *Index*

Abbreviations

Add. MSS	Additional Manuscripts, British Library, London.
ADM	Admiralty Records, Public Record Office, London.
ARA	Algemeen Rijksarchief, The Hague.
BL	British Library, London.
BL Loan	British Library Loan Manuscripts, British Library, London.
BOD	Bodleian Library, Oxford University, Oxford.
Cal. Hist. MSS	*Calendar of Historical Manuscripts in the Office of the Secretary of State, Albany, New York*. Vol. 2, *English Manuscripts, 1664–1776*. Albany: Weed, Parsons, 1866.
CO	Colonial Office Papers, Public Record Office, London.
Commons *Journals*	*Journals of the House of Commons, 1547–1714*. 17 vols. London, 1742.
CSPC	*Calendar of State Papers, Colonial Series, America and West Indies, 1574–1738*, ed. Noel Sainsbury et al. 42 vols. London: Her Majesty's Stationery Office, 1860–1969.
CSPD	*Calendar of State Papers, Domestic Series*. London: Her Majesty's Stationery Office, 1858–.
DNB	*Dictionary of National Biography*, ed. Leslie Stephen and Sidney Lee. London: Oxford University Press, 1885–1900.
Doc. Hist.	*Documentary History of the State of New York*, ed. E. B. O'Callaghan. 4 vols. Albany: Weed, Parsons, 1849–51.
HCA	High Court of Admiralty Records, Public Record Office, London.
HEH	Henry E. Huntington Library, San Marino, California.
HMC	Historical Manuscripts Commission.
IOR	India Office Records, India Office, London.

Journal of the General Assembly	*Journal of the Votes and Proceedings of the General Assembly of the Colony of New York. Vol. 1, 1691–1743.* New York, 1764.
NYCD	*Documents Relative to the Colonial History of the State of New York*, ed. E. B. O'Callaghan and Berthold Fernow. 15 vols. Albany: Weed, Parsons, 1856–87.
NY Col. MSS	New York Colonial Manuscripts, New York State Library, Albany.
NYHS *Collections*	New-York Historical Society *Collections*. New York, 1811–.
Orig. Corr.	Original Correspondence, East India Company Records, India Office, London.
PRO	Public Record Office, London.
State Trials	*A Complete Collection of State Trials and Proceedings for High Treason and Other Crimes and Misdemeanors, from the Reign of King Richard II to the End of King George I.* London, 1730.
Vernon Letters	Vernon Letters, Buccleuch Manuscripts, Northhamptonshire Record Office, Northhampton, England.
VOC	Verenigde Oostindische Compagnie Records, Algemeen Rijksarchief, The Hague.

Notes

1. The Sea Peoples

1. The capture of *La Paix* is recounted dramatically in Captain William Passenger's letter to the Admiralty, May 3, 1700. ADM 1/2277, 4086, fols. 835–880, PRO. For the trial of the crew see HCA 26/1; 32/1; 1/32, fols. 44–47, PRO. For the order to display the bodies of Guittar and his men see ADM 2/1048, fol. 20.

2. Such a large number of hangings cost the Admiralty a good deal extra for the hangman and the carpenters, who had to build not only additional gallows but also a rail to keep the audience at bay. ADM 1/3666 and ADM 2/1048, PRO. Early newspapers reported the hangings: the *Postman*, May 24, 1701; the *Post Boy*, May 10, 22, 24, 27, 1701; the *Flying Post*, no. 937, pp. 941–943.

3. F. J. Tritsch, "The 'Sackers of Cities' and the Movement of Population," in *Bronze Age Migrations in the Aegean*, ed. P. A. Crossland and Ann Birchall (London: Duckworth, 1973), pp. 233–238; Nancy K. Sandars, *The Sea Peoples: Warriors of the Ancient Mediterranean, 1250–1150 B.C.* (London: Thames and Hudson, 1978), pp. 116–137, 186–187, 197–202; Aristotle, *Politics*, 1256B; Thucydides, *History of the Peloponnesian Wars*, I, 2–6; Herodotus, *The Persian Wars*, I, 1–5.

4. Henry A. Ormerod, *Piracy in the Ancient World: An Essay in Mediterranean History* (reprint ed., Chicago: Argonaut, 1967), pp. 102–103.

5. Ibid., pp. 190–210, 231–241; Thomas R. Holmes, *The Roman Republic and the Founding of the Empire* (Oxford: Clarendon Press, 1923), I, 167–175; Arthur M. Shepard, *Sea Power in Ancient History: The Story of the Navies of Classic Greece and Rome* (Boston: Little, Brown, 1924), pp. 169–185, 195–205.

6. Neville Williams, *Captains Outrageous: Seven Centuries of Piracy* (London: Barrie, 1961), pp. 3–30; W. Branch Johnson, *Wolves of the Channel* (London: Wishart, 1931), pp. 1–18; Georges Duby, *The Early Growth of the*

European Economy (Ithaca: Cornell University Press, 1974), pp. 120, 127, 142.

7. W. H. Moreland, *India at the Death of Akbar: An Economic Study* (Delhi: Atma Ram, 1962), pp. 189–193, 223–225; Gopal Lallanji, *The Economic Life of Northern India, c. A.D. 700–1200* (Delhi: Motilal Banarsidass, 1965), pp. 119–160; Dipakranjan Das, *Economic History of the Deccan: From the First to the Sixth Century A.D.* (Delhi: Munshiram Manoharlal, 1967), pp. 208–270.

8. Kwan-wai So, *Japanese Piracy in Ming China during the Sixteenth Century* (East Lansing: Michigan State University Press, 1975), pp. 145–156.

9. Gunther E. Rothenberg, "Venice and the Uzkoks of Senj, 1537–1618," *Journal of Modern History*, 33 (1961), 148–156.

10. As one official put it, "Wars at sea are merchants' affairs and of no concern to the prestige of kings." Charles R. Boxer, *The Portuguese Seaborne Empire, 1415–1825* (New York: Knopf, 1969), p. 50.

11. G. J. Marcus, *A Naval History of England* (London: Longmans, 1961–71), I, 113–115, 137–139; W. L. Clowes et al., *The Royal Navy: A History* (London: S. Low, Marsten, 1897–1903), I, 348–349.

12. Bailey W. Diffie and George D. Winius, *Foundations of the Portuguese Empire, 1415–1580* (Minneapolis: University of Minnesota Press, 1977), pp. 223–226; K. M. Panikkar, *A History of Kerala, 1498–1801* (Annamalaingar: Annamalai University Press, 1960), pp. 48–49; Boxer, *Portuguese Empire*, pp. 39–64.

13. The Portuguese historian Joao de Barros wrote, "It is true that there does exist a common right to all to navigate the seas and in Europe we recognize the rights which others hold against us; but the right does not extend beyond Europe and therefore the Portuguese as Lords of the Sea are justified in confiscating the goods of all those who navigate the seas without their permission." Quoted in K. M. Panikkar, *Asia and Western Dominance: A Survey of the Vasco da Gama Epoch in Asian History* (New York: Collier, 1969), p. 42.

14. Diffie and Winius, *Foundations of the Portuguese Empire*, pp. 243–271; Holden Furber, *Rival Empires of Trade in the Orient, 1600–1800* (Minneapolis: University of Minnesota Press, 1976), pp. 1–78.

15. For the history of India see R. P. Tripathi, *Rise and Fall of the Mughal Empire* (Allahabad: Central Book Depot, 1963); Ashirabadi Lal Srivastava, *The Mughal Empire, 1526–1803* (Agra: S. L. Agarwala, 1959). For accounts of the naval conflict see Auguste Toussaint, *History of the Indian Ocean* (Chicago: University of Chicago Press, 1966), pp. 140–144; O. K. Nambiar, *The Kunjalis: Admirals of Calicut* (London: Asia Publishing House, 1963); Panikkar, *Kerala*, pp. 126–130; Andrew C. Hess, "The Evolution of the Ottoman Seaborne Empire in the Age of Oceanic Discoveries, 1453–1525," *American Historical Review*, 75 (1970), 1892–1919; Louis Dermigny,

La Chine et l'Occident: La commerce à Canton au XVIII siècle, 1719–1833 (Paris: S.E.V.P.E.N., 1964), pp. 92–103.

16. Huan Ma, *Ying-yai Sheng Lan "The Overall Survey of the Ocean's Shores,"* ed. J. V. G. Mills, trans. Feng Ch'eng-chun (Cambridge: Hakluyt Society, University Press, 1970); Joseph Needham, *Science and Civilization in China*, vol. 4, *Civil Engineering and Nautics* (Cambridge: Cambridge University Press, 1971), pt. 3, pp. 478–528. For an assessment of the conditions in each of the empires that proved so favorable to the Europeans see E. L. Jones, *The European Miracle: Environments, Economies and Geopolitics in the History of Europe and Asia* (Cambridge: Cambridge University Press, 1981).

17. John H. Parry, *The Age of Reconnaissance* (New York: New American Library, 1963), pp. 193–206, 243–273; Ralph Davis, *The Rise of the Atlantic Economies* (Ithaca: Cornell University Press, 1973), pp. 37–87, 143–156; David B. Quinn, *North America from Earliest Discovery to First Settlements: The Norse Voyages to 1612* (New York: Harper and Row, 1977), pp. 240–288; J. C. A. De Meij, *De Watergeuzen en de Nederlanden, 1568–1572* (Amsterdam: North-Holland, 1972); Kenneth R. Andrews, *The Spanish Caribbean: Trade and Plunder 1530–1630* (New Haven: Yale University Press, 1978); idem, *Trade, Plunder and Settlement: Maritime Enterprise and the Genesis of the British Empire, 1480–1630* (Cambridge: Cambridge University Press, 1984); Arthur P. Newton, *The European Nations in the West Indies, 1493–1688* (reprint ed., New York: Barnes and Noble, 1967); Cornelis Goslinga, *The Dutch in the Caribbean and on the Wild Coast, 1580–1680* (Assen: Van Gorcum, 1971).

18. Fernand Braudel describes the piracy of this era as a substitute for war that resulted from the fact that the Spanish and Turks failed to carry the heavy burdens of empire and cut costs by encouraging private warfare against the enemy. Braudel, *The Mediterranean and the Mediterranean World in the Age of Phillip II*, trans. Sian Reynolds (New York: W. W. Norton, 1973), II, 865–891. See also John F. Guilmartin, *Gunpowder and Galleys: Changing Technology and Mediterranean Warfare at Sea in the Sixteenth Century* (Cambridge: Cambridge University Press, 1974), pp. 81–83, 221–258; Andrew C. Hess, *The Forgotten Frontier: A History of the Sixteenth Century Ibero-American Frontier* (Chicago: University of Chicago Press, 1978), pp. 71–99, 127–155; Jack Beeching, *The Galleys at Lepanto* (New York: Scribner, 1982).

19. Newton, *European Nations*, pp. 45–49.

20. Reginald G. Marsden, "Early Prize Jurisdiction and Prize Law in England," *English Historical Review*, 24 (1909), 675–697; 25 (1910), 243–263; 26 (1911), 34–56. See also idem, *Documents Relating to Law and Custom of the Sea, 1205–1767* (London: Navy Record Society, 1915–16).

21. Robert W. Kenny, *Elizabeth's Admiral: The Political Career of Charles Howard, Earl of Nottingham, 1536–1624* (Baltimore: Johns Hopkins University Press, 1970), pp. 266–271; David Mathew, "The Cornish and Welsh Pirates in the Reign of Elizabeth," *English Historical Review*, 34 (1924),

337–348; C. L. Ewen, "Organized Piracy around England in the Sixteenth Century," *Mariners Mirror,* 34 (1949), 29–42; C. L. Kingsford, "West Country Piracy: The School of English Seamen," in *Prejudice and Promise in Fifteenth Century England* (London: F. Cass, 1962), pp. 78–105; Kenneth R. Andrews, *Elizabethan Privateering: English Privateering during the Spanish War, 1585–1603* (Cambridge: Cambridge University Press, 1964), pp. 22–31; Reginald G. Marsden, "The Vice-Admirals of the Coast," *English Historical Review,* 22 (1907), 468–774; 23 (1908), 736–757.

22. See the accounts of two captains who were confronted by ships of greater force and decided discretion was the better part of valor. ADM 51/291 and State Papers 14/154, fol. 43, PRO. On the general background see Christopher D. Penn, *The Navy under the Early Stuarts and Its Influence on English History* (London: J. Hogg, 1920), pp. 46–49, 81–87.

23. There are many accounts of Drake's voyage. See for example Derek Wilson, *The World Encompassed: Francis Drake and His Great Voyage* (New York: Harper and Row, 1977).

24. Wesley F. Craven, "The Earl of Warwick, A Speculator in Piracy," *Hispanic American Historical Review,* 10 (1930), 457–479; Andrews, *The Spanish Caribbean,* pp. 134–170.

25. Kenneth R. Andrews, "Sir Robert Cecil and Mediterranean Plunder," *English Historical Review,* 87 (1972), 513–532. Cecil's conduct elsewhere was equally lacking in a sense of ethics; see Lawrence Stone, *Family and Fortune: Studies in Aristocratic Finance in the Sixteenth and Seventeenth Centuries* (Oxford: Clarendon Press, 1973), pp. 3–15, 32–49.

26. Stone, *Family and Fortune,* pp. 55–58; Sir John Neale, "Elizabethan Political Scene," in idem, *Essays in Elizabethan History* (London: J. Cape, 1958).

27. Charles Grey, *Pirates of the Eastern Seas, 1618–1723: A Lurid Page of History* (London: S. Low, Marston, 1933), pp. 76–78.

28. Paul E. Hoffman, *The Spanish Crown and the Defense of the Caribbean, 1535–85: Precedent, Patrimonialism and Royal Parsimony* (Baton Rouge: Louisiana State University Press, 1980); Newton, *European Nations,* pp. 108–124; Andrews, *The Spanish Caribbean,* pp. 81–107, 198–223.

29. Quinn, *North America from Earliest Discovery,* pp. 240–261; Arthur P. Newton, *The Colonizing Activities of the English Puritans* (New Haven: Yale University Press, 1914), pp. 80–100, 294–313.

30. Clarence H. Haring, *The Buccaneers in the West Indies in the Seventeenth Century* (London: Methuen, 1910), pp. 79–231; Stephen S. Webb, *The Governors General: The English Army and the Definition of the Empire, 1569–1681* (Chapel Hill: University of North Carolina Press, 1979), pp. 151–312.

31. Nellis M. Crouse, *French Struggle for the West Indies, 1665–1713* (New York: Columbia University Press), pp. 133–147; Goslinga, *Dutch in the Caribbean,* pp. 304–404.

32. James Vernon to Earl of Shrewsbury, November 28, 1696, in

G. P. R. James, *Letters Illustrative of the Reign of William III from 1696–1708 addressed to the Duke of Shrewsbury* (London: H. Colburn, 1841), I, 87.

33. Andrews, *Elizabethan Privateering*, pp. 104–109.

34. Gordon Connell-Smith, *Forerunners of Drake: A Study of English Trade with Spain in the Early Tudor Period* (London: Longmans, Green, 1954), pp. 136–151.

35. Heyn was later killed in action while fighting the Dunkirk pirates. S. P. L'Honore-Naber and Irene A. Wright, *Piet Heyn en de Zilvervloot* (Utrecht: Kemink and Zoon, 1928); Robert F. Marx, *The Capture of the Treasure Fleet* (New York: McKay, 1977); Goslinga, *Dutch in the Caribbean*, pp. 141–194.

36. Sir William Foster, ed., *The Voyages of Sir James Lancaster to Brazil and the East Indies, 1591–1603* (London: Hakluyt Society, 1940).

37. Braudel, *The Mediterranean*, II, 865–891.

38. Among the many accounts of the Barbary corsairs two are notable: Peter Earle, *Corsairs of Malta and Barbary* (London: Sidgwick and Jackson, 1970); John B. Wolf, *The Barbary Coast: Algiers under the Turks, 1500–1830* (New York: Norton, 1979).

39. Even in the remote province of New York a "Turk's rate" was levied in 1678. NY Col. MSS, 27, fol. 179. For the organized ransom business see Ellen G. Friedman, *Spanish Captives in North Africa in the Early Modern Age* (Madison: University of Wisconsin Press, 1983); Braudel, *The Mediterranean*, II, 877–879. For a firsthand account of the slavery business see *Mr. Roberts his Voyage to the Levant* . . . in William Hacke, ed., *A Collection of Original Voyages* (London, 1699), pp. 9–20; also the correspondence of John Ealisman, English consul at Algiers, State Papers, 71/3, PRO; Wolf, *Barbary Coast*, pp. 151–174.

40. Earle, *Corsairs of Malta*, pp. 97–144; Braudel, *The Mediterranean*, II, 877–879; Hacke, *Roberts his Voyage*, p. 11.

41. The new pirates had a serious impact on Venice. See Alberto Tenenti, *Piracy and the Decline of Venice, 1580–1615*, trans. Janet and Brian Pullan (Berkeley: University of California Press, 1967), pp. 56–73.

42. Richard Gifford to Lord Buckhurst, June 28, 1601, State Papers, 98/1, fol. 187, PRO. See also Thomas Wilson to Buckhurst, August 9, 1601, ibid., fols. 203–204; and the correspondence in Add. MSS, 24107, fols. 190–191; Rawlinson MSS, A/343, fols. 1–10, BOD; Cotton MSS, E/8, fol. 358, BL.

43. Sir Leoline Jenkins discussed this case in his writings on Admiralty Court jurisdiction. There was even a resident trader or factor operating in Salé on behalf of the merchants. Add. MSS, 18206, fols. 95–96, 108, BL.

44. R. Coindreau, *Les corsairs de Salé* (Paris: Société d'éditions géographiques, maritimes et coloniales, 1948); Earle, *Corsairs of Malta*, pp. 72–94; Wolf, *Barbary Coast*, pp. 55–150.

45. Williams, *Captains Outrageous*, pp. 97–110; Clive Senior, *A Nation of Pirates: English Piracy in Its Heyday* (New York: Crane, Russak, 1976), pp.

36–46; G. E. Manwaring, *The Life and Works of Sir Henry Mainwaring* (London: Navy Records Society, 1920), I, 1–32.

46. J. M. Perkins, "Piracy in Iceland," *American Scandinavian Review,* 47 (1961), 259–265; Earle, *Corsairs of Malta,* pp. 47–71; Senior, *Nation of Pirates,* pp. 102–107; Clowes et al., *Royal Navy,* II, 49–50. Six Algerian pirates were reported in the English Channel during the spring of 1686. CSPD, II, nos. 602, 721.

47. There is an extensive literature on the buccaneers, which includes the following: John Exquemelin, *The Bucaniers of America* (London, 1684); Phillip Ayres, *The Voyages and Adventures of Captain Bartholomew Sharp and others in the South Sea* (London, 1684); William Dampier, *A New Voyage Round the World* (London, 1694); Vincent T. Harlow, ed., *The Voyages of Captain William Jackson, 1642–1645* (London: Hakluyt Society, 1923); Marguerite E. Wilbur, ed. and trans., *Raveneau de Lussan: Buccaneer of the Spanish Main and Early French Filibuster of the Pacific* (Cleveland: Arthur H. Clark, 1930). For secondary accounts see Haring, *Buccaneers;* Crouse, *French Struggle;* James Burney, *History of the Buccaneers in America* (London: Payne and Foss, 1816); P. K. Kemp and Christopher Lloyd, *The Brethren of the Coast: The British and French Buccaneers in the South Seas* (London: Heinemann, 1960); Dudley Pope, *Harry Morgan's Way: The Biography of Sir Henry Morgan, 1635–1684* (London: Secker and Warburg, 1977).

48. My account is based on the interrogation of Dangerfield conducted while he was a prisoner in the Carolinas. CO, 1/57, fol. 381, PRO.

49. See the account of Alexander Selkirk, model for the fictional Robinson Crusoe, in Woodes Rogers, *A Cruising Voyage Around the World* (London, 1712), pp. 123–129. Another instance of abandoning a man on Juan Fernandez is in the journal of Basil Ringrose; see Exquemelin, *Bucaniers,* II, 122.

50. Shirley C. Hughson, *The Carolina Pirates and Colonial Commerce, 1670–1740* (Baltimore: Johns Hopkins University Press, 1894), pp. 5–46. Hughson explains piracy in the colony as a matter of low moral character among the colonists. For a more balanced view that takes into account Charleston's economy, see Converse D. Clowse, *Economic Beginnings in Colonial South Carolina, 1670–1730* (Columbia: University of South Carolina Press, 1971), pp. 87–90.

2. From Pirate to Friend of the Junto

1. Hard evidence about Kidd's life before 1689, when he participated in Codrington's campaign, is difficult to obtain. As he became a mythic figure, layer after layer of fantasy obscured the few facts we have. Kidd never left a full record of his career: not until his arrest in 1699 did he require such an account, and then he wrote only what he thought his audience desired or what was self-serving. See for instance his statement in BL Loan, 29/207, fols. 106–107. The remaining evidence comes from those who were ac-

quainted with certain aspects of his career, usually after 1689. But many of these individuals were induced to testify during the numerous pirate trials in 1700 and 1701 on the promise of a pardon; therefore the evidence they gave needs careful consideration.

It is possible to reconstruct some aspects of Kidd's career before he enters the records of New York in 1691. See the depositions of Samuel Burgess, HCA 1/98, pt. 1, fols. 42–50, PRO; Council's Brief in the trial of Burgess, Rawlinson MSS, A/270, no. 1, BOD; testimony of John Brown, HCA 1/16, pt. 1, fol. 1; and finally, testimony of Robert Culliford, HCA 1/16, pt. 1, fol. 5, and ADM 1/3666, fol. 100, no. 4, PRO; Paul Lorrain, *The Ordinary of Newgate, His Account of the Behavior, Confessions and Dying Words of Captain William Kidd, and Other Pirates, that were Executed at the Execution Dock in Wapping, Friday, May 23, 1701* (London, 1701). Other works dealing with William Kidd are the following: John S. Abbott, *Captain William Kidd, and Others of the Pirates and Buccaneers Who Ravaged the Seas, the Islands, and the Continents of America Two Hundred Years Ago* (New York: Dodd, Mead, 1874); William H. Bonner, *Pirate Laureate: The Life and Legends of Captain Kidd* (New Brunswick, N.J.: Rutgers University Press, 1957); Graham Brooks, ed., *The Trial of Captain Kidd* (London: William Hedges, 1930); William W. Campbell, *An Historical Sketch of Robin Hood and Captain Kidd* (New York: C. Scribner, 1853); Cornelius Dalton, *The Real Captain Kidd: A Vindication* (New York: Duffield, 1911); Dunbar M. Hinrichs, *The Fateful Voyage of Captain Kidd* (New York: Bookman Associates, 1955); Clarence Milligan, *Captain William Kidd, Gentleman or Buccaneer?* (Philadelphia: Dorrance, 1932); Don C. Seitz, ed., *The Tryal of Captain William Kidd for Murther and Piracy* . . . (New York: R. R. Wilson, 1936); Harold T. Wilkins, *Captain Kidd and His Skeleton Island* (London: Cassell, 1935); Alexander Winston, *No Man Knows My Grave: Sir Henry Morgan, Captain William Kidd, Captain Woodes Rogers in the Great Age of Privateers and Pirates, 1665–1715* (Boston: Houghton Mifflin, 1969).

2.   Vaughan to Lords of Trade, April 4, 1676, CO 5/36, fol. 71, PRO.

3.   Wilbur, *Raveneau de Lussan*, p. 88.

4.   Deposition of Francis Tippet, November 1699, CO 323/3, fol. 112, PRO. Exquemelin, *Bucaniers*, pt. 2, 46, 55–56, relates a similar struggle between French and English buccaneers.

5.   Haring, *Buccaneers*, pp. 258–269; Crouse, *French Struggle*, pp. 176–245; Nelson, *European Nations*, pp. 320–329.

6.   CSPC (1689–92), nos. 585, 655, 718. For an overall view of campaign see Thomas Spencer, *A True and Faithfull Relation of the Proceedings of the Forces of Their Majesties King William and Queen Mary in their Expedition Against the French in the Caribby Islands in the West Indies under the Conduct of His Excellency Christopher Coddrington, 1689 and 1690* (London, 1691).

7.   Spencer, *True Relation*. Hewetson wrote a long account of the action, CSPC (1689–92), no. 789.

8. Hewetson characterized Kidd in this fashion at Kidd's trial. See *State Trials*, V, 326.

9. Codrington, in recording this loss, wrote of Kidd, "He behaved himself well" CSPC (1689–92), no. 789. See also the depositions of Burgess, Brown, and Culliford cited in note 1 to this chapter.

10. Statement by Kidd (no date), BL Loan, 29/207, fols. 106–107. These are the papers of Sir Robert Harley and his family.

11. Culliford reports that the two thousand pieces of eight were from coconuts; but it seems likely he meant cacao nuts, which were far more valuable. HCA 1/16, pt. 1, fol. 5, PRO.

12. Robert C. Ritchie, *The Duke's Province: A Study of Politics and Society in New York, 1664–1691* (Chapel Hill: University of North Carolina Press, 1977), pp. 198–234.

13. See the various depositions in note 1.

14. Entry for January 10, 1690, in the log of the *Archangel*, ADM 51/55, pt. 1, PRO. Captain Caspar Hicks noted that he sighted Bermuda on the ninth and then ran aground on the eastern end of the island. He anchored at Sandy Hook on March 18.

15. Ingoldsby to Leisler, NYHS *Collections* (1868), p. 300; Leisler to Ingoldsby, February 14, 1691, ibid., pp. 302–303; Joseph Dudley to Leisler, March 11, 1691, CO 37/25, no. 25, PRO; Chidley Brooke to Sloughter, March 14, 1691, CO 37/25, no. 37, PRO; Stephanus van Cortlandt to Sir William Blathwayt, April 6, 1691, Blathwayt MSS (New York), vol. 9, HEH. These papers are held by the Institute for Early American History and Culture, Williamsburg, Virginia, with a microfilm copy on file at the HEH. See also the order to Abraham de Peyster to deliver guns and ammunition to Kidd, March 20, 1691, Cal. Hist. MSS, p. 202. For an account by one of Leisler's adherents, see also the depositions in the Amsterdam Notarial Archives MSS, N. 357, 4752, no. 79, and N. 359, 4753, no. 135, Queens College, New York City. See also Lawrence H. Leder, "Records of the Trials of Jacob Leisler and His Associates," *New-York Historical Society Quarterly*, 36 (1952), 431–457; idem, "Captain Kidd and the Leisler Rebellion," ibid., 38 (1954), 48–54.

16. Major Ingoldsby was only awarded £100 for his part in the overthrow of Leisler. *Journal of the General Assembly*, I, 13.

17. The records of the capture and subsequent struggle over the *Pierre* are in Doc. Hist., II, 250–251, 291–295, 304–307. See also N.Y. Col. MSS, 34, pt. 2, fol. 80; 36, 106–112, New York State Library; HCA 24/124, no. 162; 125, no. 27. PRO. Kidd almost went to work for the colony of Connecticut as a privateer hunter. See the proposal by Captain Kidd, June 8, 1691, Massachusetts Historical Society, *Collections*, ser. 3, I, 122–123.

18. Isaac N. Phelps-Stokes, *The Iconography of Manhattan Island, 1698–*

1909 (New York: R. H. Dodd, 1916–28), VI, 132–133, 142–143. The wills of her two previous husbands are in NYHS *Collections,* 25 (1892), 157–158, 180, 183, 197, 204, 207. Cox left two houses, one on Wall Street, the other on Pearl Street.

19.   Robert C. Ritchie, "Some Effects of King William's War on New York" (in a volume forthcoming from Princeton University Press).

20.   Ibid.

21.   HCA 1/16, pt. 1, fols. 1, 5; CO 5/1040, fols. 141–143, 162; ADM 1/3666, fol. 1, no. 4; Rawlinson MSS, A/270, fol. 1, BOD; Add. MSS, 9837, fol. 113, BL. PRO.

22.   Jacob Judd, "Frederick Philipse and the Madagascar Trade," *New-York Historical Society Quarterly,* 55 (1971), 354–374; Robert C. Ritchie, "Samuel Burgess, Pirate," in *New Approaches to the History of Colonial and Revolutionary New York,* ed. Conrad Wright and William Pencak (Charlottesville: University of Virginia Press, forthcoming).

23.   For a dyspeptic view of Fletcher's character see Peter de la Noy to [unknown], June 13, 1695, NYCD, IV, 221–224. Regarding the bribes, see Weaver's reply, CO 391/11, fols. 215–216; also HCA 1/98, pt. 1, fol. 55; CO 5/1040, fols. 138, 162, PRO.

24.   Fletcher to Board of Trade, June 30, 1696, NYCD, IV, 150–151; and ibid., pp. 466–470, 479–486. See also James S. Leamon, "Governor Fletcher's Recall," *William and Mary Quarterly,* ser. 3, 20 (1963), 527–542.

25.   In nearby East Jersey, Benjamin Bullivant reported, "I lay that night almost killed with musquettos, and disturbed by some privateers [pirates] who brought theyr girls thither to make merry, and were so until 2 in the morning in the same room where I was in bed." Wayne Andrews, ed., "A Glance at New York in 1697: The Travel Diary of Dr. Benjamin Bullivant," *New-York Historical Society Quarterly,* 60 (1956), 55–73.

26.   While most supplies came from New York and other colonial ports, there are references to a few ships from England going to Madagascar. The Dutch at Cochin sometimes supplied pirates, because the brigands were regarded by the Mughal government as being English, and it was the *English* East India Company that usually suffered the consequences of the pirates' actions. Account of Richard Lasinby, Orig. Corr., E/1/13, fol. 97, IOR. See the petition of the East India Company, Add. MSS, 25098, fol. 473, BL.

27.   Log of the *Richmond,* ADM 51/4310, PRO. James Graham related that Kidd was in the privateering business. Graham to Sir William Blathwayt, May 29, 1695, Blathwayt MSS (New York), vol. 10, HEH.

28.   Phelps-Stokes, *Iconography of Manhattan,* III, 950; IV, 329, 345, 349, 392. See also Conveyance Libers, L21/155, 75–76, New York City Hall of Records. On Kidd's pew and his support of the new Anglican church, see Clifford P. Morehouse, *Trinity: Mother of Churches; An Informal History of Trinity Parish in the City of New York* (New York: Seabury Press, 1973).

29. Lawrence H. Leder, *Robert Livingston, 1654–1728, and the Politics of Colonial New York* (Chapel Hill: University of North Carolina Press, 1961), pp. 93–94; Chidley Brooke to [unknown], November 24, 1694, CO 5/1038, fols. 421–422, PRO; Paul Hamlin and Charles E. Baker, eds., *Supreme Court of Judicature of the Province of New York, 1691–1704*, NYHS, *Collections* (1952–59), I, 150, 163–164.

30. See Browne's deposition, June 17, 1702, HCA 1/16, pt. 1, fol. 1, PRO.

31. Graham mentioned Kidd's role in capturing islands in the West Indies and in helping Governor Sloughter. He praised his "unquestioned courage" in many engagements. Graham to Sir William Blathwayt, May 29, 1695, Blathwayt MSS (New York), vol. 10, HEH.

32. Livingston kept a journal in Dutch from December 9, 1694, until October 3, 1695, which has been translated by A. J. F. van Laer and is now in the New-York Historical Society. On the *Antigua* in London see Exchequer 190 (Port Books), 150/1, PRO.

33. For background on Livingston's trip see Leder, *Livingston*, pp. 46, 48, 49, 50–51, 110–111; Captain John Evans to the Admiralty, July 5, 1698, ADM 1/1754, PRO. The ship-seizing episode is described in a letter of Chidley Brooke, November 24, 1694, CO5/1038, fols. 421–422, PRO.

34. John Ehrman, *The Navy in the War of William III, 1689–1697: Its State and Direction* (Cambridge: Cambridge University Press, 1953), pp. 341–516; Clowes, *The Royal Navy*, II, 325–360. For French naval policy see Geoffrey Symcox, *The Crisis of French Sea Power, 1688–1697: From the Guerre d'Escadre to the Guerre de Course* (The Hague: M. Nijhoff, 1974).

35. Patrick Crowhurst, *The Defence of British Trade, 1689–1815* (Folkstone: Dawson, 1977), pp. 46–80.

36. For the dispute over privateering see ADM 1/5144, fols. 501, 577; 5145, fols. 399–401, 419, 423; 5146, fols. 409–445; ADM 2/1046, fols. 251, 280, 287, 297, PRO. At times during the crisis even watermen (who made their living by carrying people on London's busiest thoroughfare, the Thames) lost their freedom from impressment. Privy Council Registers 2/74, fols. 369, 389; 75, fol. 123, PRO. In the summer of 1695 ships returning from the Levant and the West Indies were stopped in the English Channel and most of the crew were impressed by the navy. ADM 3/12, July 5, 1695, PRO. The East India Company succeeded in getting commissions because of its powerful political friends and its vital trade. See CO 324/24, fols. 232, 238–241, 294–296, for the commissions granted to its ships.

37. For English politics in this period see Thomas B. Macaulay, *The History of England, from the Accession of James II* (London: Longmans, 1849–65), vol. 5; B. W. Hill, *The Growth of Parliamentary Parties, 1689–1742* (London: Allen and Unwin, 1976); Henry Horwitz, *Parliament, Policy and Politics in the Reign of William II* (Manchester: Manchester University Press, 1977); Keith Feiling, *A History of the Tory Party, 1640–1714* (Oxford:

Clarendon Press, 1924); Dennis Rubini, *Court and Country, 1688–1702* (London: Rupert Hart-Davis, 1967); J. H. Plumb, *Origins of Political Stability, England 1675–1725* (Boston: Houghton Mifflin, 1967).

38. Macaulay, *History of England*, V, 2400–4; DNB, XX, 1329–34.

39. Macaulay, *History of England*, V, 2397–2400; DNB, XIII, 665–670; *The Works and Life of the Right Honorable Charles, late Earl of Halifax* (London, 1715).

40. DNB, XVIII, 217–219; Henry Sidney, *Diary of the Times of Charles the Second . . .* (London, 1843).

41. William L. Sachse, *Lord Somers, a Political Portrait* (Manchester: Manchester University Press, 1975); DNB, XVI, 51–61.

42. DNB, XVII, 429–431.

43. DNB, XIX, 301–307; Dorothy H. Somerville, *King of Hearts, Charles Talbot, Duke of Shrewsbury* (London: Allen and Unwin, 1962); T. C. Nicholson and A. S. Tuberville, *Charles Talbot, Duke of Shrewsbury* (Cambridge: Cambridge University Press, 1930).

44. Stephen S. Webb, "William Blathwayt, Imperial Fixer: From Popish Plot to Glorious Revolution," *William and Mary Quarterly*, 25 (1968), 3–21; idem, "William Blathwayt, Imperial Fixer: Muddling Through to Empire, 1689–1717," ibid., 26 (1969), 373–415.

45. DNB, IV,1088–89. On Coote in the Netherlands see his letters to Lord Middleton, Add. MSS, 41820, fol. 273; 41821, fol. 74, BL. For his appointment as Queen Mary's treasurer see Rawlinson MSS, C/983, fol. 123, BOD; also Rawlinson MSS, A/306, fol. 9, and Add. MSS, 21505, fol. 56, BL. His presence in Holland displeased King James; see N. Japiske, ed., *Correspondence of William III and Hans W. Bentinck, Duke of Portland* (The Hague: M. Nijhoff, 1934), II, 761. Coote was raised from Baron of Coloony to Earl of Bellomont in November 1689; see CSPD, William III, I, 308. But his estate was in dispute; Stowe MSS, 202, fol. 194, BL. For Bellomont and Locke see Somers to Locke, March 5, 1690, Locke MSS, c. 18, fol. 154, BOD. Bellomont consulted Locke on the education of his children; Locke MSS, c. 7. For the Coningsby affair see Privy Council Register 2/75, fols. 189, 192, 198, PRO; Narcissus Luttrell, *A Brief Historical Relation of State Affairs from September, 1678 to April, 1718* (Oxford: Oxford University Press, 1857), III, 65, 121, 123, 153, 164; BL Loan 29/206, fol. 146, and Add. MSS, 37992, fol. 15, BL; Anchitel Grey, *Debates of the House of Commons from the year 1667 to the year 1694* (London, 1763), X, 364–368.

46. Coote to Archbishop of Armagh, November 19, 1661, Hardwicke MSS, 14590, HEH. In 1688 he had to get Chief Justice North to protect him from a suit over a £4,000 debt; Hardwicke MSS, 1611, HEH. On the difficulties with his marriage settlement see Add. MSS, 34730, fol. 81–82, and 36730, fol. 95, BL. Shrewsbury's intercession is described in William Coxe, ed., *Private and Original Correspondence of Charles Talbot, Duke of Shrewsbury with King William and Leaders of the Whig Party* (London, 1821), p. 40.

Shrewsbury mounted a campaign to get Bellomont office and lands because of his loyalty; see Sunderland to Portland, August 5, 1694, Portland MSS, PWA 1240/1, Nottingham University Library.

47. CO 391/8, fols. 51, 53, 59–61, PRO.

48. Coxe, *Original Correspondence*, pp. 93–94. Blathwayt advised against the joining of the two governments and defended Fletcher; see Add. MSS, 37992, fols. 101–112, BL. Another report, defending the union on the basis of mutual defense, is Add. MSS, 21494, fol. 37, BL.

49. Leamon, "Fletcher's Recall," pp. 531–532.

50. August 10 and 11, 1695, Livingston's Journal MSS, New-York Historical Society.

51. CO 391/8, fols. 100–104, 110, 113–114; 9, 98–99, PRO. Also Shrewsbury to Fletcher, August 12, 1697, Add. MSS, 9837, fol. 98, BL. Blathwayt protected his client by writing to Shrewsbury that the king wanted the words "taking care of Him and otherwise employing him" written in the recall letter to Fletcher. See Blathwayt to Shrewsbury, July 29, 1697, Blathwayt MSS, Osborne Collection, Beinecke Library, Yale University.

52. August 11, 1695, Livingston's Journal MSS, New-York Historical Society.

53. Bellomont to Vernon, October 18, 1700, NYCD, IV, 760, and December 6, 1700, ibid., 815–817; also statement by Kidd, BL Loan, 29/207, fols. 106–107. Hewetson testified to the threats against Kidd; *State Trials*, V, 326. For Bellomont's account see *A Full Account of the Actions of the Late Famous Pyrate Captain Kidd* (London, 1701); Gilbert Burnet, *History of His Own Time* (Oxford: Oxford University Press, 1833), IV, 433–434; John Oldmixon, *The History of England during the Reigns of King William and Queen Mary, Queen Anne and King George I* (London, 1735), pp. 205–206.

54. Livingston discussed his activities in his journal from August 12 to October 3; Journal MSS, New-York Historical Society.

55. Somerville, *King of Hearts*, p. 149.

56. Precedent already existed for the plotters' design. Medieval and early modern governments simply did not have the resources to combat piracy even in local waters. Fleets were ruinously expensive and were laid up in peacetime. During the reign of James I the magnificent navy created by Queen Elizabeth rotted because of the king's parsimony. So low did English naval power sink that James was forced to agree to a Dutch proposal to send a squadron to attack the English pirate bases. Some monarchs, such as Edward IV, had actively pursued the pirates and swept the seas clean, but all too often piracy had a low priority, particularly in wartime. If the state did not have sufficient resources, it turned to the private sector. It was not unusual for an individual or a group or a town to get a commission or orders to hunt down pirates. Often the orders were ignored unless they promised profit to the recipient. Attacking pirates was not the same as pouncing upon a merchant-

man. These commissions acted as a precedent for the Kidd plan, because the government lacked the will and the resources to do much about piracy far beyond European waters. Penn, *Navy under Early Stuarts,* pp. 1–50, 81–87. See Robert Cotton's report on the navy, State Papers, 14/41, fols. 1–71, PRO; Marsden, *Documents Relating to Law,* II, 219–220. On special commissions to seize pirates see State Papers, 14/141, fols. 57, 289, 351, and HCA 14/41, fols. 91, 92, 199; Somerville, *King of Hearts,* pp. 172–174. On Kidd's statement see BL Loan, 29/207, fols. 106–107. Hewetson took him to Romney; see *Memoirs of the Life of John, Lord Somers* (London, 1716), pp. 78–80.

57. Kidd's sureties are listed in a document dated December 11, 1695, HCA 25/12, PRO. Copies of this agreement and the bonds are numerous. See BL Loan, 29/207, fols. 72–74, 133, 134; miscellaneous MSS, 14148, HEH; NYCD, IV, 762–765.

58. Bellomont to Somers, October 16, 1697, Somers Papers, Corporation of Reigate, City Hall, Surrey, England. For Bellomont's later proposals see James, *Letters Illustrative,* I, 117, 428–429; and Bellomont's letters to Vernon and Somers, March 7, 1699, BL Loan, 29/207, fols. 84–93. Another secret partner and likely financier was Sir Richard Blackham; see Leder, *Livingston,* 198–199.

59. CO 323/4, fols. 639–640, PRO; Admiralty to Hedges, December 30, 1695, Add. MSS, 25098, fol. 298, BL. On Holmes see CO 324/5, fols. 5–6; State Papers, 44/337, fols. 349–350, PRO; Ellesmere MSS, 9794, HEH.

60. CO 323/4, fols. 639–640, PRO. The patent is enrolled in Chancery 66/3391, PRO. For the order for the Great Seal see William A. Shaw, *Calendar of Treasury Books* (London: Her Majesty's Stationery Office, 1904–1962), XI, 115–116.

61. BL Loan, 29/207, fols. 72–74.

62. Shrewsbury to King William, August 15, 1696; Coxe, *Original Correspondence,* pp. 136–137. For the navy's reward and encouragement to attack pirates see, for example, ADM 7/339, 3, PRO.

63. King William to Shrewsbury, August 24, 1696, and reply, September 1, 1696; Coxe, *Original Correspondence,* pp. 137–140; James, *Letters Illustrative,* I, 144, 154, 190; grant to Bellomont and others, May 27, 1697, Rawlinson MSS, A/241, fol. 251, BOD.

3. Voyage to Madagascar

1. Whenever the partners needed information, they had to go to Harrison, who kept all the records. Sir James Vernon to Shrewsbury, November 26, 1698, in James, *Letters Illustrative,* II, 112. Harrison had power of attorney to act for all the others. Vernon to Shrewsbury, October 9, 1697, ibid., I, 428–429.

2. Ralph Davis, *The Rise of the English Shipping Industry in the Seventeenth and Eighteenth Centuries* (London: Macmillan, 1962), pp. 110–158. For examples of taking guns out of the hold, see logs of the *London*, Sloane MSS, 3668, and the *Barnardiston*, Sloane MSS, 854, BL.

3. J. Delumeau, "La guerre du course française sous l'ancien régime," in *Course et piraterie, Etudes présentés à la Commission Internationale d'Histoire Maritime* (1975).

4. For the registration of the *Adventure Galley* with the Admiralty see HCA 26/3, fol. 59, PRO. See also R. C. Anderson, *Oared Fighting Ships: From Classical Times to the Coming of Steam* (London: P. Marshall, 1962), pp. 86–87. Both depictions of the *Charles Galley* are in Bruce S. Ingram, *Three Sea Journals of Stuart Times* (London: Constable, 1936). For Roch's remarks on the ship and its speed under oars see ibid., pp. 116–117, 131.

5. The story of the "family men" is related in *A Full Account of the Actions of the late Famous Pyrate Captain Kidd. With Proceedings against Him, and a Vindication of the Right Honourable Richard Earl of Bellomont, Lord Coloony, . . . by a Person of Quality* (Dublin, 1701), p. 5. The author of this pamphlet asserts that Harrison recruited the crew, which is not unlikely given his knowledge of London's labor market. HCA 25/12, PRO.

6. There are a number of copies of this agreement dated September 10, 1695: one is in HCA 1/15, pt. 1, fol. 8, PRO; another is in BL Loan, 29/207, fols. 134–135. Exquemelin describes his first contract in *Bucaniers of America*, pp. 42–43.

7. Wilbur, *Raveneau de Lussan*, pp. 135–136.

8. Ibid., p. 215.

9. For this tradition see the journal of John Strong, Harleian MSS, 5101, fol. 46, and Sloane MSS, 3295, BL. See also the examination of Thomas Phips, CO 1/53, fol. 33, PRO. And for a late example of the same activity on a merchant ship see Nathaniel Uring, *The Voyages and Travels of Captain Nathaniel Uring*, ed. Alfred Dewar (London: Cassell, 1928), p. 117.

10. During the war the demand for experienced men was so great that trained mariners were assigned ship by ship in order to spread them around. See the discussions by the Lords of the Admiralty, ADM 1/5148, January 25, 29, and March 9, 1702, PRO. See also CO 5/861, no. 17, PRO; and T. S. Bromley, *The Manning Problem of the Royal Navy: Select Published Pamphlets, 1693–1873* (London: Navy Records Society, 1974).

11. See Bellomont's instructions to Kidd in *The Trial of Captain Kidd*, ed. Graham Brooks (London: W. Hodge, 1930), pp. 16–17.

12. Conveyance Libers (records of property transfers), 21/139–140, New York City (NYC) Hall of Records. Vernon to Shrewsbury, June 19, 1697, in James, *Letters Illustrative*, I, 276–277.

13. Bellomont's Instructions, Brooks, *Trial of Kidd*, pp. 16–17.

14. BL Loan, 29/207, fols. 47–48.

15. The Admiralty issued a proclamation on July 12, 1694, setting

forth the regulations on flags and pendants. CO 323/3, fol. 290, PRO. A trial of a captain for not striking the colors to a navy ship is in *An Exact Narrative of the Tryals of the Pyrates, January 7 and 9, 1675*. Kidd swore to obey the regulations. HCA 25/12, PRO.

16. BL Loan, 29/207, fols. 47–48. For another example of this time-honored salute see *Ramblin' Jack: The Journal of Captain John Cremer, 1700–1774*, ed. R. Reynell Bellamy (London: J. Cape, 1936), p. 96.

17. The order was issued on February 29, 1696. ADM 3/12, PRO.

18. February 23, 1696, ADM 1/5145, fol. 827, PRO.

19. Kidd to Russell, April 11, 1700, BL Loan, 29/207, fols. 106–107. Kidd identified the *Duchess* as the ship that had received his men. See Kidd's statement, ibid., fol. 104. Orford was later accused of weakening the ship in the face of the enemy when he removed the men from the *Duchess*—a charge he denied. *State Trials*, V, 542–543.

20. He left Plymouth on April 23, 1696. See Kidd's Instrument of Protest, *Report on the Manuscripts of His Grace the Duke of Portland, Welbeck Abbey* (London: Historical Manuscripts Commission, 1923), IX, 403–406.

21. Ibid. When the banker was condemned as a prize in New York, the ship and its cargo brought £312. *Adventure Galley*'s Accounts, BL Loan, 29/206, fols. 132–133, 246–247.

22. A copy of the New York broadsheet is in HCA 1/15, pt. 1, fol. 8, PRO.

23. On the situation in New York see Ritchie, "Some Effects of King William's War."

24. James Boswell, *The Life of Samuel Johnson* (London, 1791), p. 86.

25. Andrew Barker, *A True and Certaine Report of the Beginning, Proceedings and now present Estate of Captaine Ward and Dansker* (London, 1609).

26. Kidd's register of his men is in CO 5/861, fols. 267–268, PRO. He omits Abeel Owen, the cook; Owen's apprentice, Robert Lamley; Richard Barlycorne, Kidd's own apprentice; William Jenkins, apprentice to George Bollen, the chief mate; and Edward Palmer. Another copy of the list is in BL Loan, 29/207, fol. 105. Most of the men remain anonymous and only in a few instances are there depositions or other records. See HCA 1/15, fols. 3–5; HCA 1/98, pt. 1, fols. 114, 123; HCA 1/53, fols. 95–96, 110–111; HCA 1/16, pt. 1, fol. 1; HCA 1/50, fol. 100; ADM 3/55; ADM 3/15; ADM 1/3666, fol. 66; CO 5/860, nos. 64, 73, PRO; Orig. Corr., E/3/54, nos. 6446, 6448, 6469, IOR.

27. For other studies of pirates see Senior, *Nation of Pirates*, pp. 13–42; Ronald Moore, "Some Aspects of the Origin and Nature of English Piracy, 1603–1625" (Ph.D. Diss., University of Virginia, 1960), pp. 255–276; Marcus Rediker, "'Under the Banner of King Death': The Social World of Anglo-American Pirates, 1716 to 1726," *William and Mary Quarterly*, ser. 3, 38 (1983), 203–227.

28. Conveyance Libers, 21/125, 127, 128, 132, 133, 135–156, NYC

Hall of Records. On Hawden's deal for his servant see CO 5/861, fol. 262, PRO.

29. On the apprentices see ADM 3/15, April 15, 1700; CO 5/860, no. 64; HCA 1/15, fol. 5, PRO. The original printed indenture for Lamley is in HCA 1/15, pt. 1, fol. 31, PRO.

30. See Lorrain, *Ordinary of Newgate.*

31. For his career see CSPC (1698–99), nos. 506, 738; NYCD, III, 586, 600, 673, 740; O'Callaghan, Cal. Hist. MSS, pp. 124, 132, 216, 227, 240, 272.

32. Franks's longest deposition was taken in India on October 20, 1697, Orig. Corr., E/3/53, no. 6448, IOR. See also Jacob R. Marcus, *The Colonial American Jew, 1492–1776* (Detroit: Wayne State University Press, 1970), II, 581; and idem, *Early American Jewry: The Jews of New York, New England and Canada* (Philadelphia: Jewish Publication Society of America, 1951), pp. 57–68. For the jewelry trade see Gedalia Yogev, *Diamonds and Coral: Anglo-Dutch Jews and Eighteenth Century Trade* (New York: Leicester University Press, 1978).

33. Conveyance Libers, 21/139–141, NYC Hall of Records.

34. Browne made two depositions that vary slightly. See HCA 1/16, fol. 1, PRO; Rawlinson A270, fol. 1, BOD.

35. Conveyance Libers, 21/139–140, NYC Hall of Records.

36. Ibid., 21/127–139. Kidd later created a set of accounts for the voyage in which he listed £1,196 as advances paid in New York. A portion of this sum may well have been for men whom he helped by financing their voyage; some is undoubtedly the £6 apiece he charged them for arms and ammunition at the start of the voyage. *State Trials,* V, 304. Kidd also made individual agreements; see the one with Jan Cornelius, CO 5/861, fol. 264, PRO.

37. HCA 1/98, fol. 74, PRO. In his deposition John Barret complained of having to buy food on Madagascar, where the pirates purchased most of their food from the local natives. HCA 1/53, fols. 102–103, PRO.

38. HCA 1/98, fol. 74, PRO. Men also went into "consortship" with one another, whereby if one died the other received his property. Ibid., fol. 193. For some of the buccaneers this relationship also meant sharing wives. See Louis A. T. Le Golif, *The Memoirs of a Bucaneer,* ed. G. Alaux and A. t'Sterstevens, trans. Malcolm Barnes (London: George Allen and Unwin, 1954), pp. 87–110.

39. Fletcher to Board of Trade, June 22, 1697, CO 5/1040, fols. 67–70, PRO.

40. NYHS *Collections* (1910), I, 9, 86, 116.

41. Fletcher to Board of Trade [July 1696], NYCD, IV, 273–276.

42. Jonathan Tredway recollected this ceremony in his deposition made in India December 17, 1697. E/3/53, no. 6469, IOR.

43. For an explanation of the monsoons see Peter J. Webster, "Monsoons," *Scientific American*, 245 (August 1981), 108–119.

44. Ingram, *Three Sea Journals*, p. 147.

45. The *Richmond*'s log records the activities of Evans and his men. ADM 51/4310, PRO. For other aspects of Evans' career while in New York see Fletcher to Board of Trade, CO 5/1040, fols. 67–70; CO 323/2, November 9, 1696, no. 15; Evans to the Admiralty, July 21, 1698, ADM 51/1754, PRO.

46. The crew's organization is in CO 5/861, fols. 267–268, PRO. Other details are in BL Loan, 29/207, fol. 136; James Emott to Kidd, June 4, 1698, HCA 1/98, pt. 1, fol. 114, PRO.

47. Benjamin Franks relates these episodes in Orig. Corr., E/3/53, no. 6448, IOR.

48. For the evolution of this route see *A Journal of the First Voyage of Vasco Da Gama, 1497–99*, trans. and ed. E. G. Ravenstein (London: Hakluyt Society, 1898); also Diffie and Winius, *Foundations of the Portuguese Empire*, pp. 74–185, and Parry, *Age of Reconnaissance*, pp. 146–157.

49. T. Bentley Duncan, *Atlantic Islands: Madeira, The Azores, and the Cape Verdes in Seventeenth Century Commerce and Navigation* (Chicago: University of Chicago Press, 1972).

50. References to the messes and their role in shipboard organization are in *State Trials*, V, 332, 334, 335, and the deposition of Bradinham, HCA 1/15, fol. 7, PRO.

51. Bradinham, HCA 1/15, fol. 7, PRO.

52. The delight of mariners in fishing during this long and tedious voyage can be seen in various sources: log of the *Sampson*, L.Mar.A. CVII, IOR; log of the *Kempthorne*, Sloane MSS, 3671, BL; Ingram, *Three Sea Journals*, pp. 149–156. One crew lived for ten days on their catches. Mariners' fear of sharks was one of the excuses they gave for not learning how to swim (in the Caribbean sharks were known by the French buccaneers as "requiems"). Le Golif, *Memoirs of a Bucaneer*, p. 33.

53. The English colonists on Providence Island relied on turtle as an important part of their diet. Diary of Nathaniel Butler, Sloane MSS, 758, BL. I should like to thank Karen Ordahl Kupperman for calling my attention to this manuscript. The English on Jamaica had a severe crisis later, when the Spanish kept the turtle-fishing fleet in the harbor. CSPC (1681–1685), no. 1938. Barbadians went as far afield as Ascension Island for turtle and kept it fresh on the voyage home, as did all mariners, by turning the turtles on their backs to immobilize them and eating them when they wanted fresh food. Sloane MSS, 3668, BL. Cremer's remarks about the effects of turtle are the most incisive. *Journal of John Cremer*, p. 83. Hans Sloane recorded that although he thought green turtle tasted best, it had a tendency to turn his skin yellow and "prodigously" stain his shirts at the armpits. *A Voyage to the Islands of Madera, Barbados, Nieves, Saint Christophers, and Jamaica* (London,

1707), p. xvii. Henry Pitman, on first being forced to eat a turtle diet, complained of the "violent looseness" that it caused. He "cured" his condition by taking advantage of the constipating qualities of opium. *A Relation of the Great Suffering and Strange Adventures of Henry Pitman, late chirurgeon to the late Duke of Monmouth* (London, 1689), p. 23. For a modern account of the turtle see James J. Parsons, *The Green Turtle and Man* (Gainesville: University of Florida Press, 1962), pp. 6–15.

54.   When the pirate Basil Ringrose fought a duel, he went ashore to do so. Exquemelin, *Bucaniers of America*, II, 165. See also Dangerfield's deposition, CO 1/57, fol. 381, PRO. For an instance of such behavior on a navy ship caught in ice see *The Diary of Henry Teonge*, ed. G. E. Manwaring (London: G. Routledge, 1927), p. 239. One of the best accounts of the casual violence on pirate ships is in William Snelgrave, *A New Account of Some Parts of Guinea and Slave Trade* (London, 1734).

55.   *Diary of Henry Teonge*, p. 206. Pitman records an episode in which the crew of a New York sloop got so drunk from liquor his men had given them that they allowed their ship to slam into his during a storm. Pitman, *A Relation*, p. 28.

56.   For examples of these ceremonies see Exquemelin, *Bucaniers of America*, pp. 2–3; *Diary of Henry Teonge*, p. 47; "Voyage to Guinea, Antego, Bay of Campeche, Cuba, Barbadoes, etc., 1714–1723," Add. MSS, 39946, fol. 27, BL.

57.   For contemporary accounts of crossing the equator see Basil Lubbock, transcriber, *Barlow's Journal of His Life at Sea in King's Ships, East and West Indiamen and Other Merchantmen from 1659–1703* (London: Hurst and Blackett, 1934), I, 181. By far the fullest description, and the one I have relied on most, is that of Robert Challe in his *Journal d'un voyage fait aux Indes Orientales, 1690–1691* (Paris: Mercure de France, 1979), pp. 189–193. I am grateful to Dana Tiffany for aiding me with the translation. For the continuation of these traditions, and some wonderful pictures and insightful comments, see Margaret Creighton, *Dogwatch and Liberty Days: Seafaring Life in the Nineteenth Century* (Salem, Mass.: Peabody Museum, 1982), pp. 45–51.

58.   The fastest ship during the day assumed the lead at night and flew a light to guide the other ships. The log of the *Sampson*, an East Indiaman, illustrates the habits of the outward-bound ships. Sloane MSS, 3814, BL.

59.   Log of the *Advice* for Saturday, December 12, 1696, ADM, 51/13, PRO.

60.   Logs of the *Windsor*, ADM 51/1072, the *Vulture*, ADM 51/4386, the *Tiger*, ADM 51/4369, and the *Kingfisher*, ADM 52/56, PRO.

61.   The rising concern of the company captains can be seen in the logs of the *Sampson*, L.Mar.A., CVII, and the *Sceptre*, L.Mar.A., CII, IOR. Edward Barlow was mate aboard the *Sceptre* (about which we shall hear) and did not like the navy's ways. *Journal*, II, 459–462.

62.   The classic discussion of scurvy is James Lind, *Treatise of the Scurvy,*

ed. Charles Lloyd (London: Naval Records Society, 1965). This work was first published in 1753 in response to the devastating death rate on Anson's famous circumnavigation (1,081 of 1,955 men died). The captain of the *Barnardiston* flew the skull and crossbones when a man died. Log of the *Barnardiston*, Sloane MSS, 854, fol. 129.

63. H. C. V. Leibbrandt, *Precis of the Archives of the Cape of Good Hope* (Cape Town: W. A. Richards, 1896), II, 115. The captain of the *Sceptre* recorded the death rate for the *Vosmaer*. L.Mar.A., CII, IOR. For contemporary comments on the problem see Leibbrandt, *Precis*, III, 3–4, 18, 30, 115. The English government asked Trinity House, the pilots' guild, to comment on the high death rate during East Indies voyages, and a copy of their report is in Rawlinson MSS, A 171, fols. 223–231, BOD.

64. See the log of the *Sampson*, L.Mar.A., CVII, IOR, and *Barlow's Journal*, II, 456–463.

65. The sad course of the squadron can be followed in Warren's log of the *Windsor*, ADM 51/1072, PRO. For examples of lost ships see the log of the *Kempthorne*, Sloan MSS, 3671, fol. 11, BL; Pitman, *A Relation*, pp. 34–35; and Butler, "Diary," Sloane MSS, 758, fol. 170, BL.

66. Log of the *Windsor* for May 19 and 25, 1696, ADM 51/1072, PRO.

67. The quotation is from a memo of John Clerke, captain of the *East India Merchant*, Orig. Corr., E/3/53, no. 6409, IOR. See also CO 328/2, fols. 346–347, PRO.

68. For the atmosphere on the *Adventure Galley* see the depositions of Tredway and Franks, Orig. Corr., E/3/63, nos. 6448 and 6469, IOR. Kidd's "escape" is noted in the logs, ADM 51/13, 1072; and 4369, PRO.

69. Leibbrandt, *Precis*, III, 34–36; Clerke's memo, Orig. Corr., E/3/53, no. 6409, IOR. Kidd met the *Loyal Russell* at sea and may have asked it to help him get supplies from the cape, but the meeting was accidental. Deposition of Hugh Parrot, HCA 1/15, IOR.

70. Catchpoole to Bowrey, January 15, 1697, Bowrey MSS, H/827, fol. 312, IOR.

4. The Pirates' Last Frontier

1. The casual reader will find a general history of Madagascar during this period in Mervyn Brown, *Madagascar Rediscovered: A History from Early Times to Independence* (London: Damien Tunnacliffe, 1978), pp. 41–91. The more diligent will profit from the massive collection of documents in the multivolume work of Alfred and Guillaume Grandidier, *Collections des ouvrages anciens concernant Madagascar* (Paris: Comité de Madagascar, 1903–7). Other sources are Raymond K. Kent, *Early Kingdoms in Madagascar, 1500–1700* (New York: Holt, Rinehart, 1970); G. Dongue, "Le climat d'une façade au vent de l'alizé: la Côte Est de Madagascar," *Madagascar Revue de*

Géographie, 24 (1974), 9–74; J. Randrianarison, "Le boeuf dans l'économie rurale de Madagascar," *Madagascar Revue de Géographie*, 28 (1976), 9–122; F. Le Bourdiec, "Géographie historique de la riziculture malagache," *Madagascar Revue de Géographie*, 31 (1977), 11–69.

2. For an eyewitness account of the Saint Augustine colony see Add. MSS, 14037, BL. On another settlement attempt farther north see the journal of Charles Wylde, James Ford Bell Library, University of Minnesota; and Sir William Foster, "An English Settlement on Madagascar, 1645–6," *English Historical Review*, 27 (1912), 239–250.

3. Louis Pauliat, *Madagascar sous Louis XIV: Louis XIV et la Compagnie des Indies Orientales de 1664* (Paris: Calmann Levy, 1886); Arthur Malotet, *Étienne de Flacourt, ou Les origines de la colonization française à Madagascar, 1648–1661* (Paris: E. Leroux, 1858).

4. J. M. Filliot, *La traité des esclaves vers les mascareignes aux XVIII siècle* (Tanarive: Office de la Recherche Scientifique et Technologie d'Outre-Mer, 1970), pp. 141–164.

5. Captain William Cowley's account of his voyage around the world is in Hacke, *A Collection of Original Voyages*. See also Sloane MSS, 54, BL; and Dampier, *A New Voyage*.

6. For advice about carrying on the slave trade see the instructions of Thomas Bowrey, M3041/3 (iii), Guildhall Library, and of an anonymous individual, Rawlinson MSS, A 334, fol. 61, BOD. Captain Jan Coin of the *Tamboer* gives an account of doing business with Edward Welsh, VOC 4043, fol. 820, ARA.

7. For Samuel's career see the deposition of Samuel Parker, CO 323/2, fols. 382–385; narrative of Henry Watson, CO 323/2, fol. 240; deposition of Adam Baldridge, CO5/1042, no. 30, PRO; VOC 4043, fol. 820, ARA. See also Robert Drury, *Madagascar; or Robert Drury's Journal during Fifteen Years' Captivity on That Island*, ed. Pasfield Oliver (London: Unwin, 1890), p. 83. For the seizure of the ship see "Journal of John Cruger," in David T. Valentine, ed., *Manual of the Corporation of the City of New York* (New York: J. W. Bell, 1853), pp. 406–408; deposition of Stephen Smith, HCA 1/53, fols. 101–102; deposition of Jeffrey Edwards, ADM 1/1462, no. 15; and HCA 1/98, fols. 143, 174, PRO.

8. For the Dutch reports see VOC 4043, fol. 820, ARA, and Leibbrandt, *Precis*, I, 113. On Littleton see log of the *Anglesea*, ADM 51/4114, PRO.

9. Captain Edward Welsh, who replaced Baldridge, had the 500-man private army. See the report of Captain Jan Coin, VOC 4043, fol. 820, ARA; deposition of Theophilus Turner, CO 5/714, fols. 373–374, 376, PRO.

10. *State Trials*, V, 7–8; deposition of John Dann, September 8, 1696, HCA 1/53, fols. 73–74, PRO.

11. *State Trials*, V, 11–12.

12. This proclamation was found and taken to India by Captain John Browne of the East India Company ship *Benjamin*. Charles S. Hill, "Notes on Piracy in Eastern Waters," *Indian Antiquary*, 55 (1926), p. 101. Many believed that they should be left alone if they intended to attack only "moors." See ibid., p. 95, and the narrative of Nathaniel Codrington, CO 5/1259, fols. 205–206, PRO.

13. K. N. Chaudhuri, *Trading World of Asia and the English East India Company, 1660–1760* (Cambridge: Cambridge University Press, 1978), p. 194.

14. CO 5/1258, fols. 166–169, PRO.

15. Deposition of Muhammad Ibrahim, Ethe MSS, 370, fol. 19, IOR. My thanks to Fereydoun L. Badrei of the University of California, Berkeley, for translating this document. See also examinations of John Dann, CO 323/2, fol. 119; HCA 1/53, fols. 73–74; HCA 1/29, fol. 73, PRO; Khafi Khan, *History of Alamgir-Muntakhab ul Lubab*, ed. S. M. Haq (New Karachi: Pakistan Historical Society, 1975), p. 419; Jadunath Sarkar, *History of Aurangzeb* (Bombay: Orient Longman, 1952), V, 460–463; Yogendra-Natha Das Gupta, *India in the Seventeenth Century as Depicted by European Travellers* (Calcutta: University of Calcutta Press, 1916), pp. 233–238.

16. HCA 1/29, fol. 73, PRO.

17. Ibid. For Avery's legend see Daniel Defoe, *The King of Pirates, Being an Account of Famous Enterprises of Captain Avery, with the Lives of Other Pirates and Robbers* (London, 1724).

18. Examination of John Brent, HCA 1/53, fols. 83–84, PRO; deposition of Benjamin Franks, Orig. Corr., E/3/53, no. 6448; and memorandum of John Clerke, no. 6409, IOR.

19. For accounts of Johanna see Challe, *Journal*, pp. 235–253; *Barlow's Journal*, I, 183–184; Sloane MSS, 3665, fol. 35; and Ingram, *Three Sea Journals*, pp. 157–161.

As stated in the text, the modern name of Johanna is Anjouan. In general, I have used place names familiar to the pirates—or even, on occasion, kept an earlier spelling of a name that has been changed slightly in present times. I regret any confusion that may result from this procedure, but I wished to avoid cluttering the text with two sets of names.

20. Memorandum of John Clerke, Orig. Corr., E/3/53, no. 6409, IOR, and further testimony by Clerke, CO 328/2, fol. 346–347, PRO. Log of the *Madras Merchant*, Marine Records, L.Mar.A., CVI, IOR.

21. In his "Instrument of Protest," July 7, 1699, Kidd claimed he lost fifty men, whereas Jonathan Tredway mentions only twenty-seven in his deposition and Nicholas Alderson reported thirty. HMC, *Report on the Manuscripts of His Grace the Duke of Portland, Welbeck Abbey*, IX, 403–406; Tredway and Alderson, Orig. Corr., E/3/53, nos. 6469 and 6446 respectively, IOR.

22. Lamport Barnard, *A Three Years' Cruise in the Mozambique Channel* (London: Dawsons of Pall Mall, 1969).

23. *Barlow's Journal*, I, 213–214.

24. Examination of John Brent, HCA 1/53, fols. 83–84, PRO; *State Trials*, V, 304; log of the *Madras Merchant*, Marine Records, CVI, IOR.

25. "Instrument of Protest," HMC, *Portland*, IX, 403–06.

26. Baldridge's deposition, CO 5/1042, no. 30, PRO.

27. Bradinham's deposition, HCA 1/15, fol. 7, PRO.

28. Palmer's testimony, *State Trials*, V, 304.

29. Deposition of Benjamin Franks, Orig. Corr., E/3/53, no. 6448, IOR.

30. Ibid; *State Trials*, V, 319.

31. *Barlow's Journal*, II, 482; Franks, Orig. Corr., E/3/53, no. 6448, IOR.

32. The *Sceptre's* log is in Marine Records, L.Mar.A., CII, IOR. The log ends on June 1, 1697, as the ship was on its way to Mocha. For the orders to the ship see Orig. Corr., E/3/53, no. 6393, IOR.

33. *Barlow's Journal*, II, 472–483. The *Gunsway* had left the harbor before Barlow arrived.

34. Hill, "Notes on Piracy," pp. 93–94. Members of the English East India Company were also well aware that the Dutch spread stories about them. Orig. Corr., E/3/53, nos. 6384, 6490, IOR.

35. For accounts of the action see *Barlow's Journal*, II, 483–485; the depositions of various of Kidd's men in Orig. Corr., E/3/53, nos. 6446, 6448, 6469, IOR; and *State Trials*, V, 322. The news that the fleet had beat off an attack boosted trade in Surat. Vaux's Diary, Add. MSS, 14253, fol. 90, BL. The Dutch also spread the rumor that Kidd and Barlow were actually in partnership. Orig. Corr., E/3/53, no. 6490, IOR.

36. President Gayer to the company directors, January 26, 1698, Orig. Corr., E/3/53, nos. 6490, 6500, IOR. See also the reports in ibid., nos. 6250, 6270. For the disputes over pepper and the men's wages see ibid., nos. 6493–94, 6498–99, IOR; *Barlow's Journal*, II, 453.

37. *Barlow's Journal*, II, 501.

38. See the various depositions in Orig. Corr., E/3/53, nos. 6446, 6448, 6469, IOR; and HCA 1/15, fol. 7, PRO.

39. John Clerke's memorandum, Orig. Corr., E/3/53, no. 6409, IOR; and another version in CO 328/2, fols. 346–347, PRO.

40. Orig. Corr., E/3/53, no. 6446, IOR; *State Trials*, V, 304, 322.

41. Pattle and Harvey's report, Orig. Corr., E/3/53, no. 6426, IOR. Mason's career can be traced in the testimony of his shipmates: Browne, HCA 1/16, pt. 1, fol. 1; Culliford, ADM 1/3666, fol. 100, no. 4, PRO; Burgess, Rawlinson MSS, A/270, fol. 1, BOD.

42. "The Diary of a European Pirate . . . ," Orig. Corr., E/3/52, no. 6318, and a further report in no. 6317, IOR.

43. Orig. Corr., E/3/52, no. 6318, IOR.

44. Ibid.

45. As quoted in Hill, "Notes on Piracy," p. 115. For the other reports on this encounter see Orig. Corr., E/3/53, nos. 6426, 6437, 6446, 6448, 6459, 6469, IOR; HCA 1/15, fol. 7, PRO; *State Trials*, V, 322–323.

46. For background on Ghafur see Arnold Wright, *Annesley of Surat and His Times: The True Story of the Mythical Wesley Fortune* (London: A. Melrose, 1918), pp. 110–160. The agents in Carwar had spread the news that Kidd intended to hunt Ghafur's ship. Orig. Corr., E/3/53, nos. 6426, 6437, IOR.

47. The Portuguese viceroy at Goa sent these ships to seek Kidd and to protect the fleet bringing the annual rice shipments to Goa. Orig. Corr., E/3/53, nos. 6437, 6438, IOR. Barlow met them while voyaging along the coast and reported that the smaller ship was "sadly" beaten. *Barlow's Journal*, II, 490. Kidd's boast is in the Narrative he prepared in Boston. CO 5/860, fols. 198–201, PRO.

48. Pennynge's report, Orig. Corr., E/3/53, no. 6439, IOR. Reacting to Pennynge's surly behavior, Kidd threatened to report him to Whitehall. *Barlow's Journal*, II, 491.

49. Orig. Corr., E/3/53, no. 6473, IOR.

50. For various reports relating to the pirates' stay see Orig. Corr., E/3/53, no. 6467, IOR; *State Trials*, V, 296, 304, 324, 332, 335; *Barlow's Journal*, II, 492.

51. Kidd's claim of going to Saint Marie is in his Narrative.

52. Kidd's Narrative; *State Trials*, V, 289–294; Orig. Corr., E/3/53, no. 6467, IOR.

53. The story of Moore's death was fully aired when Kidd was tried for Moore's murder. *State Trials*, V, 287–296.

54. *Barlow's Journal*, II, 491; report in Orig. Corr., E/3/53, no. 6467, IOR.

55. Kidd gives only minimal details of this capture. He stresses that the ship was a "moor's ship" with only three Dutch men in the crew, the rest being lascars. Kidd's Narrative; Orig. Corr., E/3/53, nos. 6459, 6473, IOR. The quotation is in *State Trials*, V, 296, 324. Further testimony is in HCA 1/15, fol. 7, PRO. The *Rupperell* pass, or at least a copy of it, is in CO 5/860, fols. 159–160, PRO. This was the second time the ship had been taken by pirates. Orig. Corr., E/3/53, no. 6309, IOR.

56. Caliquilon was known to the pirates as a "free port," or safe harbor for them to trade. Sir Richard Carnac Temple, *New Light on the Mysterious Tragedy of the Worcester, 1704–1715* (London: E. Benn, 1930), pp. 126–138; Alexander Hamilton, *A New Account of the East Indies*, ed. Sir William Foster (London: Argonaut Press, 1930), I, 184; and Orig. Corr., E/3/54, nos. 6543, 6553, 6556, IOR. The men described the sharing ceremony at their trial. *State Trials*, V, 304, 324, 332, 335. See also the deposition of Edward Palmer, April 15, 1700, ADM 3/15, PRO. Europeans were not above profiting from cheap pirate goods. The leaders of the Dutch East India Company even proposed that the Cape Colony trade with the pirates on

Madagascar to obtain cheap goods from the East Indies. Leibbrandt, *Precis,* II, 262. As late as 1719 the Dutch in Cochin still accepted goods from pirates. Orig. Corr., E/1/13, fols. 97–98, IOR; Bradinham's deposition, HCA 1/15, fol. 7, PRO; *State Trials,* V, 301–302, 317. Kidd never mentions either the ketch or the Portuguese ship in his various depositions.

57.   There is testimony on the hiring of the *Quedah Merchant* for this voyage in HCA 24/127, no. 107, PRO; and the claim of Coji Babba is in Rawlinson MSS, B 383, fols. 547–548, 550, BOD. On the capture of the ship and the aftermath see Orig. Corr., E/3/54, nos. 6543, 6545, 6547, 6553, 6556, IOR; *State Trials,* V, 302, 304, 307, 324–325. Kidd's own account is in his Narrative, CO 5/860, fols. 198–201. A copy of the French pass is in CO 5/860, fols. 161–162, PRO.

58.   The ship's condition is described in Kidd's Narrative, and Orig. Corr., E/3/54, no. 6544, IOR.

59.   Kidd ends his account of the voyage after the capture of the *Quedah Merchant,* maintaining silence about these events. But see the reports in Orig. Corr., E/3/53, nos. 6430, 6484; E/3/54, no. 6543, IOR; HCA 1/53, fols. 75–76, PRO.

60.   Orig. Corr., E/3/54, no. 6553, IOR; and Records of Fort Saint George, *Diary and Consultation Book of 1697* (Madras: Madras Record Office, 1921), XXVII, April 4, 1698.

61.   Orig. Corr., E/3/54, no. 6543, IOR; Bradinham's deposition, HCA 1/15, fol. 7, PRO. Normally pirate ships used slaves to do the hard work; but while they were in the East Indies, they used lascars just as Kidd did in this instance. One of these men left an account of his voyage with some pirates. See "Information of a Lascar," Orig. Corr., E/3/52, no. 6325, IOR. For accounts of slaves on ships see Pitman, *A Relation,* p. 34; Exquemelin, *Bucaniers of America,* pt. 2, 14–16, pt. 3, 43; *State Trials,* V, 211; Add. MSS, 11410, fol. 354, BL; examination of Richard Arnold, Blathwayt MSS, 327, HEH; Dangerfield's examination, CO 1/57, fol. 381, PRO.

62.   The governor of Mauritius wrote numerous letters about the appalling conditions, including the "thousands of millions" of rats. For an example see Leibbrandt, *Precis,* II, 167–169. The colony was recalled in 1707; ibid., pp. 436–437. The quote on the dodo birds is from the log of the *Berkeley Castle,* which visited the island in 1681. Sloane MSS, 3668, BL. The Dutch made another mistake by introducing rabbits to Robbins Island in the bay of the Cape of Good Hope. The rabbits proceeded to denude the island, forcing the Dutch to remove their cattle. Leibbrandt, *Precis,* II, 10–11.

5. Life in a Pirate Settlement

1.   Captain Henry Fowlis of HMS *Scarborough* cruised around the island in 1703 and recorded his impressions of the weather. Sloane MSS, 3674, BL.

For a more scientific account see Dongue, "Le climat d'une façade," and J. P. LaPaire, "Contribution à l'étude morphologique de l'île Sainte-Marie de Madagascar," *Madagascar Revue de Géographie*, 34 (1979), 90–91. A contemporary visitor has found the island idyllic, but still plagued by heavy rainfall. Brown, *Madagascar Rediscovered*, p. 82.

2. Realistic appraisals can be found in Bowrey MSS, M3041/3(iii), Guildhall Library, London; report of Captain Jan Coin, VOC no. 4043, fol. 820, ARA; deposition of Theophilus Turner, CO 5/714, fols. 373–374; deposition of John Finlinson, CO 391/10, fols. 432–433, PRO; examination of Samuel Perkins, SOU 18, Southwell MSS, National Maritime Museum, Greenwich, England.

3. For the transformation of the encampment into a fort see examination of Otto van Toyle, CO 5/1042, fol. 299, and examination of John Blacon, CO 391/11, fol. 169, PRO. On the fear of a pirate state see a representation of the Board of Trade, January 17, 1698, CO 324/6, fols. 222–225, PRO. The board reported the most extreme statistics on the island: 1,500 men, 40 to 50 guns, and 17 ships.

4. Baldridge left a very long deposition about his career on Saint Marie. CO 5/1042, no. 30; see also CO 391/10, fols. 432–433; CO 323/2, no. 90, PRO.

5. On the general background of the slave trade see Virginia B. Platt, "The East India Company and the Madagascar Slave Trade," *William and Mary Quarterly*, 26 (1969), 548–577. Philipse's role is chronicled in Jacob Judd, "Frederick Philipse and the Madagascar Trade," *New-York Historical Society Quarterly*, 47 (1963), 66–74.

6. Burgess' involvement with Kidd is in Ritchie, "Samuel Burgess."

7. Typically, when men died their clothes were sold. *A Relation of Three Years' Sufferings of Robert Everard upon the Coast of Africa near Madagascar in a Voyage to India in the year 1686* (London, 1693), p. 275. John Quelch and his men made their breeches out of captured silk. *State Trials*, VIII, 212. When two pirates faced execution in 1615, they gave away their fancy clothing: breeches of crimson taffeta, velvet doublets with gold buttons, and velvet shirts with gold lace. John Stow, *The Annals or General Chronicle of England* (London, 1615), p. 657.

8. The men with Raveneau de Lussan had a particularly difficult time keeping ships together. Wilbur, *Raveneau de Lussan*, pp. 112–126, 252–255. On Ringrose's ship they used Osnaburg, a cheap cotton cloth, for sails. Exquemelin, *Bucaniers of America*, II, 83. On silk sails see John Ovington, *A Voyage to Surat in the Year 1689* (London, 1696), pp. 102–104.

9. A remarkable letter has survived: Philipse to Baldridge, February 26, 1695, HCA 1/98, fols. 57–58, PRO.

10. Testimony of John Lenard, E/3/53, no. 6321, IOR.

11. Theophilus Turner reported that the captains really made money from selling liquor and food to the men on the way home. HCA 13/82, 314–

316, and 312–313, PRO. If a man could not afford passage, he was put off the ship. Examination of Samuel Perkins, SOU 18, Southwell MSS, National Maritime Museum, Greenwich, England.

12. The logs of the navy ships in Warren's squadron register Burgess' coming and going. ADM 51/56, 4369, 13; Warren's certificate to Burgess, HCA 1/98, fol. 78, PRO.

13. On this aspect of Philipse's entrepreneurship see the documents relating to the capture in Hamburg of his ship, the *Frederick*. HCA 15/17; HCA 24/126; HCA 1/14, pt. 2, no. 140, PRO.

14. Baldridge's deposition, CO 5/1042, no. 30, II, PRO. See also the examination of Perkins, as above, and that of Blacon, CO 391/11, fols. 169–171, PRO.

15. Welsh is recorded as having come to Madagascar from New England as a boy. On his career see CO 5/714, fol. 373–374, PRO; VOC, 4043, fol. 820, ARA; HCA 1/98, fol. 62, PRO.

16. There is a fine late-eighteenth-century drawing of the harbor in Add. MSS, 15319, fol. 34, BL. Kidd recorded the arrival of his ships in his Narrative, CO 5/860, fols. 198–201, PRO. The best modern map is that of the Institut Géographique National in Paris, Centre à Madagascar.

17. *State Trials*, V, 303, 306, 334–335; Bradinham's deposition, HCA 1/15, fol. 7, PRO.

18. *State Trials*, V, 303, 306.

19. For Culliford's career see his depositions: HCA 1/16, pt. 1, fol. 5; ADM 1/3666, fol. 100, no. 4, PRO. For the testimony of others see John Browne, Rawlinson MSS, A/270, fol. 1, BOD; HCA 1/16, pt. 1, fol. 1, PRO; John Barrett, HCA 1/53, fols. 102–103; John Hales, HCA 1/53, fols. 75–76, PRO. A Captain Willocks in the East India Company's service, who was forcibly detained by Stout and Culliford because of his navigational skills, testified about his experiences aboard the *Resolution*. Orig. Corr., E/3/53, no. 6484, IOR. And two of the supercargoes on the *Dorrill* wrote about their brush with the *Resolution*. Orig. Corr., E/3/53, no. 6430, IOR.

20. Bradinham's deposition, HCA 1/15, fol. 7, PRO; *State Trials*, V, 322.

21. Kidd's Narrative, CO 5/860, fols. 198–201, PRO.

22. Johannes de Peyster to Abraham de Peyster, June 11, 1698, de Peyster MSS, New-York Historical Society; examination of Otto Van Toyle, CO 5/1042, fol. 299, PRO. Many men claimed that their loot was largely won at play, perhaps to lessen their culpability in the eyes of the law. See, for example, the depositions in HCA 1/53, 102–103, 95–99, PRO.

23. Bartholomew Sharpe's journal, Add. MSS, 11410, fol. 357, BL. The men later abandoned the ship because they could not get enough slaves to do the hard labor. De Lussan was lucky. Five men who were also carrying their booty were killed before they reached the coast. Wilbur, *Raveneau de Lussan*, pp. 256–257, 281.

24. Examination of Samuel Perkins, CO 323/2, fols. 382–385, PRO. Perkins survived the attack on Baldridge's fort. Baldridge later picked him up and took him to Saint Augustine; he left the ship to settle there.

25. Burgess made the mistake of sailing into the harbor at the Cape of Good Hope without giving all due honor to Captain Lowth. Angry and suspicious, Lowth boarded and captured the *Margaret* with the pirates and their loot still on board. See Ritchie, "Burgess." A listing of the men's fortunes is in State Papers 34/7, fols. 12–13, PRO. Seven men made it to shore, but they fared no better, as the Dutch government seized their money. VOC 4043, fol. 676, ARA. For Eldridge see HCA 24/127, no. 3. For Samuel Bradish see CO 5/1042, no. 26 (7), PRO. Robert Bradinham, another member of the crew of the *Adventure Galley,* was later captured in Pennsylvania. He filed a claim against the governor, whom he charged with taking his fortune. It is an extensive list that includes 2,058 Lion dollars, 1,185 pieces of eight, and a variety of broken pieces of currency and plate. HCA 24/127, no. 110, PRO.

26. HCA 1/98, fols. 98–101, PRO.

27. Of the four ships that sailed for Madagascar in 1698 only one returned safely. Two were taken by pirates who needed new ships and simply took the ones from New York. On July 1, 1698, Stephanus van Cortland reported the ships as leaving New York. CO 5/1042, fols. 242–243, PRO. For the fate of the *Prophet Daniel,* see "Journal of John Cruger," in Valentine, *Manual,* pp. 406–408; for the *Peter,* see the deposition of its captain, George Reveley, HCA 1/98, fol. 22, PRO. One of the men who did make it back was Giles Shelley, who had been with Kidd in London in 1695. When he arrived off Cape May on May 27, 1699, he wrote a long letter to his chief owner, Stephen de Lancey, detailing his voyage, including the process of transferring returning men to shore. CO 5/1258, no. 29, II, PRO. On the fate of some of the men see Jeremiah Basse to William Popple, June 9, 1699, CO 5/1258, no. 29, PRO. John Browne, one of Kidd's crewmates in the 1689 West Indies campaign who went out with him in 1696, returned with Shelley. HCA 1/53, fols. 110–111, PRO. One can see the blurred moral dimension of the time in the comment of a merchant that piracy was an "honest occupation." Samuel Staats to Johannes de Peyster, July 10, 1699, de Peyster MSS, NYHS.

28. For Wilday see HCA 1/98, fol. 116; for Horne, HCA 1/98, fol. 118, PRO. While Kidd lingered at Saint Marie, at least one trading ship came into the port. Gabriel Loffe recorded that a New York ship commanded by a Captain Coster carried home some of the men's booty. CO 5/860, fols. 198–201, PRO. It is also possible that a ship commanded by the delightfully named Tempest Rogers visited the harbor. Deposition of John Hales, High Court of Delegates, 2/62, PRO.

29. HCA 1/98, fol. 154, PRO.

30. HCA 1/98, fol. 172, PRO.

31. Jones was captain of the *Beckford Galley*, but after it was burned by natives he stole the New York ship the *Peter*. HCA 1/98, fol. 22; for the letter to his wife, see HCA 1/98, fols. 183–184, PRO.

32. Examination of Gabriel Loffe, CO 5/860, no. 64, PRO.

33. HCA 1/98, fol. 187, PRO.

34. For examples of the wills see HCA 1/98, fols. 87–88, 108; for Culliford's letter, HCA 1/98, fol. 171, PRO.

35. HCA 1/98, fols. 110, 175, PRO. Unfortunately, John Dodd had retired on Madagascar; all Rowse could do was write to him telling him to pay Mrs. Breho her 400 pieces of eight. For other examples see HCA 1/98, fols. 90–97, 104, 158.

36. F. E. Baldwin, *Sumptuary Legislation and Personal Regulation in England* (Baltimore: Johns Hopkins University Press, 1926); N. B. Harte, "State Control of Dress and Social Change in Pre-Industrial England," in *Trade, Government and Economy in Pre-Industrial England: Essays Presented to F. J. Fisher*, ed. D. C. Coleman and A. H. John (London: Weidenfeld and Nicolson, 1976). For examples of legislation in the colonies see Nathaniel B. Shurtleff, *Records of the Governor and Company of Massachusetts Bay in New England* (Boston: W. White, 1853), I, 126, 183, 274.

37. For Le Golif's problems see his *Memoirs of a Buccaneer*, pp. 31, 54–55. For other examples of homosexual practices see *Barlow's Journal*, II, 68; Turner's deposition, CO 5/714, fols. 373–374, PRO; Exquemelin, *Bucaniers of America*, II, 121, 137. On the Navy and buggery see Arthur N. Gilbert, "Buggery and the British Navy, 1700–1861," *Journal of Social History*, 10 (1976), 72–98. Richard Burgh claims in his *Sodomy and the Perception of Evil: English Sea Rovers in the Seventeenth-Century Caribbean* (New York: New York University Press, 1983) that the vast majority of the buccaneers were practicing homosexuals. Although I agree that homosexuality existed, there is too much evidence of pirate heterosexuality in too many sources for me to accept his thesis.

38. Leibbrandt, *Precis*, II, 135; and for a similar sentiment see ibid., III, 5–6.

39. For the navy's interest in the pirate settlement see HCA 1/98, fols. 28–30; ADM 1/3666, fol. 100; correspondence of Captain Thomas Warren, ADM 1/2637, no. 16, PRO. A squadron that visited Madagascar and Saint Marie in May 1700 reported that the pirate town sat on a hill and had one "great" house in the middle of it. On this occasion the pirates blew up their ships in the harbor rather than allow them to fall into the navy's hands. Logs of the *Hastings*, ADM 51/3859, of the *Anglesea*, ADM 51/4114, and of the *Lizard*, ADM 51/3886, PRO. See yet another expedition in 1703–4, log of the *Scarborough*, Sloane MSS, 3674, BL.

40. Buckmaster deposition, CO 5/1042, fol. 297, PRO. Kidd made a list of the men who left his ship at this point, BL Loan, 29/207, fol. 105. See also *State Trials*, V, 303; Bradinham's deposition, HCA 1/15, fol. 7; Cul-

liford's depositions, HCA 1/16, pt. 1, fol. 5; ADM 1/3666, fol. 100, no. 4, PRO.

41. Kidd's Narrative, CO 5/860, fols. 198–201, PRO.

42. Ibid. For other examples see *The Grand Pyrate: Or, The Life and Death of Captain George Cusack* (London, 1675) and *The Arraignment, Tryal, and Condemnation, of Captain John Quelch and Others of his Company . . .* (London, 1705).

43. Kidd's Narrative, CO 5/860, fols. 198–201, PRO; report of Jan Coin, who visited the island in 1699; Leibbrandt, *Precis*, II, 229; *State Trials*, V, 303.

6. Revenge of the Company

1. Agaperry Callendin to Annesley, April 16, 1698, Orig. Corr., E/3/54, no. 6545, IOR.

2. Ovington, *Voyage to Surat*, pp. 226–236; Ishwari Prasad, *India in the Eighteenth Century* (Allahabad: Chugh Publications, 1973), pp. 62–63.

3. Chaudhuri, *Trading World of Asia*, pp. 421–422, 507–509.

4. Shafaat Ahmed Khan, *The East India Trade in the Seventeenth Century in Its Political and Economic Aspects* (London: H. Milford, 1923), pp. 150 ff., 206–207; Macaulay, *History of England*, V, 2096–2101.

5. Khan, *East India Trade*, pp. 202–205; Susil Chaudhuri, *Trade and Commercial Organization in Bengal, 1650–1720; with Special Reference to the English East India Company* (Calcutta: K. L. Mukhopodhyay, 1975), pp. 37–39; Sir William Wilson, *A History of British India* (reprint ed., New York: AMS Press, 1966), pp. 241–271.

6. Chaudhuri, *Trading World of Asia*, pp. 81–97, 421–422, 507–509.

7. For an excellent general background to these issues see Chandra Mukerji, *From Graven Images: Patterns of Modern Materialism* (New York: Columbia University Press, 1983), pp. 166–209; William Foster, *East India House; Its History and Associations* (London: John Lane, 1924), pp. 68–79; Audrey W. Douglas, "Cotton Textiles in England: The East India Company's Attempt to Exploit Developments in Fashion, 1660–1721," *Journal of British Studies* 8 (1969), 28–43.

8. Wilson, *History of British India*, pp. 283–298, 301–322; A. F. W. Papillon, *Memoirs of Thomas Papillon of London, Merchant, 1623–1702* (Reading, England: J. J. Beecroft, 1887).

9. On the bribes see *An Exact Collection of the Debates and Proceedings in Parliament in 1694 and 1695 Upon the Inquiry into the late Briberies and Corrupt Practices* (London, 1695); Wilson, *History of British India*, pp. 306–322.

10. The consequences of the seizing of Ghafur's ship are recorded in Ovington, *A Voyage to Surat*, pp. 410–419. On Ghafur's importance see

Hamilton, *A New Account of the East Indies*, I, 89; Das Gupta Ashin, "The Merchants of Surat, c.1700–1750," in *Elites in Southeast Asia*, ed. E. Leach and S. N. Mukherjee (Cambridge: Cambridge University Press, 1970).

11. Wright, *Annesley*, pp. 158–188; reports from the company's representatives, Orig. Corr., E/3/52, nos. 6201, 6205, 6226, 6290, IOR.

12. Annesley's report, November 2, 1696, Orig. Corr., E/3/52, no. 6329, IOR.

13. Leibbrandt, *Precis*, II, 253–254, 275; Orig. Corr., E/3/53, nos. 6384, 6490, IOR.

14. Orig. Corr., E/3/52, nos. 6279, 6311, 6329, IOR.

15. Various reports, Orig. Corr., E/3/53, nos. 6309, 6409, 6426, 6437, 6438, 6439, 6442, 6446, 6448, 6459, 6469, 6473, IOR.

16. Orig. Corr., E/3/53, no. 6467, IOR.

17. Orig. Corr., E/3/53, nos. 6545, 6547, IOR.

18. Orig. Corr., E/3/53, no. 6472, IOR; Gayer to company directors, Orme MSS, OV/155, fols. 52–57, IOR.

19. Orig. Corr., E/3/53, nos. 6556, 6591, IOR; Wright, *Annesley*, pp. 210–223.

20. Orig. Corr., E/3/53, nos. 6585, 6591, IOR. The representatives of the New East India Company also spread rumors that the old company had lost its charter in England because of its involvement with pirates—a rumor that only helped confirm opinions in Surat. Needless to say, local merchants identified with the company abandoned it to its fate. CO 77/16, fol. 241, PRO.

21. Orig. Corr., E/3/53, nos. 6598, 6601, 6602, IOR.

22. Orig. Corr., E/3/53, nos. 6592, 6593. See also Gayer to Bombay, February 2, 1699, Orme MSS, OV/155, fol. 141; and also his earlier letters to Surat July 7 and 21, fols. 71–72, 72–75, IOR.

23. Orig. Corr., E/3/53, nos. 6604, 6610, 6563, IOR. The final surrender came after another round of beatings administered to the company's servants and brokers, and a threat from the governor that the company members would all be "chawbuckt," or whipped. See also Wright, *Annesley*, p. 223.

24. Orig. Corr., E/3/53, nos. 6270, 6611, IOR. There is a good description of this series of events in Harikar Das, *Norris Embassy to Aurangzeb, 1699–1702* (Calcutta: Mukhopodhyay, 1959), pp. 34–36.

25. East India Company minutes of meetings, Minute Book, B1/41, fols. 78–79, 155–156, IOR; Robert Steele, *A Bibliography of Royal Proclamations of the Tudor and Stuart Sovereigns and of other publications under authority, 1485–1714* (New York: B. Franklin, 1967), I, nos. 4199, 4200, 4262.

26. John Dann details the experiences of Avery and his men after they left the Indian Ocean, and also the trial where he and Phillip Middleton testified against their crewmates. HCA 1/29, fol. 73, PRO; *State Trials*, V, 8–10. Dann, at age twenty-five, was among the youngest and the least guilty

of Avery's crew. The prosecution typically seized on such a man and had him turn state's evidence on promise of a pardon. The East India Company did everything it could to aid the prosecution, even to the point of buying new clothes for Middleton and paying his mother a pension for his testimony. Court Minutes B/41, fols. 168, 208, IOR. The legend of Avery can be found in Defoe, *King of the Pirates.*

27. An account of the trial is in *State Trials,* V, 2–17; Newton's statement is on p. 2.

28. *State Trials,* V, 2–3.

29. Aspects of this campaign are evident in the records of the Board of Trade. CO 323/2, fols. 268–269, 276–278, 342–376; CO 324/6, fols. 106–107, 111–113, 157, 159; CO 391/10, fols. 389–394, 413, 434–436, 442–443, PRO. For general background on this campaign see P. Bradley Nutting, "The Madagascar Connection: Parliament and Piracy, 1690–1701," *American Journal of Legal History,* 22 (1978), 202–215. The proclamation, with the exception for Kidd and Avery, was passed by the Privy Council on December 8, 1698. Privy Council 2/77, fols. 276–277, PRO. Surprisingly, the government feared that the pirates would come "under a formed Government" of their own, which obviously it did not want.

30. Coxe, *Original Correspondence,* pp. 569–571.

31. Ian K. Steele has an excellent discussion of the war on piracy, and Kidd's role, in his *Politics of Colonial Policy: The Board of Trade in Colonial Administration, 1696–1720* (Oxford: Clarendon Press, 1968), pp. 42–59.

32. On the general background of the merchant community at this time, see D. W. Jones, "London Merchants and the Crisis of the 1690s," in Peter Clark and Paul Slack, eds., *Crisis and Order in English Towns, 1500–1700* (London: Routledge and Kegan Paul, 1972). See also Gary S. De Krey, "Trade, Religion, and Politics in London in the Reign of William III" (Ph.D. diss., Princeton University, 1978). On specialization in trade see the example of naval supplies in Ehrman, *Navy in the War of William III,* pp. 56–61.

33. P. G. M. Dickson, *The Financial Revolution in England* (New York: St. Martin's Press, 1967), remains the best treatment of the new financial institutions. On ideological change see Joyce Oldham Appleby, *Economic Thought and Ideology in Seventeenth-Century England* (Princeton: Princeton University Press, 1978), pp. 242–279. Daniel Defoe, who wrote a great deal about buccaneers and sided with them, had a dyspeptic view of the new financiers and the world of stocks, bonds, and jobbers. At one time he wrote, "it would make a sad chasm on the Exchange of London, if all Pyrates should be taken away from among the merchants there." *A Review of the State of the British Nation,* October 18, 1707, IV, 107.

34. The records of the "Gentlemen Planters" are in CO 31/2, fols. 11–49, PRO. Other merchants also were organizing into more formal groups. See Alison G. Olson, "The Virginia Merchants of London: A Study in Eighteenth-Century Interest-Group Politics," *William and Mary Quarterly,*

40 (1983), 363–388. For the activities of the East India Company see Arnold A. Sherman, "Commerce, Colonies, and Competition: Special Interest Groups and English Commercial and Colonial Policy, 1660–1673" (Ph.D. diss., Yale University, 1972).

35. Merchant organization is particularly visible in the many petitions filed with the government. There is a large collection of such documents in CO 388/1–4, PRO.

36. This growing affiliation of merchants and bureaucracy is visible in the minutes of the Admiralty, ADM 1, and other Admiralty records such as ADM 7, plus the Lords of Trade and Plantations/Board of Trade, CO 391, PRO; and for Parliament in the Commons *Journals*.

37. Merchants were particularly interested in continuing naval protection for their ships after the war. The discussions are in CO 391/10, CO 324/6, ADM 3/13, ADM 1/5146, PRO. As usual, the East India Company joined in. State Papers 44/275, fols. 314–315, PRO.

38. Bradshaw was designated as the merchant representative, but the Admiralty would have none of it. The discussions were held in March 1697. ADM 3/13, PRO.

39. Penn, *Navy under the Early Stuarts*, pp. 46–49.

40. Chudleigh to Sir Edward Conway, November 18, 1623, State Papers 14/154, fol. 43, PRO; Senior, *Nation of Pirates*, pp. 70–71. Robert Cotton wrote a biting report on the state of the navy and characterized its sailors as "aged, impotent, vagrant, lewd and disorderly . . . a ragged regiment of Tapsters, Tinckers, Coblers, and many common rogues." State Papers, 14/41, fols. 39, 1–71, PRO.

41. HCA 14/41, fols. 91–92, 99, 149, 150; HCA 14/42, fols. 2, 50, 100, 149, 150; State Papers, 14/141, fols. 57, 66, 289, 351, PRO.

42. John Godolphin, *A View of Admiralty Jurisdiction* (London, 1661); Richard Zouch, *The Jurisdiction of the Admiralty Court of England Asserted* (London, 1663). For more recent assessments see Joanne Mathiason, "Some Problems of Admiralty Jurisdiction in the Seventeenth Century," *American Journal of Legal History*, 2 (1958), 25–36; George F. Steckley, "Merchants and the Admiralty Court during the English Revolution," *American Journal of Legal History*, 22 (1978), 137–175; Brian Levack, *The Civil Lawyers in England, 1603–1641: A Political Study* (Oxford: Clarendon Press, 1973).

43. 28 Henry 8, c. 15, *Statutes of the Realm*, III, 671.

44. Reginald G. Marsden, "The Vice-Admirals of the Coast," *English Historical Review*, 22 (1907), 468–477; 23 (1908), 736–757.

45. Paul L. Hughes and James F. Larkin, *Tudor Royal Proclamations, 1485–1603* (New Haven: Yale University Press, 1964–69), I, nos. 24, 40, 83, 317, 323, 362; II, nos. 450, 479, 482, 499, 513, 519, 526, 562, 563, 573, 585, 620, 742, 743, 797, 813.

46. Steele, *Bibliography of Royal Proclamations*, nos. 3729, 3857, 4199, 4200.

47. April 4, 1676, CO 1/36, fol. 71, PRO. On the general background see Haring, *The Buccaneers*, pp. 150–231; Crouse, *French Struggle for the West Indies*, pp. 146–175; and A. P. Thornton, *The European Nations in the West Indies, 1493–1688* (New York: Barnes and Noble, 1933), pp. 171–308.

48. Vaughan to Lords of Trade, April 4, 1676, CO 1/36, fol. 71, PRO.

49. Marsden, *Law and Custom*, II, 92–93; Haring, *The Buccaneers*, 200–201.

50. Helen J. Crump, *Colonial Admiralty Jurisdiction in the Seventeenth Century* (London: Longmans, Green, 1931), pp. 91–95.

51. CSPC (1675–1676), no. 295.

52. Crump, *Colonial Admiralty Jurisdiction*, pp. 97–116. On the use of the court-martial see Hill, "Notes on Piracy," p. 93.

53. Lloyd's report, July 30, 1676, CO 138/3, fols. 80–83, PRO.

54. The policy machinations can be followed in ibid., fols. 83–86; CO 1/41, fol. 254; CSPC (1677–80), no. 500; CO 138/3, 192–194; CO 1/17, fols. 199–200. For the text of the law see CO 139/8, 9–11, PRO.

55. CSPC (1681–85), 1210, 1718. Lynch applied for and received permission to conduct these negotiations. CO 138/4, fols. 91–94, PRO.

56. CSPC (1681–85), nos. 1065, 1249, 1938.

57. The report was filed March 4, 1684, CO 1/54, fol. 116, PRO.

58. CO 324/4, fol. 103, PRO.

59. CSPC (1681–85), nos. 1582, 1711, 1712, 1812, 1813; CSPC (1685–88), no. 1463; Privy Council 2, fol. 63, PRO.

60. *Earliest Printed Laws of South Carolina, 1692–1734*, I, 75. A copy of the Massachusetts law is in CO 1/55, fol. 98, PRO. NY Col. MSS, 35, fol. 36, NY State Library. Barbados, CSPC (1681–85), no. 1920. Pennsylvania, CO 5/1258, fol. 153, PRO.

61. 22 and 23 Carolus II, c. 11, *Statutes of the Realm*, V, 720–722.

62. The following works all deal with aspects of the rise of the state: J. H. Plumb, *The Growth of Political Stability in England* (London: Macmillan, 1967); J. R. Western, *Monarchy and Revolution* (Totowa, N.J.: Rowman and Littlefield, 1972); Geoffrey Holmes, *Augustan England: Professions, State and Society, 1680–1730* (London: George Allen and Unwin, 1982).

63. Hedges to William Blathwayt, August 29, 1701, Blathwayt Papers, Osborne Collection, Beineke Library, Yale University. Needless to say, this is a sentiment close to the heart of every historian. Holmes, *Augustan England*, pp. 237–287, has the best discussion of the new "civil service." On taxation see Edward Hughes, *Studies in Administration and Finance, 1558–1825, with special Reference to the History of Salt Taxation in England* (Manchester: Manchester University Press, 1934). And on finance see Stephen Baxter, *The Development of the Treasury, 1660–1702* (Cambridge, Mass.: Harvard University Press, 1957).

64. See Horwitz, *Parliament, Policy and Politics*, for a detailed account of the House of Commons' activities.

65. A complete account of the embassy to India is in Das, *Norris Embassy*. On the new diplomatic service see D. B. Horn, *British Diplomatic Representatives, 1689–1789* (London: Camden Society, 1932).

66. Charles McLean Andrews, *British Committees, Commissions and Councils of Trade and Plantations, 1622–1675* (Baltimore: Johns Hopkins University Press, 1908); Steele, *Politics of Colonial Policy*, pp. 3–41.

67. Charles McLean Andrews, *The Colonial Period of American History*, IV, 144–271.

68. "The Case of Nicholas Trott," Sloane MSS, 2902, fol. 269, BL; and also CSPC (1697–98), no. 928. On Fletcher see James S. Leamon, "Governor Fletcher's Recall," *William and Mary Quarterly*, 20 (1963), 527–542; and on Markham, CO 391/10, fols. 268, 271–274, 286–287, 332–333. See also the king's circular letter, April 22, 1697, CO 324/6, fols. 140–141, PRO.

69. After a six-hour fight Basse was captured by a buccaneering ship commanded by a German. The captives were taken to Hispaniola, where they were made to careen the ship. The pirates treated the men harshly, keeping them in water barrels at night, and did not release their captives until they left for Africa. Basse to William Popple, CSPC (1696–97), no. 1203. Basse wrote a detailed account of the piracy trade. CO 323/3, no. 44A, PRO.

70. CO 324/4, fols. 138–140, PRO.

71. CSPC (1675–76), nos. 431, 693, 729, 730; (1677–80), nos. 503, 577, 581. A similar case can be followed in CO 1/35, fols. 248, 251, 252, 261, PRO. A wealth of information on privateering and reprisal may be found in Marsden, "Early Prize Jurisdiction."

72. CO 1/51, fol. 69; CO 138/4, fols. 91–92, 117–118; CO 1/42, fol. 320, PRO.

73. The best account of the evolution of French naval policy is in Symcox, *Crisis of French Seapower*. Francis M. Stark, *The Abolition of Privateering and the Declaration of Paris* (New York: Columbia University Press, 1897), discusses the general background of privateering. George N. Clark, *The Dutch Alliance and the War against French Trade* (Manchester: Manchester University Press, 1923), is the best survey of the privateering war.

74. 4 William and Mary, c. 25, *Statutes of the Realm*, VII, 419–423; Marsden, "Early Prize Jurisdiction," pp. 51–53.

75. CO 391/10, fol. 350; CO 324/6, fols. 106–107, PRO; DNB, XXV, 362–363.

76. CO 391/10, fols. 350–354; CO 324/6, fols. 211–212, PRO. William Penn was particularly upset by the "interference" with his colony. Penn to Robert Harley, August 6, 1701, BL Loan, 29/190, 185–190; CO 5/1287, fols. 16–17, 18, 31, PRO. For examples of the laws see *Charter of William Penn and the Laws of the Province of Pennsylvania; Passed 1682–1700* (Harrisburg, 1879), pp. 284–285; Massachusetts, CO 5/770, fols. 87–88, PRO; East Jersey, CSPC (1699), no. 512.

77. CO 391/10, fol. 353. See the complaints in CO 323/2, fols. 40, 90;

CO 324/3, fols. 108–110; CO 324/7, fols. 94–97. On Parliament see CO 324/6, fols. 68–69, PRO.

78. CO 324/4, fol. 104, PRO.

79. Vernon's memo is dated March 28, 1698, CO 324/6, fols. 261–263; CO 323/2, fol. 278; CO 391/11, fols. 8, 11, 17–19. The draft of the bill is in 323/2, fols. 283–292, 314–317, PRO, and another copy is in Add. MSS, 24107, fol. 159, BL.

80. Commons *Journals*, XIII, 57, 132, 142, 265, 267, 275, 286, 289, 293, 296, 305.

81. 11 William and Mary, c. 7, *Statutes of the Realm*, VII, 590–594; CO 324/6, fols. 142, 284–285, PRO.

82. Orders for Larkin, CO 389/17, fols. 240–242; Privy Council 5/2, April 1701. For Larkin's work in one colony see CO 390/12, fols. 361–385, PRO.

83. CO 324/7, fols. 75–76, 78–79, 80–81, 85–94; CO 389/17, 50–51, PRO.

84. For a broad look at the navy during this period see M. Oppenheim, *A History of the Administration of the Royal Navy and of merchant shipping in relation to the navy from 1509 to 1660* (London: J. Lane, 1896); Ehrman, *Navy in the War of William III;* J. R. Tanner, *Samuel Pepys and the Royal Navy* (Cambridge: Cambridge University Press, 1920). For the size of the fleet in 1675 see ADM 8/1, PRO. This class of papers records the number of ships in sea pay, which is not a reflection of total fleet size; but it does state the total number of ships that were manned and ready for service.

85. Accounts on January 1685, ADM 8/1, PRO.

86. Accounts on January 1689, ADM 8/1–4, PRO.

87. ADM 8/4, June 1, 1696, PRO.

88. Symcox, *Crisis of French Sea Power*, pp. 143–220. One of the outstanding French privateers, and a man much hated by the English, was the redoubtable Jean Bart. Henri Malo, *Les corsaires dunkerquois et Jean Bart*, 2 vols. (Paris: Mercure de France, 1913–14).

89. Crowhurst, *Defence of British Trade*, pp. 45–63.

90. For an example of the detailed work and cooperation needed to run the convoy system, see ADM 1/5148; CO 388/2, PRO. These volumes record merchant petitions relating to the problems of the emerging convoy system.

91. See Admiralty to Board of Trade, September 20, 1697, CO 323, fol. 192. There were also later petitions: ADM 3/16, November 26, 1700, and CO 323/3, fol. 108. In 1699 the Board of Trade petitioned the king for more ships. CO 324/7, fols. 106–109, PRO.

92. R. D. Merriman, ed., *The Sergison Papers* (London: Naval Record Society, 1950), p. 362. By January 1701 there were still seventy-two ships in pay. ADM 7/335, PRO. The Admiralty actually wanted eighty. Vernon to Shrewsbury, September 28, 1697, in James, *Letters Illustrative*, I, 414.

93. On the emergence of the navy as a profession see Holmes, *Augustan England*, pp. 274–287. On one occasion during the conflict the men-of-war attached to a convoy abandoned it to go hunt prizes. Blathwayt Papers, 74/ 6.16, fol. 25, Osborne MSS, Beineke Library, Yale University. King William had to allow the customs officers to search royal ships because of suspicions that they were smuggling gold. ADM 2/4080, fol. 737, PRO. For one captain who embezzled when he could, see the various court cases involving Christopher Billop: CO 391/4, fols. 71–72; CO 391/5, fols. 235–236, PRO; CSPC (1681–85), nos. 572, 762, 1105, 1106; Mayor's Court Depositions, Box 36, November 7, 1682, London Record Office; Privy Council 2/ 74, 88, PRO.

94. See the material on Billop in note 93.

95. Vernon wrote this letter to Shrewsbury after an attempt to take the *Queensborough*, October 1, 1698; James, *Letters Illustrative*, II, 186–188. This was not an isolated episode. A later expedition to Saint Marie removed the captain of the *Hastings* when it seemed his ship would turn pirate. Logs of the *Hastings*, ADM 51/3859, the *Anglesea*, ADM 51/4114, and the *Lizard*, ADM 51/3886, PRO.

96. Vernon to Board of Trade, December 23, 1698, CO 324/6, fol. 113.

97. Planning for the Warren expedition began in the spring, under pressure from the East India Company. It testified to the demands that would be put on the ships and also agreed to supply the ships. Accompanying the fleet would be a three-man commission that was to oversee the pardoning of pirates on Madagascar. The group never visited the island, as the ships went straight to India. An account of part of the expedition is in Das, *Norris Embassy*, pp. 31–32. Discussion regarding the expedition can be followed in CO 324/6, CO 323/2, CO 391/10 and 11; see also Privy Council 2/77, fols. 276–277; ADM 1/3666, fol. 100; HCA 1/98, fol. 28, PRO. The lords justices rightly thought the ships would do little good. Robert Yard to William Blathwayt, August 30, 1698, Blathwayt Papers, Box 20, Osborne MSS, Beineke Library, Yale University. The directors of the New East India Company had such strong doubts about the navy's ability to do the job in the East that they wanted to send their own ships and officers. Vernon to King William, August 26, 1698, PWA 1478, Portland of Welbeck MSS, Nottingham University Library.

98. Log of the *Essex Prize*, ADM 51/291, PRO. Captain Richard Burgess of the *Maryland Merchant* was aboard the *Providence Galley* during the chase. CO 323/3, no. 21, PRO. The captain of the pirate ship was Evan Jones, the person noted earlier as having written his wife that he would return in five years. Actually he set out for home after a year; when one of his captives asked who he was, he answered, "I am Kidd," a sign of Kidd's growing notoriety in the colonies.

99. Captain Passenger's letters are in ADM 1/2277 and his letter of May 3, 1700, details his fight; PRO.

100. W. L. Grant and J. Munro, *Acts of the Privy Council; Colonial Series, England* (London: Her Majesty's Stationery Office, 1910), II, 349.

7. Cat and Mouse

1. In his Narrative of July 1699 Kidd states that Culliford left Saint Marie about June 15, 1698, and that he had to wait five months for a "fair wind." CO 5/860, fols. 198–201, PRO.

2. Examination of Hugh Parrot, July 10, 1699, CO 5/860, fols. 187–188, PRO.

3. In his "Instrument of Protest," of July 7, 1699, Kidd listed most of the men who returned with him and asserts their innocence. HMC, *Portland,* IX, 403–406. They were John Ware, Hugh Parrot, Michael Galloway, Samuel Ayers, Abeel Owen, Humphrey Clay, Martin Shrink, Gabriel Lane, William Whattley, Samuel Bradley, English Smith, Richard Barlycorne, William Jenkins, Robert Lamley, John Arris, and Richard Wood. There were also two "negroes": Ventura, who had joined the crew, and Dundee, whom Kidd bought at Madagascar. The men excluded from the list were mostly the notorious characters such as Kelley and Davis, with whom Kidd did not want to be associated.

4. This version is based on Kelley's own account, delivered by his wife to the printer: *A Full and True Discovery of all the Robberies, Pyracies and other Notorious Actions of that Famous English Pyrate, Captain James Kelley, who was executed on Friday 12 July 1700* . . . (London: July 11, 1700). The original manuscript of Dampier's journal is Sloane MSS, 3236, and of Cowley's, Sloan MSS, 1050 and 1054, BL. Cowley's journal was later published by William Hacke as *Cowley's Voyage Round the Globe* (London, 1699). There are many editions of the Dampier journal.

5. On the murder of Leonard Edgecombe see June 14, 1700, HCA 1/53, fol. 73, PRO. In Kelley's examination at the time of his trial he was reported as forty years old, born in Hartlepool, Durham. He admitted to leaving Rhode Island and going to Madagascar, where he remained for fourteen months before meeting Kidd. HCA 1/14, fol. 203, PRO.

6. On Harrison see the examination of Hugh Parrot, CO 5/860, fol. 187, PRO; deposition of John Hales, Court of Delegates, 2/62; deposition of Edward Davis, April 15, 1700, HCA 1/14, fol. 205, PRO. Bellomont suspected Davis when he arrived in New York, and it was he who commented on Davis' girth. CO 5/860, fols. 330–333. See also Kemp and Lloyd, *Brethren of the Coast,* pp. 94–96, 124–132.

7. Report of Stephanus van Cortlandt, July 1, 1698, CO 5/1042, fols. 242–243, PRO.

8. The *Peter* was taken by Evan Jones, to replace his ship after it burned. HCA 1/98, fol. 22, PRO. The *Prophet Daniel* suffered a similar fate, which has already been recounted in the discussion on "King" Abraham Samuel. The *Margaret* was seized at the Cape of Good Hope. Log of the *Loyal Merchant*, L.Mar.A., 132, fols. 11–12, IOR; Leibbrandt, *Precis*, I, 17–21.

9. Given the dangers of the sea on such a long voyage and the slim likelihood of finding a specific individual, correspondents usually sent multiple copies of their letters. HCA 1/98, fols. 114, 123, 128, PRO. Captain George Revelly of the *Peter* also carried copies; ibid., fols. 189, 192. There are even copies of two of the letters to Kidd in The Hague. VOC, 4043, ARA. The Dutch administration at the Cape colony returned to Holland copies of the important documents that fell into its hands.

10. Emott to Kidd, June 4, 1698, HCA 1/98, fol. 114, PRO.

11. Ibid.

12. Ibid., fols. 123, 128.

13. Examination of Gabriel Loffe, CO 5/860, no. 64, PRO.

14. There is an ink drawing that shows the place on Ascension Island for leaving messages in Add. MSS, 15738, fol. 2. For accounts of visits there see the logs of the *Caesar*, Sloane MSS, 3668, and the *Kempthorne*, Sloane MSS, 3670, BL. See also *Barlow's Journal*, I, 200; and *A Relation of Three Years Sufferings of Robert Everard upon the Coast of Africa near Madagascar in a Voyage to India in the year 1686* (London, 1693), pp. 292–293.

15. It is possible that for all or part of this leg of the voyage Kidd was accompanied by the *Fidelio*, under Captain Tempest Rogers. Rogers had a private meeting with Kidd on Saint Marie and then left. Examination of Edward Davis, HCA 1/14, fol. 205, PRO. The only report that specifically connects the two men in the West Indies is that of Richard Oglethorpe, but his letter is dated January 27, 1706. CSPC (1706), no. 53. William Syme bought the *Fidelio* from Rogers at just about the time Kidd was in the West Indies, however, purchasing the ship at Crabb Island, which Kidd briefly visited. Bellomont seized the ship in Boston and managed to capture some East Indies goods, which he suspected were Kidd's. Examination of William Syme, October 22, 1699, CO 5/860, fols. 330–333, 343, PRO.

16. Council of Nevis to Vernon, February 4, 1699, CSPC (1699), no. 75 and also no. 72. Rupert Billingsley, captain of the navy ship *Queensborough*, was sent out after Kidd even though he had just lost twenty-seven men to disease and had only twelve fit for service. He reported that when Kidd was in Anguilla he had offered the governor £200 to be allowed to stay. ADM 1/1462, PRO.

17. Dunbar Maury Hinrichs, "Captain Kidd and the St. Thomas Incident," *New York History*, 37 (1956), 266–280; information of Peter Smith, CO 152/3, no. 31, PRO; Governor John Laurents to Bellomont, September

1, 1699, BL Loan, 29/207, fols. 124–126. On the voyage of *La Trompeuse* and its destruction, see the examination of Thomas Phips, CO 1/53, fol. 33, and the "account" of the burning, ibid., fol. 30.

18. Smith, CO 152/3, no. 31, PRO.

19. Council of Nevis to Vernon, May 18, 1699, CO 152/3, fol. 91, PRO. The council reported, erroneously, that Kidd had suffered a mutiny on the return voyage that killed thirty and left Kidd with only twenty-five men.

20. Governor Yeamans to Bellomont, September 1, 1699, CO 29/209, fols. 123–124, PRO.

21. Bolton's deposition, February 4, 1700, BL Loan, 29/207, 128–131.

22. Ibid.

23. For the continuing contact with Curaçao see "Calendar of Bills of Lading for Shipments by Jacobus van Cortlandt, 1699–1702," *New-York Historical Society Quarterly Bulletin,* 20 (1936), 113–121.

24. Examination of Henry Bolton, February 4, 1700, BL Loan, 29/207, fols. 128–131; Smith, June 27, 1699, ibid., fol. 30; examination of Gabriel Loffe, CO 5/860, no. 64, PRO; examination of Samuel Wood, CO 5/860, fols. 179–180, PRO.

25. Ibid. Examination of John Everitt, State Papers, 42/6, fols. 53–54, PRO. For the Brandenburgh Company see Laurents to Bellomont, BL 29/207, fols. 124–126; Admiral Benbow to Vernon, October 28, 1699, CO 318/3 no. 1, PRO.

26. For estimates see Smith, BL Loan, 29/209, fol. 30; memo of John Ruggles, August 25, 1699, BL Loan, 29/207, fol. 122; examination of John Everitt, State Papers, 42/6, fols. 53–54; also HCA 1/15, fol. 13, PRO.

27. Examination of Samuel Wood, CO 5/860, fols. 179–180; examinations of Jenkins, CO 5/860, fols. 176–177, PRO; Bolton, BL Loan, 29/207, fols. 128–131; Smith, CO 152/3, fol. 91, PRO. Six of Kidd's men left the ship at this point and went to Curaçao in the sloops. John Weir was later captured in Charlestown. HCA 1/53, fol. 90, PRO.

28. Examinations of Bolton, BL Loan, 29/207, fols. 128–131, and Smith, ibid., fol. 30. Governor Beeston to the Admiralty, August 7, 1700, HCA 1/15, fol. 13, PRO.

29. Journal of Nathaniel Cary, who went to the West Indies searching for Kidd's treasure. He recorded a rumor that the *Quedah* had burned for six hours on about June 9. CO 5/860, fols. 372–373, PRO. Other reports about the ship and its cargo filtered back to New York. Abraham Wendell to Abraham de Peyster, July 10 and 23, 1699, de Peyster MSS, New-York Historical Society. The cargo of the *Quedah* apparently was taken to Curaçao and Saint Thomas. Wendell reports that three ships at Curaçao transshipped the goods to Holland. The governor of Curaçao denied that the goods ever went through his colony, and when he questioned Lamont and Cribble,

Kidd's friends, they declared they knew nothing. CO 5/860, fol. 370, PRO. For contradictory testimony see CO 5/860, fol. 172, PRO.

30. Governor Grey to the Admiralty, June 19, 1699, ADM 1/4086, fol. 551, PRO; Livingston's estimate, Nanfan to Bellomont, June 1, 1699, CO 5/1042, fol. 301, PRO. Warren's comment was made before the Board of Trade. CO 391/19, fol. 395, PRO.

31. John D. Runcie, "The Problem of Anglo-American Politics in Bellomont's New York," *William and Mary Quarterly*, 26 (1969), 191–217; John C. Rainbolt, "The Creation of a Governor and Captain General for the Northern Colonies," *New-York Historical Society Quarterly*, 57 (1973), 101–120; Leamon, "Fletcher's Recall," pp. 527–542.

32. Captain John Evans describes Bellomont's arrival and relates the tale of the nose tweaking in Evans to Admiralty, July 5, 1698, ADM 1/1754, PRO. For a full account of Livingston's activities and problems at this time see Leder, *Robert Livingston*, pp. 96–147.

33. Bellomont to Lord Bridgewater, June 27, 1698, Ellesmere MSS, 9747, HEH.

34. CO 5/1040, fols. 138–151, PRO.

35. Fletcher collected a number of loyal addresses. Add. MSS, 9837, fols. 92–97, BL; Berthold Fernow and A. J. F. van Laer, *Calendar of Council Minutes, 1668–1783* (Albany: University of the State of New York, 1902), II, 130–131. Bellomont published a printed version of the minutes to stop rumors. CO 5/1040, fol. 162, PRO. His letter of May 18, 1698, to the Board of Trade relates how the councilors avoided him. CO 5/1115, fols. 312–322, PRO.

36. Fernow and van Laer, *Council Minutes*, II, 130–131. Frederick Philipse, at this time seventy-three years old and undoubted king of the pirate traders, sat on the council. *Journal of the Legislative Council of the Colony of New York* (Albany: Weed, Parsons, 1861), pp. 130–131.

37. Bellomont published this speech. CO 5/1040, fols. 133–134, PRO. He also issued a proclamation that ordered all pirates arrested. CO 5/1040, fol. 153, PRO.

38. On the *Fortune* see the various documents in CO 5/1040, fols. 224–249, PRO; Bellomont to the Board of Trade, May 18, 1698, CO 5/1115, fols. 312–322. Other letters of the period comment on this affair. CO 5/1115, fols. 323–337; CO 5/1040, fols. 138–157, 224–225; NYCD, IV, 306–310, 320–326, 354–358. The Board of Trade considered all of this worthwhile evidence that affirmed the tales about New York, so they in turn sent summaries to the lords justices. NYCD, IV, 542–544, 583–584.

39. Bellomont to Board of Trade, June 22, 1698, NYCD, IV, 320–326.

40. Frederick Philipse was a prominent member of the mob, perhaps because van Sweeten was his son-in-law. CO 5/1040, fols. 242–249, PRO.

41. For the reinterring see the accounts in CO 5/1042, fol. 26, PRO; Add. MSS, 9837, no. 28, BL.

42. Add. MSS, 9837, fols. 93, 110, 113, 116–119, 120–121, BL. Also "Heads of Accusation against the Earl of Bellomont," March 11, 1700, NYCD, IV, 620–623.

43. "Heads of Accusation," March 11, 1700, NYCD, IV, 620–623.

44. Blathwayt to [Vernon?], December 20, 1698, State Papers 105/52, no foliation, PRO; Stepney to Blathwayt, January 18, 1699, ibid., PRO.

45. Bellomont to John Locke, May 12, 1699, Locke MSS, c. 7 fol. 174, BOD; Bellomont to Bridgewater, October 12, 1699, Ellesmere MSS, 9767, HEH; Bellomont to Board of Trade, August 24, 1699, NYCD, IV, 549–556; Bellomont to Lowndes, November 14, 1698, Treasury 1/57, fol. 267, PRO.

46. Bellomont to Board of Trade, June 22, 1698, NYCD, IV, 320–326; also Fernow and van Laer, *Council Minutes*, II, 131; Board of Trade to Bellomont, October 4, 1698, NYCD, IV, 412–441.

47. Bellomont to Board of Trade, May 15, 1699, CO 5/1042, fols. 203–208, PRO.

48. Examination of Giles Shelley, March 29, 1701, HCA 1/53, fols. 79–81, PRO; Shelley to de Lancey, May 27, 1699, CO 5/1258, fols. 147–149; also CO 323/3, fol. 130, PRO; examination of Otto van Toyle, June 14, 1699, CO 5/1042, fol. 299, PRO.

49. Johannes de Peyster to Abraham de Peyster, June 11, 1699, de Peyster MSS, New-York Historical Society. It was estimated that Culliford's men had between £500 and £600 apiece. Examination of Otto van Toyle, CO 5/1042, fol. 299, PRO.

50. Correspondence between Nanfan and Bellomont in June 1699, CO 5/1042, fol. 301, PRO; NYCD, IV, 557. Bellomont urged Nanfan to do all in his power to jail Shelley and the men who accompanied him, but Nanfan equivocated because he had no proof of criminal activity. Nor did he get much help in obtaining proof. Mr. Hungerford, the customs collector, looked the other way rather than investigate the *Nassau*, which lay within sight of the city. CO 5/1045, fols. 271–272, PRO. For other reports on Shelley see the June letters of James Graham, Samuel Staats, and Johannes de Peyster to Abraham de Peyster, de Peyster MSS, New-York Historical Society. With pirates in the city, rumors were renewed that Kidd was still somewhere in the West Indies, but there was no clue to his intentions. CO 5/1042, fol. 301, PRO.

51. *Council Minutes*, II, 140. For an account of the meeting see Samuel Staats to Abraham de Peyster, June 12, 1699, de Peyster MSS, New-York Historical Society; William Sharpas to Abraham de Peyster, June 26, 1699, ibid. Some cloth and sixty-nine "elephants' teeth" were found in houses on Long Island. See the account of goods taken by Mr. Hungerford, CO 5/1045, fol. 283, PRO.

52. *Council Minutes,* II, 140. Examination of Edward Buckmaster, June 5, 1699, CO 5/1042, fol. 297, PRO.

53. William Stoughton to Vernon, April 12, 1699, CSPC (1699), no. 247.

54. Bellomont's correspondence during this period is full of information on Bradish's affairs. CSPC (1699), no. 343, 549, 678, 890, 1011. On Bradish's career see *A True Relation of a most Horrid Conspiracy and Running away with the Ship Adventure, Having on Board 40,000 Pieces of Eight* (London, 1700); William Stoughton to Vernon, April 12, 1699, CO 5/860, fols. 130–131, PRO; and discussion in CO 323/4, fols. 68–69, PRO.

55. Quary to Board of Trade, June 6, 1699, CO 5/1258, no. 31, PRO.

56. Basse to William Popple, June 9, 1699, CO 5/1258, no. 29. Basse had intercepted one of the copies of a letter sent by Shelley to his owners, revealing the true nature of his cargo. He also spread a rumor that Kidd was off the coast in a large sloop manned by sixty crew members.

57. Examination of William Jenkins, CO 5/860, fols. 174–176; Barlycorne, CO 5/860, fol. 176, PRO. James Kelley sent a large chest ashore at Whorekills. Examination of Gabriel Loffe, CO 5/860, fols. 170–171, PRO. Quary found out about Kidd because local people rushed to do business with him, and the men who left the *Saint Antonio* scattered into the countryside. CO 5/1258, no. 31, PRO.

58. CO 5/1042, fols. 203–208, PRO.

59. Emott's testimony before the Massachusetts council, June 19, 1699, CO 5/787, fols. 214–215, PRO. Emott stated that Kidd had a strong sense of honor and wanted very much to fulfill his commission. Bellomont to Board of Trade, July 8, 1699, CO 5/860, fols. 145–151, PRO.

60. Examinations of Hugh Parrot, John Gardiner, William Jenkins, Richard Barlycorne, Samuel Wood, Thomas Way, and Gabriel Loffe, CO 5/860, fols. 187–188, 192–193, 174–176, 176–177, 179–180, 181, 170–171, PRO. Campbell's newsletter claimed that Kidd shot at a ship sent out by the governor of Rhode Island. Massachusetts Historical Society, *Proceedings,* 12 (1871, 1873), 422.

61. Council minutes, CO 5/787, fols. 214–215, PRO; memorandum of Duncan Campbell, June 19, 1699, CO 5/860, fol. 163. Robert Yard, secretary to the lords justices, wrote to Bellomont on November 26, 1698, about Kidd. CO 324/24, fol. 637, PRO. Vernon wrote to him on November 23, CO 324/26, fols. 235–236. At the same time Yard told the Admiralty to order Admiral Benbow to capture Kidd. ADM 1/4086, fols. 346, 355, PRO. The Board of Trade also wrote to Bellomont on January 5, 1699, telling him that Kidd had been exempted from the recently issued pardon. CO 5/1116, fols. 213–214, PRO. In his letter to the Board of Trade, Bellomont wrote that he had kept this news secret, fearing that if he publicized it, Livingston and other "countrymen" of Kidd would warn him away. Of

course, all the surrounding governments had received the same message and the news was known in New York. CO 5/860, fols. 145–151, PRO.

62. CO 5/860, fol. 165, PRO. What Bellomont did not admit to Emott was that the pardon exempted Kidd. Bellomont did state that he was "tender" of using this power "because I want to bring no staine on my Reputacion." In this same letter, written to justify his actions, Bellomont called Emott "a cunning Jacobite, a fast friend of Fletcher and my avowed enemy"—hardly an appropriate emissary. Bellomont explained his dealing with Kidd as being necessary to discover the exact location of the *Quedah*. Until he knew that, he could hardly arrest him. CO 5/860, fols. 145–151, PRO.

63. CO 5/860, fol. 167, PRO.

64. CO 5/860, fols. 145–151, PRO.

65. Ibid.; CO 5/787, fols. 217–219, PRO.

66. Bellomont to Bridgewater, November 12, 1698, Ellesmere MSS, 9756, HEH.

67. Bellomont to Sir John Stanley, his personal agent, BL Loan, 29/207, fol. 66. See also his complaints to Sir Henry Ashurst, ibid., fol. 63.

68. Bellomont to Bridgewater, November 12, 1698, Ellesmere MSS, 9756, HEH.

69. These are all estimates. That of Kidd's loot is in a letter from the Board of Trade to the lords justices, NYCD, IV, 583–584. Bellomont's estimate of what actually came into his hands later on was £14,000. Bellomont to Trade, July 26, 1699, CO 5/860, fols. 154–156, PRO. What he also hoped to obtain was the £70,000 he believed to be still on the *Quedah Merchant*.

70. Bellomont proposed just such a deal to Sir James Vernon and to Stanley, March 7, 1700, BL Loan, 29/207, fols. 65–66, 86–93.

71. CO 5/860, no. 15, PRO. Bellomont accused Livingston, along with Campbell, of trying to "embezzle" Kidd's loot and of trying to "jiggle," or plot, together. BL Loan, 29/207, fols. 145–151. Livingston denied these "aspersions" under oath. NYCD, IV, 883–884; CO 5/787, fol. 223, PRO; Samuel Staats to Abraham de Peyster, July 3 and 10, 1699, de Peyster MSS, New-York Historical Society.

72. Council minutes, CO 5/787, fol. 219, PRO.

73. Ibid., fols. 220–221.

74. Ibid.

75. Bellomont to Board of Trade, July 8, 1699, CO 5/860, fols. 145–151, PRO; Livingston to Board of Trade, June 21, 1701, NYCD, IV, 883–884.

76. Bellomont to Board of Trade, July 8, 1699, CO 5/860, fols. 145–151, and his letter of July 20, ibid., fols. 154–156, PRO. Bellomont gave as his final reason for ordering Kidd's arrest the rumor that Kidd was about to

give Bellomont's wife £1,000 in gold. Upon arresting Kidd, Bellomont immediately ordered a group of officials to inventory the *Saint Antonio;* he turned over to them the presents Kidd had already made to Lady Bellomont.

8. Winners and Losers

1. Massachusetts Council minutes, CO 5/787, fols. 217, 222, 227, PRO; Bellomont to Board of Trade, October 20, 1699, NYCD, IV, 591–595. Kelley was arrested on November 29. Bellomont to Board of Trade, January 5, 1700, CO 5/860, fols. 77–78. Bellomont made much of the fact that Kelley had become a "moor" and was circumcised.

2. For Bellomont's search see his letters to the Board of Trade of July 26 and October 20, 1699, CO 5/860, fols. 154–156, PRO, and NYCD, IV, 591–595. Even Mrs. Kidd was jailed and interrogated. CO 5/787, fol. 223. It was John Cary who went to the Caribbean to search for the *Quedah Merchant.* CO 5/860, fol. 372.

3. Vernon sent Shrewsbury a copy of the *Postman* of June 10, 1697, which carried a story from Cadiz that the *Slaughter Galley,* newly arrived from Alexandria, reported that Kidd had already turned pirate in the Red Sea. Kidd did not arrive there until August, so the tale is very unlikely unless it originated with John Clerke or one of the other East India captains. If it did, it is so remarkable an example of rapid communications that even Harrison doubted it. Vernon to Shrewsbury, June 10, 1697, Vernon Letters. I examined these letters on a microfilm kindly loaned to me by Henry Horwitz. *Postman,* June 10–12, 1697, no. 330.

4. Governor Grey of Barbados was the one who quoted the £400,000 sum. ADM 1/4086, fol. 551, PRO. Vernon used the same figure in a letter to William Blathwayt, August 4, 1699. Blathwayt Papers, Osborne MSS, Beinecke. But Vernon doubted the validity of the amount quoted; see his letters to Shrewsbury in James, *Letters Illustrative,* II, 319–320, 322–324, 332–333. Even the supreme gossip Narcisus Luttrell repeated it. *A Brief Historical Relation,* IV, 543.

5. Vernon to Shrewsbury, August 8, 1699, in James, *Letters Illustrative,* II, 335–338.

6. Vernon reported to the king as early as July 14 that Kidd was in the West Indies; then on August 8 he recounted rumors that Kidd had made a deal with Bellomont. He confirmed those rumors on September 1, when Bellomont's first letters arrived, and by the end of the month the king had all the details. Blathwayt stated that the capture of Kidd pleased King William: "it could not but well please his Maj." Add. MSS, 40774, fols. 97, 136, 164, 184, BL; Blathwayt to Vernon, September 5, 1699, Add. MSS, 37992, fol. 235. On the day the story was confirmed, the directors of the Old East India Company decided to file a claim for £100,000 of Kidd's supposed treasure. Director's minutes, B/43, fol. 81, IOR.

7. ADM 3/15, September 12, December 4, PRO. (Admiralty 3 is a record of the meetings of the board; the volumes are not foliated, so all references will be made by specific date.)

8. Letters of Gerard Elwes to the Admiralty, ADM 1/1754, PRO; House of Commons' order, ADM 3/15, December 5, 1699. After Kidd's trial, pamphlets were published arguing the merits of his case and those of the Junto members; they report every rumor relating to the case. *A Full Account of the Actions of Captain Kidd,* p. 14; and *A Full Account of the Proceedings in Relation to Captain Kidd in Two Letters* (London, 1701), pp. 12–13.

9. ADM 3/15, December 5, 1699, PRO. The *Advice* was the same ship that had first spotted Kidd in the South Atlantic.

10. Hill, *Growth of Parliamentary Parties,* pp. 66–80. For excellent discussions of parliamentary affairs see Horwitz, *Parliament, Policy and Politics,* pp. 222–310; and Rubini, *Court and Country,* pp. 178–235.

11. The Somers quote is in Somers to Shrewsbury, December 15, 1698, in Coxe, *Original Correspondence,* pp. 569–571. For the enmity of the Old Company see Oldmixon, *History of England,* I, 205; and Feiling, *History of Tory Party,* pp. 328–329.

12. CO 391/11, fols. 87–88, PRO.

13. Vernon to Shrewsbury, November 29, 1698, in Vernon Letters, II, fol. 113. On the *Frederick* see HCA 24/126; Lansdowne MSS, 1153E, fol. 89, BL.

14. Vernon to Shrewsbury, November 26, 1698, Vernon Letters, II, fol. 112.

15. Vernon to Shrewsbury, December 13, 1698, ibid., fol. 120; Somers to Shrewsbury, December 15, 1698, in Coxe, *Original Correspondence,* pp. 569–571. A little earlier Montague fell into a dispute with the company over another matter in Parliament and wrote to Shrewsbury that while he was not "insensible of the Opposition I should meet with from such a set of men . . . but really the dispute was more obstinate than I did expect." Coxe, *Original Correspondence,* p. 543.

16. Biography of Sir James Vernon in the DNB, XX, 277–278. The quotation is from Vernon to Shrewsbury, September 11, 1697, in James, *Letters Illustrative,* I, 358–360.

17. Vernon to Shrewsbury, October 11, 1697, in James, *Letters Illustrative,* I, 380.

18. Vernon to Shrewsbury, September 21, 1699, in James, *Letters Illustrative,* II, 353–354.

19. H. M. Colvin et al., *The History of the King's Works* (London: Her Majesty's Stationery Office, 1976), V, 400–405.

20. Commons *Journals,* XIII, 10; Vernon to Shrewsbury, December 2, 1699, in James, *Letters Illustrative,* II, 371–374. On the orders see CO 391/12, fol. 269; CO 323/3, fol. 119, PRO.

21. Vernon to Shrewsbury, December 2, 1699, in James, *Letters Illustrative*, II, 371–374.

22. Commons *Journals*, XIII, 11–15. The journal then proceeds to print all of these documents: ibid., pp. 15–39; Vernon to Shrewsbury, December 5, 1699, in James, *Letters Illustrative*, II, 374–376.

23. Writings of Sir Richard Cocks, 1682–1701, English Historical MSS, b. 209, fol. 85, BOD.

24. Ibid.

25. Ibid.

26. Ibid. Vernon to Shrewsbury, December 7, 1699, in James, *Letters Illustrative*, II, 376–381; Robert Price to the Duke of Beaufort, December 6, 1699, Carte MSS 130, fol. 405, BOD; Edward Clarke to John Locke, December 7, 1699, Locke MSS, c. 8, fol. 230, BOD. One report states that the king, on hearing about this session, said that if the law had allowed him to be a witness he would "of my own knowledge justify the Lords concerned in all that they have done." Oldmixon, *History of England*, II, 206.

27. Vernon to Shrewsbury, December 7, 1699, in James, *Letters Illustrative*, II, 376–381.

28. Kidd was not Vernon's subject when he wrote these words, but they capture the spirit of the moment. Vernon to Shrewsbury, September 27, 1697, in James, *Letters Illustrative*, II, 404–406.

29. Log of the *Advice*, Driscoll Piracy Collection, Wichita (Kansas) Public Library.

30. Vernon to Shrewsbury, April 6, 1699, in James, *Letters Illustrative*, III, 6–9.

31. Wynn's correspondence during this period contains a large number of references to the Kidd affair, as Wynn strove to meet all of the demands on him. ADM 1/2638, PRO; minutes of the Privy Council, Add. MSS, 40781, fol. 147, BL. For the Admiralty's response see ADM 3/15, April 6, 1700.

32. The *Advice* arrived in England on April 2, a very fast voyage but not rapid enough for Kidd. Log of the *Advice*, Driscoll Piracy Collection, Wichita Public Library. Josiah Burchett reported Kidd's condition to the Admiralty as "dangerously Ill," April 15, 1700, ADM 3/15, PRO. Upon first touching land, Captain Wynn sent Thomas Gullock, luckless captain of the ship stolen by Joseph Bradish and his men, to London with news of Wynn's arrival in the channel. Gullock had been sent to New England by the owners of the ship to claim all of Bradish's treasure. CSPC (1699), no. 834.

33. Kidd to Orford, April 11, 1700, BL Loan, 29/207, fol. 104. Kidd wrote that the hulk of the *Quedah* still had £90,000 worth of goods in the hold. His "Instrument of Protest" is in HMC, *Portland*, IX, 403–406.

34. ADM 3/15, April 8, 1700; ADM 2/398, fol. 141; ADM 2/1048, fol. 5, PRO.

35. Vernon to Shrewsbury, April 9 and 13, 1700, in James, *Letters Illustrative*, III, 9–17; and Vernon to Shrewsbury, April 9, Vernon Letters, III, fol. 56.

36. Bellomont to Vernon, March 7, 1699, BL Loan, 29/207, fols. 86–93; Vernon to Shrewsbury, April 11, 13, and 16, 1700, in James, *Letters Illustrative*, III, 17–19, 26–36.

37. Bellomont to Shrewsbury, March 5, 1699, BL Loan, 29/207, fol. 70. Once the Admiralty knew who all the correspondents were, the board ordered them to attend one of their meetings. ADM 2/398, fol. 151, PRO. Vernon to Shrewsbury, April 13, 1700, in James, *Letters Illustrative*, III, 26–29. In commenting on these events, Ashurst, an old ally of Bellomont, wrote that the person Bellomont trusted with his affairs (Vernon) was a "nimble man [who] switched from a losing side to a more prosperous one." Ashurst to Bellomont, April 30, 1700, Ashurst Letterbook, Ashurst MSS, BOD.

38. Ashurst to Bellomont, April 30, 1700, Ashurst Letterbook, Ashurst MSS, BOD. The interviews at the Admiralty were conducted on April 12, 13, 15, and 18. ADM 3/15, PRO. William Popple, who retrieved Locke's letter, wrote at length to Locke about the experience, April 13, 1700. Locke MSS, c. 17, BOD.

39. Bellomont to Harrison, March 5, 1699, BL Loan, 29/207, fols. 67–68. Bellomont's note is nothing if not curt. He complains about his gout, tells Harrison that he has sent Kidd's goods to Vernon, and affirms that the "principles" could not object to that. He concludes by thoughtfully providing Harrison with a list of the pirates he had captured. Harrison must have been touched by his consideration.

40. Bellomont to Stanley, March 5, 1700, BL Loan, 29/207, fols. 65–66; Bellomont to Shrewsbury, same date, ibid., fol. 70.

41. Bellomont to Stanley, March 5, 1700, BL Loan, 29/207, fols. 65–66. Bellomont also railed at Harrison in his letter to Somers. He tempered his remarks by stating that if the partners could get a new grant from the king for the treasure he was sending, Harrison should be "reimbursed" and "I would for my own part make him a good present besides." In this letter he even wanted to reimburse Livingston. BL Loan 29/207, fols. 84–85.

42. Harley's copies are all in BL Loan, 29/207.

43. Vernon to Shrewsbury, April 16, 1700, in James, *Letters Illustrative*, III, 29–36; quotation on p. 34.

44. ADM 2/398, fols. 141, 151, 157–159; ADM 3/15, meetings of April 6, 8, 11, 14, 1700, PRO.

45. ADM 3/15, April 14, 1700, PRO. By way of corroborating Kidd's story, the board interviewed Edward Palmer on April 15, along with the young servants Jenkins, Barlycorne, Lamley, and Arris (Kidd's steward). The same day they also examined Kelley and Davis. ADM 3/15.

46. ADM 3/15; ADM 2/398, fols. 157–159, PRO.

47. Vernon to Shrewsbury, April 16, 1700, in James, *Letters Illustrative*, III, 29–36; quotation on p. 32.

48. Ibid.

49. ADM 2/1048, fols. 5–7, PRO.

50. ADM 3/16, April 23, 25, 26, 1700, PRO.

51. ADM 2/398, fols. 176, 182, 186; ADM 3/16, April 23, 1700, PRO. In a related piece of business Captain Wynn was removed from his command because the Commons might want to question him. The *Saint Antonio*, now referred to as the *Saint Anthony*, which had accompanied the *Advice* on the way to England, was ordered laid up at Sheerness. ADM 3/16, April 27, 1700, and ADM 2/398, fol. 176.

52. ADM 1/4086, fols. 759–760; ADM 3/16, May 6 and 7, 1700, PRO.

53. While much has been written about Newgate, I have relied on W. J. Sheehan, "Finding Solace in Eighteenth Century Newgate," in J. S. Cockburn, *Crime in England, 1550–1800* (Princeton: Princeton University Press, 1977), pp. 229–245, and Arthur Griffiths, *The Chronicles of Newgate* (London: Chapman and Hall, 1884), I, 259–285.

54. ADM 3/16, May 3, 7, and 13, 1700, PRO. John Cheeke, the Admiralty Court marshal, continued to carry out all of the court's orders for Kidd. ADM 2/1048, fol. 8.

55. Kidd to Admiralty, July 16, 1700, ADM 1/2002. For the responses see ADM 2/398, fols. 382–383; ADM 3/16, July 17, 1700, PRO.

56. Ibid.

57. See Wynn's correspondence, ADM 1/2638, memo of May 4, 1700; ADM 2/398, fol. 194, PRO.

58. Kidd's letter, ADM 1/2002, and the response ADM 3/16, January 4, 1701; ADM 2/399, fol. 190, PRO.

59. Vernon received a report in August of 1700 that Kidd showed little concern for his situation. Whether this was a show of bravado in front of a relative or Kidd's true feeling is hard to tell, but perhaps he still believed that the Whig lords would rescue him. If so, perhaps this faith helped him to survive his constant ill health. Vernon to Shrewsbury, August 3, 1700, in James, *Letters Illustrative*, III, 120–126.

60. Horwitz, *Parliament, Policy and Politics*, pp. 275–282; Feiling, *History of Tory Party*, pp. 333–343; Hill, *Growth of Parliamentary Parties*, pp. 82–84; Robert Walcott, "East India Company Interest in the General Election of 1700–01," *English Historical Review* 71 (1956), 223–259.

61. Horwitz, *Parliament, Policy and Politics*, pp. 282–287.

62. Commons *Journals*, XIII, 380. Burchett had to scramble to comply with this order, for some of the letters sent by Bellomont were now in the hands of others. The Admiralty's policy of controlling all matters relating to Kidd seems to have had some holes. Burchett to Popple, March 10, 1701, CO 5/862, fol. 153, PRO; and similar letters to others on the same day, ADM 2/399, fol. 365, PRO.

63. Commons *Journals*, XIII, 416, 424. Even the "secret" examination before the Admiralty was opened and read. Ibid., 409; Vernon to Shrewsbury, March 21, 1701, Vernon Letters, II, 48.

64. *Memoirs of the Life of John, Lord Somers* (London, 1716), pp. 87–89.

Because of the excitement engendered by the struggle between the parties, large crowds attended anything political. Feiling, *History of Tory Party*, p. 338.

65. After his capture Bolton had been shipped back to England as a witness against Kidd. When he first arrived, the Admiralty had no idea who he was and had to ask the Board of Trade what to do with him. ADM 2/399, fol. 168, PRO. He arrived in December 1700 and was jailed until Parliament could interrogate him about Kidd's ship and cargo. After the Solicitor General had interviewed Bolton, he did not think there was enough evidence to convict him. ADM 3/16, December 24, 1700, PRO. As soon as he had been bailed out by Whitaker, who had no orders to hold him and no special reason to keep him in jail, Bolton went into hiding, never to reappear in England.

66. Whitaker was driven from office as solicitor of the Admiralty Court, lost his house, and spent time in jail for his indiscretion. Commons *Journals*, XIII, 441, 444–445; ADM 1/3666, fols. 39, 46, 53, 68, 70, 74, 128, 170, PRO.

67. Ellis to Stepney, March 28, 1701, Add. MSS, 7074, fols. 7–8, BL; quotation on p. 7.

68. Commons *Journals*, XIII, 441–442; *Memoirs of Somers*, pp. 78–82.

69. *Memoirs of Somers*, pp. 87–89.

70. Commons *Journals*, XIII, 444–445; Ellis to Stepney, March 28, 1701, Add. MSS, 7074, fols. 7–8, BL; quotation on fol. 8.

71. Horwitz, *Parliament, Policy and Politics*, pp. 184–188.

72. Commons *Journals*, XIII, 450.

73. Ibid., 460, 465; *Memoirs of Somers*, pp. 84–86; quotation on p. 86.

74. Commons *Journals*, XIII, 480, 482; *Memoirs of Somers*, p. 86.

9. The Trial

1. John A. Langbein, "Criminal Trials before Lawyers," *University of Chicago Law Review*, 45 (1978), 263–316.

2. Edward Whitaker to Josiah Burchett, June 18, 1700, ADM 1/3666, fol. 14, PRO. For records of Kelley's trial see HCA 1/14, 203, 213–217; HCA 29, 180, 190, 194–195, PRO. Kelley's companion in death was Joseph Bradish, who was executed and displayed with Kelley along the banks of the Thames. ADM 2/1048, fol. 12. The quote is a standard admonition that was used whenever the government decided to display a body.

3. ADM 2/398, fol. 372; ADM 3/16, July 12, 1700, PRO; Vernon to Shrewsbury, July 23, 1700, in James, *Letters Illustrative*, III, 116–118.

4. ADM 3/16, April 19, 1701, PRO. Bradinham was captured in Pennsylvania. William Penn to Vernon, February 26, 1700, CO 5/1260, no. 17, PRO. The official examinations of Palmer and Bradinham were held on April 25, 1701. HCA 1/15, no. 7, PRO. They did not receive their pardons

until after the trial. See List of Pardons, August 28, 1701. HCA 1/15, no. 94. Bale, Admiralty solicitor at the time, noted that they gave testimony "voluntarily" against Kidd. HCA 1/29, fol. 268, PRO.

5. Bale to Crawley, April 30, 1701. HCA 1/29, pt. 2, fol. 274; ADM 3/16, April 24, 1701, PRO.

6. Kidd to Admiralty, March 20 and April 9, 1701, ADM 1/2002; also ADM 3/16, March 20, April 11, 12, 16, 1701; Burchett to Mr. Fells, the keeper of Newgate, April 16, 1701, ADM 2/400, fol. 2, PRO.

7. ADM 3/16, April 16, 1701, PRO.

8. Kidd to Mr. Fells, April 18, 1701, ADM 1/2004, PRO; Burchett to Jodrell, April 18, 1701, ADM 2/400, fol. 10; Kidd to Admiralty, April 23, 1701, ADM 1/2002, PRO; J. C. Sainty, *Admiralty Officials, 1660–1870* (London: Athlone Press, 1975), p. 63.

9. ADM 2/399, fol. 365, PRO. Burchett also asked Popple, secretary to the Board of Trade, for the papers in his possession. CO 5/862, fol. 153, PRO; ADM 3/16, March 6 and 7, 1701; Burchett to Wynn, May 3, 1701, ADM 2/400, fol. 94. Wynn had turned over all the papers brought with him in April of 1700. ADM 1/2638, PRO.

10. This theory is conjecture on my part; despite persistent searching I have never found substantiation for Vernon or other officials' withholding evidence from Kidd. Nonetheless, the passes were in London and they were kept from Kidd. My best guess is that Vernon, who had both access and motive, played a role. The passes found in London were copies and were sent to the Board of Trade. Ralph D. Paine, *The Book of Buried Treasure: Being a True History of the Gold, Jewells and Plate of Pirates . . .* (New York: Sturgis and Walton, 1911). The originals probably went to the Admiralty in the package carried by Wynn. These papers passed through many hands in their various trips around London; even so, my culprit is still Vernon. Copies of the passes were sent by Bellomont to the Board of Trade in his letter of July 26, 1699. They were received on September 20, read by the board on September 26, and then filed. CO 5/860, fols. 159–162, PRO.

11. Richard B. Morris, *Fair Trial* (New York: Knopf, 1953); Wilkins, *Captain Kidd*, pp. 173–200; Milligan, *Captain William Kidd*. The most balanced account is Brooks, *Trial of Captain Kidd*.

12. The Admiralty sent the warrant to Hedges on April 23 for the Court of Oyer and Terminer. Hedges was to choose the judges and alert the sheriff of London to pick the jurors. ADM 2/1048, fol. 26, PRO. Most piracy trials took place in the Marshalsea prison, the Admiralty jail, but important trials were held in the Old Bailey. Furthermore, when London merchants were the victims, the Admiralty solicitor did not like to take the chance that the pirates might be freed in another county (the Marshalsea was in Kent), which would have outraged the merchants. In London the merchants could attend the trials and the judges would have less trouble. ADM 1/3666, fol. 21, PRO.

13. Although the letter is addressed to "My Lord," there is no way of identifying which lord. A copy of the letter exists in HCA 1/29, fol. 285, PRO.

14. Bellomont even had papers collected in New York and sent to England. Bellomont to Board of Trade, April 23, 1700, CO 5/861, no. 32, PRO.

15. For a general background to court procedure at this time see Langbein, "Criminal Trials." See also Cynthia B. Herrup, "Law and Morality in Seventeenth Century England," *Past and Present*, 106 (1985), 102–123; and idem, "New Shoes and Mutton Pies: Investigative Responses to Theft in Seventeenth Century East Sussex," *Historical Journal*, 27 (1984), 811–830. The complete trial record is in *State Trials*, V, 287–338, and was also printed as a pamphlet. My account of the trial is based on this record. See Brooks, *Trial of Captain Kidd*, pp. 43–48, for an informed commentary. The records of the trial are in HCA 1/15, fols. 7, 8, 46–55, 69–70, 84–85, 108; 1/29, fols. 179, 282, 284, 285, 287; 32/48, PRO.

16. DNB, XV, 10–11. For his party affiliation see Horwitz, *Parliament, Policy and Politics*, p. 352. On Cowper see DNB, XII, 389–393.

17. *State Trials*, V, 307, 312, records these men as being present.

18. Langbein, "Criminal Trials." Oldys was an ex-Admiralty advocate who lost his office in 1693 because of his Tory sympathies. His presence at the trial indicates that Kidd was getting sophisticated advice from some quarter. DNB, XLII, 119.

19. Among the other judges were Sir John Turton, chief judge of the King's Bench; Henry Gould, judge of the King's Bench; Baron Sir Henry Hatsell of the Exchequer; Sir John Powell, chief judge of Common Pleas.

20. Accounts of these cases, dated between 1696 and 1699, are in HCA 1/29, fols. 72, 87, and CO 1/15, fol. 9, PRO.

21. All of the testimony and quotations that follow on Kidd's murder trial are from *State Trials*, V, 289–294.

22. Thomas Warren testified in favor of Culliford. HCA 1/15, pt. 1, fol. 14, PRO. For his instructions see ibid., fol. 15. A copy of the proclamation was given to Culliford and signed by Warren; the pardon was accepted by Culliford and eighteen others. HCA 1/15, pt. 1, fols. 36, 39, PRO. Oxenden himself had asked for a pardon for Culliford in order to try Samuel Burgess for piracy. ADM 7/364, fols. 48–49, PRO. See also the correspondence of various legal officials relative to Culliford. ADM 1/3666, fols. 100, 112, 125, 134, 320, PRO; Hedges to Admiralty, April 2, 1701, Add. MSS, 24, 107, fol. 207, BL.

23. Kidd had to disallow some of the members of the former juries that had already found him guilty. *State Trials*, V, fol. 330.

24. Ritchie, "Burgess." Burgess was tried for piracy.

25. Hedges to Admiralty, May 15, 1701, ADM 1/4087, fol. 235, PRO. By long-standing tradition, only captains, quartermasters, masters,

and ringleaders went to death, usually four at a time. Mass executions were rare, except for cases such as that of Quittar's crew, who because they were French could be put away. At this time the government was trying to impress the merchant community, so the more executions the better. During the spring of 1701 the merchants had good reason to celebrate: in addition to the French pirates, Kelley, Bradish, and now Kidd went to the gallows. On the tradition of four at a time, see Manwaring, *Life and Works of Mainwaring,* II, 3–49.

26. ADM 2/1048, fol. 29; HCA 1/29, fols. 288–289, PRO.

27. Kidd to Harley, May 12, 1701, BL Loan, 29/190, fol. 66. Kidd also apologized for not giving the Commons satisfaction, "as was expected from me," and attacked Bellomont for leaving him defenseless. Kidd to Harley, n.d., BL Loan, 29/190, fol. 64.

28. HCA 1/29, fol. 287, PRO.

29. HCA 24/127, no. 57, PRO.

30. Sheehan, "Finding Solace," pp. 229–245. Lorrain took his monopoly of the condemned seriously, for financial and spiritual reasons. Once he repeatedly came to blows with a Catholic priest while accompanying a youth to Tyburn for hanging. The priest at the last moment kicked Lorrain off the cart and gave the boy a proper Catholic send-off. Dr. Doran, *London in Jacobite Times* (London: R. Bentley, 1877), I, 303–306.

31. Peter Linebaugh, "The Ordinary of Newgate and his Account," in Cockburn, *Crime in England,* pp. 246–269.

32. See Lorrain's advertisement announcing his publication of Kidd's account in the *Post Boy,* May 24, 1701.

33. Lorrain, *The Ordinary of Newgate.*

34. Lorrain's rival publication noted the rumors about a pardon for Kidd: *A True Account of the Behavior, Confession and Last Dying Speeches of Captain William Kidd, and the rest of the Pirates that were executed at Execution Dock in Wapping, on Friday the 23 of May 1701.*

35. According to the author of *A True Account,* Eldridge did not hear about the pardon until the day before the execution. His pardon was final on June 19, 1701. HCA 1/15, fol. 63, PRO.

36. Linebaugh, "The Ordinary," pp. 246–269.

37. All of the newspapers covered the execution; however, the *Post Boy* and the *Flying Post* carried earlier reports on the progress of the case. These periodicals are in the Burney Collection, 115b, BL. Foreigners were amazed at the spectacle of the Tyburn executions and commented on it often. See for example François Misson, *M. Misson's Memoirs and Observations in his Travels over England* (London, 1719), pp. 123–124; and Beat L. de Muralt, *Letters Describing the Character and Customs of the English and French Nations* (London, 1726), pp. 42–44.

38. Lorrain, *The Ordinary of Newgate.*

39. On the role of the last speech see J. A. Sharpe, "'Last Dying

Speeches' Religion, Ideology and Public Execution in Seventeenth Century England," *Past and Present*, no. 107 (1985), 102–123.

40. Because of inexperience, executioners made mistakes in handling the rope. This happened in the hanging of the pirate John Gow. Griffiths, *Chronicles of Newgate*, I, 279.

10. *Of Death, Destruction, and Myths*

1. John Cheeke, the Admiralty marshal, charged £4.0.0 for transporting the condemned to the gallows in three carts; James Southwood, £10.0.0 for building the gibbet at Tilbury; Thomas Sherman, £3.2.6 for the gallows and £1.5.2 to carry the body and hang it in chains; James Smith, £4.0.0 for making the chains. Men not put on display were buried at Lyme House. The Admiralty spent a total of £154.18.7 for Kidd's incarceration and death. ADM 1/3666, fols. 210–211, PRO.

2. ADM 1/3666, fol. 79, PRO.

3. Bale wrote a long summary of the court session for Burchett, relating the court's actions toward each man. See HCA 1/15, pt. 2, fols. 96–97; HCA 1/16, fols. 43, 46–51, PRO. Giles Shelley, imprisoned for trading with pirates, was tried and convicted, then pardoned. HCA 1/15, fol. 60; 29/265, fol. 284; 24/127, no. 84. In order to sue for their pardons, the men had to find sureties for good behavior and give bail before appearing at the next court session to plead their case. They were then included in the next general pardon. Most of Kidd's men were not pardoned until July 25, 1701. HCA 1/15, pt. 2, fols. 96–97.

4. Ritchie, "Burgess"; HCA 1/16, fol. 43, PRO.

5. Nicolas Bayard, long an enemy of Bellomont, quickly spread the news of his death. Bayard to Sir Philip Meadows, March 8, 1701, NYCD, IV, 848. Lady Bellomont was served a summons to prevent her leaving New York on the *Advice* because of her husband's debts. She was allowed to leave only after posting a £10,000 bond. Lord Cornbury to the Treasury, June 22 and 24, 1701, Treasury 1/91, fols. 43–49, 80, PRO.

6. DNB, XXXVIII, 218–223; XLIX, 429–431; L, 221–229; LV, 301.

7. Leder, *Robert Livingston*, pp. 198–199.

8. For Mrs. Kidd's family genealogy see Dunbar M. Hinrichs, *The Fateful Voyage of Captain Kidd* (New York: Bookman, 1955), p. 134. Her marriage license to Christopher Rousby dated November 4, 1703, is in NYHS, *Collections* (1892), 380. Her will and death are noted in Berthold Fernow, ed., *Calendar of Wills, 1626–1836* (New York: Knickerbocker Press, 1896), p. 318. On her imprisonment see J. Franklin Jameson, *Privateering and Piracy in the Colonial Period: Illustrative Documents* (New York: Macmillan, 1923), pp. 223–224; CSPC (1699), no. 678.

9. Few ex-pirates (or mariners of any sort) appear in the records in later

years. Fairly typical of the men who escaped from the rigors of the sea were John Hales, who opened a victualing house, and Theophilus Turner, who returned to his trade as a joiner. Court of Delegates 2/62, PRO.

10. See Kidd's Narrative, CO 5/860, fols. 198–201, PRO. One estimate put the value of the goods on the *Quedah* at £20,000. HCA 24/127, no. 107, PRO.

11. Narrative of John Gardiner, July 17, 1699, CO 5/860, fols. 191–192, PRO; Thomas Way, July 8, 1699, CO 5/860, fol. 181; Jameson, *Privateering and Piracy,* pp. 223–224; New York, *Council Minutes,* I, 142–144; John Rigg to Robert Livingston, January 1700, Livingston-Redmond MSS, Franklin D. Roosevelt Library, Hyde Park, New York; Phelps-Stokes, *Iconography,* IV, 418. Bellomont raised the amount Selleck reputedly received from £5,000 in October 1700 to £10,000 by November. Bellomont to Trade, October 20, 1700, NYCD, IV, 595; November 28, 1700, CSPC (1700), no. 953.

12. Narrative of John Gardiner, July 17, 1699, CO 5/860, fols. 191–192, PRO.

13. Campbell's statement, July 12, 1699, CO 5/860, fols. 185–186, 189.

14. Ibid., fols. 181, 189; New York, *Council Minutes,* II, 141–144; Phelps-Stokes, *Iconography,* IV, 418, 422, 423; CSPC (1699), no. 678; New York council meeting, July 20, 1699, CO 5/1042, fol. 306, PRO; Massachusetts council meeting, July 20, 1699, CO 5/787, fol. 229.

15. Inventory, July 25, 1699, CO 5/787, fol. 189, PRO.

16. Deposition of Livingston, July 12, 1699, CO 5/787, fol. 182, PRO.

17. Kidd to Harley, May 12, 1701, BL Loan 29/190, fol. 66, and Kidd to Orford, April 11, 1700, ibid., 29/207, fol. 104. In the letter to Orford, Kidd mentions £90,000 as the amount he could recover. Bellomont reported Kidd's offer in a letter to the Board of Trade, January 5, 1700, NYCD, IV, 601–602. In Kidd's examination of July 3, 1699, he stated that there was no gold or silver on the *Quedah,* only 130 bales of textiles, 70 to 80 tons of sugar, 10 tons of iron, 40 tons of saltpeter, and 20 cannon. CO 5/860, fol. 196. Two men reported seeing him remove his chest from the ship, but this was never verified. CO 5/860, fols. 174–176.

18. The London *Times* and other newspapers published stories in August and September of 1983 about the adventures of two men who searched for Kidd's treasure on an island in the South China Sea and ended up as uninvited guests of the Republic of Vietnam!

19. Vernon to Old East India Company, May 14, 1700, State Papers 44/131, fol. 123; minutes of the directors of the company, July 18, 1701, B/43, fol. 460, IOR. For the City of London see ADM 1/3666, fols. 78, 81, 85; ADM 1/4086, fol. 759, PRO.

20. Admiralty to Vernon, May 7, 1700, ADM 7/564, fols. 15–16,

PRO. See statement about Kidd's treasure, March 26, 1705; Treasury 1/94, fol. 383, PRO. On Coji Babba's case see HCA 24/127, no. 107; Rawlinson B/383, fols. 547–548, 550, BOD. Babba may have received partial restitution when certain textile products were distributed by the court upon condemnation, but these goods have not been positively identified as Kidd's. HCA 24/128, no. 140, 141, PRO.

21. Treasury 1/94, fols. 381, 383, PRO. This sum is the value of the gold, silver, and precious stones; the textiles had been previously disposed of. The Admiralty deducted from this amount all of the cost of keeping and trying Kidd, and the expenses in New England (£840.8.5). CO 5/787, fol. 273, PRO.

22. Minutes of the directors of Greenwich Hospital, ADM 67/3, fols. 59, 80, 84, 100, 169, PRO.

23. The fates of the *Peter,* the *Prophet Daniel,* and the *Margaret* have been discussed. Merchants also wrote proposals to push the campaign. See *Piracy Destroy'd, or a Short Discourse shewing the Rise, Growth and Causes of Piracy of late; with a sure Method of to put a Speedy stop to that Growing Evil* (London, 1701). This pamphlet argued that the best way to stop piracy was through the granting of better conditions to the sailors in the merchant fleet. A more bloodthirsty proposal was that of Thomas Bowery, who proposed sending navy ships and armed merchantmen to Madagascar to defeat the pirates and then pardon them in order to "reclaim ye Wicked and Debauched lives of so many hundred souls." Bowery MSS, MS 3041/2–5, Guildhall, London. Josiah Burchett, secretary to the Admiralty, proposed granting pirates their freedom and property if they left areas where they threatened trade. See Burchett, "Reasons for Reducing the Pyrates at Madagascar and Proposals humbly offered to the House of Commons, for effecting the same" (1704).

24. Quotation from Leibbrandt, *Precis,* II, 262; Commons *Journals,* XV, 382–384. The testimony in the Commons in 1707 was by a Joseph Duckett, who had spoken with Samuel Burgess in 1702. Burgess said pirates would not surrender because of past "treachery."

25. June 1703, ADM 8/7, ADM 8/14, PRO.

26. Uring, *Voyages and Travels,* pp. 179–181.

27. William Snelgrave, *A New Account of Some Parts of Guinea and the Slave Trade* (London, 1734), p. 225.

28. Ibid., p. 227. My analysis has benefited greatly from the work of Marcus Rediker, whose "Under the Banner of King Death" is an excellent discussion of the pirate community of this period. See also idem, "Society and Culture among Anglo-American Deep Sea Sailors, 1700–1750" (Ph.D. diss., University of Pennsylvania, 1983); and Christopher Hill, "Radical Pirates?" in *The Origins of Anglo-American Radicalism,* ed. Margaret Jacob and James Jacob (London: George Allen and Unwin, 1984), pp. 17–32.

29. Rediker, "Under the Banner of King Death," pp. 215–218. For examples see John Barnard, *Ashton's Memorial: An History of the Strange Adven-*

tures, and Signal Deliverances, of Mr. Philip Ashton, who, after he had made his Escape from Pirates, liv'd alone on a Desolate Island for about Sixteen Months, etc. (Boston, 1725); William Jenning's testimony, Commons *Journals*, XV, 382–384; Snelgrave, *A New Account*, pp. 193–285.

30. Rediker, "Under the Banner of King Death," pp. 222–223.

31. Index to HCA 1, PRO.

32. Account of Ogle to the Admiralty, ADM 1/2242, PRO. For details see *Account of the Tryal of all the Pyrates, Lately taken by Captain Ogle, on board the Swallow, man-of-war, on the Coast of Guinea* (London, 1723).

33. Hughson, *Carolina Pirates*, pp. 44–45, 69–111.

34. Spotswood to Secretary Craggs, October 22, 1718, in *The Official Letters of Governor Alexander Spotswood, Lieutenant-Governor of the Colony of Virginia, 1710–22* (Richmond: Virginia Historical Society, 1882), pp. 305–308.

35. Hughson, *Carolina Pirates*, pp. 84–111; *Tryals of Major Stede Bonnet and Other Pirates* (Charlestown, 1718); *Trials of Major Stede Bonnet and 33 Others . . .* (Charlestown, 1718); *State Trials*, VI, 156–188.

36. Hughson, *Carolina Pirates*, pp. 116–134.

37. The sermons cited were published in Boston. Mather preached two other sermons to condemned pirates, "The Converted Sinner" and "Instructions to the Living from the Condition of the Dead." See "Diary of Cotton Mather," Massachusetts Historical Society, *Collections*, ser. 7, VIII, 491, 729.

38. Among the trials at this time was that of Captain John Rackham. He and eight other men were executed, but two of his crew escaped: Ann Bonney and Mary Read were found guilty, but allowed to plead their "bellies." In other words, they got off because they were pregnant. CO 137/4, fols. 9–18, PRO.

39. W. A. Speck, *The Butcher: The Duke of Cumberland and the Suppression of the '45* (Oxford: Blackwell, 1981); John Prebble, *Culloden* (London: Secker and Warburg, 1961); idem, *Highland Clearances* (London: Secker and Warburg, 1963).

40. The best discussion of the evolution of the buccaneer figure is Bonner, *Pirate Laureate*, pp. 151–201.

41. These are listed in ibid., pp. 74–81.

42. The first work was published in Boston in 1844 and the second in New York in 1859.

43. Bonner, *Pirate Laureate*, pp. 13–48.

Index

Abd-ul-Ghafur: and pirates, 88, 104, 106, 127, 130, 132, 134, 271n10; and English, 102–103, 131, 133

Admiralty: and merchants, 139, 156; and Royal Navy, 145, 157; and privateering, 151, 152; and Kidd, 184, 192, 194–202; symbols, 210, 224; and Kidd's execution, 224, 228; and Kidd's treasure, 232

Admiralty Courts: and Kidd's execution, 1, 224; and civil law, 140–141, 143; and piracy trials, 144, 145–146, 153, 235; in colonies, 150, 153, 154, 172; and Kidd's trial, 198, 206–227; and king's pardon, 217

Adventure Galley (ship), 58–62, 63, 224; fitting-out of, 54; crew, 64–68, 70, 124, 126, 221, 228, 269n25; departure from New York, 69–70; voyages, 70–80, 98–100, 217; in Madagascar, 89, 112, 116, 124; battles in Red Sea, 96–97; in Indian Ocean, 101, 110, 111; sinking of, 160, 176

Adventure Prize (ship), 116, 118, 126. See also *Quedah Merchant*

Advice (ship), 185, 194, 209, 287n9, 295n5; Kidd's return to London on, 192, 193, 201, 288n32; treasure on, 198–199, 231

Africa, 1, 4, 32, 37, 72, 235. *See also* Barbary Coast; Mediterranean Sea

Ahmanet Khan, 131, 133, 134

Aldred, Captain John, 159

Algiers, 20, 21

Anderson, Joseph, 24, 25

Anderson, Nicholas, 132

Anne, Queen, 202, 233

Annesley, Samuel, 131, 132, 133, 134

Antigua (ship), 32, 35, 39, 40, 51

Arris, Samuel, 228, 289n45

Asad Khan, 134

Ascension Island, 164, 174, 259n53, 280n14

Ashurst, Sir Henry, 49, 195, 289n37

Aurangzeb, Emperor, 95, 102, 127, 129, 133, 134, 149

Avery, Henry, 85–88, 95, 102, 117, 131, 280n15; escape, 135, 137; trial, 209, 272n26; in popular culture, 238

Babba, Coji, 108, 202, 203, 211, 218, 221, 225, 232, 297n20

Babs-al-Mandab, strait of, 5, 88, 94, 95, 96, 125, 132

Baldridge, Adam, 113, 114–115, 116, 269n24

Bale, Thomas, 207, 295n3

Bank of England, 36, 44

Barbarie, John, 173

Barbary Coast, 20–21, 247n38

Barker, Andrew, 63

Barlow, Edward, 95–98, 106, 131, 260n61

Barlycorne, Richard, 160, 211, 215, 218, 257n26, 279n3, 284n60

Barrow, George, 223

Basse, Jeremiah, 150, 175, 216, 218, 276n69, 284n56

Bayard, Nicholas, 171
Bellomont, Earl of (Richard Coote), 47–
48; and Livingston, 49–50, 51, 52; as
Kidd's sponsor, 52–54, 60, 163, 197,
204; as colonial governor, 93, 168–
173, 192; and Kidd's return to New
York, 165, 166, 173, 176–178; and
piracy, 170–171, 173, 175, 210; and
the Junto, 172; and arrest of Kidd,
184, 188, 191, 284n61, 285nn62,76,
286n6; papers, 194, 293n11; letters,
194–196, 202, 204; and Kidd's trial,
208, 256n11, 294n27; Kidd on, 209–
210; Kidd's proposal to, 221, 232;
death, 228–229; and Kidd's wife, 229;
and Kidd's treasure, 230, 231, 280n15,
285n69
Bellomont, Lady, 178, 180, 231,
285n76, 295n5
Benbow, Admiral John, 207
Berk, William, 221–222
Billingsley, Captain Rupert, 85
Blackham, Robert, 229, 255n58
Blathwayt, Sir William, 40, 47, 48, 50,
54, 172, 190, 195, 254nn48,51,
286n6
Blessed William (ship), 30, 31, 32–33, 35;
sale of, 34; crew, 37, 66, 93, 100,
113, 116, 162
Blydenburgh, Joseph, 66
Board of Trade, 149–150, 152, 154, 156,
169, 172, 176, 186, 187, 209
Bohun, George, 129–130
Bollen, George, 70, 110, 257n26
Bolton, Henry, 166, 167, 168, 203,
291n65
Bond, Captain, 219
Bonnet, Stede, 235, 236
Bradinham, Robert, 70, 106, 207, 214,
215, 217, 218, 220, 269n25; capture,
291n4
Bradish, Joseph, 174–175, 179, 183,
284n54, 291n2, 294n25
Bradley, Samuel, 160, 165, 279n3
Bridgewater, Earl of, 196
Brooke, Chidley, 39, 170, 171
Browne, John, 40, 66, 67, 100, 262n12,
269n27
Buckmaster, Edward, 65, 124, 160, 174
Burchett, Josiah, 202, 208, 290n62
Burgess, Samuel, 33, 38, 40, 67, 113,
115, 228; capture, 120, 121, 163,

269n25; return to Madagascar, 123;
trial of, 220, 293nn22,24
Burk, William, 167

Caesar, Julius, 4
Campbell, Duncan, 177, 180, 181, 231,
284nn60,61, 285n71
Caribbean, see West Indies
Carter, William, 47, 49, 50
Cecil, Robert (Earl of Salisbury), 13–14,
21
Charles I, 14
Charles II, 16, 43, 155, 187
Cheeke, John, 193, 196, 198, 224,
290n54, 295n1
Cheng-ho, Admiral, 9
Childe, Sir Joseph, 128–129, 130, 138
China, 6, 8–9
Chivers, Captain Dirck, 100, 132, 238
Christians, 20, 21
Chudleigh, Captain John, 140
Churchill, George, 194, 207
Churchill, Michael, 220
Churchill, Nicholas, 211, 212–213, 216,
228
Cilicians, 4–5, 6
Clarke, Thomas, 230, 231
Clerke, Captain John, 90, 99, 106, 132,
286n3
Coates, Henry, 37, 38
Cocks, Sir Richard, 191
Codrington, Governor Christopher (of
Nevis), 30, 32, 248n1, 250n9
Colman, Benjamin, 236
Commissions: privateering, 11–12, 13,
16, 30, 34, 42–43, 140, 151, 252n36;
reprisal, 11–12, 151
Coningsby, Lord, 48
Convoys, 74–75, 156–157
Cook, John, 161
Cooke, Captain Edmund, 151
Cooly, Issa, 131
Cooper, James Fenimore, 237
Coote, Richard, see Bellomont, Earl of
Cordyne, Frans, 66
Courteen, Sir William, 82
Cowley, Ambrose, 161
Cowper, Sir William, 211
Cribble, Walter, 166
Cromwell, Oliver, 155
Culliford, Robert, 33, 116, 117–118,
122, 162, 173, 219; and Kidd's crew,

37, 124–125, 160, 176, 193, 207;
    pardon, 216, 217, 220, 225, 228,
    293n22
Cutts, Lord, 49

da Gama, Vasco, 7, 71
Dampier, William, 161
Dangerfield, Robert, 23–25, 248n48
Dann, John, 135, 272n26
Davis, Edward, 162, 213, 218, 279n3,
    289n45
Dawson, Joseph (crewman), 228
Deane, John, 144
Defoe, Daniel, 223, 273n33
de Graff, Laurent, 23, 144–145
de Lancey, Stephen, 170, 173
de Lussan, Ravenau, 119–120, 268n23
Dickers, Captain Michael, 107, 110
Dongan, Governor Thomas (of New
    York), 33, 42
Don Juan of Austria, 10
Drake, Sir Francis, 12, 149
Dudley, Joseph, 49, 169
Dutch East India Company, 18, 96, 131,
    265n56
Dutch West India Company, 17, 33, 166

East India Company, 18, 51, 66, 87, 96,
    97, 99, 138, 187; and India, 14, 100–
    102, 107, 109, 117, 130–134, 135,
    137, 210, 211; and privateering com-
    missions, 43, 252n36; and hostility to
    Kidd, 127–128, 132, 159, 165, 184,
    186, 187; profits, 128–129; decline,
    129–135; charter, 130, 172; campaign
    against piracy, 135–140, 158, 170,
    186; and Vice Admiralty Courts, 143–
    144; and Tories, 172, 201; and arrest
    of Kidd, 188, 189, 190, 193; and
    Kidd's treasure, 199, 202, 221, 232,
    286n6; and Kidd's trial, 206, 225
East India Merchant (ship), 90, 92, 106
Edgecomb, Leonard, 86, 162, 279n5
Edward IV, 254n55
Egypt, 5, 8
Eldridge, John, 120, 220–221, 223, 228,
    294n35
Elizabeth, Queen, 12, 13, 254n55
Elwes, Captain Gerard, 184
Emott, James, 70, 163, 173, 176–177,
    230, 285n62
England, 7, 9–10, 11; Sea Hawks, 12–

13, 67; in Caribbean, 14–16, 29; in
    Mediterranean, 20; war with France,
    29, 36, 42, 44, 61, 63, 147, 155,
    156; politics, 43–47, 185–186; and
    Spain, 57, 151; as imperial state, 128,
    236; merchant lobbies, 139; modern
    bureaucracy, 147–148; modern diplo-
    macy, 148–149. *See also* Admiralty;
    Royal Navy
Evans, Captain John, 39, 69

Fath Mahmamadi (ship), 88, 102
Fletcher, Governor Benjamin (of New
    York), 39, 42, 63; and piracy, 38, 69,
    146, 173; and Bellomont, 48, 49,
    169–171, 172, 179; recall, 50, 150;
    on Kidd's crew, 67, 68
Fleury, Jean, 11
France, 9–10, 11, 14, 202; in Caribbean,
    15, 16, 29, 30, 142, 161; war with
    England, 29, 33, 36, 42, 61, 63, 156;
    and India, 131, 133, 134
Franks, Benjamin, 65–66, 101–102,
    132, 186
French, Philip, 49, 50

Gambling, 119–120
Gandaman, Gillam, 107
Ganj-i-Sawai (Gunsway; ship), 88, 95, 96,
    98, 131, 135
Gardiner, John, 230, 231
Gardiner's Island, 177, 230
Gayer, Sir John, 132, 133–134
Gifford, Richard, 13, 21, 90, 105
Gilliam, James, *see* Kelley, James
Glorious Revolution (1688), 33, 43
Gould, Judge Henry, 293n19
Governeur, Abraham, 49
Graham, James, 39, 40
Graham, Dr. John, 23–24
Gravenraedt, Henry, 173
Greenwich Hospital, 233
Grey, Governor (of Barbados), 168
Grotius, Hugo, 149
Guittar, Captain Louis, 1–2, 243n1
Gullock, Captain Thomas, 174, 288n32

Hales, John, 162, 296n9
Halifax, Earl of, *see* Montague, Charles
Harley, Sir Robert, 186, 190, 194, 196,
    201, 221, 232

Harrison, Sir Edward, 53; sponsorship of Kidd, 54, 56, 60, 93, 138, 180, 184, 187, 204, 255n1, 256n5; and Bellomont, 194, 195, 289nn39,41
Harrison, John, 162, 177
Harvey, John, 100
Hatsell, Sir Henry, 219, 293n19
Haversham, Lord, 196
Hawkes, Sir John, 211
Hawkins, Mathew, 200
Hawkins, Mrs., 41, 200, 224
Hedges, Sir Charles, 53, 136, 148, 152, 153, 196, 198, 207, 292n12
Hewetson, Captain Thomas, 30–31, 60, 211, 219, 225, 250n8
Heyn, Piet, 18
Hickman, Robert, 220
Hoar, John, 84, 93
Holmes, Sir Robert, 53, 54
Holt, Lord Chief Justice, 136
Hormuz, strait of, 3, 5
Houblon, Sir James, 85
How, Captain, 105
Howe, Jack, 189, 190
Howe, James, 211, 216, 220, 228
Hunt, Lieutenant Daniel, 199

Ibrahim, Muhammad, 88
India, 66, 193; pirates, 5–6, 37, 85, 89, 95, 98–99, 137; Mughal government, 8, 14, 87, 107, 129, 135, 136, 137, 216, 238, 251; East India Company, 127, 129, 130–135, 137, 193, 199
Ingoldsby, Colonel Richard, 34–35
Ingraham, Joseph: *The Spanish Galleon*, 237–238; *Captain Kyd*, 238
Irving, Washington, 237

Jacob (ship), 34, 37, 38, 40, 52, 66, 69, 100; crew of, 113, 117, 169
Jacobs, Cornelius, 39
Jamaica, 15–16, 19, 23, 29, 65, 142, 162, 203; piracy law, 144–145, 152, 153; navy, 155; turtles, 259n53
James I, 13, 140, 254n55
James II, 29, 33, 43, 47, 185
Japan, 6, 8
Jenkins, William, 211, 218, 257n26, 279n3, 289n45
Jersey, Earl of, 192, 193, 194
Jodrell, Paul, 202, 208
Johanna (island), 86, 90, 92

Johnson, Governor Robert (of South Carolina), 236
Jones, Captain Evan, 85, 122, 278n98
Junto (Whig leadership), 46, 188; partnership with Kidd, 50–51, 56, 187, 189–190, 191, 203; decline, 137, 172, 179, 185, 186; and Tories, 172, 201, 202, 204, 229; and Kidd, 184, 194, 197, 209, 221, 226

Kelley, James, 161–162, 183, 195, 206, 279nn3,4,5, 289n45, 291n2, 294n25
Kidd, Captain William: hanging, 2, 221, 224–227, 294nn25,37, 295n1; and problem of piracy, 26; birth, 27; in West Indies, 28–33, 160, 164–168; in New York, 34–36, 39–40, 60, 62, 63, 126, 176–178; marriage, 36; and Robert Livingston, 40, 42, 43, 50–51; in London, 40, 42, 49, 50–55, 60; privateering commission, 40, 50, 52, 53–55, 58, 62, 68, 103, 107, 132, 159, 189, 190, 208, 218, 224; crew, 64–68, 70, 72, 257n26, 279n3; voyage to Madagascar, 70–80, 89; in Arabian Sea, 90–94; in Red Sea, 93–98, 193; turned pirate, 93–100, 103, 108–111, 116, 125, 190, 286n3; sea battles, 96–97, 103; as ship captain, 102; on Saint Marie, 112, 116, 124, 160, 163, 193, 199; and division of loot, 118–119, 122, 124, 179–180; and East India Company, 127–128, 132, 135, 137, 138; arrest, 153, 181–182, 183, 184, 191, 231; in Caribbean, 164–165, 166; reunion with family, 176; in Boston, 176–183; House of Commons debate on, 189–192; imprisoned in England, 192, 196, 197–203, 290n59; hearings in Parliament, 203–205; trial, 203–227; treasure, 229–232, 296n18; and popular culture, 237; accounts of, 258n36. See also *Adventure Galley; Quedah Merchant*
Kidd, Elizabeth (daughter), 229
Kidd, Sarah (daughter), 229
Kidd, Sarah Bradley Cox Oort (wife), 36, 229, 230, 231, 295n8
King, John, 113
King William's War, 16, 44, 129, 139, 151
Kynnaston, Thomas, 82

Lamley, Robert, 160, 211, 218, 257n26, 279n3, 289n45
Lancaster, James, 18
La Paix (ship), 1, 159, 221, 243n1
Larkin, James, 154
Laurents, Governor John (of Saint Thomas), 165, 167
Le Golif, Louis, 123–124, 270n37
Leisler, Jacob, 34–35, 37, 42, 49, 65, 169, 171
Leisler, Jacob, Jr., 49
Lemmon, Mr., 212, 213
Lepanto, battle of, 10, 19–20
le Roy, Monsieur, 107, 108
Letters of marque, 11, 40, 42–43, 208. *See also* Commissions
Leursen, Carsten, 163, 177
Littleton, Captain, 85
Littleton, Sir Thomas, 195
Livingston, Robert, 39–40, 41–43, 47, 48; and Bellomont, 49–50, 51, 52, 285n71; and Kidd, 60, 163, 168, 180, 181, 191, 208, 229; and Fletcher, 169; and Kidd's treasure, 231, 232
Lloyd, Dr. Richard, 144
Locke, John, 48, 195
Loffe, Gabriel, 122, 160, 211, 228, 269n28
Lorrain, Paul, 27, 222–224, 225, 226, 227, 294n30
Loundes, William, 190, 195
Lovell, Sir Salathiel, 211, 212, 213
Lowth, Captain Mathew, 120, 269n25
Lynch, Governor Thomas (of Jamaica), 144–145, 151

Machworth, Sir Humphrey, 203
Madagascar, 80, 82, 112–113, 261n1, 262n2; pirates on, 26, 120, 162, 216; and American colonists, 37, 38, 137, 150, 170, 171, 172, 177, 186, 233; slave trade, 37, 74, 82–83, 84, 89, 113, 114, 115, 171, 174, 228; Kidd on, 111, 176; voyages to, 121, 122, 163, 173, 251n26, 258n37, 269n27. *See also* Saint Marie
Madeira, 70–71
Mainwaring, Henry, 21, 142, 149
Malta, 19, 20
Marauders, deep-sea, 2, 19–26, 67–68; organized, 19–23; anarchistic, 19, 23–26, 67

Markham, Governor William (of Pennsylvania), 150
Marshall, Sampson, *see* Kelley, James
Marshalsea prison, 197, 198, 199, 292n12
Mason, William, 32–33, 35, 37, 100, 101, 102, 117
Mather, Cotton, 236, 298n37
Mauritius, 110–111, 124, 174, 266n62
May, William, 86–87
Mead, Henry, 70, 221–222
Mecca, 5, 131
Mediterranean Sea, 3–5, 10, 13, 19–20
Menendez, Pedro, 14
Merchants, 17–19, 39, 244n10; and pirates, 1, 2–6, 7, 17, 128, 138, 139, 186, 189, 294n25, 297n23; and sailors, 42; government protection of, 155–157, 274nn35,36,37,38. *See also* Piracy, commercial
Middleton, Henry, 18
Middleton, Philip, 135, 272n26
Milborne, Jacob, 35, 49, 171
Mitchell, Sir David, 194, 196
Mocha, 134, 158
Monmouth, Duke of, 188
Montague, Charles (Earl of Halifax), 45, 185, 186, 189, 193, 196, 197; and impeachment, 187, 204; and East India Company, 287n15
Moore, Arthur, 189
Moore, William, 70, 106, 213, 214, 215, 226
Morgan, Sir Henry, 23, 161, 238
Muklis Khan, 127, 133, 134
Mullins, Darby, 64–65, 211, 216, 220–221, 223, 226
Munden, Captain Have, 61
Musgrave, Sir Charles, 189
Muslims, 5, 7, 8, 10, 20, 87, 132, 133

Nanfan, Lieutenant Governor John (of New York), 171, 173, 174, 283n50
Netherlands, 9–10, 11, 12, 20, 25, 29; and New York, 33–34, 41, 171; and England, 44, 254n55; colonies, 110–111, 142; and India, 131, 133, 134; capital market in, 138
New East India Company, 130, 186, 201, 272n20, 278n97
Newgate prison, 199–201, 213, 221, 225; Kidd in, 27, 197, 198, 200, 204,

Newgate prison (*continued*)
207; chapel, 222; *Accounts*, 222–
223
Newton, Dr. Henry, 135, 136, 211, 216,
217
New York City, 33; piracy and, 34–39,
51, 53, 150, 163, 169, 170–171, 233;
depression of 1690s, 36, 63, 67; slave
trade, 115; Kidd's return, 164, 230,
231; cost of living, 179
Nicholson, Governor William (of Virginia), 159
Nicolls, William, 169
Nine Years War, *see* King William's War
Norris, Ambassador (to India), 216,
276n65
November (ship), 107, 108, 109, 110, 119,
124

Ogle, Captain Chaloner, 235
Old Bailey, 209, 292n12
Oldys, Dr. William, 212, 213, 293n18
Oort, John, 36
Orford, Earl of (Edward Russell), 46, 52,
53, 54, 185, 186, 257n19; and Kidd,
61, 138, 187, 192, 203, 221, 232; and
Kidd's trial, 189, 193, 196, 197; vote
of impeachment, 204
Ottoman Empire, 8, 10, 20
Owen, Abeel, 211, 215, 219, 228,
257n26, 279n3
Oxenden, Dr. George, 211, 212, 220–
221, 293n22

Paine, Thomas, 177, 230, 231
Palmer, Edward, 257n26, 289n45
Palmer, Joseph, 207, 214, 218, 220,
291n4
Papillon, Sir Thomas, 130
Parker, Captain Thomas, 99–100, 101,
110
Parrot, Hugh, 211, 215, 228, 279n3
Passenger, Captain William, 159, 243n1
Patronage, 32, 36, 40, 55, 183
Pattle, Thomas, 100
Penn, William, 150
Pennynge, Thomas, 103–104, 106
Pepys, William, 155
Perrin, Captain Charles, 100, 101, 104
Persia, 5, 6
Philipse, Frederick, 35, 38, 113–114,
115–116, 282nn36,40

Phipps, Constantine, 49
Pierson, Colonel Henry, 175
Piracy: and profits, 3, 138; officially sanctioned, 10–16, 26; commercial, 10,
17–19, 26; and marauding, 19–26;
and colonies, 36–37, 137, 143, 144,
146, 154, 233, 235–236; treatment of
crews, 59; fortunes in, 120–121; and
hierarchy, 123, 124; and British im-
perialism, 128, 146; and British government, 138–143, 149, 159, 191;
and British law, 141–144, 148–150,
152–154, 191; and royal proclamation,
142, 143, 212–213, 216, 217, 220,
233–234; and ordinary seamen, 147;
vs. privateering, 152; suppression of,
233, 236–237, 238, 254n55; changes
in eighteenth century, 233–235; as
substitute for war, 245n18; myths of,
327
Pirates: hanging of, 1–2, 243n2, 294n25;
history, 2–14; in popular culture, 2,
237–238; shipboard life, 72–74,
259nn52,53, 260n55; in Indian Ocean,
83–89; creed, 101; clothing, 114,
267n7; fraternity, 117; and gambling,
119–120, 230; families, 121–123,
234, 258n38; and homosexuality, 123–
124, 270n37; pardon for, 133, 137,
142, 159, 162, 178, 184, 212–213,
216, 217, 220, 233–234; and Lord
Admiral, 191; and treatment of loot,
229–230; flags, 234–235. *See also*
Madagascar; Mediterranean Sea; West
Indies
Poe, Edgar Allan, 237
Pompey, 4, 6
Popple, William, 195
Portuguese, 7–8, 9, 18, 70, 71, 103,
193, 244n13, 265n47
Povey, John, 50
Powell, Sir John, 214, 216, 217, 293n19
Privateering, professional, 11–14, 16,
17–19, 162; regulations for, 151–152;
vs. piracy, 152. *See also* Commissions

Quary, Robert, 175
Quedah Merchant (*Adventure Prize;* ship):
seizure of, 108, 109, 127, 132, 133,
134, 202; voyages, 110, 116, 160,
164; in Caribbean, 165–167, 178;
abandonment of, 168, 230, 232,

281n29; cargo, 176, 181, 199, 296n17; and Kidd's trial, 216, 217, 218, 221; and Bellomont, 285n62
Queen Anne's War, 157, 233

Ransoms, 20, 24, 57, 247n39
Renegar, Robert, 17
Revelle, Jeremy, 23
Rhett, Colonel William, 236
Roch, Captain Jeremy, 58
Rock, Captain John, 214
Rogers, Tempest, 162, 269n28, 280n15
Rome, 4–5, 6
Romney, Earl of (Henry Sidney), 45–46, 52, 54, 138, 197, 203, 204
Rooke, Admiral Sir George, 196, 197
Roper, Richard, 120, 228
Rousby, Christopher, 229, 295n8
Royal African Company, 37, 143, 235
Royal Navy, 75–77, 85, 91, 140, 154–155; and Kidd, 61, 165; and homosexuality, 123, 270n37; and pirate communities, 124; and India, 134; and commerce, 145, 155–157, 159; standards, 157; and Kidd's crew, 219, 228; impressment of crews for, 252n36
Russell, Edward, *see* Orford, Earl of

Saint Antonio (ship), 167, 168, 178, 183, 290n51; cargo, 181, 230, 285n76
Saint Helena, 77, 115, 158, 164
Saint Marie: as pirate base, 26, 112–116, 117, 118–119, 123, 124, 137, 158, 162, 163, 216, 238, 270n39; Kidd on, 92, 93, 104, 110, 112, 116, 124, 160, 163, 193, 199, 207, 217, 269n28. *See also* Madagascar
Samuel, Abraham ("King"), 84–85
Savoy, Grand Duke of, 21
Sceptre (ship), 76, 95–98, 106
Scuder, Thomas, 24
Scurvy, 75–76, 77, 79, 83, 91, 188, 260n62
Sea Hawks, 12–13, 67
Selden, John, 149
Selleck, Major Jonathan, 230
Seymour, Sir Edward, 190, 204–205
Shelley, Giles, 174, 175, 207, 269n27, 283n50, 295n3; and Fletcher, 49, 50, 173; and Kidd, 60, 163, 173, 211
Ships, 6–7, 8–9, 20, 21, 56–58

Shivers, Captain Richard, 93
Shrewsbury, Duke of (Charles Talbot), 46–47, 50, 185–186, 188; and Bellomont, 48, 194, 195; and sponsorship of Kidd, 52, 53, 54, 138, 187, 197, 203, 209
Sidney, Henry, *see* Romney, Earl of
Simpson, Captain Rowland, 151
Slaves, 20, 22, 82–83, 262n6, 267n5; on pirate ships, 3, 24, 25, 34, 37, 86, 88, 110, 160, 235, 266n61, 268n23; and navy, 91, 157; and American colonies, 143
Sloughter, Colonel Henry, 34–35, 38, 65, 252n31
Somers, John, Lord, 46, 185; and Bellomont, 48, 195; and sponsorship of Kidd, 52, 54, 138, 187, 190, 194, 196, 197, 203; and Tories, 191; vote of impeachment, 204
Spain, 9, 12–13, 26, 161, 202; in Mediterranean, 10, 21; in Caribbean, 14–16, 29, 32; and England, 57, 142, 151
Spotswood, Governor Alexander (of Virginia), 236
Stanley, Sir John, 195
Stonehouse, John, 166
Stoughton, Lieutenant Governor (of New York), 181
Stuart, Mary, 29, 34, 45–48, 129
Stuyvesant, Peter, 33
Sunderland, Earl of, 48
Swann, John, 124

Talbot, Charles, *see* Shrewsbury, Duke of
Teach, Edward (Blackbeard), 235–236
Thornhill, Sir Thomas, 30, 31
Trade: and piracy, 2–6, 7, 17–19, 128; French war on American, 36; and government, 138–139, 155–157; sugar, 139; colonial, regulations, 150
Treaty of Madrid (1670), 16, 142
Tredway, Jonathan, 132, 186, 263n21
Trenchard, Sir John, 44
Trott, Governor Nicholas (of Providence Island), 89, 150
Tunis, 20, 21
Turner, Theophilus, 228, 296n9
Turton, Sir John, 293n19
Tuscany, Grand Duke of, 13, 21

Uring, Captain Nathaniel, 234
Uzkoks, 6

van de Velde, Willem the Younger, 58
van Horn, Gerrard, 119
van Horne, Captain, 23, 151, 238
van Hulst, Mr., 195
van Rensselaer, Alida, 41
van Sweeten, Ouzel, 171, 282n40
van Toyle, Otto, 174
Vaughan, Governor Thomas (of Jamaica), 27, 142, 144
Vernon, Sir James, 46, 153, 187–188; and buccaneers, 16; on navy, 158; and Kidd, 184, 193, 194, 196, 197, 199, 286nn3,6, 292n10; and House of Commons debate, 189, 190, 191, 192; and Bellomont, 195, 285n70, 289n37; and Kidd's papers, 202, 208, 209
Viele, Humphrey, 120, 228
Vikings, 5

Walker, John, 70, 94, 95, 96–97, 98, 99, 103, 107
War of the Spanish Succession, *see* Queen Anne's War
Ward, Sir Edward, 213–214, 215, 216, 217, 218, 219
Warren, Commodore Thomas, 75, 77, 115, 132, 158, 216–217, 278n97; and Kidd, 78, 89, 95, 99, 168, 219

Warwick, Earl of, 13, 14–15
Watts, Sir John, 17
Watts, Captain Lockyer, 109
Way, Thomas, 230, 231
Welsh, Edward, 116, 118, 119, 125
West Indies, 14–16, 18–19, 142, 146; marauders, 19, 22, 23, 26, 89, 119, 161, 162; and Captain Kidd, 27–33, 160, 165, 176, 183, 193, 221, 230, 232, 252n31; smuggling, 167
Wharton, Thomas, Lord, 45
Whitaker, Edward, 203, 206, 291nn65,66
Wildey, Captain, 214
William and Mary College, 162
William of Orange, 29, 34, 45–46, 47, 51, 54, 148, 162, 202; and East India Company, 129; navy under, 157, 158, 278n93; and Captain Kidd, 184, 193, 220, 286n6; and Junto, 185, 186
Windsor, Lord, 16
Wo-k'ou (Chinese and Japanese pirates), 6
Wren, Christopher, 41, 189
Wright, John, 24, 25, 108, 110, 132
Wynn, Captain Robert, 192, 199, 201, 208, 288n31, 290n51

Yankee, Captain, 161
Yard, Mr., 195